LONDON RECORD SOCIETY
PUBLICATIONS

VOLUME XII
FOR THE YEAR 1976

THE LONDON EYRE
OF 1276

EDITED BY
MARTIN WEINBAUM

LONDON RECORD SOCIETY
1976

© *London Record Society, 1976*
SBN 9009 5212 1

Printed in Great Britain by
W & J MACKAY LIMITED, CHATHAM, KENT

CONTENTS

PREFACE	vii
ABBREVIATIONS	ix
INTRODUCTION	
The Nature of the Documents	xi
The Crown Pleas	xiv
The Articles of the Eyre and the Responses	xx
Civil Pleas *extra coronam*	xxiii
London Custom	xxv
The Financial Issues of the Eyre	xxviii
A Note on Wards	xxxii
Appendix A: Articles of the Eyre	xxxiii
B: Fines and Amercements	xxxv
C: Felons' Chattels	xxxvii
D: Deodands	xxxviii
E: Extracts from the Pipe Rolls	xxxviii
EDITORIAL NOTES	xli
THE PLEA ROLL	1
THE ESTREAT (THE EXCHEQUER SUMMONS)	122
INDEX	153
LONDON RECORD SOCIETY	189

PREFACE

The present volume contains the record of crown and civil pleas for the City of London held before the justices in eyre at the Tower in 1276 together with an exchequer summons listing persons fined or amerced in the eyre. The summons is published by permission of the Corporation of London.

Professor Martin Weinbaum, whose enthusiasm for medieval London has endured for nearly five decades, has not only prepared the volume but has also made a very generous grant towards the cost of printing it. He has asked me to thank a number of people who assisted him in various ways: Dr. Helena M. Chew, who did much basic work upon the text of the plea roll; Mrs. Angela Conyers, who prepared the translation which is here printed; Mr. C. A. F. Meekings, who answered many questions and commented upon an early draft of the Introduction; Dr. M. T. Clanchy, who made detailed comments upon both the Introduction and the translation of the plea roll; and Mr. C. Blair, Dr. P. A. Brand, Dr. Diana E. Greenway, Professor R. B. Pugh and Dr. Elspeth M. Veale, who gave advice on a variety of specialised matters.

William Kellaway
Hon. General Editor

ABBREVIATIONS

Beaven	A. B. Beaven, *The Aldermen of the City of London*, 2 vols. (1908–13)
C66	Public Record Office: Patent Rolls
C.C.R.	*Calendar of Close Rolls*
C.F.R.	*Calendar of Fine Rolls*
C. Letter-Book (*A-L*)	*Calendar of Letter-Book*(*s*) *A-*(*L*), ed. R. R. Sharpe, 11 vols. (1899–1912)
CP40	Public Record Office: Common Plea Rolls
C.P.R.	*Calendar of Patent Rolls*
C.R.	*Close Rolls of the reign of Henry III*. 14 vols. (1902–38)
C. Wills	*Calendar of Wills proved and enrolled in the Husting*, ed. R. R. Sharpe, 2 vols. (1889–90)
Cam, *Studies*	Helen M. Cam, 'Studies in the Hundred Rolls', *Oxford Studies in Social and Legal History*, ed. P. Vinogradoff, vi (Oxford, 1921)
E 159	Public Record Office: Memoranda Rolls (King's Remembrancer)
E 368	Public Record Office: Memoranda Rolls (Lord Treasurer's Remembrancer)
E 372	Public Record Office: Pipe Rolls
E 401	Public Record Office: Receipt Rolls
Eyre of London, 1321	*The Eyre of London, 14 Edward II, A.D. 1321*, ed. Helen M. Cam, 2 vols. (Selden Society, lxxxv–lxxxvi, 1968–9)
Lib. Albus } *Lib. Cust.* }	*Munimenta Gildhallae Londoniensis*, ed. H. T. Riley, 3 vols. in 4 (Rolls series, 1859–62)
Lib. Ant. Leg.	*De Antiquis Legibus Liber*, ed. T. Stapleton (Camden Society, xxxiv, 1846)
London Eyre, 1244	*The London Eyre of 1244*, ed. Helena M. Chew and M. Weinbaum (London Record Society, vi, 1970)
Meekings, *Crown Pleas*	*Crown Pleas of the Wiltshire Eyre, 1249*, ed. C. A. F. Meekings (Wilts. Archaeological Society Records Branch, xvi, 1961)
Rotuli Hundredorum	*Rotuli Hundredorum*, 2 vols. (Record Commissioners, 1812–18)
Tout, *Chapters*	T. F. T. Tout, *Chapters in the Administrative History of Mediaeval England*, 6 vols. (1920–33)

INTRODUCTION

The judicial sessions of the London eyre of 1276 were held at the Tower from 3 February to about the middle of March[1] before Roger de Seyton and his fellow justices Ralph de Fremingham, John de Cobham, Geoffrey de Leukenore and Master Thomas de Sedington.[2] The present volume contains the text of two documents relating to the eyre: a plea roll and an estreat of debts. The plea roll, now British Library Additional Charter 5153, contains crown pleas arranged chronologically together with a number of miscellaneous enrolments (**1–294**), replies to the articles of the eyre (**295–469**) and civil pleas *extra coronam* (**470–523**). Attached to the plea roll is a later schedule of legal notes (**524**). The second document, now Corporation of London Records Office Miscellaneous Roll BB, is an estreat of fines and amercements relating to the plea roll (**525–786**).

The Nature of the Documents
The appearance of the plea roll is similar to that of, and has several features in common with, plea rolls of the same period preserved in the Public Record Office. It consists of twenty membranes,[3] nineteen of which are the work of four or more thirteenth-century clerks; (m. 20 is in a fourteenth-century hand and will be considered separately). Entries **1–294** comprising the crown pleas and several miscellaneous enrolments are the work of three clerks who were responsible respectively for mm.1–6d, 7–12d, and 13–15. The civil pleas (**470–523**) may be in more than one hand but were not written by the clerks responsible for the crown pleas. The intervening entries (**295–469**) appear to be in several hands. The name of the principal justice 'Seyton' is written on m.6 (at **108**) and m.17 (at **470**) and twice in the middle of m.19d (at **519**). The margins of the membranes bear the familiar notations – *infortunium, ad judicium, misericordia* and so on. Those with fiscal implications and certain others are usually crossed through, indicating that the roll was used in the financial sessions immediately following the judicial business of the eyre. All of these features, the variety of hands, the presence of the name of the presiding justice and the deleted marginations suggest that the document is Seyton's main roll.

Two features of the roll are, however, unlike other thirteenth-century plea rolls. In the margins of mm.1–15 and 17–19d are a remarkable series of legal notations ordered as a sequence of *notae*, numbered in arabic

---

1. C. *Letter-Book B*, 256 contains copies of the coroner's roll recording inquests held after the eyre, the earliest of which is dated 19 March. However, at three points the roll was substantially augmented after the judicial sessions had ended: in June 1276 two pleas were heard by the justices (**208, 523**) and in 1277 an inquisition was taken by the mayor (**75**). See also **146, 293, 493**.
2. Commission dated 17 Jan. 1276 (*C.P.R. 1272–81*, 131).
3. They measure 22–26 inches in length and $8\frac{1}{2}$–$9\frac{1}{2}$ inches in width. The roll is well preserved and little of it is damaged or illegible.

Introduction

numerals, frequently inserted around the normal marginations and occasionally continued in the spaces between enrolments. The *notae* themselves are in a variety of thirteenth-century hands.[1] Explanatory but not always reliable references to regnal years are added in the margin to the lists of mayors and sheriffs (**3–4**). But beside the legal notations apposed to various entries between **6** and **273** are added a bold *N*, *Nota* or *Scribatur* and occasionally a pointing hand (e.g. **18, 20–2, 24–5, 112**). These admonitions are written in an ink different from, and fainter than, that used elsewhere in the roll, and bear a striking resemblance to similar admonitions in the margins of Liber Ordinationum.[2] Indeed, we may safely assume that they are the work of Andrew Horn, chamberlain of the City from 1320 until his death in 1328. The second unusual feature of the roll is the fourteenth-century schedule of legal notations on m.20 (**524**) which are either word-for-word transcripts of, or closely related to, the thirteenth-century *notae* on the margins of the roll and, for the most part, have corresponding numbers. In writing on the dorse of m.20 the clerk began at the foot of the membrane. It may be assumed that the injunctions *Scribatur* or *Nota* in the hand of Andrew Horn although not applied to all numbered *notae* were directions to the clerk who wrote m.20.[3]

The rolls in Seyton's custody at the time of his death were delivered by his clerk, William de Wynterse, to the exchequer on 5 June 1279, into the hands of Thomas Bek, the king's treasurer, and John de Kirby. Among the documents was the roll of the London eyre of 1276 together with its writ file.[4] In the presence of William de Wynterse the rolls were then delivered under chirograph by Thomas Bek and John de Kirby to Walter de Wymburn, the king's justice, to be kept for the king's use.[5] If the roll printed in the present volume is in fact Seyton's roll it must have been borrowed at some time after 5 June 1279 and have passed into the hands of the City at some time before 1300. How this came about remains a mystery. It has recently been suggested[6] that our roll was transcribed for the use of the City authorities. This suggestion is based at least in part upon the mistaken assumption that the thirteenth-century *notae* were in a fourteenth-century hand and were the work of Andrew Horn. In 1244 a request by the mayor and citizens for a transcript of the roll of the preceding eyre was denied them as being contrary to law.[7] As the City custumals are silent upon the subject it is unlikely that a transcript could have been made with the consent of the justices. If the roll were a transcript it would imply that Seyton's roll was

---

1. At whose instigation they were made is unclear. Three possible candidates are Gregory de Rokesle, mayor during and after the eyre; Ralph Crepyn, common clerk (for whose career see B. R. Masters, 'The Town Clerk', *Guildhall Miscellany*, iii (1969), 55) and William de Durham, an alderman, who was perhaps recorder in fact if not in name (see below, p. xxviii).
2. *London Eyre, 1244*, pp. xxii, xxiv.
3. A similar compilation for the 1244 eyre appears as part of Horn's collection (c. 1321) imbedded in Liber Albus (*London Eyre, 1244*, pp. xi–xvi).
4. Also various rolls made before and after 1276 including Laurence de Broke's Newgate delivery roll.
5. *C.C.R. 1272–9*, 566–7.
6. *Eyre of London, 1321*, i, p. xv, but when Helen Cam first used the document she described it as 'the official eyre roll' (Cam, *Studies*, 26).
7. *London Eyre, 1244*, nos. 36, 194.

Introduction

borrowed[1] for the purpose of making a copy and that the copying was done by a number of clerks who carefully crossed through the appropriate fiscal marginations and even copied the name of the presiding justice several times.

After the judicial business of the eyre had been concluded the justices held fiscal sessions at which they determined the amounts to be paid for fines and amercements incurred during the eyre. Their assessments were recorded in a roll of fines and amercements, a copy of which, known as an estreat, was sent to the exchequer. (Neither of these documents has survived.) The exchequer then sent a further copy of the estreat, at the head and foot of which were the opening and closing phrases of the writ of summons, ordering the sheriff(s) to collect the debts listed and pay them into the exchequer. It is the text of this document (**525–786**) which is printed after the plea roll in the present volume. The document consists of seven membranes attached head to foot; only one side of the parchment is written upon, the dorse being blank except for one small note.

The writ of summons (**525, 786**) is dated 14 June 1276 and was therefore addressed to the sheriff(s) of 4 Edward I, namely John Horn and Ralph le Blund. It must have been first answered at the exchequer during the Michaelmas 1276 and Easter 1277 exchequer sessions (5 Edward I) by Robert de Araz and Ralph le Fevre, the last of whom died in office. The sheriffs of 6 Edward I, Walter le Cornwaleis and John son of John Adrian continued to work upon the summons[2] and the sheriffs of the following year referred to it although the estreat was resummoned[3] in that year (**564**).

The list of exactions (**526–785**) was heavily annotated by the sheriffs or their clerks particularly in the left hand margin but also in the right hand margin and by interlineation. In addition, the sheriffs attached to the left hand margin of the roll, usually at the appropriate point, a number of writs of respite, pardon or attermination, addressed to them on behalf of individual debtors (e.g. **547, 591, 608, 615**). Other writs were frequently referred to in the margins of the document.[4]

A comparison of the names of debtors with the names in the plea roll reveals many of those discrepancies of spelling and occasional confusion to be expected in a text which originated at the fiscal sessions held by the justices and was then twice re-copied. Of far greater importance are the names in the estreat which are nowhere to be found in the plea roll. These discrepancies may be categorised as follows. The names of several mainpernors lacking in **245** can be supplied from **564**.[5] The list of violators of the assize of wine in **292** is extended by sixteen names in the summoned estreat (**527**). Similarly the names of violators of the assize of cloth in **294** are matched only by those in **663–4**, whereas **665–7** provide a further sixty names. Of the fifty-eight entries in the estreat (**668–725**) concerning disseisin

1. For irregularities concerning the custody of Seyton's rolls, see *Select cases in the Court of King's Bench under Edward I*, ed. G. O. Sayles, i (Selden Society, lv, 1936) p. cxviii.
2. This may be inferred from an attached acquittance dated 16 Nov. 1278 (**666**).
3. The resummoned estreat has not survived.
4. The shrieval annotations on the estreat are discussed at greater length below.
5. Conversely, a number of pledges who were amerced do not appear in the summoned estreat: e.g. **41** cf. **534**; **222** cf. **548**; **252** cf. **568**; **266** cf. **576**; **279** cf. **583**. Occasionally there is a discrepancy so glaring as to make identification impossible (e.g. **284** Geoffrey le Feverer, cf. **584** John le Cuver).

Introduction

only seventeen can be matched with the plea roll leaving sixty-five names unaccounted for. Finally there are three exactions for purprestures (**731, 747, 771**) which are not represented in the plea roll (**342–467**).[1]

It is clear then that certain membranes of the plea roll are defective, notably m.15 containing the lists of violators of the assizes of wine and cloth (**292, 294**) and to a lesser extent m.13 (**245**) and m.16 or m.16d (**342–467**). Seyton himself was disarmingly frank about the quality of his rolls: 'I cannot vouch for them for various reasons, because sometimes one thing is done and another thing more or less is written in the rolls by the clerks, who continually fail to understand the lawyers and litigants correctly.'[2]

We know that our roll was marginated after 1279 and before 1300 with *notae* of interest to Londoners. The roll was undoubtedly in the hands of the City authorities in 1321 and was one of the documents used by Andrew Horn to prepare for the coming of the justices itinerant in that year. Of the later history of the roll's whereabouts little is known. John Carpenter, clerk of the City from 1417 to 1438, listed in his *pro-oemium* to Liber Albus[3] the documents he intended to include in his great custumal and mentioned twice that among them would be 'Responsiones factae ad quaestiones per justiciarios itinerantes apud Turrim Londoniarum civibus ejusdem civitatis propositas anno regni regis Edwardi filii regis Henrici quarto'. In the event he failed to make good his intention. If Carpenter had our roll before him as he wrote it was the last occasion upon which City officials seriously considered drawing upon it to establish precedents in customary law. Thereafter it is lost to sight until 1841 when it was acquired by the British Museum. The estreat, on the other hand, appears to have remained in the City's custody at Guildhall since the thirteenth century.

The Crown Pleas

The commissions enrolled on the Chancery Rolls of Henry III clearly demonstrate that London was excluded from ordinary eyres.[4] Although a limited number of civil pleas *extra coronam* were heard in 1276,[5] London eyres were essentially crown plea sessions. Whereas the usual interval between visitations of the justices in circuit eyres was about seven years, London eyres were more infrequent. During the reigns of Henry III and Edward I eyres were held in 1221, 1226, 1244, 1251 and 1276. Thus the 'new' pleas of the crown reviewed by the justices in 1276 (**6–290**) were presentments of death by felony and misadventure and appeals since the previous eyre in 1251 together with a number of indictments. The headings in the plea roll dividing the 'new' crown pleas, in accordance with exchequer practice, use the regnal year in which the sheriffs relinquished office. The chamberlain[6] and sheriffs answered for the pleas dating from their term of office and were obliged to produce their rolls on the first day of the eyre. A

1. John Prudford keu (**550**) is also unaccounted for.
2. *Select cases in King's Bench*, i, p. clxviii.
3. *Lib. Albus*, i. 11–12.
4. For an explanation of normal practice in eyres, see Meekings, *Crown Pleas*.
5. See below pp. xxiii–xxv.
6. For the office of chamberlain, who in London performed the duties of coroner, see W. Kellaway, 'The coroner in medieval London', *Studies in London History*, ed. A. E. J. Hollaender and W. Kellaway (1969), 75–87.

Introduction

chamberlain who failed to do so until 'the fifth day' was amerced (**202**). The heirs of a deceased chamberlain who failed to answer were distrained (**18**). The mayor and citizens, or more often, the mayor and aldermen performed the duties of a presenting jury, not under oath, but 'in the faith in which they are bound to the king'.

Criminal presentments far outnumber any other category of crown plea. Homicide by unknown malefactors (e.g. **24, 26, 56, 86–7, 104**) accounts for about ten per cent of such presentments. Two cases of homicide in which the felons carried off goods or money were probably premeditated (**87, 203**); the only certain instance of premeditation concerned a man, who, with his wife, beat a woman and then at nightfall completed the work with a knife (**250**). Where circumstantial detail is provided by the record, it is evident that many homicides were committed in anger. Quarrels were frequent, sometimes after drinking (e.g. **83, 102, 158, 236**) or a celebration (**60**), over women (e.g. **39, 119, 138, 181, 219, 230**), or, in two instances, after a game of chess (**48, 151**). On one occasion, some Londoners went to Bermondsey for a wrestling match with the prior's men; a quarrel broke out among them and the Londoners chased the prior's men into the priory, whereupon some monks who had entered a solar above the priory gate threw stones at the Londoners and killed one of them (**116**). Unusual cases concern a woman who bit a man's finger so that he died, apparently from the infected bite (**113**); a man who, at target practice, accidentally shot another in the head with an arrow (**61**); and two doctors and an apothecary whose patient and his servant died of eating an excess of pills (**257**). Occasionally the presentment provides detail about the actual blow which caused the death: a man passing a brothel was pulled in by three prostitutes who took from him a buckle, whereupon he drew his knife and intending to strike one of them with its handle instead struck her with the blade (**134**). Of implements used, knives are the most frequently mentioned (13 times); then swords and staffs (7 times each); arrows and axes (twice each) and an anlace (once). Suffocation and strangulation are both mentioned once as the cause of death (**231, 258**). The deed did not necessarily occur in the City (**?118, 127, 200**) but the victim lived long enough to return there to die; in one case a man beaten as far afield as Winchester died in the City and was thus the subject of a presentment (**180**). It may also be observed that women were very rarely presented for homicide (**16, 117**). Only two presentments of suicide, both by hanging, were made (**206, 213**).

Abjurations of the realm taken by the chamberlain and sheriffs, or exceptionally, in the absence of the chamberlain, by the constable of the Tower, the sheriffs and aldermen (**52**) were the frequent subject of presentments. Churches in which a fugitive might take sanctuary[1] were plentiful in London, no fewer than twenty-eight being used for the purpose between 1251 and 1276. The church nearest to hand appears to have been most favoured by the fugitive.[2] Escapes from sanctuary were not uncommon, but

---

1. I. D. Thornley, 'Sanctuary in medieval London', *Journal of the British Archaeological Association*, new series, xxxviii for 1932 (1933) 293–315.
2. The churches most used were St. Mary Woolchurch (5 times); Friars Minor (4 times); St. Lawrence Jewry, St. Mary Conyhope, St. Paul's and St. Thomas London Bridge (3 times each).

Introduction

there is no evidence to suggest that fugitives had time to consider whether escape would be easier from one church than another. The Londoners claimed that they were not obliged to keep watch over persons who took sanctuary and that the sheriffs should not be amerced for their escape (**20**). The claim, which was sustained, was more trenchantly expressed than it had been in 1244 when some attempt at guarding churches had been made.[1] Those who took sanctuary but failed to escape sent for the chamberlain, confessed their felony and abjured the realm; no case of turning approver is recorded in the plea roll. Most felons confessed to theft (34 instances) while confessions of homicide (4 instances), robbery, forgery, harbouring of felons, and escape from prison were unusual. Nearly two-thirds of the abjurors were vagabonds or strangers and only two were women. Those who abjured the realm were assigned ports of departure, a matter upon which the plea roll is silent except in one instance (**115**).

About one third of the new crown pleas were presentments of misadventure. Causes of death were varied. Death by drowning, fatal falls from ladders, steps, horses, carts, trees, or exceptionally, from the belfry of St. Paul's, and scalding by hot water or mash were common causes.[2] The collapse of solars, walls and beams also took their toll, while the fall of St. Mary le Bow's bell-tower killed no fewer than thirteen people (**221**). Starvation, fever and falling sickness were less common.[3] Death by accidentally self-inflicted wounds (**22, 133**) or by the bite of a sow (**44**) were rare. The Londoners claimed successfully, as they had in 1244, that they were not obliged to present the first finder of a corpse (**21**). The animal or object which was the cause of death was declared deodand, that is, given to God.[4] Its value was assessed at the inquest by the ward but the justices frequently discovered that the valuation was false (e.g. **40, 43, 54, 67, 129–30**). The sheriffs were normally answerable for the value of the deodand but not to the exchequer; the justices apparently bestowed it, with the king's authority, upon some charitable object.[5] The dean and chapter of St. Paul's and the master of the Temple who took objects declared deodand without warrant (**162, 184**) may have been anticipating such a grant. The only other bane taken without warrant was taken by a servant of Robert Burnell, the king's chancellor (**240**). The collapse of the bell-tower of St. Mary le Bow (**221**), already referred to, throws interesting light upon the granting of deodands. The tower itself was valued at 20 marks; a house destroyed by the fall of the tower was not valued, but the materials of which it was built were granted by the king to the prior and convent of Christchurch Canterbury, to whom the house had belonged.

All of the appeals of felony[6] on our roll appear to have been first heard in the husting with the exception of one which was heard in a county court (**131**). Homicide was the most frequent subject of appeal,[7] battery, wounding, mayhem and rape being far less frequent. Over half of the appellors

---

1. *London Eyre, 1244*, nos. 70, 148.
2. & 3. See Index.
4. See Appendix D.
5. Meekings, *Crown Pleas*, 67. See below, p. xxxi.
6. Meekings, *Crown Pleas*, 69–90.
7. See Index under Appeals.

Introduction

were women: two of their appeals concerned miscarriage as a result of battery (**222, 261**)[1] and another, the death of a child by abortion (**187**). Appellors often defaulted, withdrew or had died before the eyre. Three appeals were quashed by the justices on procedural grounds (**140, 147, 261**). In only one case did the parties agree (**273**). About one quarter of the appeals were adjudged false and only two were remitted to the husting.

Apart from the crown pleas already discussed, presentments of felony and misadventure, and appeals, a number of indictments[2] were heard by the justices. Fifty-seven persons were indicted of homicide (**98, 264, 275–6, 281, 284–5**), robbery (**278, 287**), theft (**77, 276, 282, 284, 287–8**), harbouring of felons (**284, 286**) or coin-clipping (**284**) of whom forty-nine were acquitted. Two Londoners indicted of arson in the Middlesex eyre had been successfully claimed for the liberty of the City by the London sheriffs (**280**). Four of the indictments concern felonies committed outside London (?**77**, ?**98, 275, 285**); in **98** the man accused had been arrested by the sheriffs of London and this may also explain why the other pleas were heard in the London eyre.

No single matter occupies more space in the record of crown pleas than mainprise and attachment. Londoners accused of homicide might be released without writ of mainprise on the pledge of twelve men, each liable to amercement of 100s. should they fail to produce the person bailed on the first day of the eyre (**29, 76, 324**). Such failure was commonplace (e.g. **116, 147, 183, 209, 219, 222, 227–8**). Sheriffs were answerable for mainprise (**37, 147**) and those who attached fewer than twelve pledges had *ad judicium* noted against them. In cases of death the sheriffs were obliged to attach those present (e.g. **15, 32, 51, 70, 87, 91, 260**) or those in the house when the death occurred (e.g. **15, 35, 181–2, 193**), the owner of the house (e.g. **21, 29, 40, 43, 159**), the owner of an animal which caused the death (**155**), relatives of the deceased (e.g. **7, 16, 44, 95, 197, 235**) and four neighbours (**26**). The chamberlain and sheriffs were answerable for these attachments (**321**). In appeals the appellor was to be attached and also the appellee in cases of grave felonies. The failure of the chamberlain and sheriffs to make attachments, to make them in the prescribed form or to enroll them caused *ad judicium* to be noted against their names (e.g. **39, 63, 67, 70, 119**). In 1244 the justices had expressed dissatisfaction with the way in which attachments were made in the City and for this reason a number of rules had been laid down by the king and his justices which were allowed by the mayor and citizens.[3] It is possible that further regulations were made in 1251, concerning attachments. At all events, the non-appearance of neighbours, to which no reference was made in the record of 1244 crown pleas, was very frequent in 1276 as was the consequential amercement of their pledges. Furthermore, the justices paid close attention to irregularities in the attachment of neighbours and *ad judicium* was noted against the chamberlain and sheriffs or whichever of them had erred. Examples of such irregularities are varied: the attachment of two neighbours by the same pledges (**154**); of four by one (**53**) or six pledges (**87**); of four, one by another (**108, 134**) or by the

---

1. This was also the subject of two presentments (**63, 76**).
2. Meekings, *Crown Pleas*, 92–8.
3. *London Eyre, 1244*, nos. 144, 242.

Introduction

same pledges (**154, 159**); and failure to attach any neighbours at all (**59–60, 62, 80, 161–2**). The ward might also have *ad judicium* noted against it for the false presentment of neighbours (**47, 88, 101, 111, 165, 206**) or because the neighbours' names were unknown to the men of the ward (**103, 197**). Finally, neighbours who falsely presented themselves were amerced (**88, 101**).

Another matter to which the justices paid close attention in reviewing crown pleas was the system of frankpledge. In 1244 the mayor and citizens had explained that no one might stay in the City for more than three nights unless he found two pledges and so put himself in frankpledge; if someone stayed one night longer without being in frankpledge, committed a felony and did not stand trial, then the alderman and ward were to be amerced for harbouring him.[1] Amercements of frankpledges are numerous in the record of the 1244 eyre[2] but in 1276 despite a much larger number of crown pleas there are only three instances (**185, 250, 258**). On the other hand, many felons outside frankpledge were in the mainpast or household of a master who was duly amerced (e.g. **102, 156, 190, 200–1, 208**). Wards were frequently amerced for harbouring felons outside frankpledge (e.g. **41, 50, 53, 75, 105, 112**) or had *ad judicium* noted against them (e.g. **29, 63, 73, 92, 102, 148**). On occasion wards harboured felons after the deed (e.g. **89, 109, 117**) and when the prior of Bermondsey (**116, 615**), the master of the Temple (**75, 596**), Hugh de Turberville (**205, 653**) and Henry de Coventry (**289, 589**) did so they were heavily amerced.

In most cases of homicide the slayer was not present in court, either because he had fled immediately after the deed or because he had escaped undetected. The Londoners claimed that they were not obliged to raise the hue and cry unless they so wished, although, in the interests of the king's peace, malefactors were pursued by the men of the neighbourhood (**24**). As to how often this occurred the record is silent.[3] If the felon or suspected felon were absent the justices ordered his exaction and outlawry (or, if the felon was a woman, her exaction and waivery). The London process of outlawry was explained to the justices in 1244: fugitives were put in exigent at three hustings held fortnightly and then outlawed by precept of the king at the folkmoot at St. Paul's. The justices considered that the time for exaction and outlawry was very short and should be amended.[4] No record of the form then provided has survived nor does the plea roll of 1276 provide further evidence concerning the process of outlawry. Although the development of the process in the fourteenth century lies outside the scope of this introduction it is instructive to observe that the explanation of the recorder in 1321 as to how the exactions following the eyre of 1276 had been made closely follows that given in 1244.[5]

1. *London Eyre, 1244*, nos. 62, 242.
2. *London Eyre, 1244*, nos. 82, 94, 108, 142, 152, 162, 178, 180.
3. An appellor's failure to raise the hue and cry might be used by an appellee in his defence (**147**; *London Eyre, 1244*, nos. 185–6).
4. *London Eyre, 1244*, nos. 45, 94.
5. *Eyre of London, 1321*, i, 31–7; *Lib. Cust.*, i, 333–8. It was said that foreigners were exacted four times but that all of those ordered to be outlawed in 1276 were English. The only felons in question appear to be those in **238** (see n. 2), **239, 243–4, 249–50, 252, 255–6, 258, 260** and **264**.

Introduction

The mayor and aldermen were sometimes called upon by the justices to say whether a person attached in connection with a death was suspected (**29, 37, 39, 47, 152, 257**). Strangers might put themselves upon the verdict of the mayor and aldermen (**199, 257, 281**). Londoners occasionally achieved the same end because the suspicion was slight (**70, 222**) or by payment of an oblation (**37**). Trial by the mayor and citizens occurred in one presentment in which the suspicion cannot have been slight (**146**). Strangers were also tried by juries of forty-two consisting of fourteen men from the three aldermanries nearest the place where the incident happened (**214, 233, 264**). In three further cases it may be safely assumed that the persons tried by juries of forty-two were not of the liberty of the City (**245, 249, 256**). One man, presumably a stranger, declined the offer of trial by jury (**107**).

According to the custom of the City, Londoners accused or appealed of homicide should wage their law thirty-six handed, eighteen oath-helpers coming from each side of the Walbrook. The great law, as it was called, had been waged in 1226,[1] 1244[2] and 1251.[3] It was waged once and for the last time[4] in 1276 (**209**); a wife appealed of poisoning her husband did not fail in her law and was acquitted.

The sheriffs were answerable at the exchequer for the value of felons' chattels.[5] *Ad judicium* was frequently noted against the chamberlain and sheriffs for failure to enquire concerning chattels (e.g. **41, 73, 75, 89, 148, 203, 215**). Sheriffs of counties other than London were ordered to enquire concerning strangers' chattels and the justices instituted enquiry by twelve men of the hundred for the same purpose (**245**). A similar enquiry into the chattels and lands of London felons was made by the mayor and aldermen (**72**). Chattels were falsely valued (**206, 223**) less often than deodands but in one case, perhaps significantly, the chattels were those of a suicide (**206**).

Seven felons were hanged as a result of the sessions at the Tower in 1276 (**98, 146, 276-7, 284**). A further ten had been hanged before the eyre, eight of whom had been convicted by the justices of gaol delivery at Newgate (**41, 49, 94, 128, 163, 197, 202**).[6] Another had been arrested by the constable of Dover Castle and infalisated, i.e. thrown from the cliffs (**203**). Claims of clergy were numerous,[7] but only three clerks were found guilty by the secular court (**116, 264, 316**). Finally, it is noteworthy that no fewer than fifteen persons accused of homicide obtained royal pardons (**6, 72, 75, 78, 170, 176, 189, 207-8, 218-19**) and another who had been present when a man had been strangled also obtained a pardon (**231**). The pardon of Robert and Ralph de Monte Pessulano did not remit their chattels (**72**), while the chattels of Thomas le Armurer were confiscated because he had absconded after the deed (**189**).

1. *Lib. Ant. Leg.*, 5.
2. *London Eyre, 1244*, nos. 63, 157-8, 179.
3. *Lib. Ant. Leg.*, 18.
4. The recorder claimed the custom in 1321 but on receiving some sharp comments from the justices abandoned the claim (*Eyre of London, 1321*, i, 76-9).
5. For a table showing the value of chattels in 1276, see Appendix C.
6. William Fot may also have been convicted before the justices of gaol delivery while the City was in the king's hand (**309**) and Geoffrey de Beverley was hanged in 1267 (**188**).
7. See Index under Clerks, criminous.

Introduction

The Articles of the Eyre and the Responses

The commission appointing Roger de Seyton and his fellow justices was issued in November 1275. Attached to the enrolment of the commission on the Patent Roll was a writ, addressed to the mayor and sheriffs of London, ordering them to proclaim the coming of the eyre.[1] The writ provided a warning to those who owed suit to appear on the first day and especially to the chamberlains and sheriffs who were to produce the rolls[2] pertaining to their terms of office. Essoins (excuses for non-attendance) might be procured from chancery but only one was entered on the Close Rolls.[3] The most important document drawn up in preparation for the eyre was the set of articles outlining the scope of the justices' enquiries. Drawn up in the king's council and delivered under seal to the justices, it was handed on the first day of the eyre to the mayor and citizens who were to reply to the questions it contained. The articles (**292, 294–342, 468**) appear in the plea roll after the crown pleas rather than in their logical position at the beginning of the roll.

As a collection these articles are closely associated with the gradually changing *Vetera capitula itineris*. However, they do not follow the rough historical order of the 'national model' set in use early in Edward I's reign, and differ from that 'model' in many respects.[4] It is clear that the particular circumstances of London necessitated some modifications and additions to the set of articles used for circuit eyres. Out of a total of seventy articles accumulated since the twelfth century in the 'national model', the plea roll contains fifty-one, or fifty-two if account be taken of *De novis placitis corone* (Cam no. 2), which was omitted although crown pleas were heard. The omission of *De veteribus placitis* (Cam no. 1) is curious but other articles omitted (Cam nos. 14, 23, 26, 33, 37–8) were, perhaps, less appropriate to London than to the counties. The most intriguing of these omissions is *De vicecomitibus* (Cam no. 14) concerning inquests in wapentakes and hundreds and the raising of hue and cry. The justices in fact enquired about hue and cry in the course of hearing crown pleas and the mayor and aldermen explained the City's custom (**24**).

Two articles which were 'unique' in 1244 appeared again in 1276 (**296, 306**). The first concerned the malicious destruction of houses, and despite the answer given by the mayor and citizens, cannot have been intended to uncover offences committed during de Montfort's rebellion because the events of that period were no longer subject to criminal proceedings.[5] Since cases of arson would have been dealt with as crown pleas (e.g. **275, 280**), it must be assumed that the king's council wished to be informed of major disturbances in the City. The second article (**306**; cf. Cam no. 16) concerned

---

1. C66/95 m.33.
2. They also needed other documents to hand: writs addressed to them (**231**) or chirographs concerning prisoners (**134**).
3. *C.C.R. 1272–9*, 262, 324.
4. Appendix A provides a comparison of the articles of 1244 and 1276 with the 'national model'. The numbers assigned to articles are those used in Cam, *Studies*.
5. The provisions of the *Dictum de Kenilworth* may be detected in two crown pleas (**170, 287**). At least three civil pleas owed their origin to the events of the period of the Barons' war (**493, 508, 521**). The prior and canons of Holy Trinity Aldgate were successful in reinstating their close which had been opened during the war (**345**).

Introduction

Christian usurers alive or dead. Two usurers were named, Nicholas le Convers who proffered a pardon and Hugh de Gisors who was acquitted on the verdict of the mayor and aldermen.

Nine articles were 'unique' to the 1276 eyre, although it is possible that some of them may have been used in 1251 (**298, 302–3, 307–8, 320–3**). An enquiry into advowsons to abbeys, priories and hospitals which belonged to the king (**298**) was no more than an extension of the old *De ecclesiis* (Cam no. 6). Five others were aimed at discovering corrupt practices among London officials who held the assizes of cloth and wine (**302–3**); who were concerned with murage and tallage (**322–3**);[1] or, who took prises in the king's name for themselves (**320**). All five articles received negative answers. A further 'unique' article was framed in the light of provisions made by the justices in 1251 concerning attachments. The mayor and citizens replied that attachments were answered for by the chamberlain and sheriffs and that they knew nothing further. As we have seen, the chamberlain and sheriffs were indeed made to answer for attachments.[2]

The remaining 'unique' articles concerned the Jews (**307–8**). On 18 January 1276 the king had ordered Seyton and his fellow justices not to permit Jews to be impleaded in the eyre; the Jews were, however, to answer concerning their lands within the City and other things, as was the custom in previous eyres.[3] For this immunity although in itself customary, the Jews made a fine of £50.[4] The first article (**307**) clearly did not infringe upon the immunity as it enquired into Christians who received goods of Jews in various forms. It was presumably intended to reveal collusion between Christians and Jews in usurious practices. In the event it revealed nothing. The other article was aimed at the discovery of cruelties inflicted by Jews upon Christian boys (**308**) and was, no doubt, inspired by the supposed ritual murder of a Christian boy in London in 1244, whose body was buried by the high altar of St. Paul's,[5] and by the notorious death of young Hugh of Lincoln in 1255,[6] for which nineteen Jews had been executed. The mayor and citizens answered by saying that two boys had been found killed by Jews, as appeared in the roll of the chamberlain and sheriffs. No date was given. On 21 February, the king ordered his justices in eyre not to molest some Jews who had previously been acquitted of the death of a Christian boy slain at Dowgate.[7] The justices received a further writ from the king on 3 March wishing them to certify him by word of mouth concerning the death of a Christian boy 'crucified' by the Jews, whose body had been washed up on the shore at Dowgate.[8] Only one crown plea reviewed by the justices concerned a body washed up by the tide; it was the body of a stranger with his throat cut and no mention was made of Dowgate (**86**).

1. Reminiscent of the enquiries made in the hundreds in 3 Edward I into complaints about those who assessed the levies.
2. See above p. xvii.
3. *C.C.R. 1272–9*, 265, 272.
4. *C.C.R. 1272–9*, 298; *C.F.R. 1272–1307*, 66–7.
5. C. Roth, *History of the Jews in England*, 3rd edn. (Oxford, 1964), 55–6.
6. G. I. Langmuir, 'The Knight's Tale of young Hugh of Lincoln', *Speculum*, xlvii (1972), 459–82.
7. *C.C.R. 1272–9*, 271–2.
8. *C.C.R. 1272–9*, 273–4.

Introduction

A number of articles received positive replies although *nihil sciunt* was the most common response. When the mayor and aldermen gave a negative answer to the article about aliens' chattels (Cam no. 17) they were told to make further enquiry (**310**). Of those in mercy who had not been amerced, the dean and chapter of St. Martin le Grand and one other were named as having been convicted of purprestures in 1251 (Cam no. 3; **295**). The replies given about churches and serjeanties are closely related to those of 1244 but the City was in mercy because they omitted one church from their recital (Cam nos. 6, 8; **299–300**). Two persons were named as holders of escheated property but both claimed that they held their properties by royal grants and retained possession (Cam no. 7; **341**). No article elicited a longer answer than that concerning purprestures (Cam no. 9; **342–467**). The Hundred enquiries of 3 Edward I[1] which embraced the question of purprestures presumably provided the City with up-to-date information and obviated the need for a perambulation of the kind made by the justices in 1246.[2] The lists of violators of the assizes of cloth and wine (Cam nos. 11-12; **294, 292**) appear to be incomplete.[3] Walter Hervy was presented for the false sealing of two quart measures (Cam no. 11; **468**). Thirty defaulters of the common summons of the eyre were named (Cam no. 28; **340**), but it is noteworthy that only fourteen of them were amerced (**526, 528**).

In response to the article about the failure of sureties to produce their man on the first day of the eyre, the mayor and citizens replied that they knew nothing at present but would enquire further (Cam no. 17; **310**). In fact the review of crown pleas provided ample answer (e.g. **116, 147, 183, 209, 227–8, 272–3**). To a number of articles the responses appear to be incomplete, suggesting that the mayor and citizens were not necessarily obliged to include matters which would emerge during the review of crown pleas. Although a coin-clipper was presented (Cam no. 19; **309**) no mention was made of an abjuror's confession of forging money (**11**). A deceased harbourer of a felon was presented (Cam no. 21; **213**) but no mention was made of persons subsequently in mercy for this offence (**75, 116, 205, 289**). Numerous escapes from prison were presented but many more emerged in the review of crown pleas.[4] Two articles concerning wrongful imprisonment (Cam nos. 53, 59; **326, 318**) produced negative answers although two crown pleas and one civil plea discovered matters which might well have been presented (**275, 289, 496**). Similarly, a negative was given to the article concerning those who did not allow sheriffs to enter their lands to make summonses (Cam no. 37; **337**) when there was at least one incident of which the commonalty must have been cognisant (**141**). Finally, it may be remarked that although no presentments were made about bail obtained by bribery (Cam no. 52; **324**) the mayor and citizens took the opportunity of explaining the City's cherished custom with regard to mainprise, an explanation which they twice repeated during the hearing of crown pleas (**29, 76**).

1. *Rotuli Hundredorum*, i (1812), 403–33.
2. *London Eyre, 1244*, nos. 349–486.
3. See above, p. xiii.
4. See Index under Escapes.

Introduction

Civil Pleas extra coronam
Pleas in the City were heard in the husting before the mayor, aldermen and sheriffs, or in the sheriff's court or in the mayor's court.[1] The husting met on Mondays, pleas of land and common pleas being heard fortnightly on alternate Mondays, an arrangement which may have originated in 1244[2] but was clearly established by 1272 when two separate sequences of rolls begin. In 1260 it was provided in full husting that all pleas of dower and of customs and services initiated by writ should be heard on the same day as common pleas.[3] Of the sheriff's court in the thirteenth century little is known but pleas of trespass appear to have been heard there.[4] Disputes between foreign merchants and pleas of debt and covenant were heard in both the sheriff's and mayor's courts. Although mention of the husting is frequent in the record of the 1276 eyre the sheriff's court is never referred to. The mayor's court appears once in its function of controlling the goldsmiths' craft (**491**), a function subsequently granted to the fellowship of goldsmiths. The justices in 1244 had made provision for the holding of pleas of intrusion in the City before the sheriffs, or at least one of them, the alderman of the place where the intrusion took place and, by implication because he was obliged to make enrolments, the chamberlain.[5] In 1276 an assize of novel disseisin was quashed because it had been held before the chamberlain in the sheriffs' absence (**516**).

The London eyres of the thirteenth century were essentially crown plea sessions. The civil pleas *extra coronam* heard by the justices in 1276 were comparatively few in number but were varied in content (**470–523**). The citizens claimed that they were not bound to answer concerning any tenement in the City unless the tenant had vouched a foreigner to warranty. The claim was twice upheld (**470, 484**). One plea of land (**485, 514**), an assize of mort d'ancestor (**494**), an assize of novel disseisin (**502**) and several pleas of dower (**477–8, 482, 515**) were heard by the justices because of foreign vouchers. It is interesting to notice, however, that these pleas were terminated before the justices (**494, 514, 502**) or respited to the Bench at Westminster rather than remitted to the husting according to later City custom.[6] The mayor and citizens claimed that a plea of customs and services should not be heard or terminated anywhere but in the husting; however, without surrendering their claim, they agreed that the action should proceed because the writ had been fully answered (**483**; cf. **489**). No claim was made by the citizens in pleas concerning disseisins allegedly committed after the summons of the eyre because the City courts were not sitting while the eyre was in progress (**499, 504**). An assize utrum was quashed because it was found that such assizes had not been heard by the justices in 1251 (**503**). Essoins and appointments of attorneys bulk large in the records of circuit eyres but in the London eyre of 1276 only one entry of each kind appears on

---

1. For a discussion of London's courts, see *Calendar of Early Mayor's Court Rolls, 1298–1307*, ed. A. H. Thomas (1924), pp. ix–xlv.
2. *London Eyre, 1244*, no. 235.
3. *Lib. Ant. Leg.*, 45–6.
4. c. 1259 (*Lib. Ant. Leg.*, 40–1).
5. *London Eyre, 1244*, no. 243.
6. *Lib. Albus*, i, 183–4.

Introduction

the roll (**480, 513**). The paucity of such entries is an index of the citizens' success in claiming, for the husting, pleas concerning tenements within the City.

Agreement between the parties was reached in pleas of covenant, customs and services and in an assize of mort d'ancestor (**483, 494–5, 505**). The concord itself might be enrolled (**489**). Similarly a litigant might consider it prudent to have a private charter enrolled so that it was placed on record (**501**; cf. **481**). A memorandum recording a covenant was enrolled (**492**) together with a recognizance of debt relating to it (**497**). Further recognizances of debt may be explained because the debt was owed to Seyton (**490**) or to the king (**475**). A man entrusted with a chest by Master William de Werblynton, who was visiting the Roman Curia, returned the chest to William's wife; she entered into a recognizance for its receipt before the justices (**498**). In view of the later popularity of aldermanic arbitration, **522** is of particular interest. Henry le Waleys and William de Durham agreed to the appointment of the mayor and three aldermen to assess the value of the timber in a room which had been demolished together with the value of William's perquisites as under sheriff of Middlesex, which William had withheld; ultimate authority was reserved to the justices (**522**).

Pleas of trespass outnumber any other kind of action among the civil pleas on our roll.[1] The charges were of abduction (**511**), carrying off chattels (**487, 491, 493, 508–9, 511**), breaking and entering (**519**), wounding (**471, 500, 506**) and wrongful imprisonment (**496**). A plea of battery and mayhem appears among the crown pleas because life and limb were in question (**265**). The earliest date given of an alleged trespass was July 1263 (**487**); two offences were committed after the summons of the eyre (**471, 500**) and for two, no date was given (**491, 509**). A number of actions were brought against City officials: by a goldsmith whose goods had been seized because he was working in latten (**491**), by a currier for wrongful imprisonment (**496**), by an armourer whose goods had been seized during Montfort's rebellion (**508**) and by a man who alleged that his goods had been carried off (**509**). Two of the pleas were foreign (**493, 511**) and both were adjourned to the Bench at Westminster. Only one plaintiff is recorded as failing to prosecute (**512**) and only one defendant defaulted (**520**). Agreement between parties was once allowed on payment of an oblation (**518**). The mayor and aldermen acted as jurors in four cases where presumably the justices considered the suspicion to be slight; at all events, the defendant, on each occasion, was acquitted (**265, 487, 491, 509**). In the remaining London cases the parties put themselves upon juries of one ward (**500, 508**) or two (**496, 506, 519**).

In civil pleas damages were frequently claimed but rarely awarded. Queen Eleanor's servant claimed £600 and Henry le Waleys, who had lost a cargo of hides during the rebellion, claimed £300 (**493**).[2] Sums ranging from 10 marks to £20 were more usual. Damages were assessed only in two pleas of trespass: a man whose hand had been cut when he was assaulted, was awarded 5s. (**471**) and a woman whose finger had been broken (and who,

---

1. For a learned discourse upon trespass see S. F. C. Milsom 'Trespass from Henry II to Edward III', *Law Quarterly Review*, lxxiv (1958), 195–224, 407–36, 561–90.
2. Henry le Waleys' plea was adjourned to the Bench, where a jury assessed the value of the cargo at 200 marks and awarded 50 marks damages (CP 40/17 m. 67).

Introduction

incidentally, had been raped) was awarded £5 although she had claimed £100 (**519**). In only one other plea were damages said to have been assessed but the amount was not entered in the record (**496**). There is little evidence to suggest that plaintiffs were encouraged to bring suit in the hope of being awarded damages. A man and his wife sought an assessment of damages suffered from an intrusion concerning which they had won an assize before the eyre; not only were they unsuccessful but the justices reversed the verdict of the assize on a technicality (**516**).

Four royal writs are cited giving rise to enrolments among the civil pleas. The first concerned a plea of land originating in the husting which, despite the writ, was remitted to the husting by the justices (**470**). The second was an inquest to determine whether the loss of a boy's ear had been caused accidentally by a bite from a horse or through his own fault (**473**). Perhaps the most remarkable entry in the entire roll is another inquest, held in compliance with a royal writ, to discover the whereabouts of royal muniments, including papal privileges, which had been in the possession of John Mansel, Henry III's confidential minister (**521**). The fourth enrolment amply illustrates the hazards of litigation. In pursuance with a royal writ the justices sat in the husting, some three months after the judicial sessions at the Tower had ended, to examine a plea already determined there. The plaintiff had sued Ralph Crepin, the mayor's clerk, by writ of right, but was adjudged in mercy for a false claim (**523**).

London Custom

As we have already seen, no discussion of crown and civil pleas in the London eyre is possible without reference to London custom. Although a survey of customary law in London is beyond the scope of the present introduction, it is perhaps desirable to outline briefly those features of London custom which are illustrated by the plea roll. The commission of November 1275 appointing Seyton and his fellow justices charged them to hear all pleas coming before them in accordance with precedent. Indeed, enquiry into local custom by royal justices was normal in circuit, as in London, eyres. Such enquiries had certainly been made by the justices in the London eyres of 1221, 1226 and 1244. No comprehensive statement of custom was formulated but many customs were the subject of enquiry by the justices, and others may be inferred from the record. Andrew Horn was well aware of the importance of the precedents provided by the plea roll and the list of legal annotations on m.20 (**524**), drawn up at his instigation, amply demonstrates the City's interest in records of custom and usage.

Apart from precedent the citizens were able to claim their liberties by virtue of a long succession of royal charters.[1] In 1268 the Londoners had received a charter from Henry III[2] containing a broadly phrased assurance that they should enjoy the liberties and free customs which they had enjoyed

---

1. Doubt has recently been cast upon the authenticity of Henry I's charter (C. N. L. Brooke, G. Keir and S. Reynolds, 'Henry I's charter for the City of London', *Journal of the Society of Archivists*, iv (1973), 558–78).
2. Preserved in the Corporation of London Records Office. For the text see *Lib. Ant. Leg.*, 102–5 and *Lib. Cust.*, ii, 251–3; for a translation *Historical Charters . . . of the City of London*, rev. edn., ed. W. de G. Birch (1887), 38–42.

Introduction

under the king's predecessors, with the proviso that the liberties should not be contrary to right, law and justice. The citizens should not be compelled to plead outside the City except in cases of foreign tenures or of trespasses committed elsewhere than in the City;[1] they were acquitted of *murdrum* and therefore not obliged to prove Englishry, a subject of frequent enquiry in many circuit eyres;[2] they were exempted from waging battle (but the process of appeal was available in London as it was elsewhere); and the cherished Great Law, although not mentioned by name, was confirmed by implication. The only custom abolished by the charter was the swearing of oaths over the graves of deceased compurgators. Only once in 1276 was the charter of 1268 invoked in defence of the citizens' liberties. The mayor and bailiffs in a plea of dower maintained that the writ should not be pleaded in eyre unless it had been initiated in the husting and then respited until the coming of the justices because the tenant had vouched a foreigner to warranty. In support of their claim they proffered a royal writ ordering the justices to allow them rights and liberties granted by Henry III in his charter; Ralph de Hengham had been sent with fuller instructions and the plea was to proceed according to his counsel. Ralph said that it was ordained before the king and the whole council that the citizens should have the liberties contained in their charter and should not plead or be impleaded by any writ unless initiated in the husting and transferred to the eyre because of foreign voucher (**484**).

If royal charters and precedent were the twin pillars of the citizens' defence of their liberties, it was upon precedent that they relied most heavily. A number of administrative and procedural specialties were based upon precedent. The Londoners' claim to have their own janitor outside the gate of the Tower and their own usher outside the door of the hall where the pleas were heard together with their own sergeants, was allowed in 1276 (**2**) as it had been in 1244 and 1251.[3] The articles of the eyre were to be administered by the mayor and citizens and not by ward juries; the chamberlain and sheriffs were answerable for 'new' pleas of the crown; and the mayor and aldermen (or citizens) were to serve as a presentment jury. In 1244 the City claimed successfully that the mayor and citizens, and the sheriffs, should answer, not under oath but 'in the faith in which they are bound to the king and according to the fealty they have done to him'.[4] In 1276 the mayor and aldermen (or citizens) answered in like manner. The justices enquired whether or not jurors should be sworn in a plea of land, to which the mayor and aldermen replied that in cases of winning or losing land, as in cases of homicide, they should be sworn (**514**). Their answer is confirmed elsewhere in the record: juries of forty-two (e.g. **214, 233, 249**) and even the mayor and aldermen (**146, 187, 222**) took an oath in cases of homicide, as

1. Accordingly, two Londoners who were indicted and one who was appealed in the Middlesex eyre of 2 Edward I were successfully claimed for the liberty of the City on the ground that they were not bound to answer outside the City (**279–80**).
2. Meekings, *Crown Pleas*, 61–5.
3. In 1321 the City's right was challenged (as it may have been in 1276 although the plea roll is silent on the point), on the ground that the marshalsy of the eyre belonged as an hereditary right to John de Dagworth (*Eyre of London, 1321*, i, p. xxvi and App. 5; H. M. Cam, *Liberties and Communities* (Cambridge, 1944), 136–49).
4. *London Eyre, 1244*, no. 6.

Introduction

did juries of twenty-four in pleas of land (**523**). The constable of the Tower claimed that no prisoner should be delivered to the sheriffs once he had entered the gate of the Tower; the mayor and citizens, on the other hand, claimed that they had always been given custody of prisoners, even though they had entered the Tower (**98**). The issue remained unresolved until 1321.[1]

During the review of crown pleas a number of customs were explained to the justices. Despite the provisions of the Statute of Westminster I the citizens successfully claimed that they were not obliged to raise hue and cry (**24**) and that persons arrested on suspicion of felony, including homicide, might be bailed without writ.[2] Mention has already been made of a number of other customs including: the presentment of first finders of corpses, escapes from sanctuary, attachments, the Great Law and outlawry.[3] The claim disallowed in 1244, that enquiries into deaths by felony or misadventure were the exclusive duty of the chamberlain and sheriffs and that no other examination should be made,[4] was repeated in 1276 but on two occasions the justices held examinations of this kind (**18, 146**).

Newgate was clearly the most populous prison; Aldgate was also used as a prison on at least one occasion (**153**) and the sheriffs sometimes used their own houses (**83, 316, 509**) or another house (**204**). A canon of Holy Trinity Aldgate was kept in chains in the priory until he was delivered to the justices of gaol delivery at Newgate (**55**). A clerk was imprisoned at Newgate by licence of the sheriff (**316**). As escapes were frequent and as the sheriffs were liable to be heavily amerced in consequence, it was important for outgoing sheriffs to be acquitted of the prisoners in their custody. This they did by means of chirographs drawn up with the incoming sheriffs (**134**). *Suet de prison* (an amenity or alleviation of imprisonment) was adjudged 'against the law and custom of the realm and the City' (**496**; cf. **257**). The keeping of watch and ward 'according to custom' is also mentioned in the review of crown pleas (**20, 138, 159**). The mayor himself is found patrolling the streets to see that a good watch was being kept early in the Barons' war in June 1263 (**146**).

The impact of custom upon civil pleas was even more marked than its impact upon crown pleas. The most important customs invoked in the hearing of civil pleas have already been mentioned[5] but several others deserve comment. In pleas of covenant and debt where there was no written agreement the plaintiff was to prove his case by witnesses rather than the defendant to clear himself by jury or twelve-handed. It further transpired that clerks might not act as witnesses in such cases (**488**). If a will was proved in the husting a legatee might take possession of land or rents without proceeding against the heirs of a testator and conversely, if a will was annulled in the husting the heirs of a testator might take possession without proceeding against the legatee (**517**). The land of a married woman could not be alienated unless she came into the husting and formally renounced it (**489**).

No mention of the office of recorder appears in the plea roll but in 1321

1. *Eyre of London, 1321*, i, 37.
2. & 3. See above, pp. xv–xix.
4. *London Eyre, 1244*, nos. 39–40.
5. See above, pp. xxiii–xxv.

Introduction

it was asserted that from time immemorial the citizens had claimed their franchises and customs in eyre by the mouth of the recorder.[1] In 1276 the mayor and aldermen are frequently said to have put their custom on record (*recordantur*) (e.g. **488, 517, 523**) and it is reasonable to suppose that the alderman most learned in City custom had this responsibility. But the first named recorder was John de Wengrave who was sworn in 1304. It has been pointed out that the oath which he took does not look like the oath of a newly created office.[2] It is also significant that every recorder until the late fourteenth century was an alderman. The holders of the office were not only learned in customary law but of high standing in the City hierarchy. If, as seems probable, the functions of the recorder were performed in 1276 by one of the aldermen, a possible candidate is at hand. William de Durham was acquitted of a debt of over £6 which he owed to the City by reason of 'his various labours' at the eyre 'undertaken on behalf of the City'.[3]

The Financial Issues of the Eyre
The exchequer summons[4] (**525–786**) is the only surviving financial record concerned exclusively with the London eyre of 1276. The judicial sessions ended before the middle of March and were followed by fiscal sessions at which the justices fixed the amount to be paid for the amercements incurred during the pleas. The order of the debtors listed on the estreat reflects the order in which the justices carried out their work. Those who had failed to answer the common summons and violators of the assize of wine were assessed first (**526–9**). Crown pleas on mm. 1–3d of the plea roll were dealt with next (**530–40**) and then those on mm. 11–15 (**541–90**). Escapes presented in response to the article on that subject were assessed (**591**) before the remaining crown pleas on mm. 4–11 (**592–662**). The concluding sessions were devoted to violators of the assize of cloth (**663–7**), disseisins and civil pleas (**668–725**), and purprestures (**726–85**). The order of the debtors within each of these groups is closely related to the order of the plea roll,[5] which suggests that the justices were assisted by the mayor and aldermen, rather than by ward juries, in determining the economic capacity of those amerced.[6] Had ward juries assisted, a less obvious relationship between the order of the two documents might be expected.

The size of amercements varied considerably.[7] The highest amercement was £260 (**591**) and the lowest, 3s. 4d. (e.g. **761–2**). Jews amerced for purprestures were assessed at the abnormally high rate of £5 (**775, 777**), half a mark being the usual rate for Gentiles. The margination *ad judicium* did not always result in amercement. Wards against whom *ad judicium* or *miseri-*

---

1. The best account of the early history of the office is in *Eyre of London, 1321*, i, pp. lviii–lxi. It should be noted, however, that G. A. Williams (in 'London and Edward I', Royal Historical Society *Trans.*, 5th series, xi (1961), 97) argues that the office was created in 1298.
2. *Eyre of London, 1321*, i, p. lviii.
3. *C. Letter-Book A*, 211. It is possible, but less probable, that the 'various labours' were those of the City's pleader or common serjeant.
4. For a description of the document, see above, pp. xiii–xiv.
5. With the exception of **706–25**.
6. Cf. *London Eyre, 1244*, p. xvi.
7. For an analysis of fines and amercements, see Appendix B.

Introduction

cordia was noted invariably escaped amercement as was often the case in circuit eyres. The valuation of chattels entered on the plea roll is, in two instances (**107, 228**), not accounted for in the estreat. In neither case had the usual marginal note been made, which may explain why these chattels were overlooked. The absence from the estreat of a number of purprestures on the plea roll may be attributed to arrentation: in return for annual rents (*firmae minutae*) owners of property might be allowed to retain buildings which had offended, or land upon which they had encroached. These 'small purpresture farms' were accounted for by the sheriffs but did not form part of the estreat.

Some mention has already been made of the entries on the estreat which cannot be matched with the plea roll.[1] A large group, comprising disseisins (**668–706**) may, however, be readily explained. Assizes of novel disseisin and of mort d'ancestor were not heard before the justices unless the disseisin had occurred after the summons of the eyre or in cases of foreign voucher. But fines and amercements arising from assizes held in the City before the eyre belonged to the crown and were assessed by the itinerant justices.[2] No possessory assize rolls survive with which to compare the amercements on the summoned estreat. The amercement of the Jews of England in £1000 *pro pluribus transgressionibus* (**551**) is unexpected. Although the functions of the exchequer and the exchequer of the Jews overlapped[3] no satisfactory explanation can be offered as to why this entry appeared on the estreat. Seyton and his colleagues were expressly forbidden to hear Jewish pleas which was the duty of the justices of the Jews. The justices itinerant were ordered to report orally to the king their findings concerning a supposed ritual murder by Jews[4] and it is just possible that this incident provided the pretext for the swingeing fine. It is noteworthy that the entry on the estreat was cleared.

Debts on the estreat total £1,808[5] (excluding the £1,000 imposed upon the Jews). Crown pleas gave rise to debts totalling £1,208, of which £770 was for escapes. With one exception (**558**) each escape was assessed at £20; no other category of offence was equally profitable to the crown. The value of chattels entered on the estreat was £129;[6] chattels to be answered for by county sheriffs, or at the wardrobe, were not, of course, entered.[7] Civil pleas, on the other hand, gave rise to debts totalling only £44. Violators of the assize of cloth were assessed at a total of £428, violators of the assize of wine at £57, perpetrators of purprestures at £33 and defaulters on common summons at £38.

The estreat might, at first sight, confirm the dictum *justicia magnum emolumentum est* but the profits of justice were easier to assess than to collect. The writ of summons which tops and tails the list of debtors,

---

1. See above, pp. xiii–xiv.
2. For later procedure, see Statute of Gloucester (6 Edward I, c. 14).
3. *Calendar of the Plea Rolls of the Exchequer of the Jews*, iii, ed. H. Jenkinson (1929), pp. xiii–xix.
4. See above, p. xxi.
5. The calculations given in the present paragraph are 'rounded up' or 'down' to the nearest pound.
6. Included in the crown pleas total.
7. See Appendix C.

Introduction

ordered the sheriffs to collect the debts and pay them into the exchequer. The sheriffs heavily annotated the roll: their marginations and interpolations (printed in italic in the present edition) vividly illustrate the difficulties confronting them, e.g. *pauper, obiit, ignotus, Hibernia, ultra mare*. No doubt the crown was cheated more often by death than by any other single cause although insolvency was common. Naturally enough, debtors used every means at hand to avoid or delay payment. Writs of respite or attermination, or even of pardon, might be procured. Attermination (abbreviated to *att'* or *atterm'*) permitted the debtor to pay by instalments. Debtors who obtained this privilege were usually important persons: e.g. Henry de Coventry (**529**), John de Northampton (**533**), Henry Walemund (**539**), Stephen de Cornhill (**547**), Henry de Frowyk (**591**), William de Durham (**650**), Richard de Araz of Lincoln (**643**), Luke de Lucca and his associates (**666**) and the master and brethren of St. Bartholomew's hospital (**685**).

The sheriffs' notes in the margins of the estreat frequently employed exchequer conventions. *Addr'* (*addressare*) indicated an order to the debtor to make amends and account for his debt. Tallies (*tall'*) were sometimes issued and when the sheriffs held security for a debt the marginal note *vad'* (*vadium*) might be added. Conversely, *nihil in ballio* indicated that the sheriffs had obtained no security for the debt. Orders to distrain (*levar' fac'*) were sometimes noted. The symbol Ø (a contraction of the older *O.Ni: oneratur nisi habeat sufficientem exoneracionem*) showed that the sheriffs had become the king's debtors and that the original debt was owed to the sheriffs. Because two or more persons were often liable for parts of the same debt and might make payment of their share at different times, notes were needed to signpost the fact (e.g. *pars, residuum*). When the debt had been cleared the entry was deleted (indicated by an asterisk in the present edition). *T.* (*totum*) announced that the full charge of an exaction would be removed to a later Pipe Roll. A cross (+) was apposed to debts which were later to be assembled for clearance in a lump sum. The symbols *d, Ro 1* and *2* and the dots preceding certain debtors' names repeated annotations in the Estreat Roll[1] showing that removal of the debt in question to the Pipe Roll was still pending. The sheriffs continued to work upon the summoned estreat until 1278 when the estreat was resummoned.

It is sometimes possible to trace the later history of individual debts in the Receipt, Memoranda and Pipe Rolls. This has been done in the editorial notes following each entry or group of entries in the present edition. Excerpts from the Pipe Rolls of 5 and 6 Edward I have been printed in Appendix E and these require some further explanation. Traditionally the amercements of an eyre were accounted for as occasional revenue under *Nova oblata* where they were listed *De amerciamentis itineris* (followed by reference to the eyre in question and the name of the presiding justice). In the first audit, after the issue of an exchequer summons, the clerk prepared the Pipe Roll according to procedures explicitly described in the Pipe Roll orders of 1270 and 1273.[2] The clerk did not repeat all the individual charges on the estreat. Instead, the sheriffs were charged and acquitted for a lump

1. For this practice, see C. A. F. Meekings, 'The Pipe Roll order of 12 February 1270', *Studies presented to Sir Hilary Jenkinson*, ed. J. C. Davies (1957), 222–53.
2. *Ibid.*

Introduction

sum payment. In addition, the Pipe Rolls of 5, 7, 9 and 13 Edward I record a number of group payments of this kind, not by sheriffs but *per diversos*.[1] The names of the debtors grouped by these arrangements were marked off on the Estreat Roll without being listed in the Pipe Roll. The London and Middlesex account of 5 Edward I enters the grouped and individual payments together among the *Nova oblata*. The account of 6 Edward I lacks any record of a lump sum payment. It contains scattered references to the eyre but places them between the entries for recurring revenues and the entries under *Nova oblata*; a note is added: *Debita et libertates huius itineris non sunt in rotulo*. In several later county accounts lump sum payments are again recorded suggesting that resummonses were issued at intervals. It remains to show the totals of the lump sum payments in the Pipe Rolls which may be directly attributed to the eyre:

	£	s.	d.
5 Edward I (see Appendix D)	137	3	4
7 Edward I (E 372/123 m.9)	40	16	8
9 Edward I (E 372/125 m.12)	7	13	4
13 Edward I (E 372/130 m.10)	35	0	0
Total	£220	13	4

The estimated totals for the eyres of 1244 (£220), 1251 (£300)[2] and 1321 (£155 to £200)[3] are of a similar order.

One other financial issue of the eyre deserves consideration, namely deodands. The sheriffs were answerable for them, but not to the exchequer. From time to time the king granted the deodands belonging to the eyres for some charitable purpose. The recipient of the deodands of the London eyre has not been traced but in 1278 the king granted all deodands adjudged during the next three years to the London Dominicans[4] in aid of building their new house on the site of Baynard Castle. In 1280 the *Domus Conversorum* was granted all deodands adjudged in eyres for the term of seven years starting at the end of the Dominicans' term;[5] in 1290 the grant was renewed but this time, at will.[6] A similar grant of Irish deodands was made to the priory of St. Mary Waterford in 1290.[7] The deodands of the London eyre amounted to £38 10s. 10d or £18 10s. 7d. if the two unmarginated items (**216, 221**) are excluded from the total. The amount compares unfavourably with the deodands received by the *Domus Conversorum* between 1281 and 1286[8] from circuit eyres when it is remembered that in 1276 the justices were reviewing misadventures which had occurred during a twenty-five year period.

---

1. According to Mr. Meekings payments *per diversos* are exceptional and are not met with in other counties.
2. *London Eyre, 1244*, pp. xvii–xviii.
3. *Eyre of London, 1321*, i, p. xvi n.
4. *C.P.R. 1272–81*, 252; cf. *C.C.R. 1272–9*, 515.
5. *C.P.R. 1272–81*, 371–2; cf. *C.C.R. 1279–88*, 107.
6. *C.P.R. 1281–92*, 363.
7. *C.P.R. 1281–92*, 356.
8. M. Adler, *Jews of Medieval England* (1939), 301–2.

Introduction

A Note on Wards

Until the late thirteenth century most of the wards into which London was divided were referred to by the name of the presiding alderman. In the plea roll of 1276 only half a dozen wards were referred to by their modern names: Portsoken, invariably (**43, 111, 156**); Cheap, in most cases (e.g. **65, 72**) and Billingsgate, Castle Baynard, Dowgate and Langbourn at least once (**365, 132, 124, 197**). In the record of pleas of the crown wards were sometimes designated by the name of the alderman holding office in 1276 rather than by the name of his predecessor who presided during the period of the case under review. For example, the name Henry le Waleys, alderman (*c.* 1269–94), is used to describe Cordwainer ward in a plea of 1252–3 (**35**) and that of Simon de Hadstock, alderman (*c.* 1269–88), to describe Queenhithe ward in a plea of 1253 (**30**). On the other hand, the names of aldermen not in office in 1276 were frequently given: the ward of Billingsgate, for example, was designated in a plea of 1254–5 by the name of Arnold fitz Thedmar (**60**) who died in 1275 and Coleman Street ward by the name of William de Essewy (**83**) who died in 1259. Thus the names of several aldermen are often used in the plea roll to describe the same ward. The problem is further aggravated by our lack of precise information about the aldermen who held office before 1276.[1] Although it is occasionally possible to confirm the identification of a ward by topographical evidence contained in the record, some of the modern ward names provided by the editor in the present edition must be regarded as tentative.

1. The Letter-Books which enable Beaven (*Aldermen*) to stand on reasonably firm ground for the period after 1276 do not exist for the earlier period. Beaven's listings of earlier aldermen, while useful, are frequently confusing.

Introduction

APPENDIX A

ARTICLES OF THE LONDON EYRE, 1244 AND 1276

The following list of articles is arranged in the order of Helen Cam's 'national model' of *Vetera Capitula* (Cam, *Studies*, 92–3) and the number preceding each article is that used by her. Articles which occur in the London set of 1244 are followed by '1244' with references to the appropriate entry numbers in *London Eyre, 1244*, while articles which occur in the 1276 set are followed by '1276' with references to the entry numbers in the present edition. Those articles which were not part of the 'national model' are listed separately at the end as 'Unique articles 1244' and 'Unique articles 1276'. It should be noted, however, that the text printed in *London Eyre, 1244* was not taken into account by Professor Cam in her work on the articles of the eyre (Cam, *Studies*, 24–8).

ARTICLES FROM THE 1190s TO THE 1240s

1. *De veteris placitis.* 1244 (7, 269); 1276 (omitted).
2. *De novis placitis corone.* 1244 (8, 270); 1276 (the article was omitted but such pleas were heard).
3. *De illis qui sunt in misericordia domini regis.* 1244 (9, 194, 271 reading *fuerunt* for *sunt*); 1276 (**295**).
4. *De valettis et puellis.* 1244 (12, 197, 274); 1276 (merged with Cam no. 5 in **297**).
5. *De dominabus.* 1244 (omitted); 1276 (merged with Cam no. 4 in **297**).
6. *De ecclesiis.* 1244 (14, 199, 276); 1276 (abridged as **299**; see also below, Unique articles 1276, **298**).
7. *De eschaetis.* 1244 (with varying scope 15, 208, 277–8, 302); 1276 (in full **341**).
8. *De serjantiis.* 1244 (13, 198, 275); 1276 (**300**).
9. *De purpresturis.* 1244 (16, 343, 348); 1276 (**342**).
10. *De denariis.* 1244 (omitted); 1276 (**301**).
11. *De mensuris* and *De pannis venditis.* 1244 (coalesced in 17, 322; *de pannis* 225); 1276 (*de mensuris* **468**; *de pannis* **294**).
12. *De vinis venditis.* 1244 (18, 223, 324); 1276 (**292**).
13. *De thesauris inventis.* 1244 (19, 200, 325); 1276 (**304**).
14. *De vicecomitibus.* 1244 (omitted); 1276 (omitted, but the justices enquired concerning hue and cry in **24**).
15. *De ballivis qui tenent placita corone.* 1244 (20, 201, 326); 1276 (**305**).
16. *De usurariis Christianis mortuis.* 1244 (21, 202, 338, amplified by unique articles aiming also at living Christian usurers, see below, Unique articles 1244, 34, 231, 314, 327); 1276 (all combined in **306** omitting *Christianis*).
17. *De catallis Francorum et Flandrensium.* 1244 (narrowed down in 22, 203, 328; cf. below, Unique articles 1244, 195); 1276 (broadly rephrased to include all foreign born **310**).
18. *De catallis iudeorum occisorum.* 1244 (23, 204, 329); 1276 (**336**).
19. *De falsonariis.* 1244 (24, 206, 330); 1276 (**309**, but see also **11**).
20. *De moneta et escambio.* 1244 (with variation of phrasing 25, 207, 331); 1276 (**311** retaining the phrasing in 1244's 25 and 331).
21. *De malefactoribus et burgatoribus* omitted in national model after 1231. 1244 (retained completely 26, 332; narrowed down 205); 1276 (retained in full **312**).
22. *De utlagatis et fugitivis* eventually omitted from national model. 1244 (27, 221, 333); 1276 (omitted).
25. *De mercede capta.* 1244 (28, 224, 334); 1276 (**313**).
27. *De novis consuetudinibus.* 1244 (29, 226, 335); 1276 (**314**).
28. *De defaltis.* 1244 (30, 227, 336); 1276 (**340**).
29. *De gaolis deliberatis* split into nos. 29 and 30 in later versions of the national model. 1244 (31, 228, 337); 1276 (retained as one in **317**).

xxxiii

Introduction

31. *De malefactoribus in parcis et vivariis.* 1244 (omitted); 1276 (enlarged **315**).
32. *De evasione latronum.* 1244 (33, 230, 340); 1276 (**316**).
34. *De prisis factis extraneis.* 1244 (extended to include *de dampnis* 35, 232, 339); 1276 (**319** retaining the 1244 version).
35. *De hiis qui non permittunt ballivos domini regis introire.* 1244 (omitted); 1276 (retained with broader phrasing in **337** and answered in the negative, but such a plea was heard among the new pleas, **141**).
36. *De ballivis qui ceperunt denarios pro recognitoribus amovendis.* 1244 (omitted); 1276 (**338** reading *recognicionibus*).

ARTICLES SINCE 1246

44. *De ballivis ambidextris.* 1276 (**325**).
51. *De hiis qui piscantur cum kidellis et skarkellis.* 1276 (**339**).
52. *De vicecomitibus . . . qui ceperint denarios . . . ut dimitterint per plevinas.* 1276 (rephrased in **324**).
53. *De vicecomitibus et aliis ballivis qui imprisonaverunt.* 1276 (**326** answered in the negative, but see **257, 289, 496**).
54. *De vicecomitibus et aliis ballivis qui bis ceperunt denarios pro uno amerciamento.* 1276 (**327**).
55. *De hiis qui manuceperunt habendi aliquem . . . primo die.* 1276 (**330**).
56. *De hiis qui extraxerunt brevia regis.* 1276 (**331**).
58. *De pontibus et calcetis fractis.* 1276 (**334**, reading *de pontibus fractibus*).
59. *De imprisonatis ad voluntatem ballivorum sine causa racionabili.* 1276 (**318**).
60. *De felonibus suspensis et dampnatis alibi quam coram justiciariis ad omnia placita.* 1276 (**335**).
62. *De hiis qui distringunt aliquem ad pacandum plus.* 1276 (**328**).
63. *De hiis qui distringunt plures habentem unum nomen.* 1276 (**329**; see also **38**).
64. *De denariis captis ab excommunicatis.* 1276 (**333**).
65. *De denariis captis pro defaltis non venientibus ad summonicionem vicecomitum.* 1276 (**332**).

UNIQUE ARTICLES 1244

De illis qui infra libertatem Civitatis maliciose domus aliquorum prostraverunt vel combusserunt contra pacem. 1244 (11, 273); 1276 (**296**).

De usurariis christianis vivis (sive mortuis). 1244 (34, 231, 327); 1276 (combined with Cam no. 16 in **306**).

De debitis domino regi patri domini regis debitis in gwerra et ante gwerram. 1244 (195); 1276 (omitted).

UNIQUE ARTICLES 1276

De abbathiis prioratibus hospitalibus que sunt et esse debent de advocacione domini regis (**298**).

De ballivis qui ceperunt mercedem ab aliquibus ut possint vendere pannos contra assisam (**302**).

De illis qui mercedem ceperunt de venditoribus vinorum ut possint vendere mixta vel putrida et de illis qui vina illa miscuerunt (**303**).

De christianis qui receperunt bona judeorum tam in cartis quam in denariis, vadiis et aliis (**307**).

De judeis qui fecerunt crudelitatem de pueris christianis (**308**).

De ballivis et aliis qui ceperunt prisas nomine regis ad opus ipsorum vel aliorum que non devenerunt ad manus regis (**320**).

Si provisiones facte per justiciarios ultimo itinerantes apud Turrim London de attachiamentis faciendis tam de placitis corone quam de assisis nove disseisine et aliis bene servate sint (**321**).

Introduction

Si aliqua magna summa pecunia fuerit collecta ad introitum et exitum portarum Civitatis London ad muros eiusdem Civitatis reparandos et ad alias operaciones eiusdem Civitatis. Et si aliqua pecunia assisa collecta fuit in ipsa Civitate per maiorem, vicecomites et aldermannos vel alios qui pecuniam illam ceperunt et quo pecunia illa devenit (**322**).
Si quod tallagium assisum fuit per quod pauperes gravati fuerunt et divites desportati (**323**).

APPENDIX B

FINES AND AMERCEMENTS

The following table analyses the fines and amercements in the estreat (**525–786**). Where only one amount is given it has been entered in the *Highest* column.

	Lowest £ s. d.	Highest £ s. d.
Pro pluribus transgressionibus		
chamberlain (**600, 624, 628**)	6 8	10 0 0
sheriffs (**531, 537, 565, 595, 600, 617, 659**)	6 8	10 0 0
Jews (**551**)		1,000 0 0
Appeals		
appellee and pledges for default (**548, 580**)	3 4	13 4
appellor and pledges for non-prosecution (**576–7, 579–81**)		6 8
appellor for false appeal (**622**)		6 8
Assize of cloth		
violators of the assize (**663–7**)	6 8	40 0 0
Assize of wine		
violators of the assize (**527, 529**)	3 4	3 6 8
Chattels (See also Appendix C)		
master of the Temple, for taking without warrant (and harbouring) (**596**)		20 0 0
sheriff, for concealment (**591**)		10 0 0
sheriff, for taking without warrant (**645**)		6 8
Contempt		
chamberlain (**650**)		3 6 8
sheriff of Suffolk (**712**)		3 6 8
Default		
of common summons (**526, 528**)	6 8	10 0 0
of neighbours, and pledges (**533, 535–6, 543–4, 547, 549, 553, 556, 559, 561–3, 567–9, 572, 574, 578, 593, 600, 604–5, 608–12, 616, 618, 620–1, 626–7, 629, 633, 635, 638–9, 642–3, 647–9, 651, 655–6, 660, 662, 721**) [normally 6s. 8d.]	3 4	1 0 0
of owners of houses in which misadventures or homicides occurred, and pledges (**530, 559, 631, 634**)	3 4	13 4
of persons attached: pledges (**724**)		6 8

Introduction

	Lowest			*Highest*		
	£	s.	d.	£	s.	d.
of persons present at homicides or suspected homicides, and pledges (**534, 558, 560, 565, 573, 605, 631, 640–1**)		3	4		13	4
of persons present at misadventures, and pledges (**532, 569–71, 602, 630, 637, 658**)		3	4	3	6	8

See also above Appeals

Detinue
of charters (**716**)					6	8
of hospitality (**719**)					6	8
unspecified (**720**)					6	8

Disseisin
defendant (**668–705**)		3	4	5	0	0
pledges (**668–705**)					6	8

Escapes
custodians of Aldgate, for an escape (**625**)				20	0	0
sheriffs of London, for each person who escaped (**533, 539–40, 555, 571, 575, 589, 591, 599, 638, 652**)				20	0	0
sheriff of Middlesex, for the escape of two persons (**588**)				10	0	0

False claim by plaintiff
in plea of intrusion (**711**)					6	8
in plea of land (**715**)					6	8
in plea of trespass (**707–10, 713**)		6	8	3	6	8

False presentation
of neighbours (**606**)					6	8

Frankpledges
for flight of felon in frankpledge (**567**)					6	8

Harbouring
in mainpast (**607, 615, 627, 653**)		3	4	20	0	0
(*after allowing escape*, **589**)				10	0	0
(*and taking chattels without warrant*, **596**)				20	0	0

Inquest, defective
sheriff (**546**)				3	6	8

Licence
to agree (in plea of trespass) (**717**)					6	8
to have an inquisition (**533**)				1	0	0

Mainpast
flight of servant in (**550, 573**)	1	0	0	2	0	0

See also above Harbouring

Mainprise
mainpernors, for failing to produce the person bailed (**545, 565, 613, 642, 657**)				5	0	0
mainpernors, for failing to do so on the first day (**552, 564, 576–7, 583–4**)		3	4	2	0	0
sheriff, ? for failing to answer earlier for mainprise (**533**)				5	0	0

Introduction

	Lowest £ s. d.	Highest £ s. d.
Purprestures (**726–85**) [normally 6s. 8d.]	3 4	5 0 0
Trespass		
acquitted of homicide but present (**619**)		3 4
? assault (and default) (**718**)		6 8
instigator of false indictment (**566**)		1 0 0
plaintiff and pledges for non-prosecution (**714**)		6 8
robbery (**587**)		1 6 8
wounding (**718**)		1 6 8

APPENDIX C

Felons' Chattels

In the following list the entry number in the plea roll is followed by that in the estreat. An asterisk (*) indicates that the value includes the year day and waste of the felons' lands.

	£ s. d.		s. d.
72[1]	78 16 8*	163, 632	10 0
138[2]	63 6 8*	172[11], 636	9 6
75, 596	40 0 0*	72, 594	6 8*
188, 644	40 0 0	163, 632	6 8
146[3]	27 10 9	228[12]	6 8
309[4]	20 0 0	276, 582	6 8
80[5], 598	13 6 8	92, 603	5 0
258, 572	5 3 0[6]	189, 645	5 0
316, 591[7]	4 10 8	284, 585	5 0
51, 538	4 0 0	41, 534	4 0
107[8]	4 0 0	112[13]	4 0
202, 650	2 14 6	214, 541	4 0
176, 638	2 14 0	206, 654	3 1
290, 590	2 0 0	29, 531	3 0
234, 557[9]	1 14 8	89, 601	3 0
60, 539	1 6 0	37, 533	2 0
9[10]	1 4 0	66, 592	2 0
194, 646	1 2 0	148, 623	2 0
218, 544	1 0 0	215, 542	2 0
231, 554	1 0 0	223, 549	2 0
286, 586	1 0 0	159, 631	1 6
213, 661	17 4	181, 640	1 6
79, 597	13 3	264, 576	1 4
163, 632	13 4	83, 599	1 2
262, 574	13 4	186, 644	1 2
50, 537	10 0	117, 614	1 0

1. Subsequently pardoned.
2. Remaining in the king's hand.
3. Sheriff of Kent to answer.
4. To be paid into the wardrobe.
5. One fourth part of a ship and 8 tuns and 1 pipe of wine.
6. Including a debt of £5.
7. £4 10s. in **591**.
8. No marginal note on plea roll perhaps explaining its absence from summoned estreat.

Introduction

9. 18s. + 6s. 8d. in **557** instead of 28s. + 6s. 8d.
10. 24 sheep; sheriff of Yorkshire to answer.
11. Also 28s. 6d. in Worcestershire (not in **636**).
12. As note 8 above.
13. Sheriff of Essex to answer.

APPENDIX D

Deodands

	£	s.	d.		£	s.	d.
horse (**67**)	3	0	0[1]	chair (**216**)			3[7]
(**161**)	1	0	0	chair and rope (**162**)	1	0	0
(**144**)		10	0	vessel (**142**)		1	2
(**178**)		8	0	(**174**)		1	0
(**10**)		5	0	leaden vessel (**13**)		4	0
horse and cart (**59**)		13	4	(**21**)		3	4
(**45**)		7	0	(**43**)		3	4
2 horses and cart (**227**)		14	8	(**14**)		2	0
2 pigs (**155**)		2	8	(**212**)		2	0
sow (**44**)		1	8	bowl (**69**)			3
bell-tower (**221**)	20	0	0[2]	bucket (**191**)			8
solar (**54**)		10	0[3]	brass pot (**210**)		1	8
wall and timber (**195**)	1	6	8	tine (**95**)			6
stone wall (**88**)		3	0	tub (**224**)			6
party-wall (**121**)		1	0	vat (**247**)		2	0
beam (**91**)		1	6[4]	pear tree (**232**)		1	6
(**8**)		1	4	pear tree and pears (**32**)		1	6
(**35**)		1	0	load of lead (**270**)		2	0
board (**101**)			6	mill-stone (**130**)	1	0	0
plank and knife (**22**)			—[5]	ship (**240**)	1	6	8
step (**254**)		6	8	(**248**)	1	0	0
(**164**)		5	0	(**259**)		6	3
(**175**)		1	0	(**139**)		3	0
(**40**)			7	boat (**184**)		10	0
(**68**)			6	(**229**)		6	0
ladder (**101**)			6	(**160**)		3	0
(**129**)			4[6]	(**251**)		2	0
ladder and timber (**64**)		3	10	boat and faggots (**220**)		6	0
wharf (**196**)		1	1	boat and wood (**12**)		15	0

1. Falsely valued by the ward at £2 13s. 4d.
2. No marginal note of deodand. In addition stone, timber and lead (unvalued) were granted to Christchurch Canterbury.
3. Falsely valued by the ward at 4d.
4. Falsely valued by the ward at 1s.
5. Not valued.
6. Falsely valued by the ward at 1½d.
7. No marginal note of deodand.

APPENDIX E

Extracts from London and Middlesex accounts in the Pipe Rolls
From the Account for 5 Edward I (E 372/121 m. 18d)

De amerciamentis coram magistro Rogero de Seyton et sociis suis apud Turrim London anno quarto.

Introduction

Iidem vicecomites reddunt compotum de 137 li. 3s. et 4d. de amerciamentis hominum quorum nominibus preponitur littera T in rotulo de predicto itinere quem predicti [justiciarii] liberaverunt. In thesauro 117 li. per diversos. Et 16 li. 15s. 8d. per vicecomites. Et debent 68s. et 4d.

Idem reddunt compotum de eodem debito. In thesauro 56s. et 8d. per diversos. Et debent 11s. et 8d.

Idem reddunt compotum de eodem debito. In thesauro di. m. pro Galfrido de Hundesdich [629]. Et debent 5s. respice infra.

Iidem vicecomites reddunt compotum de 5s. de Johanne de Gowington[1] [631] sicut supra continetur [sic]. In thesauro lib' per eundem. Et quieti sunt.

Henricus de Coventre 5m. pro vino vendito contra assisam [529]. Et 20 li. pro evasione Nicholai de Saunford[2] [589]. Et 10 li. pro receptamento [589]. Et 20 li. pro evasione Arnaldi Petri [591]. Et 20 li. pro evasione Thome de Barton [591]. Et 10 li. quia concelavit catalla et evasionem [591]. Et 10 li. pro pluribus transgressionibus. Et 4 li. 19s. et 11d. de pluribus debitis sicut continetur in rotulo precedenti.[3] Summa 98 li. 6s. et 7d.[4]

Hubelettus de Araz reddit compotum de di. m. pro pannis venditis contra assisam.[5]

Roes de Watford reddit compotum de di. m. pro iniusta detencione [719]. Et di. m. pro transgressione purpresture [?741]. Et debet di. m.

Johannes de Northht' 20 li. pro evasione Radulfi le Parmenter [533]. Et 40 li. pro evasione [591] quator latronum[6] sicut infra continetur. Et 100s. pro transgressionibus.[7]

Robertus de Kidderminstre quia non venit, Willelmus le Engleis et Walterus de Welles plegii reddunt compotum de di. m. [567]. In thesauro 2s. 2d. et ob. pro Roberto. Et debent alii 4s. 5d. ob.

Stephanus de Cornhull vicinus 20s. quia non venit [547]. Et 20 li. pro panno vendito contra assisam [663].

Reimundus de Burdeus 20s. pro fuga [573].

Johannes de Northht' et Ricardus Picard debent 80 li. pro evasione quatuor latronum sociorum Rogeri de Clere de quibus Johannes respondebat supra de 40 li. Et debet Ricardus 40 li. [591].

Henricus de Frowik et Lucas de Batencourt 280 li. pro evasione Rogeri Drinkwater et 12 sociorum suorum [591].

Reginaldus de Suffolk camerarius 100s. pro pluribus transgressionibus [624]. Et di. m. pro uno solio [757].

Robertus de Linton reddit compotum[8] quia non venit. Et debet di. m. pro pluribus transgressionibus [537 or 663]. Et debet 10 li. pro evasione [591] sicut infra continetur. In thesauro 11 li. per tres tallias. Et debet 4 li. et di. m.

Johannes de Wautham magister hospitalis Sancti Bartholomei London' et fratres sui annotati in rotulo de eodem itinere reddunt compotum de 100s. pro disseisina [685]. In thesauro nichil. Et in perdonis eidem magistro 100s. per breve regis. Et quieti sunt.[9]

From the Account for 6 Edward I[10] (E 372/122 m. 20d)

De amerciamentis per magistrum Rogeri de Seiton.

Debita et libertates huius itineris non sunt in rotulo.

Humfridus le Tailur et Johannes Cristemesse debent di. m. pro fuga Johannis le Gaunter [567]. De quibus Humfridus respondet infra de 40d. Et debet Johannes 40d. Humfridus le Tailur 40d. pro fuga sicut supra continetur.

Totus comitatus Midd' 10 li. 2s. 8d. [?552, ?569, ?564] pro falso iudicio et aliis transgressionibus. Robertus de Araz et Radulfus le Fevre 68s. 4d. de remanente eiusdem summe totalis sicut continetur in rotulo precedenti.

Robertus de Suffolk debet 20s. pro vinis venditis contra assisam[11] [527].

Introduction

De amerciamentis coram magistro Rogero de Seiton.
　　　　　　　　　　　Debita et libertates huius itineris non sunt in rotulo.
Robertus de Essex bureler reddit compotum de 100s. quia non habet Ceciliam que fuit uxor Jollani de Dunelm quam manucepit [657]. In thesauro 1 m. Et debet 6 m. et di.
Nicholaus de Wilton reddit compotum de di. m. pro plegio [687]. In thesauro liberavit. Et quietus est.
Henricus de Coventre reddit compotum de 98 li. 6s. 7d. de pluribus debitis sicut continetur in rotulo precedenti.[12] In thesauro 20 li. Et debet 78 li. 6s. et 7d.
Hubelettus[13] de Araz debet di. m. pro panno vendito contra assisam [663].
Roesia de Watford di. m. pro iniusta detencione [719].
Willelmus le Engleis et Walterus de Welles 4s. 5d. ob. pro plegio [567].
Reimund de Burdeus pro fuga 20s. [573].

1. *Godington* (**631**).
2. Staunford (**589**).
3. i.e. for 4 Edward I.
4. Cf. the entry for 6 Edward I printed below.
5. *Hubelinus de Araz pro vino vendito contra assisam* (**292, 527**).
6. *sociorum Rogeri de Clere* interlined.
7. Not traced.
8. ? *de 100s.* (**657**).
9. Lower down the membrane the county account concludes with the passage discussed by C. A. F. Meekings, 'The Pipe Roll order of 12 February 1270', *Studies presented to Sir H. Jenkinson*, 239.
10. Entries scattered between the audit of the City's farm and *Nova Oblata*.
11. *sed respice infra* interlined.
12. Printed above.
13. Recte *Robertus*.

EDITORIAL NOTES

The Plea Roll has been printed in English but shortened in several ways: words such as 'the said', 'the aforementioned' etc. have usually been omitted and regnal years have been rendered in an abbreviated form; charters and writs have been summarised. Three dots (. . .) indicate the omission of illegible words or phrases. The more common Christian names have been translated but the original spelling of surnames has normally been retained with the exception of some common latin place names which have been translated. A serial number printed in bold type has been assigned to each plea. Cross reference to other pleas and to entries in the estreat appear at the end of the plea in square brackets. Square brackets within an entry enclose matter supplied by the editor. Italic type in the text has been used exclusively to indicate the presence of a word or phrase appearing in the margin of the roll. For example, in the phrase 'So they are in *mercy*', the word *misericordia* appears in the margin. If the word or phrase in the margin does not appear in the text it is inserted there in round brackets, e.g. *2 marks* (*deodandum*). Where the margination was crossed through an asterisk (*) has been inserted in front of the italicised word or phrase in the text. The numbered series of marginal legal notations or *notae* have been printed in smaller type at the end of the entries to which they relate. Cross reference is made in each instance to the list of these annotations on m.20 (**524**). If the text of the *nota* in the margin does not differ from that in **524** it has not been repeated there but has been replaced by a cross reference.

The Estreat (*the Exchequer Summons*) has been printed in latin. The text is in roman type. Shrieval annotations are in italic;[1] those in the left hand margin of the roll precede the line to which they refer; those in the right hand margin follow it. Interlineations are enclosed in pointed brackets. An asterisk(*) precedes lines which are crossed through in the document. Words in square brackets are supplied by the editor. The phrase 'pro eodem' has been omitted where the sense is obvious. For convenience a number of headings printed in small capitals have been supplied by the editor, and the text has been divided into paragraphs each of which has been assigned a serial number printed in bold type. Cross references to the appropriate entry in the plea roll follow each paragraph. References citing Memoranda, Receipt and Pipe Rolls, together with certain other sources are printed in small type following the paragraph to which they relate. The more important discrepancies[2] between the plea roll and the estreat are also mentioned in the notes.

1. For an explanation of some of the abbreviations used by the sheriffs, see above p. xxx.
2. For a discussion of these, see above, pp. xiii–xiv, xxix.

LONDON EYRE, 1276
PLEA ROLL

(British Library Add. Charter 5153)

1. [m. 1] PLEAS BEFORE MASTER ROGER DE SEYTON, RALPH DE FREMINGHAM, JOHN DE COBHAM, GEOFFREY DE LEUKENORE AND MASTER THOMAS DE SODINGTON, JUSTICES ITINERANT FOR PLEAS OF THE CITY AT THE TOWER OF LONDON ON THE MORROW OF THE PURIFICATION 4 EDWARD I [3 Feb. 1276].

2. Be it known that it is found by the rolls of the last eyre[1] of the itinerant justices at the Tower of London that it was allowed to the barons of London that they might begin pleas before the justices as soon as they had their door-keeper outside the gates of the Tower and the king's door-keeper was inside the gates; and likewise that they might have their usher outside the door of the hall where the pleas are to be heard to introduce the barons and others of the City who have to plead and of whom he has notice; and the king's usher is to be inside the door; and that they are to have their serjeants with their rods, and no serjeant is to meddle on the king's behalf before the justices in any matter touching the office of serjeant.

   1. No record of the eyre of 1251 survives, but the wording in this paragraph differs little from *London Eyre, 1244*, no. 2.

3. The names of the mayors since the last pleas:
John Norman who was mayor during the last eyre (*35 Henry III*) [1250–1][1]
Adam de Basinges for one year (*36 Henry III*) [1251–2]
John de Tholosane for one year (*37 Henry III*) [1252–3]
Nicholas Bat for one year (*38 Henry III*) [1253–4]
Ralph Hardel for three years and more from the feast of SS. Simon and Jude until the feast of St. Valentine (*39–41 Henry III*) [1254–Feb. 1258][2]
William son of Richard for two years [1259–61]
John de Gisorz for one year [1258–9][3]
Thomas son of Thomas for four years [1261–Aug. 1265][4]
Hugh son of Otto [warden, Oct.–Nov. or Dec. 1265][5]
John de Lynde and John Walerand [wardens, Nov. 1265–June 1267][6]
Alan la Zouche [warden, June 1267–Apr. 1268][7]
Thomas de Ipegrave from Easter in the year [blank] until the feast of St. James [warden, Apr.–July 1268][8]
Stephen de Edesworthe [warden, July 1268–?1269][9]
John Adrian [mayor, June 1270–Oct. 1271][10]
Walter Hervy for one year [sic] [1271–3]
Henry de Frouwyk[11]
Henry le Waleys for one year [1273–5]
Gregory de Rokesle who is now mayor [1275–81]

1

1. Regnal and mayoral years coincided during the reign of Henry III.
2. On 1 Feb. 1258 Ralph Hardel was removed and the constable of the Tower appointed warden; on 13 Feb. William fitz Richard became mayor for the remainder of the term (*Lib. Ant. Leg.*, 32, 36, 177).
3. *Lib. Ant. Leg.*, 39. The name is out of place presumably because William fitz Richard held office in 1258.
4. The City was in the king's hand Aug. 1265 – June 1270. Roger de Leyburn and Robert Walerand were wardens before 15 Oct. 1265 (*C.P.R. 1258–66*, 461, 463; *Lib. Ant. Leg.*, 77).
5. *C.P.R. 1258–66*, 463, 512; *Lib. Ant. Leg.*, 79–80.
6. *C.P.R. 1258–66*, 512; *Lib. Ant. Leg.*, 80; *C.P.R. 1266–72*, 78.
7. *C.P.R. 1266–72*, 78, 215; *Lib. Ant. Leg.*, 93.
8. *C.P.R. 1266–72*, 215, 248; *Lib. Ant. Leg.*, 102.
9. *C.P.R. 1266–72*, 248; *Lib. Ant. Leg.*, 106. Hugh fitz Otto was warden March 1269–June 1270 (*Lib. Ant. Leg.*, 108, 124).
10. *Lib. Ant. Leg.*, 124.
11. ? Warden, ?11–18 Nov. 1272 during Henry's disputed election (*Lib. Ant. Leg.*, 151–4); warden during the absence of Henry le Waleys (*ibid.*, 171).

4. The names of the sheriffs who held office since the last eyre:

Nicholas Bat and Laurence de Frouwyk were sheriffs for one year, both have died, and John son of Laurence answers for them [36 Henry III.[1] cf. **6**]

William de Durham and Thomas de Wymbourne who has died and William answers [37 Henry III. cf. **14, 18**]

John de Norhamton who now answers and Richard Picard who has died [38 Henry III]

Robert de Lynton who now answers. William Esswy mercer who has died [39 Henry III: to Feb. 1255]

Stephen de Oistergate [and] Henry Waleman who have died for whom no one answers [39 Henry III: Feb.–Mich. 1255]

Matthew Bokerel who has died for whom William his son answers and John le Minur who has died for whom no one answers [40 Henry III]

Richard de Ewell who now answers. William Asswy draper who has died [41 Henry III]

Thomas son of Thomas and Matthew Bukerel[2] [and] William Gratefige[3] who have died [42 Henry III]

John Adrien who now answers. Robert de Cornhull who has died for whom Robert his son answers [43 Henry III. cf. **86**]

Adam Broning who has died for whom John his son answers and Henry de Coventre who now answers [44 Henry III]

Richard Picard who has died and John de Norhamton who now answers [45 Henry III]

Philip le Taillur who now answers. Richard de Walebrok who has died and for whom no one answers [46 Henry III. cf. **119**]

Robert de Monte Pesulano [and] Osbert de Suffolk who now answer [47 Henry III]

Gregory de Rokele who now answers and Thomas de la Forde who has died [48 Henry III]

Edward le Blund and Peter Aunger who have died [49 Henry III]

Gregory de Rokele [and] Simon de Adestok who now answers[4]

John Adrian and Walter Hervi who now answer

William son of Richard who has died for whom no one answers
John Adrian who now answers and Luke de Batencourt who has died
William de Durham and Walter Hervy who now answer
Thomas de Basyng who now answers and Robert de Cornhull who has died for whom Robert his son answers
Philip le Taillur and Walter le Poter who now answer [54 Henry III: July–Mich. 1270]
Henry le Waleys and Gregory de Rokele who now answer [55 Henry III]
Richard de Paris who now answers and John de Bodele who has died [56 Henry III]
John Horn and Walter le Potter who now answer [57 Henry III and 1 Edward I]
Peter Cosyn and Robert de Meldebourne who now answer [2 Edward I: Mich.–Nov. 1273]
Henry de Coventre and Nicholas de Wynton who now answer [Nov. 1273–Mich. 1274]
Luke de Battencourt who has died and Henry de Frouwyk who now answers [3 Edward I]
John Horn and Ralph le Blund who are now [the sheriffs] and answer [4 Edward I]

> 1. Dates supplied from P.R.O. *List of Sheriffs* (Lists and indexes, ix, Kraus reprint, 1963), 201. A number of regnal years appear on the margin, many of which are incorrect.
> 2. Bukerel succeeded Robert de Catalone, 19 Oct. 1257 (*Lib. Ant. Leg.*, 29).
> 3. Michael Tovy and John Adrian, bailiffs, 1–13 Feb. 1258 (*Lib. Ant. Leg.*, 32). Thomas fitz Thomas was reinstated on 13 Feb. 1258.
> 4. Elected but not admitted (*Lib. Ant. Leg.*, 77). The City was in the king's hand, Aug. 1265–June 1270. For the bailiffs during this period, see *List of Sheriffs*, 201.

5. The names of the chamberlains since the last eyre:
Arnold de Gereudon[1]

> 1. Large space left blank. For a list of chamberlains, see W. Kellaway, 'The coroner in medieval London', *Studies in London History*, ed. A. E. J. Hollaender and W. Kellaway (1969), 88.

PLEAS OF THE CROWN 36 HENRY III [1251–2]

6. In the same year, Arnold de Geraudon and Thomas Esporon being chamberlains, Nicholas Bat and Laurence de Frowik being sheriffs, for whom no one answers; Maud wife of John de Taterig and Richard his brother appealed John le Gerdeler of London in the husting of the death of John de Tateregge. They do not come and do not prosecute their appeal, so *let them be arrested* and their pledges to prosecute are in mercy. They have not found pledges except by faith (nisi per fidem). John le Gerdlere now comes and proffers a charter[1] of King Henry pardoning him his suit for breach of the peace arising from this death on condition that he stands to right in the king's court if anyone wishes to implead him. Publicly and solemnly it is proclaimed. And there is no one. So he is granted firm peace. It is testified that John was arrested and detained at Newgate and afterwards was released by the king's writ to twelve men on pledge to have

The Plea Roll

him here on the first day and they did not have him. The sheriffs do not answer for the pledges, so *to judgment* on the sheriffs. The sheriff of Essex is ordered to distrain John son and heir of Laurence de Frowyk then sheriff, on all his lands and from the profits and to have his body here on Monday in the third week of Lent [9 Mar. 1276].

> *Nota 1. . . . manucaptus usque ad iter justiciariorum . . . hoc primo . . .*
> 14th cent.: *nota scribatur* [cf. **524** no. 1].
> 1. *C.R. 1251–3*, 55, 22 Feb. 1252 (cancelled).

7. John son of Aubery (Albredi) killed John del Perer. He at once fled and is suspected, so *let him be exacted and outlawed*. No chattels nor frankpledge but he was in the mainpast of John whom he killed, so nothing from the mainpast. All the neighbours have died. Adam son of Aubery [does not come] and is not suspected. He was attached by Adam de Witebi 'paternostrer' and Robert de Notingham (**misericordia*).

8. Thomas de Michem fell from a ladder and was crushed by a beam . . . value of the beam 16d. for which the sheriffs are to answer. All the neighbours have died. No one is suspected. Judgment: *misadventure*.

9. [m. 1d] William son of Robert le Clerk of Tresk and Richard son of Geoffrey Boleng of the same took sanctuary in the church of St. Thomas on London Bridge, confessed that they were thieves and *abjured* the realm before the chamberlain and sheriffs. Richard's chattels are twenty-four sheep worth **24s.* for which the sheriff of Yorkshire is to answer. He also had two bovates of land in the vill of Tresk in the same county. So the sheriff of *Yorkshire* is ordered to take the land into the king's hand and to *enquire* about the intervening period.

10. Hamo Suuthall servant of Nicholas Bat fell from a horse into the Thames and was drowned. Value of the horse 5s. (*deodandum*) for which Nicholas Bat then sheriff is to answer. No one is suspected. Judgment: *misadventure*.

11. Gocelin de Colon' took sanctuary in the church of St. Paul's London, confessed that he was a forger of money and *abjured* the realm before the chamberlain and sheriffs. No chattels.

12. Robert Russel, Geoffrey de Wyndesores and Walter de Oxford were in a boat loaded with wood (*busca*). The boat sank because of its weight and Robert with it. Geoffrey and Walter escaped, were attached and do not come. They were attached by Roger Inkel 'mariner', William Nichol 'mariner', Ralph de Holebod and William de Okele[1] who was from Berkshire. So they are all in *mercy*. Value of the boat and the wood 15s. (*deodandum*) for which the sheriffs are to answer. (*Infortunium*).

> 1. *Willelmum de Okele* deleted; *obiit* interlined.

13. A woman named Cecily and her maid Juliana were fighting in a house, next to a leaden vessel full of hot water. During the fight both fell into the

The Plea Roll

vessel and were scalded to death. Value of the vessel *4s.* (*deodandum*) for which the sheriffs are to answer. William de Haverynge, attached for the death, does not come and is not suspected. He was attached by Richard de[1] Basing mercer and Roger de Derby 'taillur'. So they are all in *mercy. All the neighbours have died. No one is suspected. Judgment: *misadventure*.

1. *Ricardus de* deleted; *obiit* interlined.

PLEAS OF THE CROWN 37 HENRY III [1252–3]

14. In the same year, Arnold de Geraudon and Thomas Sporon being [chamberlains], for whom no one answers but Alice la Blund has their lands, William de Durham, who answers now, and Thomas de Wymbourn, for whom his son Michael answers, being sheriffs; Edith de Dumowe fell into a leaden vessel full of mash and was scalded to death. Value of the vessel **2s.* (*deodandum*) for which the sheriffs are to answer. All the neighbours come except Alexander Aberdas and he is not suspected. Alexander was attached by Adam But of Melkstrete tailor and Gilbert de Hospitali tailor. So they are all in *mercy*. No one is suspected. Judgment: *misadventure*.

15. Four unknown malefactors encountered Richard son of the Parson on London Bridge. A quarrel arising among them, they killed Richard and at once fled. It is not known who they were. Richard Kyngesfeld and Ralph de Bradele were then in company with Richard and were attached. They do not come and are not suspected. Richard was attached by Ivor la Suche and William la Suzche and Ralph by Simon Godewe and William Megucer. So they are all in *mercy. Richard Wildelyfe, Robert Vivien and Adam de Grescherche were attached for the death because they were staying in the house in which Richard was found killed. They do not come and are not suspected. Richard was attached by Vincent Bonenfaunt and John Wilde, Robert by Walter Godinou and Simon Leuman, and Adam by Nicholas Anaine and Jordan le Frankeleyn. So they are all in *mercy. All the neighbours have died, so nothing from them. [cf. **530**]

16. Alice wife of Ralph Mercer beat to death a boy named John in the ward of Michael Tovy.[1] She at once fled and is suspected, so *let her be exacted and waived*. No chattels. Her husband Ralph was attached for the death. He does not come and is not suspected. He was attached by Ralph Sire, Richard de Rumford, Nicholas Pyning, Richer de Erebourwe, Nicholas Sely, Gilbert Golet, Richard le Wollemanger, Alfred le Surgien, Wakelin le Dubbur, Warin le Bocher, Lorekin Slipertop and Silvester Daniel. So they are in *mercy.

1. In 1246 purprestures were found in the ward of Michael Tovy *versus Turrim*; Tower ward was tentatively suggested in *London Eyre, 1244*, no. 466. However, as William fitz Richard was alderman of Tower ward in 1253 (**22**), Aldgate ward seems to be a more plausible identification.

17. Charter of the earl of Gloucester of acquittance from common summons.

'Henry by the grace of God; we have granted on behalf of ourselves and our heirs to Gilbert de Clare that for his lifetime he shall have this liberty, namely, that he shall not be molested by reason of a general summons before any of our justices and shall not at any time be amerced for this reason; at Westminster, 17 September 47 Henry III [1263].'

1. *C.P.R. 1258–66*, 278, 18 Sep. 1263.

PLEAS OF THE CROWN 37 HENRY III [1252–3]

18. Arnold de Gerowedon and Thomas Sporon being chamberlains, for whom no one answers, Thomas de Wymborn and William de Durham, who answers now, being sheriffs; on Monday before the feast of SS. Simon and Jude [21 Oct. 1252] Richard Norman was found drowned in a pit in the garden of his father William Norman in Aldresgate street in the aldermanry of John le Minur.[1] Because it is not known and cannot be ascertained by any inquest held by the chamberlain and sheriffs whether he died by misadventure or felony, the justices wish to examine twelve men from the aldermanry where the incident occurred concerning the death. The mayor and barons say that it is not for the justices to hold an examination concerning a man's death. Because it is found in the rolls[2] of William de York that the mayor and barons in eyre have granted that the justices should hold enquiry at will, notwithstanding any inquest held by the chamberlain and sheriffs, the mayor and commonalty are in *mercy. Because no one answers for Arnold and Thomas, the sheriff of Essex is ordered to distrain Arnold's heirs and have their bodies here in fifteen days from the Purification [16 Feb.]. And likewise the bishops of Lincoln, Salisbury and Chichester are ordered to cause Thomas to come at the said term, as he is a clerk.

Nota 2. De maiore et communitate amerciatis quia in isto itinere dedixerunt id quod prius in alio itinere concesserunt.
14th cent.: *Nota scribatur* [cf. **524** no. 2].
1. Presumably Aldersgate ward.
2. *London Eyre, 1244*, nos. 39–40.

19. In the same year John de Gisors being chamberlain and the same being sheriffs; Alice de Enefeud was found drowned on Sunday after the feast of St. Matthew [28 Sep. 1253]. The neighbours have died. No one is suspected. Judgment: *misadventure*. Because the chamberlain makes no mention in his roll of the attachment of neighbours, whereas he should always enrol attachments of this kind on his roll and answer for them before the justices, *to judgment* on John son and heir of John de Gisors because he answers for his father. [cf. **628**]

20. On Wednesday before the feast of St. Gregory [5 Mar. 1253] Thomas son of William the Smith of Faversham took sanctuary in the church of St. Lawrence Jewry, confessed that he had cut purses and stolen a surcoat of russet at (? Barnet) and abjured the realm. No chattels. He was not harboured in the City, but was there because he was a vagabond. In addition the mayor and barons were asked how watch and ward should be kept over such thieves who took sanctuary in a church and who should answer for

The Plea Roll

any escape. They say in the faith in which they are bound to the king that there should be no watch and ward over such men and that no one should be amerced for their escape except only if any of them should escape from prison and then the sheriffs will answer for the escape. So *let there be a discussion.*

    Nota 3. *Quod nullus latro qui fugit ad ecclesiam debet per cives vigilari nec custodiri.*
    14th cent.: *Nota scribatur* [cf. **524** no. 3].

21. On Thursday before the Annunciation [20 Mar. 1253] Agnes de Barkyng, wishing to draw hot water from a leaden vessel in the house of John Makerel, fell into the vessel by accident. She was scalded and died forthwith. Value of the vessel *40d. (deodandum).* William Wade[1] and Thomas le Laster, neighbours, do not come. William was attached by Henry de Canterbury and Geoffrey Gypes, Thomas le Laster by Walter de Oxford tailor and Adam le Fuster. So they are in *mercy.* Be it known that the mayor and barons say in the faith in which they are bound to the king that they are not bound to present the finder; and this is found in the rolls of the last eyre.[2] John Makerel and his wife Felice, in whose house the incident occurred, were attached for the death elsewhere... Judgment: misadventure.

    Nota 4. *Quod nullus presentabitur inventor in Civitate pro morte hominis.*
    14th cent.: *Nota scribatur* [cf. **524** no. 4].
    1. *obiit* interlined.
    2. Cf. *London Eyre, 1244,* no. 37 for a similar claim.

22. [m. 2] On Thursday after the Annunciation [27 Mar. 1253] in his own house in the ward of William son of Richard [Tower ward], Nicholas de Hallyngber', wanting to make a hole in a plank (plana) with a knife, accidentally wounded himself in the thigh and cut his veins so that he bled to death. Arnold de Geredon and Thomas Sporon chamberlains and William de Durham and Thomas de Wymbourn sheriffs did not value the plank and knife when they held the inquest on the death, so *to judgment* on them. Alexander le Bowyer and Hervey de Martilane, neighbours, do not come and are not suspected. They were attached by Thomas de la Sale, Nicholas de Len, William le Minur and Walter le Pestour. So they are all in **mercy*.* The mayor and barons are asked whether all persons of twelve years old and over should attend inquests before the chamberlain and sheriffs and say in the faith in which they are bound to the king that when such an event occurs in the City they themselves hold the inquest with the more discreet neighbours and it is not customary in the City for all those of twelve and over to attend. So *let there be a discussion.*

    Nota 5. *Quod non est necesse ut omnes de etate xii annorum veniant ad inquisiciones de morte hominis coram coronatore et vicecomitibus.*
    14th cent.: *Scribatur nota* [With a pointing hand. Cf. **524** no. 5].

23. John son of Geoffrey Bosse of Warwickshire fled to the church of St. Bartholomew the Less in London, confessed that he had stolen 20s. from a servant near Coventre and committed many other thefts and *abjured* the realm before the chamberlain and sheriffs. No chattels because he was a vagabond and stranger.

24. On Friday before the feast of St. Dunstan [16 May 1253] in the aldermanry of William Viel [Bread Street ward] in Westchepe a stranger out riding tried to take from Henry de Westhamme a staff which he held in his hand and threw him down onto the pavement. He fell on his head as though half dead and died forthwith. The stranger at once fled. It is not known who he was and no one pursued him or raised the hue and cry. Geoffrey de Hallyngber' and Richard le Tayllur, neighbours, do not come and are not suspected. They were attached by William Viel, William Page, Richard Damyas and Martin de Waldene (*obierunt*). So they are in *mercy. Because this happened by day and the stranger was not arrested nor pursued, to judgment on the aldermanry. The mayor and aldermen are asked how pursuit should be made through the neighbourhood when a man is killed and whether the men of the neighbourhood should raise the hue and cry in such an event. They say that the neighbourhood need not raise the hue and cry unless they wish but in order to preserve the king's peace the men of the neighbourhood pursue the malefactors to arrest them if they can; though even if they do not pursue them they will not suffer any penalty on that account. So *let there be a discussion*. Because John le [sic] Gisors chamberlain made no mention in his rolls of the pledges of the neighbours, *to judgment* on his son John who answers for him. [cf. **628**]

> Nota 6. *Si secta debeat fieri post latrones aut hutesium levari.*
> 14th cent.: *Scribatur* [With a pointing hand. Cf. **524** no. 6].

25. On the feast of St. Urban [25 May 1253] an unknown beggar was found dead, apparently from hunger, in the ward of John de Blakethorn [Aldersgate ward] outside Aldresgate. Nicholas de Herlauwe and Roger de Celario, neighbours, do not come and are not suspected. Nicholas was attached by Philip de Wynton' and Alan de Pelham, Roger by Nicholas le Lorimer and John de Gatesdene. So they are in *mercy. No one else is suspected. Judgment: *misadventure*. Because John de Gisors chamberlain does not answer for the attachments of the neighbours and makes no mention of them in his roll, *to judgment* on him. Because the mayor and aldermen testify that the beggar was living among them in the ward, and the men of the ward made no mention of his name at the inquest held before the chamberlain and they do not even yet know what he is called, *to judgment on the ward. [cf. **628**]

> Nota 7. *Quod oportet nominare interfectum.*
> 14th cent.: *Scribatur* [cf. **524** no. 7].

26. Ranulf de Brinkele came out of his house at night to light a candle in Wollelane[1] in the ward of Ralph Sparling [Billingsgate ward] and an unknown malefactor waylaid him and struck him with a knife so that he died forthwith in his own house. The malefactor at once fled and it is not known who he was. Henry le Keu, Richard Boles, Walter Jur', and William de Faversham, the four neighbours who were attached, do not come and are not suspected. Henry was attached by Austin de Wrotham and Alfred Oysel, Richard by Ralph le Portur and Reginald Wytside, Walter by Christian the Clerk and Henry le Reus, William by Simon le Reus and Walter Skete. So they are in *mercy*. Be it known that four neighbours should always be attached when anyone is killed feloniously. Because the chamberlain makes no mention of the neighbours in his roll, *to judgment* on him. [cf. **628**]

> Nota 8. De quatuor vicinis semper attachiandis.
> 14th cent.: *Scribatur* [cf. **524** no. 8].
> 1. Unidentified.

27. Robert Bord, a beggar suffering from the falling sickness, suddenly fell down dead in the ward of John Horn [Bridge ward]. No one is suspected. Judgment: *misadventure*. Adam Capes and Austin Ballard, neighbours, do not come and are not suspected. Adam was attached by John Godhale and John le Cuneyse, Austin by Henry Beaupyne and Ralph Smalehunte. So they are in **mercy*.

28. Morkin de Enefeud of Middlesex took sanctuary in the church of St. Katherine outside London,[1] confessed that he had harboured a thief, Reginald de Beverley, with his stolen goods, and *abjured* the realm before the chamberlain and sheriffs. Nothing is known of frankpledge or chattels because he is from Middlesex. Therefore the sheriff of Middlesex is ordered to inquire about chattels and frankpledge and to answer for the amercements. Later the sheriff testifies that he had no chattels and was not in frankpledge because he was a vagabond.

> 1. Presumably the hospital of St. Katherine by the Tower, still regarded as part of Portsoken ward in the 13th century.

29. On Friday after the feast of SS. Peter and Paul [4 July 1253] Guyot servant of Master Matthew Boby encountered Arnato de Garsie, a Roman, and, a quarrel arising between them, Arnato hit Guyot on the arm and wounded him in other parts of the body so that he died on the third day after in the house of Master Sylvester de Anania in the ward of Nicholas de Wynton' [Langbourn ward]. Arnato at once fled and is suspected, so *let him be exacted and outlawed* according to the law and custom of the City. Chattels **3s.* for which William de Durham sheriff is to answer. Because the mayor and aldermen testify that Arnato was harboured in the ward for a long time outside frankpledge, *to judgment* on the ward. Master Sylvester and his servant Bernard de Chaors were attached for the death because Guyot died in Sylvester's house and they do not come. Master Sylvester was attached by Andrew le Fraunceys and William Prest, Bernard by John Theoland and Richard Faukes. So they are in **mercy*. The sheriffs are ordered to *arrest* Sylvester and Bernard if they can be found. Because William de Durham and Thomas de Wymbourn then sheriffs attached Sylvester and Bernard each by only two pledges whereas anyone suspected of a man's death should be attached by twelve, *to judgment* on the sheriffs. Afterwards the sheriff[1] testifies that they have not been found. The mayor and aldermen say in the faith in which they are bound to the king that they do not suspect them and that they did not abscond because of the death. Therefore nothing from them. [cf. **531**]

> Nota 9. Ad iudicium quia quidam receptatus fuit extra francum plegium.
> Nota 10. De vicecomitibus amerciatis quia dimiserunt quemdam attachiatum pro morte hominis per duos plegios ubi deberet [sic] invenisse xii plegios.
> 14th cent.: *Scribatur* [cf. **524** nos. 9–10].
> 1. Viz. William de Durham, surviving.

The Plea Roll

30. On the feast of St. Margaret the Virgin [20 July 1253] Lettice la Waleys, who suffered from the falling sickness, accidentally fell dead at the gate of a canon of St. Paul's London. No one is suspected. Judgment: *misadventure*. William Synod and Robert de Bray,[1] neighbours, do not come and are not suspected. William was attached by Ellis de Gynges and Simon le Frank, Robert by Nicholas Synot and Master William le Carpenter. So they are in **mercy*. The men of the ward of Simon de Hadstok [Queenhithe ward] where the incident occurred are asked how it happened and say they know nothing. So *to judgment* on the whole ward.

    1. *Robertus de Bray* underlined; *obiit* interlined.

31. Henry Vennair died suddenly of the falling sickness in the ward of Anketin de Auvergne [Farringdon ward]. No one is suspected. Judgment: *misadventure*. Gilbert de Cambridge, a neighbour, does not come and is not suspected. A second neighbour has died, so nothing from him. Gilbert was attached by Robert le Marchaunt and Ralph de Wyteby. So they are in **mercy*. Because the men of the ward do not know who the neighbours are and cannot name them, *to judgment* on the ward.

    Nota 11. Oportet nominare vicinos.
    14th cent.: *Scribatur nota* [cf. **524** no. 11].

32. [m. 2d] Nicholas de Berkyng while gathering pears in the garden of the prior of St. Bartholomew fell from a tree and died. Value of the tree and the pears **18d*. (*deodandum*). No one else is suspected. Judgment: *misadventure*. The men of the ward of John de Blakethorn [Aldersgate ward] are asked who was with him when he fell and say they do not know, so **to judgment* on the whole ward. Afterwards it was found in the rolls of the chamberlains and sheriffs that Henry de Wimbeldon, William de Leuesham, Gilbert de Wimbeldon and Thomas Randal were with him and were attached, but they do not come and are not suspected. Henry was attached by William Albyn and Peter Dunkan, William by Roger le Wolf 'pessoner' and Ranulf Canon, Gilbert by William de Berkyng and William Dibel, Thomas by Ralph Canon 'puleter' and John Randolf. So they are in **mercy*. Two neighbours have died, so nothing from them. Because the chamberlain and sheriffs falsely valued the deodand, **to judgment* on them. [cf. **532**]

    Nota 12. De warda amerciata quia nesciverunt qui fuerunt cum quodam qui oppressus fuit per quemdam [sic] *arborem per infortunium.*
    14th cent.: *Scribatur* [cf. **524** no. 12].

33. Alice de Lichefeld, who was suffering from some infirmity, accidentally fell dead in the ward of Simon de Hadstok [Queenhithe ward]. The men of the ward are asked how this incident occurred and say they know nothing, so **to judgment* on the whole ward. No one is suspected. Judgment: *misadventure*. Thomas Everard and Jordan de St. Pauls, neighbours, do not come. Thomas was attached by Adam the Sealmaker (Factorem sigillorum) and Gilbert le Cordwainer, Jordan by Ralph Paternoster and Simon le Cuverur. So they are in **mercy*.

34. Theobald de Melton was found drowned in the ward of Walmar de

Essex [Billingsgate ward]. As the justices cannot discover by inquest how he was drowned, the men of the ward are asked how it happened and say in the faith in which they are bound to the king that they know nothing, so *to judgment on the whole ward. No one is suspected. Judgment: *misadventure*. Robert Dagun and William Egrith, neighbours, do not come and are not suspected. Robert was attached by William Fros and Robert le Sachier, William by Michael the Clerk and John Sperlyng. So they are in *mercy.

35. A woman called Agnes was crushed by a beam in the house of Ralph Bullok in the ward of Henry le Waleys [Cordwainer ward]. Value of the beam *12d. (deodandum). No one is suspected. Judgment: *misadventure*. Two neighbours have died, so nothing from them. Ralph was attached for the death but has died. William de Neuport and Isabel de Haverhull who were in the house were attached, but do not come and are not suspected. William was attached by John le Bas and Peter le Botoner, Isabel by Geoffrey le Botoner and Thomas de Norhamton tailor. So they are in *mercy*.

PLEAS OF THE CROWN 38 HENRY III [1253–4]

36. In the same year the same being chamberlain, Richard Pikard and John de Norhamton being sheriffs; Robert de Haselyngfeud, walking on the bank of the Thames, fell in and was drowned. No one is suspected. Judgment: *misadventure*. Robert le Cornmonger and Roger Edrith, neighbours, do not come. Robert was attached by Henry le Engleys and John Ters, Roger by William Edrith and Richard de Billing. So they are in *mercy.

37. On the morrow of St. Andrew the Apostle [1 Dec. 1253] in the ward of Simon de Hadstok [Queenhithe ward], Ralph the Parmenter and William Gille quarrelled in the house of Walter de Exeport and later went out of the house and during the dispute Ralph hit William on the head with a wooden staff, so that he quickly died. Ralph was arrested by Walter de Exeport and handed over to Richard Picard and John de Norhamton then sheriffs, who imprisoned him in Newgate. Because it is testified that Ralph is still alive and living in the City and no one knows how he was delivered from prison, to judgment on the sheriffs for the *escape. The sheriffs are ordered to *arrest* Ralph and have his body in court on the following day (? *hic cras*). Walter de Exeport, John Milneward, Adam Scot and Ralph le Joynur, four neighbours, do not come. Walter was attached by Laurence le Brocher and William Dibel, John by Nicholas Hunde and William Hog, Adam by William Baterell and William Forain, Ralph by Laurence le Brocher and Baldwin le Tymbermonger. So they are in *mercy. The mayor and aldermen, asked if they suspect the neighbours, say in the faith in which they are bound to the king that they do not. Ralph comes on the following day and says when asked how he was delivered from prison, that it was by royal writ in the shrievalty of John de Norhamton. Asked where the writ of mainprise is, he says that it was taken from him in time of war, but that he was handed over to Paulin de Thorp skinner and William de Evesham who are present and acknowledge the fact; likewise to Richard de Batewell, William de

The Plea Roll

Batewell, Simon de Norhamton, Geoffrey Poteys, John de Garst, Thomas Prest 'peleter', Henry de Cestfeud, Thomas de Barton, Siward de Hertford and Thomas de Cambridge who were to have him here on the first day and did not have him. So they are in *mercy. *To judgment on John de Norhamton because he did not answer earlier for the mainprise, but nothing because the mainprise is not found in the coroner's roll. Asked how he wishes to clear himself, Ralph denies the death and everything and offers the king *20s. for enquiry to be made by the mayor and aldermen; by licence of the justices this is permitted. The mayor and aldermen say in the faith in which they are bound to the king that he is not guilty. So he is *quit*. But they say that Richard Fukelape of Northamptonshire killed William, so *let him be exacted and outlawed according to the custom of the City. Chattels *2s. for which the sheriffs are to answer. [cf. 533]

> Nota 13. *Quod ambo vicecomites responderunt de evasione licet aliquis evadat ab uno eorum.*
> Nota 14. *Quod oportet quod manucapcio irrotuletur in rotulo camerarii.*
> 14th cent.: *Scribatur* [cf. 524 nos. 13–14].

38. Agnes Daythef took sanctuary in the church of St. Mary le Bow London, confessed that she had stolen a surcoat and committed many other thefts and *abjured* the realm before the chamberlain and sheriffs. Nothing is known of chattels because she was a vagabond from Oxfordshire. Afterwards it is testified that a woman of this name is living in the City, so let her be arrested. Later a woman called Agnes comes, and asked by the justices what her name is and how long she has lived in the City, says she is called Agnes de Leic' and does not know by what surname others call her. Because the justices agree that at the time that the event occurred she was not yet born (non fuit in residencia nativa), she is *quit*.

39. On Friday after the feast of St. Scholastica the Virgin [13 Feb. 1254] in the ward of Laurence de Frowick [Farringdon ward], Lambert de Cologne and Walter esquire of Master Philip de Cancellis clerk were taking Philip's sister Alice home and when they came to the churchyard of St. Dunstan in the West (iuxta Novum Templum) they met Henry de Merston, a clerk of the chancery, and his servant Robert [de Kyngeston]. A quarrel ensued among them about the woman and Robert de *Kyngeston*, by Henry's order, stabbed Lambert with a knife below the right shoulder, so that he died on the third day after in the house of Master Henry the Versifier (Versificatoris). Robert at once fled and is suspected; because he was not of the City but of the county of Stafford, the sheriff of Stafford is ordered to have him *exacted and outlawed* in his own county. Henry is a clerk and lives in Bedfordshire in the diocese of Lincoln. Therefore the bishop of Lincoln is ordered to cause him to appear in three weeks from the Purification [23 Feb. 1276]; and the sheriff of Bedford is to *arrest* him if he can be found. Walter and Alice and the others who were present when the incident occurred do not come and were not attached, so *to judgment on the chamberlain and sheriffs for not attaching them. The mayor and aldermen are asked if they suspect Walter and Alice of the death and say that they do not, but that they were present. So they are in *mercy. Afterwards Henry comes, and asked how he

The Plea Roll

wishes to clear himself of incitement, says that he is a clerk and is not bound to answer here. Thereupon Richard de Berues minor canon of St. Paul's London comes and claims him as a clerk by virtue of letters of the bishop of London in which the bishop entrusted to him his authority for claiming clergy. Because it is provided by the king's council that no one is bound to answer a charge of incitement[1] before the committer of the deed (factor) has been convicted, let Henry be handed over to the bishop to have him before the king or his justices on summons on penalty of £100.

> Nota 15. De coronatore et vicecomitibus amerciatis quia non attachiaverunt illos qui presentes fuerunt in lite ubi quidam interfectus fuit percussus.
> Nota 16. De clericis liberandis ordinariis per justiciarios sub pena centam librarum ab episcopo loci levandarum.
> 14th cent.: Scribatur nota [cf. **524** nos. 15–16].
> 1. Cf. **70, 219**; Statute of Westminster I, c. 14.

40. [m. 3] James le Chaucer fell from a step in the house of William de Norfolk in the ward of William son of Richard [Tower ward], so that he died. Value of the step *7d. (*deodandum*). William de Norfolk was attached for the death, but has died and is not suspected. The neighbours have died, so nothing from them. No one is suspected. Judgment: *misadventure*. The men of the ward falsely valued the step, so *to judgment* on them.

41. Ralph de Worstede and Peter de Richemund were standing together by the church of St. Michael by Westchepe in the ward of Laurence de Frowyk [Farringdon ward] and, a quarrel arising between them, Ralph wounded Peter in several places with a sword, so that he died soon afterwards. Ralph was at once arrested while fleeing by near neighbours and taken to Newgate where before Peter the Constable[1] and Roger de Boyland justices of gaol delivery he was convicted and hanged. Chattels *4s. Because the justices cannot find out about the chattels from any inquest held by the chamberlain and sheriffs, *to judgment* on them. All the neighbours have died. Because it is testified that Ralph was harboured in the ward outside frankpledge before he committed the crime the whole ward is in *mercy*. Alecot de Wyteby, attached for the death because he was present when it occurred, does not come and is not suspected. He was attached by Thomas le Paternoster and Stephen le Chapeleyn. So they are in *mercy*. [cf. **534**]

> Nota 17. De warda amerciata pro quodam commorante in eadem extra francum plegium.
> Nota 18. Et de camerario et vicecomitibus amerciatis quia camerarius et vicecomites non inquisiverunt de catallis felonum.
> 14th cent.: Scribatur [cf. **524** nos. 17–18].
> 1. i.e. constable of the Tower.

42. Thomas de Sanzdamage of Yorkshire took sanctuary in the church of St. Botolph without Aldresgate, confessed that he had plundered certain men in Essex and *abjured* the realm before the chamberlain and sheriffs. Nothing is known of chattels nor of frankpledge because he was a stranger.

43. A woman called Alditha, wanting to draw hot water from a leaden vessel in the house of Roger Crepyn outside Alegate in the ward of Porsokene, fell into the vessel and was at once scalded to death. Value of the

The Plea Roll

vessel *3s. 4d. (deodandum). Roger was attached for the death but has died, so nothing from him. All the neighbours have died, except John de Stebenhuthe who does not come and is not suspected. He was attached by Thomas Pynnot and Roger Haring. So they are in *mercy. No one else is suspected. Judgment: misadventure. Because the men of the ward falsely valued the deodand before the justices, to judgment on them. [cf. 535]

> Nota 19. De warda amerciata quia male appreciaverunt deodandum.
> 14th cent.: Scribatur nota [cf. 524 no. 19].

44. A sow bit a one-year old child called Amice in the ward of Laurence de Frowyk [Farringdon ward] so that she died. Value of the sow *20d. (deodandum). The neighbours have died. No one is suspected. Judgment: misadventure. Walter le Soper, the child's father, and his wife Alditha were attached for the death but have died, so nothing from them. Because the chamberlain and sheriffs make no mention in their roll of their attachment, *to judgment on them.

45. On the feast of St. Dunstan [19 May 1254] Nicholas the Carter (Carettarius) of Shordich was driving a cart and horse beyond London Bridge and when he came to a ditch outside Bisshopesgate the cart overturned on him and crushed him to death. Value of the horse and cart 7s. (deodandum) for which Richard Pycard is to answer. No one is suspected. Judgment: misadventure. Thomas Mutton and Henry le Tuler, neighbours, do not come and are not suspected. Thomas was attached by Richard le Tuler and Walter Frebodi, Henry by John of Waldegrave and Richard Frere of the same. So they are in *mercy. [cf. 536]

46. Jaket servant of John de Gysors, Fulk [?servant] of John Amerb', Reginald de Wautham and William Picard were together in a boat on the Thames when the boat overturned. Jaket was drowned, but the others escaped. All the neighbours have died. Fulk and the others who were with him in the boat were attached for the death, but do not come and are not suspected. Fulk was attached by Bartholomew le Ferur and Geoffrey de Waldegrave, Reginald by John Burel and Richard Heryng. So they are in *mercy. William Picard has died, so nothing from him or his pledges (omnes obierunt). No one else is suspected. Judgment: misadventure. Asked what became of the boat, they say that it was never found, so nothing from the deodand.

47. William de Suffolk was suddenly found dead in bed in the ward of Henry le Galeys [Cordwainer ward]. The mayor and aldermen, asked if they suspect anyone of the death, say they do not. The aldermanry falsely presented the neighbours, so *to judgment on them. The first neighbour has died, but Ralph Adrian the second neighbour comes and is not suspected. So he is quit. Judgment: misadventure.

48. On the morrow of the Assumption [16 Aug. 1254] William de Wendene of Essex was playing chess (ad scaccarium) with Robert son of Bernard, a knight of Essex, in Robert's house in the ward of Ralph Sperling [Billingsgate ward] when a quarrel arose between them. Robert the knight's squire intervened with the intention of striking William because he was arguing with his master and William, perceiving this, struck Robert in the stomach with a knife so that he died. William at once fled and took sanctuary in the church of St. Mary atte Hulle where he remained for three days and then escaped. The mayor and aldermen are asked who should answer for the escape and say that an answer has been given elsewhere.[1] Therefore *let there be a discussion*. Because William was not of the City but of the county of Essex the sheriff of Essex is ordered to have him exacted and outlawed in his own county, and to inquire about chattels and frankpledge. Thomas de Hales, Henry the Cook, William Baudri and Simon Crul, four neighbours, do not come and are not suspected. Thomas was attached by John Sperlyng and Roger Heryng, Henry by John Frere and William Pikeman, William by Reginald Fresheryng and William le Fhismongere [sic], Simon by Richard le Rus and Thomas de Oystergate. So they are in *mercy. Robert son of Bernard was attached for the death but does not come. The mayor and aldermen, asked if they suspect him, say they do not. He was attached by Walter de Coumbes and Henry de Waleton baker. So they are in *mercy.

Nota 20. Quod nemo tenetur respondere de evasione in Civitate.
14th cent.: *Scribatur nota* [cf. **524** no. 20].
1. See **20**.

49. John le Tawyer killed Henry de Plumstede in the ward of Simon de Hadstok [Queenhithe ward] and was at once arrested and hanged for the death at Newgate. No chattels. Simon le Candeler, Stephen the Capper (Capellarius) and William Russell, three neighbours, do not come and are not suspected. The fourth neighbour has died. Simon was attached by John the Cook and Ralph Pertrix, Stephen by Henry de Gotham and Eustace le Fruter, Eustace[1] by Lovekin le Chapeler and Godman the Cook. So they are in *mercy.

1. *Recte* William.

PLEAS OF THE CROWN 39 HENRY III [1254–5]
50. In the same year, John de Gysors being chamberlain, William de Esewy mercer and Robert de Lynton, who now answers for him, being sheriffs; Thomas de Halstede killed Jordan de Cristchirche in the ward of John de Norhamton [Aldgate ward], at once fled and is suspected. So *let him be exacted and outlawed* according to the form (forma) of the City. Chattels **10s.* for which the sheriffs [are to answer]. He was harboured in the ward outside frankpledge, so the whole ward is in *mercy. Because the chamberlain and sheriffs made no mention of neighbours or frankpledge, to judgment on them. Afterwards it is testified that all the neighbours have died, so nothing from them. [cf. **537**]

Nota 21. De warda amerciata quia receptaverunt quemdam extra francum plegium.
14th cent.: *Scribatur nota* [cf. **524** no. 21].

51. [m. 3d] On the feast of St. Edmund [20 Nov. 1254] John le Joven and Robert de Pontefract were eating together with John de Butteley knight in the house of Walter the Marshal in Candelwykstrete in the ward of Thomas de Basynges [Candlewick ward] and on their departure a quarrel arose between them. Robert struck John with an anlace beneath the breast so that he died forthwith. Robert at once fled and is suspected of the death, so *let him be exacted and outlawed* according to the form etc. Chattels *6 marks for which the sheriffs are to answer. He was not in frankpledge because he was always coming and going (iens et rediens). John de Boteley of the county of *Southampton* was attached for the death, but does not come and is not suspected. He was attached by William de Abyndon of the county of Southampton and Geoffrey de Caumpes of the same county. So they are in **mercy*. [cf. **538**]

52. Walter son of Henry de Normanton of Lincolnshire took sanctuary in the church of St. Bartholomew the Less in London, confessed that he had robbed an agent (nuncium) of his cloths (pannis) to the value of 5s. and abjured the realm. No chattels, nor frankpledge because he was a stranger. Be it known that it is found in the rolls of the eyre[1] of William de York that the constable of the Tower, the sheriffs and the aldermen may receive abjurations without the chamberlain, if he should be absent on the king's business.

Nota 22. De abiuracione recipienda per constabularium Turris et vicecomites London' si camerarius absens fuerit [cf. **524** no. 22].
1. *London Eyre, 1244*, no. 93.

53. John de Berkeley servant of Bartholomew le Tayllur went out at night from Bartholomew's solar and came upon Simon de Lemynstre servant of Godman the Tailor in Cheap in the ward of William de Durham [Bread Street ward]. He struck him repeatedly on the head with a staff so that he died forthwith. He at once fled and is suspected, so *let him be exacted and outlawed*. No chattels, but he was harboured in the ward outside frankpledge; so the whole ward is in **mercy*. Because Walter de Vaus openly stated before the justices that John was not living with anyone in the ward, and afterwards it was testified that he was the servant of Bartholomew and a member of his household, *to judgment* on Walter. William of Bedford, Hugh of the same, Richard le Tayllur and Henry le Tayllur of Cristeshale, neighbours, do not come and are not suspected. William was attached by William del Hale and Ralph le Tayllur, Hugh by Gilbert le Tayllur and Robert Davy, Richard by William le Tayllur and Henry le Tayllur, Henry by William de Ware. So they are in **mercy*. Bartholomew and Godman have died, so nothing from them. Because the chamberlain and sheriffs attached the fourth neighbour Henry by only one pledge, *to judgment* on them.

Nota 23. De camerario et vicecomitibus amerciatis quia attachiaverunt quartum vicinum per unum plegium tantum.
14th cent.: *Scribatur nota* [cf. **524** no. 23].

54. Stephen son of John the Clerk, and his sister Agnes, both children, were crushed to death by their father's solar. Value of the solar *10s. (deodandum)* for which the sheriffs are to answer. No one is suspected.

The Plea Roll

Judgment: *misadventure*. All the neighbours have died. Because the ward of Henry de Coventre [Vintry ward] earlier valued the deodand at 4d. and now on examination by the justices at 10s., *to judgment* on the whole ward for the false valuation.

> Nota 24. De tota warda amerciata pro falsa appreciacione deodande [sic].
> 14th cent.: *Nota* [cf. **524** no. 24].

55. In the same year, William de Haselbech [being chamberlain] and the same being sheriffs; John de Bordray and Roger de Thele canons of Holy Trinity London were together in the priory and a quarrel arising between them Roger struck John on the head with a staff so that he died forthwith. Roger was at once arrested and kept in chains at the priory until he was delivered to Newgate gaol where before Laurence de Brok justice of gaol delivery he was handed over to Fulk Basset then bishop of London who claimed him as his clerk. The mayor and aldermen say in the faith [in which they are bound to the king] that such was the procedure in this case and that Roger is dead. Therefore nothing.

56. In the same year the same being chamberlain, Stephen de Oystergate and Henry de Walemond being sheriffs, for whom no one answers; unknown malefactors waylaid Simon de St. Pauls clerk of William le Moyne in the ward of John Norman [? Cordwainer ward] killed him and at once fled. It is not known who they were. William does not come now and was not attached, so *to judgment on the sheriffs. No neighbour was attached, so *to judgment on the sheriffs.

57. John son of Adam the Carpenter of Huthe took sanctuary in the church of St. Mary Conehop, confessed that he had stolen ecclesiastical books at Hertford and other goods and *abjured* the realm before the chamberlain and sheriffs. Nothing is known of chattels or frankpledge because he was a stranger.

58. Roger de Donewyz goldsmith took sanctuary in the church of St. Mary Conehop and Richard le Aguiler of la Haye in the church of St. Thomas Acon. They confessed that they had committed many thefts and *abjured* the realm. Nothing is known of chattels or frankpledge because they were strangers.

59. Robert son of Gerard and Peter Peitel of Bernate were driving a cart outside Bisshopesgate near a ditch when Robert fell from the cart into the ditch and died forthwith. Value of the horse and cart *1 mark* for which the sheriffs are to answer; but because the sheriffs have died, no one answers. Because the chamberlain did not value the deodand, *to judgment on him. Peter and the neighbours do not come and were not attached, so *to judgment on the sheriffs.

> Nota 25. De camerario amerciato quia non fecit appreciare deodandum [cf. **524** no. 25].

60. Michael brother of Albod the Fleming was having a celebration (in quodam tripudio) with others in a lane in the ward of Arnald Thedmar

[Billingsgate ward] when William Longman, Ralph Longman, Henry Smyth, William Heyroun, Richard Bosse and William de Orewell came up, a quarrel arising among them, William Longman and the others killed Michael and struck and wounded the others who were celebrating with him. William Longman, Ralph Longman and Henry Smyth were at once arrested and taken to Newgate, but they do not come now and it is not known how they were delivered from prison, so to judgment on the sheriffs for the *escape*. They have now absconded and are suspected, so *let them be exacted and outlawed* according to the custom of the City. Chattels *26s. (deodandum [sic]) for which the sheriffs are to answer. William Heyroun, Richard Bosse and William de Orewell fled immediately after the deed and are suspected, so let them be exacted and outlawed according to the custom of the City. No chattels and they were not in frankpledge because they were strangers. No neighbour comes because they were not attached, so *to judgment* on the sheriffs. [cf. **539**]

Nota 26. *Quod non oportet quod extranei sint in franco plegio* [cf. **524** no. 26].

61. Richard son of Avelin was shooting at targets with a crossbow in the parish of Holy Trinity when he accidentally hit Walter Sanzstere on the head with an arrow (tela) so that he died. Richard at once fled to the church of St. Magnus where he remained for three days and then escaped from the church and has now absconded. Therefore *let him be exacted and outlawed*. No chattels nor frankpledge because he was a vagabond.

62. A male infant was drowned in the Thames. William Croll found the boy and tied him by the foot to the quay of Nicholas Bat,[1] for which he was arrested and taken to Newgate, but now he does not come and it is not known how he was delivered from prison, so to judgment on the sheriffs for the *escape*. No neighbour was attached, so *to judgment* on the sheriffs. [cf. **540**]

1. ? At the end of Batteslane, alias Haywharf Lane (E. Ekwall, *Street-names of the City of London* (1954), 133).

[m. 4] PLEAS OF THE CROWN 40 HENRY III [1255–6]
63. In the same year John Gisors being chamberlain, Matthew Bukerel, for whom his son William answers, and John le Minur, for whom no one answers, being sheriffs; on Sunday before the feast of St. Martin [7 Nov. 1255] in the ward of Wolmar de Essex [Billingsgate ward] towards Billynggesgate Robert le Cordwaner beat Sarah wife of Henry the Tailor so that she gave birth to a female child. He at once fled and is suspected, so *let him be exacted and outlawed* according to the form of the City. He was harboured in the ward for a long time outside frankpledge, so **to judgment* on the whole ward. Asked if he had any chattels, they say he did not. All the neighbours have died. Because the chamberlain and sheriffs did not enrol the names of the neighbours, *to judgment* on them.

64. Simon the Carpenter fell from a ladder onto some timber in the ward of [Henry] le Waleys [Cordwainer ward], so that he died. Value of the ladder

The Plea Roll

and the timber *3s. 10d. (*deodandum*) for which the sheriffs are to answer. All the neighbours have died and no one is suspected. Judgment: *misadventure*.

65. Philip son of Richard le Tressere of Staunford and William son of Roger le Teler of Warwyk took sanctuary in the church of St. Lawrence Jewry, confessed that they were thieves and cut-purses and *abjured* the realm. No chattels. The men of the ward of Cheap are asked where the incident occurred for which they abjured the realm and say they know nothing, so *to judgment* on the whole ward.

> Nota 27. De warda amerciata quia nesciunt ubi casus accidit pro quo quidam abiuraverunt regnum.
> 14th cent.: *Scribatur* [cf. **524** no. 27].

66. William de Langeford of Oxfordshire took sanctuary in the church of St. Matthew Fridaistrete, confessed that he had stolen a surcoat value *2s.* and committed many other thefts and *abjured* the realm. Chattels *2s. for which the sheriffs are to answer. [cf. **592**]

67. Bartholomew de Gascony (Vasconia) was riding a horse in Holebourne in the ward of Laurence de Frowyk [Farringdon ward] when the horse stumbled and fell on top of him, crushing him so that he died on the fifth day after. Value of the horse *60s.* (*deodandum*) for which the sheriffs are to answer. Thomas le Waleys 'puleter', Robert de Cardoil, Manasser le Parmenter and Richard de Wilinghale, four neighbours, do not come and are not suspected. Thomas was attached by Ralph de Bedford parmenter and Henry de Staunton, Robert by Luke le Parmenter and Henry le Feroun, Manasser by Kyng le Parmenter and Ambrose le Parmenter, Richard by Serle le Tuler and a man called Richard whose surname is not known. So they are in *mercy. *To judgment* on the chamberlain and sheriffs because they do not know the surname of the pledge. Judgment: *misadventure*. Because the men of the ward say that the horse was only valued at 4 marks and it is found in the rolls of the chamberlains that it was valued at 60s., *to judgment* on them. [cf. **593**]

> Nota 28. De warda amerciata pro discordancia inter presentacionem suam et rotulos camerarii [cf. **524** no. 28].

68. Beatrice wife of William de Holeborn fell from a step in her house in the ward of Laurence de Frowyk [Farringdon ward] and broke her neck. Value of the step *6d.* (*deodandum*) for which the sheriffs are to answer. The neighbours have died and no one is suspected. Judgment: *misadventure*.

69. In the same year William de Haselbeche being chamberlain and the same being sheriffs; on Friday before the feast of St. James [21 July 1256] a boy named John son of Richard was scalded to death by a [bowl] full of hot water which fell on him in his father's house. Value of the bowl *3d. (*deodandum*) for which the sheriffs are to answer. Richard de Wycumbe, a neighbour, comes and is not suspected. He was attached by Niel the Measurer (Mensuratorem) and Geoffrey de Wautham. So they are in

*_mercy_. The other neighbour has died and no one is suspected. Judgment: _misadventure_.

70. Thomas le Jovene, who has died, and Peter de Micheham, who is present, sent [John] de Berkyng, Peter de Cray and Walter Halveclerk, who are dead (abierunt), to the house of Robert de Haraz to distrain Robert for the trespass of making cloths contrary to the assize in the ward of Thomas de Basynges [Candlewick ward]; because of the crowd of people that went with them, John son of Philip de Wynton', a child, was trampled to death under foot. All the neighbours have died, so nothing from them. Peter de Micham comes and is committed to Newgate _gaol_ until the morrow. Because the chamberlain and sheriffs did nothing about John de Berkyngg and the others, and, when they held their inquest did not attach them or enquire who the people were who went with them to the place, _to judgment_ on them. Because the justices want to examine the matter more openly by the aldermen, the case is adjourned until the following day. Afterwards the mayor and aldermen testify that William Samuel and Gerard le Paumer went with John de Berkyng and the others to the house, so _let them be arrested_. Afterwards it is testified that they have all died, so nothing from them. Then Peter comes and, asked how he wishes to clear himself, says that although he is not bound to answer any charge of incitement[1] or instigation before those accused of the deed are convicted, nevertheless he puts himself for good or ill upon the verdict of the mayor and aldermen; although he is of the liberty of the City, as the suspicion is small and slight, it is granted to him by licence of the justices. The mayor and aldermen say in the faith in which they are bound to the king that he is not guilty and was never an accomplice in the death, so he is _quit_.

<small>Nota 29. Quod oportet ille qui manucaptus est usque ad iter justiciariorum pro morte hominis vel alia felonia acquietet se per magnam legem.
14th cent.: _Scribatur_ [cf. **524** no. 29].
1. Cf. **39, 219**.</small>

71. An unknown woman was found floating in the Thames. She was brought out alive but died soon afterwards. No one is suspected. Judgment: _misadventure_. Roger le Mareschall, a neighbour, does not come and is not suspected. He was attached by Robert de Rotherhull and Gilbert Pavely. So they are in _mercy_. The other neighbour has died, so nothing from him.

72. In the same year John Gysors being chamberlain and [the same] being sheriffs; Alice wife of Robert de Langley appealed Robert de Mumpelers and Ralph de Mumpelers, who has died, in the husting of London of the death of her husband Robert. She does not come or prosecute her appeal, so let her be arrested and her pledges to prosecute are in mercy. She did not find pledges except by faith (nisi per fidem) because she was poor. The mayor and aldermen say that the parties have not come to an agreement. Robert de Monpelers[1] comes and, asked how he wishes to clear himself of the death, says that King Henry pardoned him his suit for breach of the peace and he proffers a royal charter[2] in these words: 'Henry by the grace of God; at the instance of our daughter Margaret queen of Scotland we have pardoned Robert de Monte Pessulano, Ralph de Monte Pessulano,[3]

The Plea Roll

Philip de Gloucester and Peter de Stanes, citizens of London, their suit for breach of our peace arising from the death of Robert de Langley lately killed in London, of which they are accused; and we grant them firm peace, on condition that they stand to right in the king's court if anyone wishes to implead them.' There is no one who wishes to prosecute him [sic] for the death, so they are granted firm peace. Because the king made no remission of chattels in the charter, let enquiry be made about the chattels by the mayor [and aldermen]. They say that in that year Robert had chattels worth 100 marks; a house in Milkstrete, year and waste worth 60s.; two shops and two solars in the ward of Cheap, year and waste worth 10 marks; a house and two shops in Honilane, year and waste worth 50s.; and the issues of all the properties in the intervening period for which the sheriffs are to answer. Likewise because Philip de Gloucester, Ralph de Monte Pessulano and Peter de Stanes previously absconded on account of the death and do not come, their chattels are to be confiscated. No chattels except a house that Philip had in the ward of Henry de Frowyk [Cripplegate ward], year and waste worth ½ mark and the issues of the intervening period for which the sheriffs are to answer. There is a mistake about the house and lands. [Blank] chaplain of St. Paul's London now holds the house and it is not known by what warrant, so to judgment on him. The sheriff is ordered to take the house into the king's hand. Peter had two houses and two cellars in Wodestrate, year and waste worth 65s. and the issues of the intervening period for which the sheriffs are to answer. [cf. **594**]

> Nota 30. *Licet rex perdonaverit sectam pacis sue tamen non remittit catalla, nisi in carta de pace expressa fiat mencio de catallis* [cf. **524** no. 30].
> 1. For his release at the instance of the queen mother, see *C.C.R. 1272–9*, 272, 28 Feb. 1276. For his connection with the royal household, see C. E. Trease, 'The spicers and apothecaries of the royal household in the reigns of Henry III, Edward I and Edward II,' *Nottingham Medieval Studies*, iii (1959), 24–30.
> 2. Cf. *C.P.R. 1247–58*, 498 where the name of Ralph de Montpellier does not appear.
> 3. *Radulfo de Monte Pessulano*, interlined.

PLEAS OF THE CROWN 41 HENRY III [1256–7]

73. In the same year Thomas Speron and Matthew Bukerel being chamberlains, William de Hassewy and Richard de Ewell being sheriffs; Thomas de St. Edmunds baker took sanctuary in the church of St. Thomas the Martyr on London Bridge, confessed that he had stolen a reliquary and other objects and abjured the realm. Because the chamberlain and sheriffs made no enquiry about his chattels, to judgment on them. Afterwards the alderman testifies that he had no chattels and was not in frankpledge, but was harboured in the ward of John Horn [Bridge ward], so to judgment on the whole ward.

> Nota 31. *De warda amerciata pro franco plegio* [cf. **524** no. 31].

74. [m. 4d] Alice le Normande appealed Frederico and Gentilio, merchants of Rome, in the husting of rape and the theft of a brooch (firmachuli) and a hood. She does not come or prosecute her appeal, so *let her be arrested* and her pledges to prosecute are in mercy. Because the sheriffs do not answer for the pledges, *to judgment on them. The mayor and aldermen testify that

The Plea Roll

Frederico and Gentilio were arrested and taken to Newgate, where they were delivered before Laurence de Brok. Therefore the sheriff is ordered to cause Laurence's son and heir Hugh to appear with his father's roll. Afterwards Hugh comes and finds six pledges to answer to the king for his father's term of office on the king's command, as appears by a writ among the 'brevia de precepto'.

75. William Asshebof merchant went to the house of Master Adam de Lynton in the ward of Richard de Ewell [Farringdon ward] to sell silk to Adam's wife Maud. Master Adam and his servant William le Waleys appeared and William Assheboef[1] and Maud hid in a room out of fright; Adam and his servant seeing this sought them out and when they found William they at once attacked him, Adam striking him with a sword so that he died forthwith. Adam and his servant William fled and are suspected, so *let them be exacted and outlawed* according to the custom of the City. Adam's chattels *20 marks (deodandum [sic]) and a house, year and waste worth *2 marks and the issues of the intervening period *38 marks for which the sheriffs are to answer. William had no chattels, but was harboured in the ward outside frankpledge, so the whole *ward* is in *mercy* (*pro franco plegio*). Because the chamberlain and sheriffs held no enquiry about the chattels, *to judgment* on them. Because the mayor and aldermen later testify that Maud and her maid Agnes were arrested and delivered[2] before the justices at Newgate and have now died, nothing from them. The sheriff is ordered to take the house into the king's hand. Richard le Parchominer the second neighbour does not come and is not suspected. He was attached by John of Pelham and Gervase of the same. So they are in **mercy*. John de Bere and Philip le Pestour, two neighbours, have died, so nothing from them. Walter de Herteford, the fourth neighbour, comes and is not suspected, so he is *quit*. Afterwards the mayor and aldermen testify that the master of the Temple in England took the chattels without warrant and that Adam returned to the master's house in London and was his clerk; he was harboured there for a long time after the crime. Therefore *to judgment* on the said master. [cf. **596**]

Afterwards the mayor and sheriffs of London were ordered by Master Roger de Seyton on the command of the king and his council to enquire whether the rents and tenements of Master Adam in the City of London were escheats of the king or not; the form of the inquisition is as follows: Inquisition held on Friday after the feast of St. Barnabas the Apostle 5 Edward I [18 June 1277] before Gregory de Roqesley mayor of London on the precept of Master Roger de Seyton and his fellow justices last on eyre in the City of London; to enquire whether the rents and tenements which once belonged to Master Adam de Lynton now deceased, at one time accused of the death of William de Assibhof merchant, are escheats of the king or not, by the following jurors: William de Assyndon, John de Vaus goldsmith, Henry le Ferur, John le Kyng, John de Horton, Walter the Marshal, Roger the Cook, Walter de St. Salvator, John de Chestehunt, Henry the Cook, William de Notyngham and Roger le Stiwr. The [jurors] say in the faith in which they are bound to the king that William de Assebof was killed in the house of Master Adam, who fled with his servant William

The Plea Roll

le Waleys; they were indicted and William at once fled overseas and was never afterwards seen in England, as far as they know; Master Adam absconded and stayed for some time with the Templars at the New Temple London, whose clerk he was, until Sir Henry de Wengham, then dean of St. Martin le Grand London and king's chancellor, procured for him a grant of the king's peace; the king granted him his peace[3] and remitted his suit and no one else proceeded against him; inasmuch as he had a royal charter and his peace was then publicly proclaimed throughout the whole City, he was restored to his rents and tenements and held them peaceably for two years after the proclamation; afterwards, in the zeal which he felt towards the dean and chapter of St. Martin's, he enfeoffed the said dean, chapter and church of the rents and tenements and from then on they were in full and peaceful seisin; thus for two years before the enfeoffment and for ten years after, Master Adam continually enjoyed the king's peace in the City, and there he died; he was never convicted of this felony or any other, so the jury say that his rents and tenements are not and ought not to be escheats of the king, because they were restored to Adam with his chattels after the proclamation of his peace on the king's command to the sheriffs of London.[4]

> Nota 32. Quod maior et vicecomites inquirant de escaetis [cf. **524** no. 32].
> 1. *Macelof* deleted; *Assheboef* interlined.
> 2. *C.P.R. 1247–58*, 547, 3 Apr. 1257.
> 3. For pardon at the instance of Conrad, archbishop of Cologne, see *C.P.R. 1247–58*, 548, 8 Apr. 1257.
> 4. For an order permitting the dean and chapter to hold the rents and tenements, see *C.C.R. 1272–9*, 437, 17 Jan. 1278. The order was made because the king had learned by the record of Master Roger de Seyton that the rents and tenements, whereof Adam in his lifetime had enfeoffed the dean and chapter, were not the king's escheats because Adam was never convicted of the said felony.

76. Richard Scharp wool-merchant beat his wife Emma so that she gave birth to a still-born boy. Because Richard has died, nothing from the outlawry. The mayor and aldermen testify that Richard was arrested and handed over to Richard de Ewell sheriff, who released him on the pledges of six men. Because according to the law of the City no one accused of a man's death should be released on bail except on the pledges of twelve men,[1] any of whom should be able to answer to the king for 100s. as amercement if he should fail, *to judgment on Richard de Ewelle. [cf. **595**]

> Nota 33. Quod rettati de morte hominis debent dimitti per xii plegios et non minus quorum quilibet sufficiens sit ad respondendum regi de centum solidis pro misericordia sua [cf. **524** no. 33].
> 1. Cf. **29**, **87**.

77. Nicholas de Duncon and John de Sutwerk, accused of theft, come and, asked how they wish to clear themselves, say they put themselves for good or ill upon the verdict of the aldermen. Because they are not of the liberty of the City, this is granted to them. The aldermen say in the faith in which they are bound to the king that they are not guilty of any misdeed, so they are *quit*.

> Nota 34. Quod forinceci rettati de latrocinio se possint acquietare per verdictum maioris et aldermannorum [cf. **524** no. 34].

The Plea Roll

PLEAS OF THE CROWN 42 HENRY III [1257-8]

78. In the same year, Peter de Gysorz being chamberlain, Thomas son of Thomas and William Gratefige being sheriffs, for whom no one answers; Michael of Spain killed Nicholas de Ireland near Castle Baynard and was at once arrested and taken to Newgate. Afterwards King Henry pardoned him his suit for breach of the peace by writ in these words: 'Henry by the grace of God; because at the instance of bishop Silvens[1] of Spain and with the consent and will of Richard de Clare, earl of Gloucester and Hertford, we have pardoned Michael of Spain, the bishop's man, his suit for breach of the peace arising from the death of Nicholas de Ireland, the said earl's man, for which Michael was in outlawry; we order you to hand over Michael, with his chattels seized on that occasion, to John Maunsel, treasurer of York, to be handed over to the said bishop; at Westminster, 4 May 43 Henry III'.[2] Therefore nothing from the outlawry or chattels. All the neighbours except William Dybel come and are not suspected. William was attached by Alan de Castello and Hugh le Bucher. So they are in *mercy*.

Nota 35. *Carta de pace regis concessa cum catallis* [cf. **524** no. 35].
1. Silves, Portugal (C. Eubel, *Hierarchia Catholica* i (1913), 452).
2. *Recte* 4 May 42 Henry III (*C.R. 1256-9*, 218).

79. Thomas son of Thomas Attewode of Barton took sanctuary in the church of St. Lawrence Candelwikstrete, confessed that he had stolen an ox and a horse and *abjured* the realm before the chamberlain and sheriffs. Chattels **1 mark* for which the sheriffs are to answer. [cf. **597**]

80. [m. 5] Oliver of Wynchelsee, Richard Fraunkeleyn and others were together in a ship on the Thames when a quarrel arose among them and Oliver killed Richard with a staff and threw him into the water. He at once fled and is suspected, so *let him be exacted and outlawed* according to the custom of the City. Chattels 20 marks which were handed over on the king's command to Stephen Andreu of Wynchilse and his son John, provided that on their behalf Henry de Bathon and Matthias de Mara undertook to pay the king the said 20 marks by royal writ[1] in these words: 'Henry [III] to the sheriffs of London; because Henry de Bathon and Matthias de Mara on behalf of Stephen of Wynchelesse and his son John have undertaken before us to pay in fifteen days from Michaelmas [13 Oct.] the 20 marks at which was valued the fourth part which pertained to Oliver [son of] Robert,[2] of the ship belonging to Stephen and John from which, it is said, Oliver threw a sailor into the Thames near the Tower of London, so that he was drowned; together with eight tuns and one pipe of wine which Oliver had on the ship and which belongs to us because of the felony committed by Oliver; we order you to hand over without delay to Stephen and John or their attorney the ship with gear and appurtenances, and eight tuns and one pipe of wine; at Westminster, 18 July 42 Henry III [1258].' Because Henry and Matthias are dead, let their heirs answer for the **20 marks*. No neighbour was attached because the incident happened on the Thames. [cf. **598**]

1. *C.R. 1256-9*, 249, 28 July 1258.
2. *Oliveri Roberti*.

The Plea Roll

81. Emma wife of John le Mazon took sanctuary in the church of St. Martin Isemongereslane, confessed that she had killed her husband John and *abjured* the realm before the chamberlain. No chattels. [cf. **84**]

82. In the same year Thomas Esperon being chamberlain and [Thomas son of Thomas and] Matthew Bukerel being sheriffs; Peter son of Geoffrey de Bosco took sanctuary in the church of St. Lawrence Jewry, confessed that he had stolen a cow at Totenham and abjured the realm before the chamberlain and sheriff. No chattels.

83. John Wodeman and Martin le Taylur were drinking together in a tavern in the ward of William de Essewy [Coleman Street ward] and when they returned home together from the tavern a quarrel arose between them as they were going towards the lodging and John killed Martin with a staff. He was at once arrested and taken to the house of Matthew Bukerel then sheriff, where he was imprisoned. Afterwards he escaped and took sanctuary in the church of St. Mary Wolmarchirch, where he remained for fifteen days and then escaped. Therefore to judgment on Matthew for the *escape*. John has not [sic] absconded and is suspected, so *let him be exacted and outlawed* according to the custom of the City. Chattels *14d.* for which the sheriffs are to answer. Nothing is known of frankpledge because he was a vagabond. All the neighbours except Robert de Kopherlee do not [sic] come and he is not suspected. He was attached by Ralph le Large 'ayler'[1] and Geoffrey Long 'bateman'. So they are all in *mercy*. [cf. **599**]

1. Garlick-seller.

84. Emma wife of John le Mazon and Joan daughter of Simon son of Mary, with other persons unknown, killed John le Mazon by night. Emma took sanctuary in the church of St. Martin Isemongerelane, confessed the deed and *abjured* the realm. No chattels. Joan fled and is suspected, so *let her be exacted and waived*. No chattels. All the neighbours have died, so nothing from them. [cf. **81**]

85. Christine daughter of John de Lincoln appealed Richard de Byllyng in the husting of rape. She does not come or prosecute her appeal, so *let her be arrested* and her pledges to prosecute are in *mercy*, viz. John her father and the others who were under oath to prosecute. Richard does not come. He was attached by John de Hungrie and Abel the Goldsmith, John Trentemars and Andrew Spereon. So they are in *mercy*. To preserve the king's peace let the truth be ascertained by the mayor and aldermen; they say in the faith in which they are bound to the king that the parties are not agreed and [Richard] is not guilty. Therefore he is quit.

Nota 36. *De appello facto in hustengo.*
14th cent.: *Scribatur nota* [cf. **524** no. 36].

PLEAS OF THE CROWN 43 HENRY III [1258–9]

86. In the same year, Peter de Gysors being chamberlain, who answers, John Adrian and Robert de Cornhull, who has died, being sheriffs, for whom John Adrian answers; a stranger was found dead on the bank of the Thames with his throat cut. The mayor and aldermen are asked who killed him and say in the faith in which they are bound to the king that they do not know, nor how he was washed up there, unless by the tide. John de Couventre, a neighbour, does not come and is not suspected. He was attached by Peter de Hamiston and Reginald le Barbur. So they are in *mercy. All the other neighbours attached for the death have died, so nothing from them. [cf. **600**]

87. John la Persone with others unknown went by night to the house of William de Clerkenwell and his wife Alice and killed them and carried off all their goods. They at once fled and John is suspected, so *let him be exacted and outlawed*. Nothing is known of chattels or frankpledge because he was from the county of Southampton, so let him be exacted and outlawed there. The mayor and aldermen are asked if they know who the men were who went with John to commit the murder and say in the faith [in which they are bound to the king] that they do not know and cannot discover by inquest because it happened by night; but they say that John's sister, Catherine, and her maid Dulcia[1] and also Maud de Horseye were attached on suspicion of the death and have now died, so nothing from them. Because it is found in the rolls of the coroner and sheriffs that the neighbours were attached by six pledges contrary to the custom of the City, *to judgment on the chamberlain and sheriffs. [cf. **600**]

Nota 37. De camerario et vicecomitibus amerciatis pro attachiamentis vicinorum per vi plegios contra consuetudinum Civitatis.
14th cent.: *Scribatur nota* [cf. **524** no. 37].
1. Cf. *C.P.R. 1247–58*, 666.

88. Theobald servant of Roger le Fuster was crushed to death by a stone wall in the ward of William Bukerell [Broad Street ward]. Value of the wall *3s. (*deodandum*) for which the sheriffs are to answer. No one is suspected. Judgment: misadventure. Thomas de St. Edmunds, one of the neighbours, does not come and is not suspected. He was attached by Reginald custodian of the houses of the abbot of St. Albans and Adam de Hormade of Hertfordshire. So they are in *mercy. Walter le Dormur falsely presented himself as a neighbour, so he is in *mercy. Likewise, because the men of the ward presented him as a neighbour, *to judgment on them.

Nota [38]. De vicino amerciato et warda amerciata pro falsa presentacione.
14th cent.: *Scribatur* [cf. **524** no. 38].

89. A woman called Felice, while passing through Wodestrate in the ward of Richard de Ewell [Farringdon ward], came upon Lucy brewster of Maunsell the Tailor standing in his doorway. Lucy seized Felice and dragged her into the house, charging her with taking away her business (*vendicionem servicie sue*). Thereupon Lucy, with William le Mercer and Alan de Cheddeworth, beat Felice so that she died on the third day after. William, Alan and Lucy have now fled and are suspected of the death, so let William and Alan be *exacted and outlawed* according to the custom of the City. They had no [chattels]. Let Lucy be *exacted and waived* according to the custom [of the City]. Chattels *3s. for which the sheriffs are to answer. Because the chamberlain and sheriffs made no enquiry about the chattels, *to judgment* on them. It is testified that they were harboured in the ward after the deed, so the ward is in *mercy*. All the neighbours attached for the death have died, so nothing from them. [cf. **601**]

90. Alan de Ireland took sanctuary in the church of St. Michael in Hoggelane, confessed that he had killed a man of Wymundeham and *abjured* the realm before the chamberlain and sheriffs. No chattels nor frankpledge because he was a stranger.

91. Adam le Hert, while building a house with many other workmen, was crushed to death by a beam in the courtyard of Simon Passelewe. Value of the beam **18d.* for which the sheriffs are to answer. All the neighbours have died. John de Chingeforde, Robert de Warr', Stephen de Smethefeud, William de Romoney and William de Upton were attached for the death because they were present when Adam was crushed, but they do not come and are not suspected. John was attached by Wibert de Opton and Walter de Plumstede, Robert by Thomas de Donstable mason and John de Middleton, Stephen by Thomas le Soper and John le Cordewaner, William by Master Andrew the Mason and John Frere, William de Opton by Adam de Lamburne and Simon Passelewe. So they are in *mercy*. Because the men of the ward of Peter de Edelmeton [Castle Baynard ward] only valued the deodand at 12d., *to judgment* on the whole ward. (*Infortunium.*) [cf. **602**]

92. Henry de Wokenden of Essex took sanctuary in the church of St. Mary de Wollochirch, confessed that he had stolen two oxen and *abjured* the realm. Chattels **5s.* for which the sheriffs are to answer. Because it is found in the rolls of the chamberlain and sheriffs that he was harboured in the ward of John Adrian [? Walbrook ward][1] in a house which he rented there, *to judgment* on the whole ward. [cf. **603**]

1. St. Mary Woolchurch is in Walbrook ward (cf. *Rotuli Hundredorum*, i (1812), 407; cf. Beaven, i, 373).

93. A man called Warin was bathing himself in the Thames when he accidentally fell in and was drowned. Peter le Fleg', the second neighbour, does not come and is not suspected. He was attached by William le Mannec' and John de Turribus. So they are in *mercy*. The other neighbour has died. No one is suspected. Judgment: *misadventure*. [cf. **604**]

94. Geoffrey le Gylour killed William le Werkeman in the ward of Richard de Ewell [Farringdon ward]. Afterwards he was arrested and taken to Newgate and there before Laurence de Brok he was convicted and hanged. All the neighbours have died, so nothing from them. *Let enquiry be made* about the chattels in the rolls of Laurence de Brok because the mayor and aldermen do not know whether he had chattels or not.

95. John son of Alexander Fresharing was scalded to death in his father's house in a tine full of hot mash. Value of the tine *6d.* (*deodandum*) for which the sheriffs are to answer. John Takepeny, a neighbour, does not

The Plea Roll

come and was attached by Paul warden of London Bridge, and John Godale 'oystrer'. So they are in mercy. John's father Alexander and his wife Margery were attached for the death, but do not come and are not suspected. They were attached by Peter the Goldsmith, John le Treyer, Reginald Fresharing and Robert de Coventre. So they are in *mercy. (Infortunium.)

96. Robert Perdriz of Weng fell and broke his neck. The neighbours come and are not suspected. Master Walter under Wall (sub Muro) and Thomas de Heltham capper were attached for the death because they were with Robert when it happened, but they do not come and are not suspected. They were attached by Philip de Neuchirch, Thomas de St. Albans, Thomas de Travers, and William le Cuver. So they are in *mercy. No one is suspected. Judgment: misadventure.

97. [m. 5d] Hamo Home was in a boat at Billingesgate in the ward of Ralph Sperling [Billingsgate ward] when William Nasegor and William le Hore came up and, a quarrel ensuing, killed Hamo. William Nasegor at once took sanctuary in the church of St. Mary de la Hulle, confessed the deed and *abjured* the realm. No chattels. William le Hore at once fled and is suspected, so *let him be exacted and outlawed*. Because he was from *Kent*, the sheriff is ordered to have him exacted and outlawed in the county and to *enquire* about chattels and frankpledge.

Nota 39. *Quod forincecus exigatur in comitatu unde est* [cf. **524** no. 39].

98. William de Torington, accused of the deaths of William de Brustowe and John de Feltham and arrested and detained by the sheriffs of London, comes and denies the death and everything and for good or ill puts himself upon his country. Because he is from Surrey, the sheriff of Surrey is ordered to cause to appear twelve [men] of the neighbourhood of Puttenheth. William is meanwhile committed to the custody of the sheriffs of London. Thereupon the constable of the Tower claims that no prisoner should be delivered to the sheriffs of London once he has entered the gate of the Tower, but that custody belongs to him until judgment has been passed. The mayor and citizens say in the faith in which they are bound to the king that in other eyres they have always been accustomed to have custody of their prisoners even though they have entered the Tower; the constable shows no reason why he should have this custody even though they have entered the Tower. So it is adjudged that William be committed to the custody of the sheriff saving the constable's claim. Afterwards on the appointed day the twelve jurors from the neighbourhood come and say on their oath that William is not guilty of the death, so he is *quit*. Then William de Allegate and his wife Alice, John Postel, Walter Morket and his wife Alice were arrested for the death, come and deny the death and everything and for good or ill put themselves upon the verdict of the twelve [jurors], because they are strangers; they say on their oath that none of them is guilty of the death except Walter Morket, so [let him be hanged] (*suspensus*) and all the others are *quit*. Walter had no chattels.

Nota 40. *Quod vicecomites habebunt custodiam prisonum licet Turrim intraverunt non obstante calumpnia constabularii et hoc patet hic* [cf. **524** no. 40].

The Plea Roll

99. Henry le Baude was killed on London Bridge; Nicholas Russell, Hugh the Butcher, Ranulf Lyne and Richard Curteys were attached for the death because they came up when he was killed, but they do not come and the mayor and aldermen say that they do not suspect them. Nicholas was attached by Ailward le Keu of Estchep and Hugh le Flaoner, Hugh by Adam de Hak and William the Goldsmith, Ranulf by Gilbert le Melker and Richard Sharp, Richard by Robert Nicholas and Laurence Soutere. So they are in *mercy. The four neighbours come except Hamond le Drawer and he is not suspected. He was attached by Fulk le Drauer and Henry le Drawere. So they are all in *mercy. [cf. **605**]

> Nota 41. *Quod illi qui attachiati sunt eo quod fuerunt presentes quando infortunium vel felonia accidit et similiter vicini attachiati se debent acquietare per veredictum maioris et aldermannorum* [cf. **524** no. 41].

PLEAS OF THE CROWN 44 HENRY III [1259-60]

100. In the same year, Peter de Gysorc' being chamberlain, Henry de Coventre, who answers for himself, and Adam Bruning, for whom his son John answers, being sheriffs; Ralph son of Robert de Catton of Norfolk, took sanctuary in the church of St. Mary Abbechirch in the ward of Richard de Ewelle [Farringdon ward], confessed that he was a sheep-thief and *abjured* the realm. No chattels.

101. Peter le Gardiner was climbing a ladder to put a board (tabulam) above the beams in his house when he fell upon his neck and died forthwith. Value of the ladder 6d. and of the board 6d. (*deodandum 12* [sic]) for which the sheriffs are to answer. Because the chamberlain and sheriffs made no enquiry about the ladder, to judgment on them. Ralph le Gardiner and Thomas le Keu [who] were in the house do not come and are not suspected. They were attached by Terry le Lorimer, Ralph de Neuport 'lorimer' and Thomas de Norhamton. So they are in *mercy. Two neighbours have died and William le Taylur and Thomas de Norhamton falsely presented themselves as neighbours, so to *judgment on them. Likewise because the men of the ward of Cheap produce (proferunt) them as neighbours and they are not, to *judgment on them. No one is suspected. Judgment: *misadventure*. [cf. **606**]

> Nota 42. *De warda et illis qui presentaverunt se vicinos et non fuerunt amerciatis.*
> 14th cent.: *Scribatur* [cf. **524** no. 42].

102. Robert de Berkyng, William de Walehop, Walter de Marlebergh, William Knith and John le Cordewaner were drinking together in the house of Albin the Baker in the ward of Richard de Ewell [Farringdon ward] when a quarrel arose among them and William and the others beat Robert de Berkyng to death and then dragged him to the Thames. They at once fled and are suspected, so let them be exacted and outlawed according to the custom of the City. They had no chattels and were not in frankpledge but William de Walehop and Walter were in the mainpast of John Skylman, and William Knyth in the mainpast of Thomas Purtre. So they are in *mercy.[1] Also because William and Walter were harboured in the ward of

The Plea Roll

Thomas son of Thomas [? Queenhithe ward], and William Knyth and John le Cordewaner in the ward of Richard de Ewell, outside frankpledge, *to judgment*[2] on the wards. The four neighbours and all the others attached for the death have died, except Eve, Albin's wife, who comes and is not suspected, so she is *quit*. [cf. **607**]

> Nota 43. De wardis amerciatis pro franco plegio et similiter de quibusdam amerciatis in quorum manupastu etc.
> 14th cent.: Scribatur [cf. **524** no. 43].
> 1. *Misericordia* twice in margin.
> 2. *Ad iudicium* twice in margin.

103. William de Hakeney who had the falling sickness fell dead in the ward of Adam de Basing [Cheap ward]. No one is suspected. Judgment: *misadventure*. Richard de Ambersbyre, a neighbour, does not come and is not suspected. He was attached by William le Chandeler and Adam the Baker. So they are in *mercy*. Because the men of the ward do not know who the neighbours are, *to judgment* on them. [cf. **608**]

104. Five unknown malefactors killed Master John le Gras and Besance the Roman outside St. Paul's churchyard towards Westchep in the ward of Richard de Ewell [Farringdon ward] and at once fled. It is not known who they were, but they[1] believe they were of the household of John de Crakehale,[2] who is dead. All the neighbours have died.

> 1. ? The mayor and aldermen.
> 2. Archdeacon of Bedford and Treasurer of the exchequer, 1258–60 (Tout, *Chapters*, i, 296 n. 3).

105. Thomas Bagard capper and William Frere were quarrelling together in the ward of Peter Aunger [Broad Street ward] and William killed Thomas and at once fled, so *let him be exacted and outlawed* according to the custom of the City. Nothing is known of chattels, but he was harboured in the ward outside frankpledge, so the ward is in *mercy*. All the neighbours have died except Humphrey le Megucer who does not come and is not suspected. He was attached by William le Megucer and Gilbert le Marischall. So they are in *mercy*. [cf. **609**]

106. Robert de Naun took sanctuary in the church of the Friars Minor in London, confessed that he was a thief and plunderer and *abjured* the realm. No chattels nor frankpledge because he was a vagabond.

107. Henry Joie was found killed on London Bridge; Robert le Taylour absconded and is suspected of the death, so let him be exacted and outlawed according to the custom of the City. Chattels 6 marks for which the sheriffs are to answer. He had a messuage and eight acres of land at Depteford in Kent and the annual value is unknown. Therefore the sheriff [of *Kent*] is ordered to produce on Monday twelve men. All the neighbours come and are not suspected. Afterwards Robert was arrested and comes now and does not wish to put himself upon the verdict of his country, so let him be committed to *gaol*[1] and nothing from his outlawry.

> 1. Cf. *C.C.R. 1272–9*, 285.

The Plea Roll

PLEAS OF THE CROWN 45 HENRY III [1260-1] Seyton
108. [m. 6] In the same year, Peter de Gisors being chamberlain, John de Norhampton, who answers now, and Richard Picard, for whom Hubert Pycard answers, being sheriffs; Gailard, servant of Gailard de Solio, John the Cook,[1] and John, Gailard's cook, were fighting together in the ward of Henry de Coventre [Vintry ward] in the house of Stephen Bukerel, who has died. Peter Arnald came up to settle the quarrel between them and Gailard, wanting to strike John with a knife, struck Peter instead, so that he died. He at once fled and took sanctuary in the church of St. Martin in the Vintry, where he remained for eight days and then escaped, so *let him be exacted and outlawed* according to the custom [of the City]. No chattels. Gailard de Solio, Bertram de la De and John the Cook were arrested for the death and delivered at Newgate before Richard de Coleworth and William Aguilon, justices [of gaol delivery], by royal writ, so nothing from them. The said [sic] Peter le Rus baker, Ralph le Large, John ad Crucem and Henry le Cordewaner, four neighbours, do not come and are not suspected. Peter was attached by Hugh le Rous and Ralph le Large, Ralph by Peter le Rus and Hugh le Rus, John by Ralph le Large and Richard le Coupere, Henry by Nicholas Hardel and Reginald de Suffolk. So they are in **mercy*. Because the sheriffs attached the neighbours one by the other, to *judgment* on them. [cf. **610**]

Nota 44. Quod nullus vicinus debet attachiari per alium et hoc patet hic [cf. **524** no. 44].
1. *Recte* Bertram de la De.

109. Robert le Girdeler, Albin de Gosewell, Hugh le Caretter, Thomas le Brid, Robert le Brid, Robert de Gosewell and Walter [sic] killed Bartholomew de Bungey one evening in the house of Alexander le Orbatour in the ward of John de Blakethorn [Aldersgate ward]. They at once fled and are suspected, so *let them be exacted and outlawed* according to the custom of the City. No chattels. Stephen son of Nicholas, Richard de Berkhamstede, Peter le Vineter, three neighbours, do not come and are not suspected. Stephen was attached by Richard de Cesterhunte goldsmith and Thomas de Edelmeton, Richard by Absolon de Haketon and Robert le Girdeler, Peter by Gervase (Servagium) de Notyngham and Walter le Quilter. So they are in **mercy*. The fourth neighbour has died. Afterwards it is testified that Robert le Girdeler was harboured in the City until he died, so to judgment. [cf. **611**]

Nota 45. Quod nullus debet receptari in Civitate postquam feloniam fecerit sub pena etc.
14th cent.: *Scribatur* [cf. **524** no. 45].

110. Philip de Sar' took sanctuary in the church of St. Michael Paternosterstrete, confessed that he was a thief and abjured the realm before the chamberlain and sheriffs. No chattels.

111. Reginald Caperoun killed Nicholas le Baud in the house of Richard le Rus, clerk, in the ward of Porsokene. He at once fled, so *let him be exacted and outlawed* according to the custom of the City. No chattels, but he was harboured in the ward in the house of Reginald le Clerk, who now has no land in the City, but holds an ecclesiastical benefice in the diocese of Exeter. So he is in *mercy for the mainpast. The men of the ward falsely presented the neighbours, so they are in *mercy. The neighbours have died, so nothing from them.

112. John son of Richard de Baldersham took sanctuary in the church of St. Mary Wolmarchirche in the ward of Walter le Poter [Cornhill ward], confessed that he had committed many thefts and *abjured* the realm before the chamberlain and sheriffs. Chattels 4s. for which Richard de Culesworth of *Essex* then constable of the Tower is to answer. He was harboured in the ward outside frankpledge, so the whole ward is in mercy.

> Nota 46. *Tota warda in misericordia quia receptaverunt quendam in warda qui non fuit in franco plegio.*
> 14th cent.: *Scribatur* [With a pointing hand. Cf. **524** no. 46].

113. Christine wife of William de Swath' bit Luke le Girdeler on the finger so that his whole hand and body swelled up and he died soon afterwards. Christine was arrested and imprisoned in Newgate, where she died, so nothing from her. Gilbert le Teynturer, a neighbour, does not come and is not suspected. He was attached by William le Bokeler and William le Correour. So they are in *mercy. All the other neighbours have died, except Thomas de Norwich who comes and is not suspected, so he is *quit*.

114. Christine daughter of Simon de Beverley was found drowned in the Thames. No one is suspected. John le Carpenter and John Smyth, neighbours, do not come. John [le Carpenter] was attached by Robert Bret and Baldwin de Gaunt, John Smyth by Robert de St. Edmunds 'cordewaner' and William Proudman. So they are in *mercy. Later John le Smyth comes and is not suspected, so nothing from him or his pledges. [cf. **612**]

115. Robert son of Nicholas de Alsithere of Cheshire and Geoffrey son of Roger de Erwell of Suffolk took sanctuary in the church of St. Mary Conehop, confessed that they had burgled a house at Camerwell and carried off all the goods found there, and *abjured* the realm before the chamberlain and sheriffs. No chattels. Because it is found in the rolls of the chamberlains and sheriffs that they assigned to Geoffrey the port of Portesmuth and to Robert the port of Dover, it is adjudged that the chamberlain and sheriffs are in *mercy*.[1]

> Nota 47. *Quod camerarius et vicecomitibus fuerunt amerciati eo quod dederunt duobus abiurantibus regnum simul et semel diversos portus transeundi.*
> 14th cent.: *Scribatur* [cf. **524** no. 47].
> 1. Despite *Nota 47*, the reason for this amercement is unclear. The assignment of different ports to felons who abjured from one church on the same day appears to have been usual (*Cal. Coroners' Rolls*, ed. R. R. Sharpe (1913), 124, 131; R. F. Hunnisett, *Medieval Coroner* (Cambridge, 1961), 47).

116. On Sunday before the Nativity of Mary [4 Sep. 1261], Richard de Borham with many other people from London went to a wrestling match (luctus) at Bermundseye outside the City and there wrestled with the men of the prior of Bermundeseye; a quarrel arose among them and Richard and

The Plea Roll

his companions chased the prior's men into the priory; then came a monk called Arnulf and other monks from the priory who entered a solar above the gate and threw stones at Richard and his companions; Arnulf the monk threw a stone upon Richard and crushed him so that he quickly died. It is testified that Arnulf is still alive and living in the priory, so let him be arrested. Likewise the prior of Bermundeseye is to be distrained by all his lands. The mayor and aldermen are told to enquire about the names of those who were present at the fight and death. Afterwards Arnulf comes and, asked how he wishes to clear himself of the death, says that he is a clerk and is not bound to answer here. Thereupon Richard de Harwes, minor canon of St. Paul's London, comes and claims him as a clerk by virtue of letters of the bishop of London which he proffers testifying that the bishop entrusted to him his authority for claiming clergy; so that it may be known for what he is to be handed over, let the truth be ascertained by the mayor and aldermen; they say in the faith in which they are bound to the king that he is guilty of the death, so as such *let him be handed over to the bishop*. Thereupon it is testified that he had previously been arrested for the death and released on bail to William de Kent mercer, William de Laufar 'espicer', Matthew de Pontefract, Walter Tovy, Robert de Monte Pessulano, James le Peverer, Robert de St. Helens, Adam de Walsyngham, Bartholomew le Espicer, John Derkyn, Peter de Frowyk and Thomas de Wymbourn, to have him here on the first day and they did not have him. (*Philippus le Tailur tunc vicecomes recepit manucapcionem*.) So they are all in mercy. Because Arnulf was harboured in the priory from the time when he killed Richard until the present and the prior and convent knew it well, to *judgment* on the prior for the harbouring. [cf. **613, 615**]

> Nota 48. *Quod manucaptus pro felonia sit coram justiciariis primo die.*
> 14th cent.: *Scribatur* [cf. **524** no. 48].

117. [m. 6d] Emma wife of Henry le Chaloner beat and maltreated Alice wife of Richard Attelithe and struck her (dedit ei orbos ictus)[1] so that she died on the fourth day after. Emma fled to the church of Fanchirche and escaped from there, so *let her be exacted and outlawed* [sic] according to the custom [of the City]. Chattels *12d.* for which the sheriffs are to answer. Because Emma was harboured after the deed in the ward of Nicholas de Wynton' [Langbourn ward] and the sheriffs did not attach her, *to judgment* on the sheriffs and the whole ward. The neighbours have died. [cf. **614**]

> Nota 49. *De vicecomitibus et tota warda amerciata quia non attachiaverunt felonissam.*
> 14th cent.: *Scribatur* [cf. **524** no. 49].
> 1. With blows which caused neither swelling nor bleeding.

118. Ellis the Clerk of Amias, Alexander de Kenesherte and Gilbert de Framelyngham assaulted and wounded John de Berners so that he died later the same day in the City. Ellis and the others fled and are suspected, so *let them be exacted and outlawed.* No chattels. Isabel Bukerel in whose house John died was attached, but does not come and is not suspected. She was attached by William le Corner and William de Waltham. So they are in *mercy.* [cf. **616**]

The Plea Roll

PLEAS OF THE CROWN 46 HENRY III [1261-2]

119. In the same year, Peter de Gysorz being chamberlain, Richard de Walebrok, for whom Thomas Bokez[1] answers, and Philip le Tayllur, who answers now, being sheriffs; Henry Peticors and Roger le Stedeman went to a house in the parish of All Hallows Colemanescherche, where lived Margery de Pyriton, Agnes de Blida, Dulcia Trye, Maud de Norfolk, Notekina Hoggenhore and Isabel la Rus, prostitutes; when they entered the house they found some foreign merchants there and, a quarrel arising between them, the merchants killed Henry and Roger and at once fled; it is not known who they were. It is found in the rolls of the chamberlain and sheriffs that the prostitutes were not attached when the inquest was held by the chamberlain and sheriffs, so *to judgment* on the sheriffs. Now the prostitutes have absconded for the death and are suspected, so *let them be exacted and waived* according to the custom of the City. No chattels. The mayor and aldermen testify that they rented the house from Alice la Blunde, who lives in the City, so *let her be arrested*. All the neighbours come except Nicholas de Worcester and he is not suspected. Nicholas was attached by Godfrey de Bramleye and William Gardiner. So they are in *mercy*. Afterwards Alice comes and for good or ill puts herself upon the verdict of the mayor and aldermen; they say in the faith in which they are bound to the king that she is not suspected, so she is *quit*. [cf. **617–18**]

Nota 50. De vicecomitibus amerciatis quia non attachiaverunt meretrices que fuerunt presentes quando quedam felonia fuit facta.
14th cent.: *Scribatur* [cf. **524** no. 50].
1. Not mentioned in **4**.

120. Idonea sister of Richard de la Batail appealed in the husting Christopher de Milkstrete tawyer (*allutarium*) and his brother Clement of the death of her brother Richard. Idonea comes, but Christopher and Clement do not and are suspected of the death. Therefore Idonea is told to prosecute them in the husting until they are outlawed according to the custom of the City etc. No chattels, but they were harboured in the ward of Henry de Frowyk [Cripplegate ward] outside frankpledge, so the whole ward is in *mercy*.

Nota 51. Tota warda in misericordia pro franco plegio.
14th cent.: *Scribatur* [cf. **524** no. 51].

121. Bartholomew Chapman was crushed by a party-wall (*parete*) in his own house in the parish of St. Benet. Value of the party-wall *12d.* for which the sheriffs are to answer. No one is suspected. Judgment: *misadventure*. Henry Sutor, a neighbour, does not come and is not suspected. He was attached by Master Robert the Mason and Thomas May. So they are in *mercy*.

122. John servant of Roger de Essewelle, Roger de Essewelle, Henry de Cane, Hugh and Adam, yeomen of the king's chapel, and a stranger were together in a boat on the Thames; John and the stranger, who were sitting in the stern of the boat and were drunk, fell into the water and drowned. Roger and the others at once fled. The mayor and aldermen say in the faith

The Plea Roll

in which they are bound to the king that they do not suspect them of the death, so *let them return* if they wish. No one else is suspected. Judgment: *misadventure*. Two neighbours come and are not suspected, so they are *quit*. Asked what became of the boat, they say that it was never found, so nothing for the deodand.

> Nota 52. *Quod attachiati eo quod presentes [fuerunt] ubi felonia vel infortunium acciderit, se debent acquietare per veredictum maioris et aldermannorum.*
> 14th cent.: *Scribatur* [cf. **524** no. 52].

123. Roger de Gayste took sanctuary in the church of St. Mary Wolmarechirche, confessed that he had stolen sheep and committed other thefts and *abjured* the realm. No chattels nor frankpledge because he was from Hertfordshire.

124. A woman called Edith, wanting to wash her hands in the Thames, accidentally fell into the water and was drowned. No one is suspected. Judgment: *misadventure*. The neighbours have died, so nothing from them. Because the mayor and aldermen testify that Edith was drowned in the ward of Douegate, and the sheriffs and chamberlain held no inquest in the ward for the death, to *judgment* on them.

125. In the same year, John de Swyneford being chamberlain, for whom no one answers, and the same being sheriffs; Robert Poyntel[1] killed Ralph de Taxstede in Bradstrete. He at once fled and is suspected, so *let him be exacted and outlawed*. No chattels nor frankpledge, but he was harboured in the ward of William de Bukerel [Broad Street ward] outside frankpledge. So [the ward] is in *mercy*. All the neighbours have died.

1. Cf. **290**.

126. Unknown malefactors struck and wounded William de Berkyngg in Westchep; the neighbours came out because of the noise, rescued William and took him to the house of William le Quilter where he died soon afterwards. The malefactors at once fled and it is not known who they were. James le Barber, the third neighbour, does not come and is not suspected. He was attached by John de Creye and Thomas Malemeyns. So they are in **mercy*. Because the sheriffs and chamberlain made no enquiry about the men who took him to William's house and did not attach William himself, to *judgment* on them.

127. [m. 7] Haukin le Munur, Haukin le Ganter of Lilleston, Bette Letherharde of Totenhalestrete and Henry le Forester of Lilleston encountered William de Creton at Hendon in Middlesex and there assaulted and wounded him so that he died on the third day after in the house of Agaline the Brewster in the City. They at once fled and are suspected. Because they are from Middlesex, *let them be exacted and outlawed* there. The sheriffs are ordered to *enquire (inquiratur in comitatu Midd')*[1] about their chattels and frankpledge and to answer for their amercements. All the neighbours and Agaline have died, so nothing from them.

1. Possibly intended as *Nota 53* (cf. **524** no. 53).

The Plea Roll

128. Simon le Suur and Richard le Decore killed Laurence de Jakeford in the market of Westchepe. Simon was at once arrested and *hanged* at Newgate before Laurence de Brok; Richard has now absconded and is suspected, so *let him be exacted and outlawed*. No chattels but he was harboured in the ward [? of Cheap] outside frankpledge. So [the ward] is in **mercy*. The four neighbours come and are not suspected, so they are quit.

PLEAS OF THE CROWN 47 HENRY III [1262–3]

129. In the same year, the same being chamberlain and Osbert de Suffolk and Robert de Monte Pesulano being sheriffs, who answer now; Alexander de Leuesham fell from a ladder in the house of Alexander le Cuver in the ward of Thomas de Pevelesdon[1] and died. Value of the ladder 4d., which are given for God. Because the men of the ward valued the deodand at three halfpennies before the chamberlain, **to judgment* on the whole ward. No one is suspected. Judgment: *misadventure*. All the neighbours have died.

1. Unidentified, cf. **293**. Not in Beaven.

130. A ship laden with mill-stones belonging to John Gisorz berthed at his quay; Simon Stanhard and others wanted to unload the mill-stones and they had pulled one up to the upper part of the ship when the rope by which they were pulling it broke and it fell back into the ship, crushing Simon to death forthwith. No one is suspected. Judgment: *misadventure*. All the neighbours have died. Walter Coleman, who was in the ship, was attached, but does not come and is not suspected. He was attached by Walter de Haliwell and John Gaugi. So they are in **mercy*. Value of the mill-stone **20s.* (*deodandum*) for which the sheriffs are to answer. Because the men of the ward of Henry de Coventre [Vintry ward] falsely valued the deodand before the chamberlain, to judgment on them. Because they valued only the mill-stone, *let there be a discussion*.

131. Adam le Peuerer killed Ralph Sinod in the ward of Henry le Waleys [Cordwainer ward]. He at once fled and is suspected, so *let him be exacted and outlawed*. No chattels. He was in the mainpast of Hugh Gratefige. So he is in **mercy*. All the neighbours have died. Afterwards it is testified that Maud, Ralph's widow, appealed Adam in the county (in comitatu) of the death, but she does not come now or prosecute her appeal, so *let her be arrested* and her pledges to prosecute are in *mercy*. Because the sheriffs and chamberlain do not answer for her pledges, *to judgment* on them.

132. In the same year, William de Purstok being chamberlain, for whom Ellis de Herteford answers, and the same being sheriffs; on Wednesday before the feast of the Nativity of St. John the Baptist [20 June 1263] Simon Godgrom went to bathe in the Thames and was accidentally drowned. No one is suspected. Judgment: *misadventure*. Adam Picard, a neighbour, does not come and is not suspected. He was attached by Thomas le Blater and Ralph Hayron. So they are in **mercy*. Because the accident happened in the ward of Castle Baynard and the sheriffs and chamberlain held their inquest

The Plea Roll

with the men of the ward of Richard de Ewelle [Farringdon ward], *to judgment* on them. Afterwards Adam Pycard comes and is not suspected, so nothing from him or his pledges.

133. William Greygrom and Adam de Benleyhe were quarrelling in the ward (custodia) of Walter Hervi [Cheap ward]. Robert Etewell came up to separate them and William drew his knife to strike Adam, but struck himself in the thigh, so that he bled to death. Adam comes now and the mayor and aldermen say in the faith in which they are bound to the king that he is not guilty of the death, so he is *quit*; but because he was present he is in *mercy. Because it is found in the rolls of the chamberlain and sheriffs that he was not attached when the inquest was held into the death, *to judgment* on the chamberlain and sheriffs. Robert Etewelle was attached for the death, but does not come and is not suspected. He was attached by Henry de Sandwich and Nicholas Braunte. So they are in *mercy. No one else is suspected. Judgment: *misadventure*. All the neighbours have died, except Adam Mollyngg, and he is not suspected. [cf. **619**]

134. Richard Valet came up to the door of a house in the ward of Philip le Tayllur [Bishopsgate ward] where lived Beatrice de Wynton', Isabel de Staunford and Margery de Karl', prostitutes; they immediately came out of the house, dragged Richard inside and took from him a buckle (firmachulum) worth 6d., whereupon Richard drew his knife and, intending to strike Beatrice with the handle, instead struck her beneath the breast with the blade, so that she died. It is found in the rolls of the chamberlain that Richard, Isabel and Margery were arrested and handed over to the sheriffs, who do not answer for them now or know what has become of them; nor do they show the chirograph by which they were handed over to the succeeding sheriffs, as is the rule (moris) according to the custom of the City. The mayor and aldermen say that the custom of the City is such that when a sheriff relinquishes his bailiwick, he has to draw up a chirograph between himself and the succeeding sheriff listing those who are imprisoned. So to judgment on the sheriffs for the *escapes. Richard, Isabel and Margery do not come and are suspected, so let Richard be *exacted and outlawed*, and Isabel and Margery *exacted and waived*. No chattels nor frankpledge. William son of Adam, John le Ber, John Skot and Roger le Tyeler, four neighbours, do not come and are not suspected. William was attached by John le Bere and Roger le Tyeler, John by William son of Adam and Richard le Cordwaner, John by Peter le Bray and Peter le Gorger, Roger by Peter le Gorger and Peter le Bray. So they are in *mercy. Because the sheriffs attached the neighbours one by the other, *to judgment* on them. [cf. **620**]

> Nota 54. *De cyrographo faciendo inter vicecomites de prisonibus tempore recessus eorum de balliva sua* [cf. **524** no. 54].

135. John de Grenewyz killed Simon le Poter in the house of William la Persone. He at once fled and is suspected, so *let him be exacted and outlawed*. No chattels. The mayor and aldermen say that William was an accomplice in the death, but he has now died, so nothing from him. All the

The Plea Roll

neighbours have died except John le Caretter. He was attached by William de Ely and Ingebert le Avener. So they are in mercy.

136. Alexander Caby was found dead, apparently from hunger in the ward (custodia) of William de Durham [Bread Street ward]. No one is suspected. Judgment: *misadventure*. Geoffrey le Santur[1] and Thomas le Barber, two neighbours, do not come and are not suspected. They were attached by John le Stilter and Thomas le Barbur. So they are in **mercy*. Because the chamberlain does not have the names of the pledges on his roll, *to judgment* on him. [cf. **621**]

1. *le Saltere* in **621**.

137. Ralph de Westminster capper was killed in the ward of Anketin de Auvergne near Ludgate [Farringdon ward] by two unknown servants who came out of the house of some prostitutes. They at once fled and it is not known who they were. All the neighbours have died. Because the prostitutes had a fixed abode where they had lived for a long time and the sheriffs and chamberlain had made no enquiry into their names, they are in **mercy*. Afterwards the mayor and aldermen testify that Cecily, Ralph's sister, appealed Robert the Goldsmith outside Ludgate of the death and the chamberlain does not put the fact on record. Therefore *let there be a discussion*.

138. [m. 7d] Geoffrey de Hattefel and several others were keeping watch in the City by night according to custom[1] when about midnight they encountered Thomas de Exeport escorting a woman; a dispute arising between them, Thomas and Geoffrey went away together quarrelling to the church of Wolmarchirche, whence came six unknown men who assaulted and wounded Geoffrey so that he died on the third day after. Thomas fled with the other malefactors, and it is not known who they were. Thomas has absconded and is suspected, so *let him be exacted and outlawed*. No chattels, but he had a house, year and waste worth *3 marks* and a rent of assize of *4 marks*; for the intervening period the house and rents amount to **91 marks* for which the sheriffs are to answer. The mayor and aldermen testify that immediately after the felony had been committed Peter de Chauvent took possession of the house and rent and afterwards for the four subsequent years he sold the rent to Robert de Monte Pessulano without warrant. So the sheriff is ordered to take the said messuages and rents into the king's hand and to cause Peter to appear. Afterwards Peter comes and says that he holds the messuages and rents by the gift of King Henry and he proffers a royal charter[2] in these words (*carta Petri de Chauvent*): 'Henry by the grace of God; we have granted to Peter de Chauvent for his faithful service those houses with appurtenances in the parish of Holy Trinity le Petit in the City of London which belonged to our enemy Thomas de Exeport, formerly citizen of London, to have and hold in perpetuity, performing the due and accustomed service; letters patent at Westminster, 16 October 49 Henry III'. Because the charter does not mention the felony, the house with the rents is to remain in the king's hand. (*Judicium*).

The Plea Roll

Nota 55. De carta regis non faciente mencionem de felonia, per quod tenementum per eamdem cartam datum remansit in manus [sic] *regis.*
14th cent.: *Scribatur* [cf. **524** no. 55].
1. See *Lib. Ant. Leg.*, 55. Again referred to in **159** and presupposed in **146**.
2. Cf. *C.P.R. 1258–66*, 624, 6 Aug. 1265.

139. John Poytevin and Robert de St. Edmunds boatmen took two unknown squires aboard their ship (in navi) at Westminster and John accidentally fell into the water and was drowned. Robert absconded and is not suspected, so *let him return if he wishes, but his chattels are to be confiscated for his flight. No chattels. It is not known who the squires were. Value of the ship **3s.* (*deodandum*) for which the sheriffs are to answer. All the neighbours have died. No one is suspected. Judgment: *misadventure.*

140. William Egrith appealed in the husting Robert servant of Ralph Pikeman of wounds and battery against the peace. William and Robert come and William appeals Robert that on Tuesday before Whitsun 46 Henry III [23 May 1262] Robert gave to William le Kyvere, who is now dead, a staff with which to beat and wound him and the same William broke three of his ribs and wounded him elsewhere in the body; and that he did this wickedly and feloniously. Robert comes and denies the felony and everything; he says that when William Egrith appealed Robert and William in the husting he said that Robert gave the staff to William on Monday before the Ascension 47 Henry III [7 May 1263] and now he says it was on Tuesday before Whitsun 46 Henry III [23 May 1262]; so Robert seeks judgment concerning the discrepancy and whether he is bound to answer before William is convicted of the deed. This being allowed, it is adjudged that the appeal be null and that William Egrith be committed to *gaol* for a false appeal. To preserve the king's peace let the truth be ascertained by jury (per patriam). Thereupon the mayor and aldermen say in the faith in which they are bound to the king that since it was adjudged that William's suit be null, no suit belongs to the king concerning the battery and trespass, unless it be in a matter touching life and limb. So Robert is *quit.*

Nota 56. De appello transgressionis quassato pro variacione dierum in narracione facta primo die in hustengo et postea coram justiciariis.
Nota 57. Et quod ad regem non pertinet aliqua secta in huiusmodi casu post appellum quassatum, nisi esset de re tangente vitam et membrum.
14th cent.: *Scribatur* [cf. **524** nos. 56–7].

141. Andrew de Aldewich appealed in the husting Richard Page of the kitchen of the prior of St. Bartholomew and William le Palfrayour and Alan le Palfrayour, the prior's men, of wounding and mayhem. Andrew does not come or prosecute his appeal, so *let him be arrested* and his pledges to prosecute are in *mercy,* viz. William de Derby and Maurice de Waltham, cobblers. Richard, William and Alan do not come and were not attached. Thereupon the mayor and aldermen say in the faith in which they are bound to the king that when Andrew first appeared in the husting and appealed them, the sheriffs were ordered to attach them and they went to the priory to do this, but the prior and his men did not allow them to enter the priory to attach Richard and the others. Therefore the sheriffs are ordered to cause

The Plea Roll

the prior to appear on the morrow. To preserve the king's peace let the truth be ascertained by the mayor and aldermen; they say in the faith in which they are bound to the king that they are guilty of wounding but not of mayhem, so they are in *mercy.

<small>Nota 58. Quod justiciarii inquisiverunt de facto licet pars appellans non fuisset prosecutus appellum suum de plagis et mahemio [cf. **524** no. 58].</small>

142. In the same year,[1] the same being chamberlain and Gregory de Roqesle and Thomas de Lafford, who has now died, being sheriffs; Simon servant of Adam de Leden fell into a vessel (patella) full of hot water in Adam's house and was scalded to death. No one is suspected. Judgment: *misadventure*. Value of the vessel **14d*. (*deodandum*) for which the sheriffs are to answer. Thomas le Cordewaner, a neighbour, does not come and is not suspected. He was attached by Robert Poygnant and William le Waleys. So they are in *mercy.

1. Viz. 48 Henry III (cf. **148**).

143. Osbert the Clerk was found dead without a wound in the ward of William Bukerel [Broad Street ward]. Michael le Oynter was attached for the death and comes. The mayor and aldermen say in the faith in which they are bound to the king that they do not suspect him of the death because Osbert died of a fever, so he is quit. The neighbours have died, so nothing from them. (*Infortunium*.)

144. Richard de Stebenhuth, wanting to water a horse in the Thames, fell from the horse into the water and was drowned. No one is suspected. Judgment: *misadventure*. Value of the horse *10s*. (*deodandum*) for which the sheriffs are to answer. The neighbours have died.

145. Maud widow of Hemming de Cestreis appealed in the husting Henry de Lewes, Henry de Mapelderfeld, Stephen de Pencestr', William de Mapelderfeld, Stacey servant of William de Say, Richard Caperoun, Gilbert de Estbus, John de Wytham and Ralph le Tayllur of the death of her husband and of robbery. She comes and withdraws from her appeal, so let her be committed to *gaol and her pledges to prosecute are in *mercy, viz. Robert Otes and Hubert de Wynton'.

146. On Friday the feast of SS. Peter and Paul [29 June 1263] John de Brittany, crossing the City by night, came upon the mayor and other good men of the City who were patrolling the streets to see that a good watch was being kept, and for a long time he walked along with them. At length he left them and when he reached the churchyard of St. Paul's London he encountered some unknown men who at once attacked him; Arnold the Cook came up to help him and the malefactors killed both John and Arnold and at once fled. It is not known who they were. All the neighbours have died. Because it cannot be ascertained by any inquest held by the chamberlain and sheriffs who the men were, the justices want to examine the men of the ward of Thomas de Wymborn,[1] where the incident occurred, concerning the names of those who were present at the death. Afterwards Michael Tovy

(*Michael Tovi*) was arrested for the death and for the theft of horses belonging to the king and to John de Gray and for thefts committed in Jewry and from William le Latimer and for other thefts and trespasses committed in time of peace; Michael comes and for good or ill puts himself upon the verdict of the mayor and citizens; they say on the oath they made to the king and in the faith in which they are bound that he is guilty of all the robberies and the death, except the robbery in Jewry, so [let him be hanged]. (*Suspensus*.) No chattels in the City but he has chattels and tenements in Kent. Therefore the sheriff of Kent is ordered to cause twelve [men] of the neighbourhood where Michael's lands, tenements and chattels were to appear before Roger de Seyton or John de Cobham when they visit these parts, to certify them of his lands, tenements and chattels and their value; in the meantime they are to be taken into the king's hand. Afterwards John de Cobbeham holds the enquiry and it is found that Michael had chattels worth £27 10s. 9d., for which the sheriff of Kent is to answer. [cf. **278, 287–8**]

> Nota 59. *De quodam magno interpositore Civitatis suspenso* [cf. **524** no. 59].
> At foot of membrane: *Placita corone anno Edwardi primi*.
> 1. Thomas de Wymborn was associated with Portsoken (Beaven, i, 365n) but presumably the ward of Castle Baynard or Farringdon was here in question.

147. [m. 8] Thomas Viel[1] appeals Robert de Esture that when he was in the (? ward) (via) of Westchepe in Soperlane on the feast of SS. Simon and Jude 47 Henry III [28 Oct. 1263] Robert came up about the hour of curfew and wounded him in the left hand with a sword of Coloyne, so that he was maimed; that Robert did this wickedly and feloniously and with premeditation he offers to prove against him. Robert comes and denies the felony and mayhem and everything; he says he is not bound to answer to the appeal because it makes no mention of raising the hue and cry or of the hour of day, but of the hour of curfew, which is an hour of night; so he seeks judgment concerning the appeal and the matters above being allowed, for good or ill puts himself upon the verdict of the mayor and aldermen; it is adjudged that Thomas be committed to *gaol for a false appeal. The mayor and aldermen put on record that Robert can not put himself upon their verdict for mayhem because he is not of the liberty of the City, but should put himself upon the verdict of twelve men of the ward where the incident occurred. The twelve [men] of the ward say on their oath that Robert did wound and maim Thomas, but that he did it in self-defence, because he could not otherwise escape. Therefore it is adjudged that he be committed to *gaol and make satisfaction for the injury. It is testified that Robert was arrested previously[2] in the time of Osbert de Suffolk and Robert de Monte Pessulano sheriffs and they released him publicly to have here on the first day and did not do so. Because the same sheriffs do not answer for him now, *to judgment* on them. [cf. **622**]

> Nota 60. *De appello quassato per varias proposiciones contra appellum de mahemio et de veritate inquisita per xii homines de warda et non per maiorem et aldermannos quia appellatus fuit extraneus*.
> 14th cent.: *Scribatur* [cf. **524** no. 60].
> 1. For Thomas Viel's pledge see **622**.
> 2. Cf. ?**487**.

The Plea Roll

PLEAS OF THE CROWN 48 HENRY III [1263–4][1]

148. Thomas de Cambridge killed Walter servant of Ralph Basset of Sapecote in the ward of Richard de Ewell [Farringdon ward]. He at once fled and is suspected, so *let him be exacted and outlawed*. Chattels *2s. (deodandum* [sic]) for which the sheriffs are to answer. He was harboured in the ward outside frankpledge, so *to judgment* on the whole ward. Because the sheriffs and chamberlains held no enquiry concerning the chattels, *to judgment* on them. All the neighbours have died, so nothing from them. [cf. **623**]

Nota [unnumbered]. *Ad iudicium pro defectu franci plegii.*
14th cent.: *Scribatur* [but not in **524**].
1. See also **142**.

149. In the same year, Reginald de Suffolk being chamberlain and the same being sheriffs; Philip son of Geoffrey killed Colin Wyther in the ward of Cheap. He at once fled and took sanctuary in the church of Wolmarechirche. Afterwards he escaped from the church and has now absconded and is suspected, so *let him be exacted and outlawed*. No chattels nor frankpledge because he was a clerk. All the neighbours come and are not suspected. Afterwards it is found in the chamberlain's rolls that Isabel de Hildringham, Colin's sister, appealed Philip of the death, but she does not come or prosecute her appeal, so *let her be arrested* and her pledges to prosecute are in *mercy*, viz. Robert Poygnant 'cordeler' and John de St. Salvators.

Nota 61. *Quod non oportet clericis esse in franco plegio.*
14th cent.: *Scribatur* [cf. **524** no. 61].

150. Simon de Hauvill killed John de Chesterhunte. Simon comes now and proffers a royal charter[1] testifying that King Henry pardoned him his suit for breach of the *peace* arising from his death, on condition that he stands to right if anyone wishes to implead him. And there is no one, so he is granted firm peace; but because previously he absconded for the death, his chattels are to be confiscated for the flight. No chattels. All the neighbours have died, so nothing from them.

1. *C.P.R. 1258–66*, 613, 5 July 1266.

151. David de Bristoll and Juliana wife of Richard le Cordwaner were playing chess (ad scaccarium) together in Richard's house, with several others present; a quarrel arising between them, David struck Juliana in the thigh with a sword, so that she died forthwith. He at once fled and is suspected, so *let him be exacted and outlawed*. No chattels nor frankpledge because he was a stranger. All the neighbours have died. Because the chamberlain held no enquiry concerning the men who were in the house with David and Juliana when the incident occurred, *to judgment* on him. [cf. **624**]

152. Simon le Parker was found killed in the ward of Adam de Brunyng [Farringdon ward]; Robert le Peleter and Walter le Fruter were arrested for the death, imprisoned at Newgate and delivered there before Hugh Bygot

The Plea Roll

justice [of gaol delivery]. Walter comes and, asked how he wishes to clear himself, says that previously he was delivered by jury before Hugh and was acquitted by judgment of the king's court. The mayor and aldermen testify to this in the faith in which they are bound to the king so he is quit. Saer de Harecourt, Geoffrey de Crek, Philip de Nothlethe and Robert de Lastebyr' were attached for the death because they were present when Simon was killed, but they do not come. They [sic] were attached by Geoffrey de Roynges [and] Richard le Coffrer, Geoffrey by John de Shordich and James le Botiler, Philip and Robert by Saer.[1] So they are in mercy. The mayor and aldermen say that they do not suspect them of the death. All the neighbours have died.

> Nota 62. *Quod cum aliquis attachiatus pro felonia deliberatus fuerit coram justiciariis de Newegate, non tenetur respondere coram justiciariis itinerantibus.*
> 14th cent.: *Scribatur* [cf. **524** no. 62].
> 1. The attachments appear to be garbled.

153. Hugh de Stamford killed John de Wautham in the ward of John de Norhampton [Aldgate ward]. He was at once arrested and handed over to Constantine le Brokour, Richard le Mercer and Henry Deubeny, then keepers of Alegate. Afterwards he escaped from their custody, so to judgment on them for the **escape*. Hugh has now absconded and is suspected, so **let him be exacted and outlawed.* No chattels nor frankpledge because he was a stranger. All the neighbours have died, except the fourth, Thomas de Suthwerk, who does not come. Thomas was attached by Walter Gaunter and Roger de Huntingdon. So they are in **mercy.* [cf. **625**]

154. John Skyleman encountered Thomas servant of Beatrice Allor and Alan le Prute baker and Thomas at once assaulted John and wounded him in the stomach with his knife, so that he died forthwith. Thomas was arrested and hanged at Newgate before Hugh le Despencer. Alan has absconded for the death; the mayor and aldermen say in the faith in which they are bound to the king that he is not guilty, so *let him return* if he wishes, but his chattels are to be confiscated for the flight. No chattels. Beatrice was attached for the death, comes and is not suspected, so she is *quit*. Geoffrey le Cordwaner and John the Smith, two neighbours, do not come and are not suspected. Geoffrey was attached by John the Smith and Adam de Wynepol tailor, and John by the same. So they are in **mercy* and the other neighbours have died. Because the sheriffs attached John by the same pledges, *to judgment* on them.

> Nota 63. *Quod vicini debent attachiari per diversos plegios et non per eosdem.*
> 14th cent.: *Scribatur* [cf. **524** no. 63].

155. In the same year,[1] the same being chamberlain and Edward le Blund and Peter Aungers being sheriffs; his son John answers for Edward and no one answers for Peter; on Wednesday after Michaelmas [1 Oct. 1264] John le Suur was driving two pigs on a rope when he was dragged into a ditch and was drowned. Value of the pigs 2s. 8d. for which the sheriffs are to answer. Because the wards of Stephen Bukerel and John Blakeney[2] [Cripplegate and Aldersgate wards] falsely valued the deodand before the chamberlain and

The Plea Roll

sheriffs, *to judgment on them. The neighbours have died. John, to whom the pigs belonged, was attached for the death but does not come and is not suspected. He was attached by William de Gloucester and Robert de St. Giles butcher. So they are in *mercy. [cf. **626**]

1. Viz. 49 Henry III (cf. **156**).
2. *Recte* Blakethorn.

PLEAS OF THE CROWN 49 HENRY III [1264–5]

156. Richard le Canner of Hattefeld encountered Thomas le Gardiner of St. Katherine's hospital at dusk in the ward of Portsok; a quarrel arising between them, Thomas struck Richard with a knife so that he died forthwith. He at once fled and is suspected, so *let him be exacted and outlawed*. No chattels nor frankpledge, but he was in the mainpast of the master of St. Katherine's hospital. So he is in *mercy. John de Kent and Roger le Tuler, two neighbours, do not come and are not suspected. John was attached by Stephen de Hundesdiche and Robert de Retherhethe, Roger by Nicholas le Tanur. So they are in *mercy. Stephen le Tanur, the third neighbour, comes and is not suspected, so he is *quit*. The fourth neighbour has died. [cf. **627, 629**]

157. Roger Rumpyng fell into a ditch and was drowned. No one is suspected. Judgment: *misadventure*. William Camelyn who was previously in a house drinking with him was attached for the death, but does not come and is not suspected. He was attached by Walter Bole and John Stacy. So they are in *mercy. The neighbours have died. [cf. **630**]

158. Hugh Scott goldsmith and Agnes wife of Robert de E . . . , were drinking together in Agnes' house when a quarrel arose between them and Hugh killed Agnes with a knife. He at once fled and is suspected, so *let him be exacted and outlawed*. No chattels nor frankpledge because he was then under age. All the neighbours have died, so nothing from them.

159. [m. 8d] Thomas de Stratford, Godfrey de Halistelle, John son of Godfrey, Geoffrey Tirrel, Walter de Sutht', Robert de Dovere and Walter de Essewell were keeping watch in the City to keep the peace according to custom; they were quarrelling together outside the door of Henry Russell, who came out of his house and struck Thomas de Stratford with a sword so that he died. Henry at once fled and is suspected, so *let him be exacted and outlawed*. Chattels 18d. for which the sheriffs are to answer. He was not in frankpledge, but was harboured in the ward of John Gisors [Vintry ward]. So [the ward] is in *mercy. Godfrey, Walter, Robert and William were attached for the death, but do not come and are not suspected. Godfrey was attached by Faukes le Bedel and William le Flaoner, Walter de Sutht' by John de Suht' and John de la Lade, Robert by Stephen le Gorger and Alan le Karl', Walter by Hugh Syppond and Godfrey de Haliwell. So they are in *mercy. John son of Godfrey and Geoffrey Tyrel were attached for the death, come and are not suspected, so they are *quit*. Robert de Derby in whose house Thomas was found dead does not come and is not suspected.

The Plea Roll

He was attached by John de Godyngton and John de Karl'. So they are in mercy. Alan de Carl' and William le Flaoner, two of the neighbours, do not come and are not suspected. Alan was attached by William le Flaoner and Geoffrey Monquey 'pessoner' and William by the same. So they are in *mercy. To judgment on the sheriffs because they attached William by the same pledges. The other neighbours come and are not suspected, so they are quit. Afterwards it is found in the chamberlain's rolls that Ralph de Stratford appealed Henry of the death, but he does not come or prosecute his appeal, so *let him be arrested* and his pledges to prosecute are in *mercy, viz. Robert de Derby and John le Lung. [cf. **628, 631**]

160. William son of Robert de Gravesende wanted to cross the Thames in a boat and was drowned. Value of the boat *3s.* for which the sheriffs are to answer. All the neighbours have died. No one is suspected. Judgment: *misadventure.*

161. John de Neuport wanted to water a horse near the house of the bishop of Salisbury[1] and was drowned. Value of the horse *20s.* (*deodandum*) for which the sheriffs are to answer. The chamberlain and sheriffs did not attach the neighbours, so *to judgment* on them. No one is suspected. Judgment: *misadventure.*

> 1. On the west side of the Fleet (C. L. Kingsford, 'Historical notes on mediaeval London houses', *London Topographical Record*, xii (1920), 14–16).

162. John de Suthwerk, while roofing the belfry of St. Paul's London, fell from the chair suspended by a rope in which he was sitting, and was killed. Value of the chair and the rope *20s.* (*deodandum*) which the dean and chapter of London took without warrant, so **to judgment* on them. The sheriff is ordered to cause them to appear. The chamberlain made no mention on his roll of the deodand, so *to judgment* on him. No neighbour was attached, so *to judgment* on the sheriffs. No one is suspected. Judgment: *misadventure.* Afterwards the dean and chapter come and say expressly (*presise*) that they claim nothing, so nothing.

163. Henry Hors, Cecily his wife, Maud wife of Henry le Lokyere, Roger Byssop, Adam son of Roger de Pampesworth and John son of Reginald le Buteler beat Thomas le Keu to death. Roger Bhissop and Cecily wife of Henry Hors were arrested and hanged at Newgate before Hugh le Despenser. Henry Hors, Maud wife of Henry le Lokier, Adam de Pampesworth and John le Buteler at once fled and are suspected, so *let them be exacted and outlawed* and Maud be outlawed [sic] and exacted (*exigatur et weyvetur*). Maud had no chattels, Henry le Hors **10s.*, Adam *½ mark, John *1 mark* for which the sheriffs are to answer. Nothing is known of the frankpledge of Henry, Adam and John, but they were harboured in the ward of Portesokon outside frankpledge, so [the ward] is in **mercy* (*defectus franci plegii*). All the neighbours have died. [cf. **632**]

164. Andrew Byssop fell from a step (*gradu*) in the house of Henry le Waleys and died. Value of the step *5s.* (*deodandum*) for which the sheriffs

The Plea Roll

are to answer. Because the chamberlain and sheriffs did not make a valuation of the deodand when they held the inquest into the death, *to judgment* on them. All the neighbours have died, so nothing from them. No one is suspected. Judgment: *misadventure*.

165. William de Kyngeston was found dead, apparently of starvation (inedia), in the ward of Castle Baynard. No one is suspected. Judgment: *misadventure*. John le Barber, a neighbour, does not come and is not suspected. He was attached by Walter de Brakeleye and John le Paumer. So they are in *mercy. Robert le Suer, the second neighbour, comes and is not suspected, so he is *quit*. The men of the ward falsely presented the neighbours, so to judgment on them. [cf. **633**]

    Nota [unnumbered]. *Ad iudicium quia falso presentaverunt vicinos.*

166. Unknown malefactors waylaid Robert de Blankmester, servant of Master Robert de Fridaystrete, at Smethefeld by night and at once assaulted and wounded him. They immediately fled and it is not known who they were. Afterwards Robert went to the house of his master Robert and there died on the morrow. Master Robert de Frydaystrete, in whose house he died, was attached for the death, but does not come and is not suspected. He was attached by Hubert the Goldsmith and Robert de Wynton' taverner. So they are in mercy. The neighbours have died, so nothing from them. [cf. **634**]

167. In the same year, Reginald de Suffolk being chamberlain and Walter Hervy and Gregory de Roqesle being sheriffs;[1] on Friday before the feast of SS. Simon and Jude [23 Oct. 1265] unknown malefactors killed John Ballard in the ward of Richard de Ewell [Farringdon ward]. They at once fled and it is not known who they were. All the neighbours come and are not suspected. Because it is testified that they were Thomas de Clare's men, the mayor and aldermen are told to enquire into their names. Afterwards the mayor and aldermen say in the faith in which they are bound to the king that they are unable to enquire who they were, so nothing.

    1. Presumably 50 Henry III but there is no record of Rokesle and Hervy serving together (cf. **4** n. 5).

PLEAS OF THE CROWN 50 HENRY III [1265–6]

168. In the same year, the same being chamberlain and John Adrien and Walter Hervy being sheriffs; on Monday before the feast of SS. Simon and Jude [26 Oct. 1265] Ralph Bekerannike was found dead without a wound. No one is suspected. Judgment: *misadventure*. Nicholas Poyntel, a neighbour, does not come and is not suspected. He was attached by Hugh le Cuver and Robert de St. Brides. So they are all in *mercy. [cf. **635**]

169. Nicholas de Suffolk 'chapeler', Adam le Milneward and William de Cambridge cappers, were fighting with Thomas de Cirencestre in the aldermanry of Richard de Ewelle [Farringdon ward] and eventually they killed him. They at once fled and are suspected, so *let them be exacted and out-*

lawed according to the custom of the City. No chattels, but they were harboured in the aldermanry of Richard de Ewell outside frankpledge, so the alderman and the whole aldermanry are in *mercy*. All the neighbours have died.

> At foot of membrane (14th cent.): *Placita corone de tempore E.R. primi et de appellis et aliis materiis.*

170. [m. 9] Maurice Crammok, William the Cook, Henry Child and William Dun waylaid Robert de Newcastle in the aldermanry of Robert de Meldebourne [Coleman Street ward] and assaulted him with intent to kill; Adinett[1] the king's tailor came up with Alan le Scot because of the noise to go to Robert's assistance and in the ensuing fight Robert de Newcastle [and the others] wounded Maurice so that he died on the third day after. Robert and the others have now absconded. The chamberlain and sheriffs proffer a writ[2] of King Henry in these words: 'Henry [III] to Hugh son of Otto, warden of the City of London, and to Walter Hervy and John Adrian; at the instance of our son Edward we have pardoned his tailor Adinett, Alan Scot and Robert de Newcastle their suit for breach of the peace arising from the death of Maurice Crammok of which they are accused and have granted them firm peace on condition that they stand to right in our court if anyone wishes to implead them; in the matter of this death no action shall be taken against them contrary to the form of our pardon; at Westminster, 12 November 50 Henry III [1265]'. Because this happened in time of war and the king pardoned them their suit and no one prosecutes them, nothing.

> *Nota* [unnumbered]: *Perdonacio secte regis.*
> 14th cent.: *Scribatur.*
> 1. See Tout, *Chapters*, vi, 142 under Adenettus.
> 2. *C.P.R. 1258–66*, 514, 28 Nov. 1265.

171. William Stoil and Richard le Orfeverer killed Ranulf de Stratton in the ward of Cheap. They at once fled and are suspected, so *let them be exacted and outlawed* according to the custom of the City. No chattels and they were not in frankpledge. All the neighbours come and are not suspected, so they are quit.

172. Robert son of Walter the Carpenter of Wys in Worcestershire took sanctuary in the church of St. Nicholas by the Shambles, confessed that he had committed many thefts and *abjured* the realm before the chamberlain and sheriffs. Chattels *9s. 6d.* for which the sheriffs are to answer. He also had chattels in Worcestershire in the house of his father Walter worth *28s. 6d.* for which the sheriff of *Worcestershire* is to answer. [cf. **636**]

173. Albreda de Wycoumbe was found killed in the house of William Basely and it is not known who killed her. William Basely in whose house she was found does not come and was not attached, so *to judgment* on the sheriffs. The mayor and aldermen say that William is dead, so nothing from him. All the others who were attached for the death do not come and are not suspected, so they are quit.

174. Alice de Hanyngton fell into a vessel (cuva) full of hot water in the house of William de Bixele. Value of the vessel *12d. (deodandum)* for which the sheriffs are to answer. William de Bixle, Agnes de Chenduth, Richard de Hanyngton, John de Brokenford and Robert Patrik [of] Burton were attached for the death because they were in the house, but they do not come and are not suspected. William was attached by Adam Peperer capper and Hamo the Moneyer, Agnes by Richard le Chapeler and Henry the Baker, and the others by William de Bixle, William de Haversham, William le Chapeler and Richard le Chapeler. So they are in **mercy*. All the neighbours except Walter le Ewer and Richard the Smith come and are not suspected. Walter was attached by Alexander le Fevere and William le Keuter, Richard by William the Hosier and William Page. So they are all in **mercy*. No one else is suspected. Judgment: *misadventure*. [cf. **637**]

175. Hugh de Dunstable fell from a step in his house and died. Value of the step *12d. (deodandum)* for which the sheriffs are to answer. The neighbours come and are not suspected. No one else is suspected. Judgment: *misadventure*.

176. Roger le Tuler killed Elicia his wife in his house and at once absconded for the death. Afterwards he was arrested and taken to Newgate, where he was imprisoned and then escaped, so to judgment on the sheriffs for the *escape*. Roger comes and proffers a royal charter testifying that King Henry pardoned him his suit for breach of the peace arising from this death, on condition that he stand to right if anyone wishes to implead him. And there is no one, so he is granted firm *peace*. Because previously he fled for the death, his chattels are to be confiscated for the flight. Chattels 54s. for which the sheriffs are to answer. Reginald de Canterbury, a neighbour, does not come and is not suspected. He was attached by John de Canterbury 'cordwaner' and Miles de Ireland. So they are in **mercy*. [cf. **638**]

> Nota 64. *Catalla confiscata pro fuga.*
> 14th cent.: *Scribatur nota* [cf. **524** no. 64].

177. Roger servant of John de Pysyng killed Adam son of William de Colecestre near the churchyard of St. Paul's London. He at once fled with two other unknown malefactors who were with him and is suspected, so *let him be exacted and outlawed*. No chattels nor frankpledge because he was a stranger. Because it is found in the rolls of the chamberlain and sheriffs that Adam was found in the house of Agnes la Cufrere and the sheriffs did not attach her nor did the chamberlains hold an inquest concerning those who removed the body from the place where he was killed, **to judgment* on them. All the neighbours have died except Geoffrey le Fruter who does not come and is not suspected. He was attached by Thomas le Tayllur and John le Peleter. So they are all in **mercy*. [cf. **639**]

> Nota 65. *Quod non licet alicui amovere corpus interfecti a loco in quo interficitur.*
> 14th cent.: *Scribatur* [cf. **524** no. 65].

178. In the same year, Reginald de Suffolk being chamberlain and William son of Richard being sheriffs [sic];[1] on the eve of the feast of St. John the Baptist [23 June 1266] a horse killed William le Pacbyndere in the seld of

The Plea Roll

Edward le Blunt. Value of the horse *8s. (*deodandum*) for which the sheriffs are to answer. No one is suspected. Judgment: *misadventure*. The aldermanry of Edward le Blunt [Bassishaw ward] falsely valued the deodand before the chamberlain and sheriffs, so *to judgment* on the whole aldermanry. The neighbours have died.

1. Cf. **4** where William is not associated with another bailiff.

179. Adam Russel, William le Harpur, John (Johanne) le Somoter and William . . . were fighting together in the market of Westchepe and William, John and William killed [Adam] . . . They at once fled and are suspected, so *let them be exacted and outlawed*. No chattels nor frankpledge because they were strangers. All the neighbours have died, so nothing from them.

180. Amisius le Poloter beat Bartholomew le Poluter at Winchester fair and afterwards Bartholomew returned to London and at once died of the beating in the City. Amisius has now absconded for the death and is suspected, so *let him be exacted and outlawed*. Because he was from *Middlesex* the sheriff of Middlesex is ordered to enquire into the chattels and frankpledge. Geoffrey le Mareschal and John le Chaucer, two neighbours, come and are not suspected, so they are quit. The other neighbours have died.

PLEAS OF THE CROWN 51 HENRY III [1266–7]

181. Thomas de Stocton was lodging in the house of Gilbert [Makeheyte][1] carpenter and brought with him there Dulcia de Gravesend, a prostitute. Because of this, a quarrel broke out between Thomas and Gilbert and Thomas hit Gilbert on the neck with an axe, so that he died forthwith. He at once fled and is suspected, so *let him be exacted and outlawed* according to the custom of the City. Chattels *18d.* for which the sheriffs are to answer. He was [not] in frankpledge, but was harboured in the aldermanry of John de Gisors [Vintry ward] outside frankpledge, so the aldermanry is in *mercy*. Henry de Kensyngton and Gilbert's widow Maud were attached for the death because they were in the house at the time, but they do not come and are not suspected. Henry was attached by Roger le Mareschall,[2] Geoffrey de Bow (de Arcubus) and William de Holebourn 'pessoner', Maud by Walter le Engleys and Roger le Mareschall. So they are in *mercy*. Dulcia has absconded for the death and is not suspected, so *let her return* if she wishes. All the neighbours come and are not suspected. [cf. **628, 640**]

Nota [unnumbered]. *Defectus franci plegii.*
1. Supplied from **640**.
2. Perhaps an error; see Maud's sureties.

182. [m. 9d] In the same year, the same being chamberlain and John Adrian and Luke de Batencurt being sheriffs; Austin de Burgh killed Beatrice maidservant of Thomasina de Ros in Thomasina's house. He at once fled and is suspected, so *let him be exacted and outlawed* according to the custom of the City. No chattels nor frankpledge because he was a stranger. Alice de Brakeley was in the house at the time and was attached, but she does not

The Plea Roll

come and is not suspected. She was attached by William Bengrant and William Swynhog. So they are all in *mercy. All the others and the neighbours attached for the death have died, so nothing from them. Be it known that no one answers for Luke de Batencurt, but it is testified that Alice la Blunde, Luke's widow, holds lands and tenements which belonged to Luke. So the sheriffs are ordered to distrain her to answer for Luke's term of office. She comes and says that all the lands and tenements which belonged to Luke are in the king's hand by order of the treasurer and barons of the exchequer; and that there she found the security to answer to the king for all that is owed to him. Brother William de Henly appears on behalf of the treasurer and barons and puts this fact on record on their behalf. (*Memorandum*.) [cf. **641**]

183. On the eve of the feast of St. Mary Magdalene [21 July 1267] John son of Roger de Aungre killed Walter le Moyne in the ward of Thomas de Basyngges [Candlewick ward]. He at once fled and took sanctuary in the church of St. Lawrence Candelwykstrete, whence he later escaped. He is suspected, so *let him be exacted and outlawed* according to the custom of the City. No chattels but he had a rent of one clove from a house which Roger le Jovene held of him in fee, year and waste worth nothing. The sheriff is ordered to take the rent into the king's hand. Stephen Boniur, a neighbour, does not come and is not suspected. He was attached by Simon de Norhamton and William le Callere. So they are all in *mercy. It is testified that Roger de Aungre and William son of Richard were arrested on suspicion of the death and imprisoned at Newgate; afterwards because they were of the liberty of the City they were released publicly according to the custom of the City. Roger was released to William Rime, Roger de Mareworth, Fulk de St. Edmunds, John le Jovene, Henry le Dubur, Nicholas Crispus 'hoder', William to Ayman [sic], William de Bakynge, John le Frounceys, Nicholas de Hallyngbur', John Deneman, Reginald de Walden, James de Halstede, Thomas de Thorroke, William de Uggle, Nicholas Crispus, Roger Junior, Thomas de Torrock, Nicholas de Hallyngbury, Reginald de Walden, William de Bakynge and Peter le Hoder, William to William Hayman, William de Bakyngg, John le Frounceys, Nicholas de Hallyngbur', John Deneman, Reginald de Waldene, James de Halstede, Thomas de Thurrek. William Ogele, Nicholas Crispes [sic], Roger and Robert le Jovene;[1] to have them here on the first day and did not have them. So they are all in *mercy, Roger and William come and, asked how they wish to clear themselves of the suspicion [blank. Cf. **642**]

Nota 66. De hominibus indictatis de morte hominis et replegiatis [cf. **524** no. 66].
1. The list of pledges is garbled. Roger has only 6; William is released twice, first to 15 and then to 12 pledges.

184. Walter Wan of Wendlesworthe was crossing the Thames in a boat near Westminster when he fell from the boat and was drowned. No one is suspected. Judgment: *misadventure*. Arnulf le Tayllur, a neighbour, comes and is not suspected, so he is *quit*. Value of the boat *10s. (*deodandum*) for which the master of the Knights Templar in England is to answer. Because the master took the deodand without warrant, *to judgment* on him. The

The Plea Roll

sheriff is ordered to cause him to appear. Because the chamberlain and sheriffs did not make a valuation of the boat *to judgment on them. Afterwards the master comes and makes satisfaction for the deodand.

185. John le Cuver killed Hugh de Norhampton in the aldermanry of Walter le Poter [Cornhill ward]. He at once fled and is suspected, so *let him be exacted and outlawed* according to the custom of the City. No chattels, but he was in the frankpledge of William le Furmager and Walter le Furmager in the said aldermanry, so the frankpledges are in *mercy. Osbert le Poleter, a neighbour, does not come and is not suspected. He was attached by Henry Scot and Richard le Seler. So they are all in *mercy. All the others who were attached for the death have died, so nothing from them. [cf. **643**]

[*Nota* unnumbered]: *Franci plegii in misericordia.*

186. John son of Robert de Euere took sanctuary in the church of All Hallows Bredstrete, confessed that he had stolen cloths and *abjured* the realm. Chattels *14d.* for which the sheriffs are to answer. Nothing is known of frankpledge because he was a stranger. [cf. **644**]

187. Philippa maid-servant of Mabel Louman appealed in the husting Henry son of Stephen the Clerk for the death of her son by abortion. She has now died, but Henry comes and, asked how he wishes to clear himself of the death, says that he is a clerk and is not bound to answer here. Thereupon Richard de Berwes minor canon of the church of St. Paul's London comes and claims him as a clerk and proffers letters of the bishop of London testifying that the bishop gave in turn to him and to William rector of the church of St. Christopher London his authority [for claiming clergy]. That it may be known for what he is to be handed over, let the truth be ascertained by the mayor and aldermen; they say on their oath that he is not guilty of the death, so he is quit and as such *let him be handed over to the bishop*. The bishop is forbidden to subject him to any purgation.

Nota 67. *De clerico acquietato et liberato episcopo* [cf. **524** no. 67].

188. From John Adrian and Luke de Batencurt sheriffs for the chattels of Geoffrey de Beverley, who has been hanged,[1] £40. [cf. **644**]

1. In 1267 (*Lib. Ant. Leg.*, 100).

Pleas of the Crown 52 Henry III [1267–8]

189. Jaket le Taylur and Thomas le Armurer came out of the house of Stephen le Taylur, keeper of the wardrobe of the earl of Gloucester, and encountered Geoffrey son of John de Hungrie; a quarrel arising between them, Jaket and Thomas attacked and beat Geoffrey, and Jaket struck him with a knife so that he died forthwith. Jaket at once fled and is suspected, so let him be exacted and outlawed according to the custom of the City. No chattels. Thomas comes and proffers a royal charter testifying that King Henry pardoned him his suit for breach of the peace arising from this death, of which he is accused, on condition that he stand to right if anyone wishes to implead him. And there is no one, so he is granted firm *peace*, but because

The Plea Roll

previously he absconded for the death his chattels are to be confiscated. Chattels 5s. for which Stephen le Taylur is to answer. Because he took the chattels without warrant, he is in *mercy. [cf. **645**]

190. Ralph de Ware and Thomas le Breton were in a boat on the Thames by night when John servant of Bartholomew le Brianzun appeared on the bank and a quarrel ensuing John shot Ralph with an arrow so that he died shortly after in the Tower of London. John at once returned to Bartholomew's house and afterwards fled and is suspected, so *let him be exacted and outlawed* according to the custom of the City. No chattels nor frankpledge but he was in the mainpast of Bartholomew. So he is in *mercy. Thomas was attached for the death, comes and is not suspected, so he is *quit*. No neighbour was attached because he died in the Tower of London.

191. John de Wynton' and Richard Sunit 'portur' were wanting to draw water from a well with a bucket when the rope by which they were pulling it up broke and they fell into the well and were drowned. No one is suspected. Judgment: *misadventure.* Value of the bucket 8d. for which the sheriffs are to answer. All the neighbours come and are not suspected.

192. [m. 10] John the Painter clerk and William clerk of the church of Colecherche killed Peter de Paris in the tavern of Henry de Coventre. They at once fled and are suspected, so *let them be exacted and outlawed.* No chattels nor frankpledge because they were clerks. Raymond de Burdagel was attached for the death because he was in the tavern at the time, and he comes and is not suspected, so he is *quit*. Peter le Cotiler, a neighbour, does not come. He was attached by Peter le Furbur and Godfrey le Botoner. So they are in *mercy.

193. In the same year, Walter de Capeles being chamberlain, for whom no one answers, and Walter Hervi and William de Durham being sheriffs, who answer now; on Friday the eve of the feast of the Translation of St. Thomas the Martyr [6 July 1268] Jolinet a king's clerk killed Nicholas servant of Philip parson of the church of Coneham[1] in the house of Henry Broning. He was at once arrested and taken to Newgate where he died in prison. Emery, Philip's brother, Henry Bruning and his wife Avice were attached for the death because they were in the house and now they have all died except Emery who does not come and is not suspected. He was attached by Thomas de Hormade and Solomon the Baker. So they are all in *mercy. All the neighbours come and are not suspected.

14th cent. heading: *Walterus Hervi et Willelmus de Dunolmia* [53 Henry III].
1. Unidentified: ? *recte* Conehop.

194. John Paternoster killed Nicholas le Paternoster in Nicholas' house in the ward of Anketin le Mercer [Farringdon ward]. He at once fled to the church of St. Mary Magdalene and afterwards escaped from there; he has now absconded and is suspected, so *let him be exacted and outlawed* according to the custom of the City. Chattels *22s. for which Walter Hervi is to answer. He was harboured in the ward of Aketin [sic] le Mercer outside

The Plea Roll

frankpledge, so the alderman and the whole ward are in mercy. The four neighbours come and are not suspected. [cf. **646**]

Nota [68]. *Warda in misericordia pro defectu franci plegii* [cf. **524** no. 68].

195. Bartholomew the Carpenter, John de Breynford, William de Merton, carpenter, and Hugh le Clerk were making a wood-yard out of timber (lignarium de meremio) near a wall when they were crushed by the wall and the timber and died. Value of the wall and the timber *2 marks* (*deodandum*) for which Walter Hervi is to answer. No one is suspected. Judgment: *misadventure*. Two neighbours come and are not suspected.

196. Muriel wife of William de Stanes fell from a bridge (ponte) into the Thames and was drowned. Value of the bridge *13d.* for which Walter Hervi is to answer. John le Clerk, a neighbour, does not come and is not suspected. He was attached by Walter Odyn and William Pepes. So they are in *mercy*. No one is suspected. Judgment: *misadventure*. [cf. **647**]

197. John de Goldweye killed Peter Messeday in Langebourn ward and was immediately arrested and hanged on the following day at Newgate. No chattels. John de Norhampton, a neighbour, does not come and is not suspected. He was attached by Robert le Cordwaner of Chesterhunte and Hugh Bereman. So they are in **mercy*. Edith wife of John was attached for the death, but does not come and is not suspected. She was attached by Robert le Hulder and Richard Roberd. So they are all in **mercy*. The alderman and ward of Langebourne do not know the names of the neighbours, so *to judgment* [on them]. [cf. **648**]

[*Nota* unnumbered: *Ad iudicium*] *quia nesciverunt nominare vicinos.*

198. Stephen de Kemesyng and Thomas le Marcheys were fighting together in a house which they rented from Richard de Paris, and Thomas beat Stephen to death. Thomas at once fled and is suspected, so *let him be exacted and outlawed* according to the custom of the City. No chattels, but he was harboured in the ward of Cheap outside frankpledge, so the alderman and his ward are in **mercy*. Richard de Paris was attached for the death because Thomas lodged in his house, and comes and is not suspected, so he is *quit*. Andrew de Dunster, a neighbour, does not come and is not suspected. He was attached by John de Berkhamstede. So he is in **mercy*. [cf. **649**]

[*Nota* unnumbered: *Misericordia*] *pro defectu franci plegii.*

199. William Russel was killed in the ward of Portesoken. Peter Baret absconded for the death and has now been arrested; he comes and, asked how he wishes to acquit himself of the death, says that for good or ill he puts himself upon the verdict of the mayor and aldermen. Because he is not of the liberty of the City it is permitted by licence of the justices. The mayor and aldermen say on their oath that he is not guilty of the death or of any crime, so he is *quit*.

200. Nicholas de Cullyng and Juliana de Ethelburg were walking together in a field outside London when John le Messer, servant of Thomas son of Adam de Basyng, came up and a quarrel broke out between him and Nicholas and John struck Nicholas on the head with an axe so that he died shortly afterwards in the City. John at once fled and is suspected, so *let him be exacted and outlawed* according to the custom of the City. No chattels nor frankpledge, but he was in the mainpast of Thomas de Basyng. So he is in *mercy*. The four neighbours have died. Because the chamberlain and sheriffs did not attach Juliana, *to judgment* on them.

PLEAS OF THE CROWN 53 HENRY III [1268-9]

201. Simon de la Brome door-keeper of the priory of St. Bartholomew killed John de Colecestre in the priory. He at once fled and is suspected, so *let him be exacted and outlawed* according to the custom of the City. No chattels nor frankpledge, but he was in the mainpast of the prior of St. Bartholomew, so *to judgment* on the prior. All the neighbours have died. Nicholas Abraham was attached for the death, but does not come and is not suspected. He was attached by Henry de Milkstrete and William son of Stephen. So they are in *mercy*. Likewise John le Bracour was attached for the death; he comes and is not suspected, so he is *quit*.

202. In the same year, Stephen de Edeworth being chamberlain and the same being sheriffs; on Monday before the feast of St. Thomas the Apostle [17 Dec. 1268] Roger le Bret and Thomas and William servants of John de Hertfeld were arguing together in John's house when John came up and, a quarrel arising between him and Roger, John struck Roger with a knife so that he died forthwith. John, Thomas and William were at once arrested and taken to Newgate and there before Laurence le [sic] Brok, Thomas and William were delivered by jury and John was convicted and hanged for the death. Chattels 54s. 6d. for which the sheriffs are to answer. All the neighbours have died, so nothing from them. Because the chamberlain did not come with his rolls on the first day on the arrival of the justices, but on the fifth day after, he is in *mercy*. [cf. **650**]

[*Nota* unnumbered]. *Camerarius debet venire primo die cum rotulis suis.*

203. William de Portu, a Roman, killed Master James de Portu, a Roman, in the house of William de Essewy. He at once fled and carried off with him about fifty marks and when he reached Dover he was arrested there by Stephen de Pencestre constable of Dover Castle[1] and thrown from the cliff (phalizatus)[2] for the death. So *let there be an enquiry* there into the chattels. Because the chamberlain and sheriffs did not hold an enquiry into the chattels and did not attach William de Esewey in whose house the incident occurred, or a servant who was in the house at the time, *to judgment* on them. Thereupon it is testified by the mayor and the aldermen that Gerard Perot and Beren[gar], James' servants, were arrested for the death and before Laurence de Brok at Newgate delivered by jury, so nothing from them. The four neighbours came except Robert Wybert and he is not suspected. He was attached by Robert de Springham and Adam Picar'. So they are in **mercy*. [cf. **651**]

Nota 69. Omnes qui fuerunt presentes in domo ubi aliquis interfectus fuerit debent attachiari [cf. **524** no. 69].
1. Appointed before 30 Jan. 1268 (*C.P.R. 1266–72*, 186).
2. On infalisation see M. Bateson, *Borough Customs*, i (Selden Soc., xviii, 1904), 76.

204. In the same year, Hugh son of Otto being chamberlain and the same being sheriffs; Henry Walemund, bailiff of the City, arrested Roger de Coventre son of Gilbert de Grimsby for theft and imprisoned him in another house (in domo alia), from which prison he afterwards escaped. So to judgment on Henry for the escape. Afterwards Roger . . . [took sanctuary and] abjured the realm before the chamberlain and sheriffs. No [chattels].¹ [cf. **652**]

    1. Membrane partly faded.

205. [m. 10d] In the same year, the same being chamberlain and Robert de Cornhull, for whom his son Robert answers, and Thomas de Bassynges being sheriffs; John the Cook and Robert the marshal of Hugh de Turbervill were fighting together in John's house and Robert killed John and at once returned to the house (hospicium) of his master Hugh; he left the City with him and stayed with him, until after the lapse of a year or more he returned to the City with Hugh and was then arrested and taken to Neugate, where he died in prison. Because he stayed with Hugh for a long time after the deed, Hugh is in *mercy. All the neighbours come and are not suspected. [cf. **653**]

Nota 70. De Hugone de Turberville qui non fuit nisi amerciatus eo quod receptaverat quemdam secum per unum annum postquam interfecerat unum hominem [cf. **524** no. 70].

206. Simon Ferol hanged himself with a rope in a house at West Smethefeld. No one else is suspected. Judgment: *suicide*. Chattels *3s. 1d. for which the sheriffs are to answer. Because the ward of Richard de Ewelle [Farringdon ward] falsely valued the chattels before the chamberlain and now has falsely presented the neighbours, the alderman and the whole ward are in *mercy. All the neighbours have died. [cf. **654**]

PLEAS OF THE CROWN 54 HENRY III [1269–70]

207. In the same year, Hugh son of Otto being chamberlain and the same being sheriffs; Laurence son of Humphrey Duket killed Master William le Fremund in the ward of John Adrian [? Walbrook ward].¹ He comes and proffers a charter of King Henry in these words: 'Henry by the grace of God; at the instance of John de Valence, our grandson, we have pardoned Laurence Duket of London his suit for breach of the peace arising from the death of Master William le Fremund, of which he is accused, and we grant him firm peace on condition that he stand to right in our court if anyone wishes to implead him; letters patent at Westminster, 4 June 56 Henry III [1272]'. And there is no one who wishes to prosecute him, so he is granted firm peace. All the neighbours have died.

Nota 71. Pax per cartam regis [cf. **524** no. 71].
1. Cf. **92**n.

The Plea Roll

208. Alan le Somoter, John and Robert, men of Giles de Arraz, with others of his household came out of Giles' house and waylaid William de Edelmeton in the parish of [St.] Mildred assaulting and wounding him so that he died forthwith.[1] Alan and the others at once returned to Giles' house and stayed there until they and about seven other members of the household were [arrested] for the death and taken to Newgate. It is not known how they escaped from prison, so *to judgment* on [the sheriffs] *for the escape*. Alan, John and Robert do not come and are suspected, so let them be exacted and outlawed according to the custom of the City. No chattels nor frankpledge, but they were in the mainpast of Giles. So he is in **mercy*. The mayor and aldermen are told to enquire the names of the others who were arrested. All the neighbours come and are not suspected. Afterwards the king notified the justices by writ that King Henry at the instance of his son Edmund pardoned Alan, John and Robert their suit for breach of the peace arising from this death; he understands by inspection of the rolls of chancery that Alan, John and Robert were delivered from Neugate prison where they were detained on account of this death; consequently the sheriffs are not to be prosecuted for the delivery. Therefore nothing for the escape of Alan, John and Robert. Afterwards on Monday on the quindene of Trinity [8 June 1276] the king ordered the justices by writ, as appears among the 'brevia de precepto' of this eyre, to hold an enquiry by good and lawful men of the City by whom the truth may better be known and who are in no way suspected by the sheriffs and aldermen of the City; according to their findings they are to proceed further in this matter as by law and by the custom of the City they see should be done. The mayor and aldermen and the good men of the City say [blank].[2]

1. Cf. *Rotuli Hundredorum*, i, 407.
2. Cf. *C.F.R 1272–1307*, 139, 2 Dec. 1280 Giles de Argenteyn. Not in the estreat.

209. Bartholomew de Durham, nephew of Jollan de Durham, appealed Cecily, widow of Jollan, that in 48 Henry III [1263–4] she gave a poisoned drink to her husband so that he died. Because he does not come or prosecute his appeal let him be arrested and his pledges to prosecute are in mercy, viz. John Duraunt; the other pledge has died. Cecily comes and, asked how she wishes to clear herself of the death, freely says that she denies the death and everything and puts herself upon the verdict of the aldermen and neighbourhood that she is not guilty thereof. The mayor and citizens are asked whether the verdict of the aldermen and neighbourhood is sufficient for her release or condemnation and say it is not because she is of the liberty of the City and that she must purge herself by the *great law* according to the custom of the City. Therefore it is adjudged that she should wage law in the hand of the justices and purge herself thirty-six-handed, with eighteen men from one side of the Walebrok and eighteen from the other; they are to be chosen before the mayor and aldermen, the chamberlain and sheriffs being absent, in the folkmoot in the churchyard of St. Paul's London with the parties present; the election is to be on the first Sunday in Lent [22 Feb. 1276] and she is to come with her law on the following Wednesday. Because she did not find pledges of law she is to be committed to the sheriffs. Afterwards on the appointed day the thirty-six men were elected at the folkmoot

The Plea Roll

in the prescribed form; on the east of the Walebrok, viz. Peter de Micheam, William de Keleweden, Henry de . . . , Maurice de Waltham, John le Fethermonger, Hugh le Wolf, Peter le Hoder, Henry le Buriler, John Wy . . . , Osbert le Puleter, Roger le Braeler, John le Batour, John Skip, Ralph le Cotiler, Henry de Faversham, Thomas de Capeneshors, Thomas de Suffolk 'peleter';[1] on the west, viz. Godfrey le Coffrer, Henry le Coffrer, Roger de Euere, Richard le Poter, Roger le Lorimer, Geoffrey Monquey, John Wake, Robert Ha . . . , Ellis of Honilane, Thomas Heyron, Roger de Cleve, Robert Curteys, Roger Fucedame, Nicholas [? Le . . .], Faukes le Taverner, Hugh de Wyndesoures, Alan le Huyrer, Thomas de Hereford. Afterwards on the appointed day Cecily comes with her law and wages it before the justices swearing in these words: viz. that she never gave any poisonous drink to her husband Alan[2] or did anything by which he was nearer to death and further from life, so help her God and these holy things (hec sauncta); afterwards six men swore that according to their conscience her oath was a true one; after the six had sworn, Cecily repeated her former oath and after her another six swore and thus Cecily swore six times and waged her law. Therefore it is adjudged that Cecily be *quit* of the death in perpetuity. The mayor and aldermen testify that Cecily was previously arrested at the suit of Bartholomew and that because she was of the liberty of the City she was handed over to twelve pledges according to the custom of the City, viz. Roger Norman 'orlatour',[3] Geoffrey de Rothyng, Henry le Burger, William Wynterington tailor, Peter de Micheham 'peterer', Robert de Essex 'borleor', Adam de Eye dyer, Mahekin de Folesham 'pessoner', Auncelin le Tronur, Robert de Lynton, Philip Frowyk, Fulk de St. Edmunds 'burler', who mainperned to have her here on the first day [and did not] have her. So they are all in *mercy. [cf. **657**]

> Nota 72. *Quod manucapti pro morte hominis usque ad iter justiciariorum non possunt se acquietare per veredictum maioris et aldermannorum et visneti, sed per magnam legem. Et quia non invenit plegios, ideo amerciatur vicecomes. Qualiter magna lex debet fieri. Quod omnes manucapti usque ad iter justiciariorum veniant primo die.* [cf. **524** no. 72].
> 14th cent. at foot of membrane: *Die Jovis apud Turrim.*
> 1. i.e. only 17 names.
> 2. *Recte* Jollan.
> 3. *Recte* orbatour.

210. [m. 11] Michael son of Warin was scalded to death in a brass pot in the house of William le Chaloner. Value of the pot *20d.* (*deodandum*) for which the sheriffs are to answer. All the neighbours have died. William le Chaloner was attached for the death, but does not come and is not suspected. He was attached by Ranulf le Chaloner and Gilbert le Chaloner. So they are in *mercy*. Because it is testified that there were others in the house when the accident happened and the sheriffs did not attach them, *to judgment* on them. No one is suspected. Judgment: *misadventure*. [cf. **658**]

211. An unknown man was found drowned in the ward of Henry de Frowyk [Cripplegate ward]. Thereupon the mayor and aldermen testify that he lay for about five weeks before he was seen by the chamberlain and sheriffs, so *to judgment* on the alderman and his ward. All the neighbours have died. No one else is suspected. Judgment: *misadventure*.

The Plea Roll

212. Isabel daughter of Richard la [sic] Paternostrer was scalded to death in a leaden vessel full of hot water in her father's house. Value of the vessel 2s. (*deodandum*) for which the sheriffs are to answer. Edmund the Goldsmith and John le Heyward, neighbours, do not come and are not suspected. Edmund was attached by Richard Pecche and Hugh le Plumer, John by Richard le Paternostrer and Robert Stroby. So they are in **mercy*. Emma de Len was attached for the death because she was in the house, but she does not come. She was attached by Alan Godard and Hugh de Rokyngham. So they are in **mercy*. Because the wards of Anketin le Mercer, William de Durham and Bartholomew de Castello [Farringdon, Bread Street and ? Cripplegate wards] falsely valued the deodand before the chamberlain and sheriffs, **to judgment* on them. No one else is suspected. Judgment: *misadventure*. [cf. **656, 660**]

213. Alexander Esprigonel hanged himself in the house of Katherine de Westminster. Chattels **17s. 4d.* for which the sheriffs are to answer. Katherine was attached for the death, comes and is not suspected, so she is *quit*. All the neighbours come and are not suspected, except Gilbert de Northbrok. He was attached by Richard de Northbrok and Laurence le Mercer. So they are in **mercy*. No one else is suspected. Judgment: *suicide*. [cf. **661**]

214. Thomas servant of Master Geoffrey, cook of sir Robert Walrant, with others from Robert's household went to Queenhithe (Ripam Regine) and there encountered Robert son of Hamo de Pystewell; urged on by Henry le Petit and his wife Margery they at once attacked and wounded Robert and Thomas struck him to the heart with a sword so that he died forthwith. Thomas immediately fled and is suspected, so *let him be exacted and outlawed* according to the custom of the City. Nothing is known of chattels or frankpledge because he was not of the household of Robert Walrant, who has died. Henry fled at the time and has now returned to the City and been arrested and imprisoned at Neugate. Because Margery is still living in the City, the sheriffs are ordered *to arrest her*. Richard le Armurer and Peter le Furbur, two neighbours, do not come and are not suspected. Richard was attached by John May and Solomon le Cotiler, Peter by Thomas Payn cobbler and John de Borham 'correur'. So they are all in **mercy*. Afterwards Henry and Margery come and deny the death and everything and put themselves upon the verdict of the aldermen and neighbourhood that they are not guilty thereof. The mayor and citizens are asked whether the verdict of the aldermen and neighbourhood is sufficient, and they say it is not, but as they are strangers the verdict of forty-two men from the three aldermanries nearest to the place where the incident occurred will suffice; so that from each ward fourteen men are to be chosen on whose oath the truth is to be ascertained; and upon their verdict they freely put themselves for good or ill. They are to be elected immediately and swear before the justices to tell the truth; they say on their oath that they are not guilty of the death, so they are *quit*. Because it is testified that Henry previously absconded for the death, his chattels are to be confiscated for the flight. Chattels **4s.* for which the sheriffs are to answer. [cf. **541, 655, 662**]

The Plea Roll

Nota 73. Quod non oportet quod extraneus sit in franco plegio. Nichil de catallis pro fuga.
Nota 74. Qualiter extraneus se debet purgare per sacramentum xlii hominum de tribus wardis.
14th cent.: *Scribatur* [cf. **524** nos. 73–4].

215. Guillot le Paternoster and his wife Lucy quarrelled with Robert le Heaumer in the house of Simon le Heaumer and Guillot struck Robert with a staff so that he died on the third day after. Guillot and Lucy at once fled and are suspected, so let Guillot *be exacted and outlawed* and Lucy be exacted and waived according to the custom of the City. Chattels *2s*. for which the sheriffs are to answer. Because the sheriffs and chamberlain held no enquiry concerning chattels, **to judgment* on them. Guillot and Lucy were harboured in the ward of Anketin le Mercer [Farringdon ward] outside frankpledge, so the ward is in *mercy* (*pro franco plegio*). It is testified in the rolls of the chamberlain and sheriffs that Thomas de Caxton was present at the fight, but he does not come and is not suspected; the sheriffs did not attach him, so *to judgment* on them. All the neighbours come and are not suspected. Afterwards the sheriffs testify that Thomas le Peleter was attached for the death and he comes and is not suspected, so he is *quit* [cf. **542**]

216. Robert le Waleys, who had the falling sickness, fell upon a chair and died. Value of the chair 3d. which are given for God. Stephen le Salter and Geoffrey le Salter, two neighbours, do not come and are not suspected. Stephen was attached by Walter de Gloucestre tawyer and Lovekin the Cook, Geoffrey by Reginald de Fridaistrete and John de Boketon. So they are in *mercy*. William le Waleys, in whose house the accident occurred, was attached for the death; he comes and is not suspected, so he is *quit*. No one is suspected. Judgment: *misadventure*. Afterwards Stephen le Salter comes, so nothing from him or his pledges.

217. Isabel daughter of William Scrul, wanting to draw water from the Thames, fell into the water and was drowned. No one else is suspected. Judgment: *misadventure*. Roger de Chesewyke and Adam le Botare, two neighbours, do not come and are not suspected. Roger was attached by William le Plastrer and Simon le Plastrer, Adam by William de Wautham and John le Deveneys, so they are in *mercy*. [cf. **543**]

218. John Russel killed Lucy widow of Adam the Woodmonger (de Wysdarii) in Estchepe. John comes and proffers a royal charter[1] testifying that King Henry pardoned him his suit for breach of the *peace* arising from this death of which he is accused and also outlawry, if it should have been promulgated against him for this death, and granted him firm peace; on condition that he stand to right in the king's court if anyone wishes to implead him. Publicly and solemnly it is proclaimed. And there is no one, so he is granted firm *peace*, but because he previously absconded for the death for about a year, his chattels are to be confiscated. Chattels *20s*. for which the sheriffs are to answer. All the neighbours come [except] Robert de Lavenham and he is not suspected. He was attached by Matthew le

Chaundeler and John le Barbour. So they are in *mercy. [cf. **544**]

1. *C.P.R. 1266–72*, 454, 15 Aug. 1270, Lucy la Queyfer.

219. [m. 11d] Symonet Spinelli, Agnes his mistress (amica ipsius) and Geoffrey Bereman were together in Geoffrey's house when a quarrel broke out among them; Symonet left the house and returned later the same day with Richard Russel his servant to the house of Godfrey le Gorger, where he found Geoffrey; a quarrel arose and Richard and Symonet killed Geoffrey. They immediately went to the house near Grescherche where they lived with Hugh Mace and Reyner Durant and then Richard at once fled and is suspected, so *let him be exacted and outlawed*. No chattels, but he was harboured in the ward of John de Norhampton [Aldgate ward] outside frankpledge, so the ward is in *mercy. Symonet, Hugh Mace and Reyner Durant were arrested and taken to Newgate, where they were imprisoned. Afterwards Hugh and Reyner on the order of the king were released publicly to Reyner Albertis merchant of Florence and James Anguillaunt of Pistoia, who do not answer for them now. So they are in *mercy. Symonet was delivered to Hugh son of Otto then constable of the Tower of London by royal writ addressed to the keeper of Neugate gaol; Hugh does not answer for him now, so to judgment on him (*evasio*). Symonet does not come and is suspected, so *let him be exacted and outlawed* according to the custom of the City. After outlawry has been promulgated against Richard, let proceedings be taken for the outlawry of Simon [sic], because it is testified that he is not guilty except of incitement and the king has lately ordained that no one accused of incitement[1] should answer or incur any penalty before the principal has been convicted. (*Inquiratur*.) Afterwards the king reported by writ that his father had pardoned Hugh Mace.[2] [cf. **545**]

Nota 75. Quod utlagaria primo promulgetur super indictatum de facto et postea super ipsum qui indictatur de auxilio. Et quod rettatus de precepto non portabit penam antequam principalis actor sit convictus [cf. **524** no. 75].

1. Cf. **39, 70**.
2. Cf. *C.P.R. 1266–72*, 401, 6 Jan. 1270, pardon of Symonet at the instance of Hugh Mace.

220. In the same year, Walter Hervy being chamberlain and Philip le Tayllur and Walter le Poter being sheriffs; Walter son of Gerard le Estrays, William le Batiler of Grenewiz, Maud le Estreys, Herman le Estrays and Alice de Grenewich were on the Thames in a boat overloaded with faggots. The boat sank because of the excessive weight of the faggots and Walter, Maud and William were drowned, but the others escaped alive. Value of the boat and faggots *6s. (*deodandum*) for which the sheriffs are to answer. The two neighbours have died. The chamberlain and sheriffs did nothing concerning Herman and Alice at the inquest, so *to judgment on them. The wards of Arnald Tedmar and William de Hadstok [Billingsgate and Tower wards] falsely valued the deodand before the chamberlain, so they are in *mercy. No one is suspected. Judgment: *misadventure*. [cf. **546**]

PLEAS OF THE CROWN 55 HENRY III [1270–1]

221. In the same year, Walter Hervy being chamberlain and Gregory de

The Plea Roll

Roquesle and Henry le Galeys being sheriffs; on Wednesday before the feast of the Purification [28 Jan. 1271] John de Gynges, Alexander de Asshewell and Maud de Haliwell, Maud their niece, Margery de Haverhulle, Philip Tilly, William de Harwes, Clemence widow of Robert de Penkerk, Agnes de Huntyngfeud, John le Poleter, Alice de Bynere, Andrew de Suthwerk, Andrea widow of John de Alorinton were crushed by the bell-tower of the church of St. Mary le Bow (de Arcubus), London,[1] which fell upon them. Value of the bell-tower 20 marks for which the sheriffs are to answer. All the neighbours come except Stephen de Cornhill. He was attached by Anketin de Bentull and Robert de Camaile. So they are in *mercy*, and he is not suspected. No one is suspected. Judgment: *misadventure*. Thereupon the sheriffs come and proffer a royal writ[2] in these words: 'Henry [III] to the sheriffs of London; because of the unfortunate accident in which men and women were crushed to death in Westchepe by the ruin of the bell-tower of the church of St. Mary le Bow and of a house belonging to the prior and convent of Christchurch Canterbury, the stone, timber, lead and everything else pertaining to the house were taken into our hand as deodand; wishing to give thanks to the prior and convent, we have granted them the stone, timber, lead etc. taken into our hand on that occasion; we order you to restore to the prior and convent, as our gift, the stone, timber and lead etc.; at Westminster, 12 March 55 Henry III [1271]'. [cf. **547**]

Nota 76. De oppressione virorum et mulierum per casum campanarii ecclesie de Arcubus. [With a sketch of the bell-tower. Cf. **524** no. 76].
1. Noted in *Lib. Ant. Leg.*, 130.
2. *C.P.R. 1266–72*, 523, 16 Mar. 1271.

222. William Sorel appealed in the husting Robert de Hakeney that he beat his wife Alice so that she gave birth to a still-born boy. He does not come or prosecute his appeal, so *let him be arrested* and his pledges to prosecute are in *mercy, viz. John Hog and Thomas the Carpenter. Thereupon it is found in the rolls of the coroner that William did proceed against him and he was attached by Ralph le Paumer, Solomon le Cotiler, John de Mimmis, John le Marbrer, Nicholas May 'coreyer', Adam le Chaundeler, Stephen le Ferun, Guillot le Rous 'cordewaner', William Bonefaunt 'seler', John May 'poter', Gladwin le Forbour and Edward the Mercer (Mercenarium) to have him here on the first day of the eyre and they did not have him. So they are in *mercy. Robert comes and, asked how he wishes to clear himself of the death, says that for good or ill he puts himself upon the verdict of the mayor and citizens. Because the suspicion is slight, although he is of the liberty of the City, it is allowed by grace of the justices. The jury say on their oath that he is not guilty of the death and the parties have not agreed, so he is *quit*. [cf. **548**]

[*Nota* unnumbered. 14th cent.]. *Appellatur in hustengo*.

223. Peter de la Mote and Dunnyng Petrus were fighting together in the ward of William de Durham [Bread Street ward] and Peter killed Dunnyng and at once fled and took sanctuary in the church of St. Paul's London; afterwards he escaped from the church and has now absconded and is

The Plea Roll

suspected, so *let him be exacted and outlawed* according to the custom of the City. Chattels 2s. for which the sheriffs are to answer. The wards of William de Durham, Henry le Waleys and Simon de Hadstok [Bread Street, Cordwainer and Queenhithe wards] falsely valued the chattels before the chamberlain and sheriffs, so they are in **mercy*. Hugh de Fridaystrete and Henry de Suffolk, two neighbours, do not come and are not suspected. Hugh was attached by John le Paumer and Richard le Chaundeler, Henry by Gregory le Pruter and Robert de Prato. So they are in **mercy*. [cf. **549**]

224. Richard de Taddesworthe and Beatrice maid-servant of Roger de Merton were carrying between them a tub full of water when the tub fell upon Richard and killed him. Value of the tub **6d*. (*deodandum*) for which the sheriffs are to answer. All the neighbours have died, and so has Beatrice, so nothing from them. No one is suspected. Judgment: *misadventure*.

225. Walter le Ferur, a man of the Earl Warenne with twelve other men from the earl's household went to the house of the abbot of Walden to claim hospitality (ad capiendum hospicium); there he found Henry de Rothyng within the gate of the house and he would not allow Walter to enter, so Walter and the others assaulted Henry and Walter killed him with a sword. Walter at once returned to the earl's house. He has now absconded and is suspected, so *let him be exacted and outlawed* according to the custom of the City. Nothing is known of chattels because the chamberlain and sheriffs held no enquiry concerning them or who the men were who went with Walter or what has become of them, so **to judgment* on the chamberlain and sheriffs. Walter was in the mainpast of the earl. So he is in *mercy*.

226. [m. 12] William, servant of Master Bonett,[1] king's clerk, killed John de Nastok in the ward of John Horn [Bridge ward]. He at once fled to Bonett's house in the City who on the following day sent him overseas. He does not come and is suspected, so *let him be exacted and outlawed* according to the custom of the City. No chattels, but he was in the mainpast of Bonett. So he is in **mercy*. All the neighbours come and are not suspected. [cf. **550**]

1. Alias Bonacius Lombardus (Tout, *Chapters*, i, 273–4).

227. John de Wastmel of Lambourn was riding an unbroken (indomitum) horse to water when he met Robert son of Peter de Stebenhuthe driving a horse and cart. John's horse jumped upon the cart and crushed him to death. Value of the horses and cart **14s. 8d*. (*deodandum*) for which the sheriffs are to answer. Robert comes and is [not] suspected, so he is *quit*; he was released publicly by William Godewyn carter to his brother William Speleman, John Spendellum,[1] Reginald Edwyne, Ralph Swetyng, John Strip, John Wytstone, William Bagel, Hugh le Poel and John de Hede, Walter de Clive, Hugh de Cruce and Henry de Fige to have him here on the first day and they did not have him. So they are all in **mercy*. No one is suspected. Judgment: *misadventure*. [cf. **552**]

1. ?*Recte* Spendelove (cf. **552**).

The Plea Roll

PLEAS OF THE CROWN 56 HENRY III [1271-2]

228. In the same year, the same being chamberlain and John de Buddle and Richard de Paris, who answers now for himself and John, being sheriffs; Adam de Ware killed Reginald Tropinel tailor. He was at once arrested and taken to Neugate and afterwards by the liberty of the City he was released on bail (*traditus fuit in ballium*) to Gilbert Cusyn 'taverner', Thomas le Mareschal 'taverner', William de Mannahole, Robert le Escot 'taverner', Roger le Rous 'braeler', John le Lung 'pessoner', Richard de Ware 'macegref', John de Salle 'mercer', Robert de Hakeneye 'cuteler', Roger de Stoppes, Roger le Mareschal 'vineter' of the Conduit[1] to have him here on the first day and they did not have him. So they are all in *mercy*. Afterwards because it is testified that Adam has died, nothing for the mainprise or outlawry; but because he absconded and is suspected, *let him be exacted and outlawed* according to the custom of the City. Chattels ½ mark for which the sheriffs are to answer. The chamberlain and sheriffs made no enquiry concerning the chattels, so they are in mercy. Richard Pel, Philip de Grascherche, John Hatche and Adam de Gandos were attached for the death because they were present and come; the mayor and aldermen say in the faith in which they are bound to the king that they are not guilty of the death, so they are *quit*. Richard de Walden, a neighbour, does not come and is not suspected. He was attached by Richard le Cuper and Geoffrey le Furbur. So they are in *mercy*. [cf. **553**]

Nota 77. *De quodam tradito in ballium per libertatem Civitatis* [cf. **524** no. 77].
1. Only 11 sureties named.

229. Hervey de Scardesborgh fell from a boat at Byllinggate into the Thames and was drowned. Value of the boat *6s. (deodandum)* for which the sheriffs are to answer. All the neighbours come except William le Wyte and he is not suspected. He was attached by John the Clerk and Roger le Marischall. So they are in *mercy*. No one is suspected. Judgment: *misadventure*.

230. Hugh cook of sir Thomas de Clare, John de Montfort and Richard Brid went to the house of a certain Richolda in Bredstrete, where they found a number of women with whom they amused themselves. Philip le Orbatour, Robert de Hadstok clerk, John Porteioye and Osbert de Kent arrived and, a quarrel arising among them, they left the house arguing. Philip seized a knife from Richard Brid and struck Hugh the Cook in the stomach so that he died. Philip at once fled and is suspected, so *let him be exacted and outlawed* according to the custom of the City. No chattels nor frankpledge, but he was harboured in the ward of William de Durham [Bread Street ward] outside frankpledge, so the ward is in *mercy (pro franco plegio)*. Robert and John Porteioye, Osbert, Richolda and also Maud la Wyte, Juliana de Wynton' and Alice Blereheye, who were with Richolda in the house, were arrested for the death and taken to Neugate. It is not known how they were delivered from prison, so *let there be a discussion*. John de Montefort and Richard Brid were not found at the time. It is testified that they afterwards returned to the City with Thomas de Clare and the sheriffs did not attach them, so to judgment on the sheriffs. The mayor and aldermen say in the faith in which they are bound to the king that they do not suspect John and Richard of the death, so nothing from them. All the neighbours come and are not suspected, so they are quit. Afterwards Osbert de Kent, Richolda and Alice Blereheye, who were arrested for the death, come and, asked how they wish to clear themselves, say that they were previously delivered as quit thereof before Laurence de Brok, justice of gaol delivery at Neugate; this is confirmed by the neighbourhood, so they are quit. Nothing for their escape. [cf. 555]

Nota 78. De fugientibus attachiandis cum proximo venerint ad Civitatem [cf. 524 no. 78].

231. Geoffrey le Mareschal and his servant Bernard Angolam, Giles Chasteloyne clerk of Lorianico, William le Messager, Gilbert de Hokyng, Philip de Hokyng, Theobald and Nicholas, Giles' packmen (sometarii), were lodging in the house of Christine widow of Robert the Cook of Flete. One night Geoffrey le Mareschall and Giles went to the stable in the courtyard, where Geoffrey's servant Bernard Angulame was, and, during a quarrel, Geoffrey strangled Bernard in Giles' presence. He at once fled and is suspected, so *let him be exacted and outlawed* according to the custom of the City. Chattels *20s. (deodandum* [sic]) for which the sheriffs are to answer. He was not in frankpledge because he was a stranger. All the others, together with Christine's servant Robert and her maid-servant Estrilda, were arrested and imprisoned at Newgate. Afterwards Giles was delivered with his chattels on the king's command by a royal writ of pardon which the sheriffs now proffer testifying to this. It is not known how the others were delivered, so *to judgment* on the sheriffs. Christine who was attached for the death, comes and is not suspected, so she is *quit*. [cf. 554]

Nota [unnumbered]. *Perdonacio secte regis.*

232. In the same year, the same being chamberlain and John Horn and Walter le Poter being sheriffs; Eustace de Laufare fell from a pear tree in the garden of Jollan de Durham and died. Value of the pear tree *18d. (deodandum)* for which the sheriffs are to answer. Lambert le Flemyng, Good Neighbour Romayn, two neighbours, come and are not suspected. Lambert was attached by William de Enefeld and Thomas son of Jordan, Good Neighbour by Richard le Carpentare and Austin de Graschirch. So they are all in mercy. James Bonacurs and Rembertinus [son] of James were attached for the death, but do not come and are not suspected. James was attached by Thomas le Pourte and Nicholas le Taverner, Rembertus [sic] by Adam de Giseburn and Richard le Paumer 'le fevere'. So they are in **mercy*. No one else is suspected. Judgment: *misadventure*. [cf. 556]

233. Margery la Huppehaldestere was found killed outside Alegate and Nicholas son of Ralph Attediche was accused of the death and comes now. He denies the death and everything, and for good or ill puts himself upon the verdict of forty-two men from the three aldermanries nearest to the place where the incident occurred. Because he is not of the liberty of the City, this is granted to him. Afterwards the forty-two men, sworn before the justices to tell the truth, say on their oath that he is not guilty of the death,

The Plea Roll

so he is *quit*. It is testified that Walter le Brewer absconded for the death and is suspected, so *let him be exacted and outlawed*. No chattels nor frankpledge because he was a stranger.

Nota 79. *Acquietacio per xlii homines* [cf. **524** no. 79].

234. 1 Edward I [1272–3].[1] Hugh Caldelwell took sanctuary in the church of St. Giles without Crepelgate in the ward of Henry de Frowyk [Cripplegate ward] and afterwards escaped from the church. Chattels *28s. (deodandum* [sic]) for which John Horn and Walter le Poter sheriffs are to answer. Hugh has now been arrested and is in prison at Newgate. Afterwards it is testified that Hugh was previously sought in the City in the shrievalty of Nicholas de Wynton' and escaped. Goods to the value of 76s. were found in the house of Denise de Lovecotes and were handed over to the king's exchequer in full by John de Cobham justice of Neugate who is present and testifies to this. Therefore nothing from the chattels. Afterwards it is testified that he had other goods or armour to the value of ½ *mark* for which John Horn is to answer. [cf. **557**]

1. See below, **238**.

PLEAS OF THE CROWN 57 HENRY III [1272]

235. [m. 12d] Roger servant of Ranulf de Waltham killed Reginald de Waltham in the house of William le Tuk. He at once fled and is suspected, so *let him be exacted and outlawed*. No chattels and he was not in frankpledge because he belonged to the household of Alan la Zuche, who has died. William Tuk was arrested for the death and delivered before Laurence de Brok at Neugate. Constance, William's wife, was attached for the death, but does not come and is not suspected. She was attached by William Foucher and Maurice de Sandwys. So they are all in *mercy*. All the neighbours come except John Bolace and he is not suspected. He was attached by Roger de Keylaston and John Snod. So they are in *mercy*. [cf. **558**]

236. William le Wyte, John servant of John de Depe, and Ralph le Taverner were drinking together with others in a tavern when a quarrel arose among them and William and John killed Ralph. John at once fled and is suspected, so *let him be exacted and outlawed*. No chattels nor frankpledge because he was a stranger. William was immediately arrested and taken to Newgate, but afterwards he was delivered to Walter de Merton chancellor with orders to produce him at the king's command. William still remains with Walter, so the sheriff is ordered *to arrest him*. Robert Torp, Thomas de Combe, John de Depe and Henry Spirhard were attached for the death because they were present in the tavern and they come now. The mayor and aldermen say in the faith in which they are bound to the king that they do not suspect them, so they are *quit*. Geoffrey Dyting was attached for the death, but does not come and is not suspected. He was attached by Roger Shaylard, Walter Shank, John Lock, Ralph de Berkhamstede, John de Malmesbur', Simon de Donyngham, Geoffrey de Retherhete, John le Paumer, Henry le Fevere, Simon le Clerk, William de Canwode, Richard Daniel, Geoffrey de St.

Salvator, William Wasem, Adam Spedel and Roger de Bedford. So they are all in *mercy*. Afterwards it is testified that all the pledges have died, so nothing from them.

237. William le Meystre killed John de Cranlegh in the ward of Henry de Coventre [Vintry ward]. He at once fled and is suspected, so *let him be exacted and outlawed* according to the custom of the City. No chattels, but he was harboured in the ward outside frankpledge, so the alderman and the whole ward are in mercy. All the neighbours come except William le Tele and he is not suspected. He was attached by Robert de Mallyng 'barber' and Thomas le Barber in Vintry. So they are in **mercy*. Gilbert de Dynton, Andrew de Pauely, Alan de Dunton and Edmund le Taverner were attached for the death because they were present when the incident occurred and they are not suspected, so they are *quit*. Likewise Ellis de Rotheley and Thomas Baron, in whose house John was found dead, were attached, but they do not come and are not suspected. Ellis was attached by Robert le Escot and Matthew le Karon, Thomas by Richard le Skinnere and Adam de Basyng. So they are all in **mercy*. [cf. **559**]

PLEAS OF THE CROWN 1 EDWARD I [1272–3][1]

238. Adam de Durham encountered Richard de Castle Baynard and Richard de Pek of Norfolk, servants of Robert de Teyford, in the ward of Henry le Waleys [Cordwainer ward]. A quarrel broke out among them and Richard and Richard killed Adam. They at once fled and are suspected, so *let them be exacted and outlawed* according to the custom of the City.[2] No chattels, but they were harboured in the ward outside frankpledge, so the alderman and the whole ward are in *mercy*. Robert de Teyford who was attached for the death, comes and is not suspected, so he is quit. All the neighbours come and are not suspected, so they are *quit*.

1. Above this heading in a different hand: *De tempore regis Edwardi filii regis Henrici.* See also **234**.
2. They were put in exigent for the first time on 20 July 1276 and twice thereafter in the husting of pleas of land (Husting Pleas of Land Roll 4, mm. 1d., 2d., 3d.) but the procedure was the subject of enquiry by the justices in 1321 (*Eyre of London, 1321*, i, 31–7; *Lib. Cust.*, i, 333–8).

239. John de Shordiche killed Peter son of John de Stonhall in the ward of Anketin de Auverne [Farringdon ward]. He at once fled and is suspected, so *let him be exacted and outlawed* according to the custom of the City.[1] No chattels nor frankpledge because he was a stranger. John, Peter's brother, was attached for the death because he was present, but he does not come and is not suspected. He was attached by Joce the king's purveyor (emptorem)[2] and William de Enefeld. So they are all in **mercy*. Hugh le Chapeyler, Peter de Durham and William the Cook, three neighbours, do not come and are not suspected. Hugh was attached by Alexander Russel and Stephen Brian, Peter by Richard le Couriur and Nicholas the Cook, William by William de Ware cobbler (sutorem) and Nicholas de Wenham. So they are all in **mercy*. Afterwards Peter de Durham comes and is not suspected, so he is quit; nothing from him or his pledges. [cf. **560**]

The Plea Roll

1. See **238** n. 2.
2. Alias Joce le Akatur (Tout, *Chapters*, ii, 7 n. 2).

240. [m. 13] Roger de Chevendre of Sheperton was sailing in a ship which belonged to Robert Burnell when he fell from the ship and was drowned. Value of the ship **2 marks* (*deodandum*) for which the sheriffs are to answer. Hubert the Tailor, a neighbour, does not come and is not suspected. He was attached by Stephen de Suffolk baker and Richard le Fevere. So they are in mercy. Afterwards the mayor and aldermen testify that Master Geoffrey de Shankerton clerk of Robert de Burnell took the ship for the use of his master, so **to judgment* on him. Because the chamberlain made no enquiry concerning the ship, *to judgment* on him. No one is suspected. Judgment: *misadventure*. [cf. **562**]

241. Adam son of Robert Monsorel killed Richard de Wycombe in a seld in the parish of St. Mary le Bow. He at once fled to the church, confessed the deed and *abjured* the realm before the chamberlain and sheriffs. No chattels, but he was harboured in the ward of Cheap outside frankpledge, so the alderman and the whole ward are in **mercy* (*pro franco plegio*). All the neighbours come except Richard de St. Botolph and he is not suspected. He was attached by Henry le Wympler and Robert Grapefig. So they are in **mercy*. Because the chamberlain made no enquiry concerning those who were present in the seld and did not order them to be attached, *to judgment* on him. [cf. **561, 721**]

242. John de Tuffel took sanctuary in the church of St. Peter Wodestrete, confessed that he had committed several thefts and *abjured* the realm. No chattels nor frankpledge because he was a stranger.

243. In the same year, the same being chamberlain and Peter Cusin and Robert de Meldeburne, who answer now, being sheriffs; on Thursday before the feast of St. Edmund the king [17 Nov. 1272] William Blauet encountered Robert son of Oskin and Walter de Wodeham in the ward of Peter de Aunger [Broad Street ward], and they immediately attacked and killed him. They at once fled and are suspected, so *let them be exacted and outlawed* according to the custom of the City.[1] No chattels, but they were harboured in the ward outside frankpledge, so the alderman and the whole ward are in **mercy*. Thereupon it is testified that John de Wodeforde, Adam de Wynton', Richard de Wautham, Robert de Tame, Robert de Beri, William de Tykenham, Richard de Rothing, Thomas Frere and William Cok' were arrested on suspicion of the death, but delivered by jury before John de Cobeham justice [of gaol delivery] at Neuwegate. John is present and proffers his rolls which testify to this. All the neighbours come and are not suspected, so they are *quit*.

1. See **238** n. 2.

244. Simon le Waleys servant of Master Reymund de Nogeriis[1] killed Laurence le Barbur near the New Temple. He at once fled and is suspected, so *let him be exacted and outlawed*.[2] No chattels nor frankpledge, but he was

The Plea Roll

in the mainpast of Reymund. So he is in *mercy. All the neighbours come except Hubert the Tailor, Ellis Picard and John le Vinere and they are not suspected. Hubert was attached by Hugh le Broier and John le Taillur, John by Richard Sotewy and Nicholas de Oxford, Ellis by William le Brewere and William de Suffolk. So they are all in *mercy. [cf. **563**]

1. Papal chaplain and nuncio (W. E. Lunt, *Financial Relations of the Papacy with England to 1327* (Cambridge, Mass., 1939), 618).
2. See **238** n. 2.

245. Alice widow of Michael le Mareschal appealed in the husting William le Noreis, Robert Randolf, Ralph the Priest (Sacerdotem) of Hakeneye, William son of Ralph le Lung clerk, William Turgis, Richard de Hoke, Robert de Hull, Robert Swain, William Tuler and Robert Prituse of the death of her husband Michael. She does not come and it is testified that she has died, so nothing from her or her pledges. Robert Randolf, William Turgis, Richard de Hoke, Robert de Hull, Robert Swain, William le Tuler and Robert Prituse come, but the others do not. So let the truth be ascertained by jury. Robert Randolf and the others who come, asked how they wish to clear themselves, say that they freely put themselves upon the verdict of forty-two men from the three aldermanries nearest to the place where the incident occurred. Because they are strangers this is granted to them. The forty-two men, sworn before the justices to tell the truth, say on their oath that none of them is guilty of the death except Ralph the Chaplain (Capellanum) of Hakeneye, William son of Ralph le Lung clerk and William le Noreys, so the others are *quit*. Ralph, William and William are to be exacted and outlawed and because they are of *Middlesex*, let them be exacted and outlawed there. There is to be an enquiry concerning chattels and frankpledge in the hundred of Osolvestane, and the sheriff is ordered to produce on the morrow twelve men from the hundred. Robert Randolf, William Turgis, Richard atte Hoke, Robert de Hull, Robert Swain, William le Tuler and Robert Prituse were previously arrested and released publicly on the king's command; Robert being released to William de Harenges, Robert le Marchaunt, John Goldeston, Robert de Shakewell, all of Hakeney, Henry Attelane of Shoredych, Richard the Clerk, John Aston, John Pode, Richard Alward, Richard le Veer, Robert le Rus, all of Hakeneye, and John de Store of Stebenheth; William Turgis to William le Veer, William Charle, Henry le Scoueler, John le Veer, Thomas le Freman, all of Hakeney, Richard le Wodere of Stebenheth, Richard Chapman of Hakeneye, William Bisshop of Hakeneye, Laurence Mauntel of Haliwell, John atte Hoke, William le Fevere, Warin Grosile, all of Hakeneye; Richard Attehoke to William atte Mersce, John atte Hegge, both of Hakeneye, Edmund Kyse of Stebenhethe, William atte Grove, Robert Roger, Warin Silketop, Richard Leuis, Adinette Merke, Richard le Canon, Richard Pige, Richard Gilbert and William Warin, all of Hakeney; Robert del Hull to William Bruning, Richard son of Robert of Hakeney, Alan son of Philip of the same, William Attebrok, Roger Bruning, Robert Attewell, Robert atte Merk, Richard Attehull, Richard son of Peter, Warin Attestile, and William Goding, all of Stebenhethe; Robert Swain to Adam de Caldelonde of Stebenhethe, Richard Attepyre of Iseldone, William Pig, Robert Coleman, Osbert

The Plea Roll

Attewell, Richard Osbern, John Atteasse, Richard Patrick, John Silketop and Walter le Wodeward, all of Hakeney; William le Tuler to Brouning Mauntel, Richard Mauntel, John le Pil, William Wranghorn, Richard atte Well, Reginald Alvene, Robert Nicol, Godfrey le Tuler, Paulinus Heron, Daniel le Tuler, all of Shordiche, Herion of Hoxton, Adam Herion of the same; Robert Prituse to Robert Atteponde of Hakeney, Henry le Nas of Stebenheth, Richard le Vair, Reginald le Neuman, Alan Dusse, William Brid, all of Hakeney, Solomon Atteclive of Stebenhethe, Richard Artur of Hakeneye, John Goding of Stebenhuthe, Hugh Goding of the same, John son of Robert of Edelmeton and John le Sondere of Stebenheth; they[1] were to have them here on the first day and did not have them. So they are in *mercy*. Afterwards twelve men from the hundred come and say on their oath that Ralph, William and William had no chattels and were not in frankpledge because they were vagabonds. [cf. **564**]

> Nota 80. *Appellum in hustengo. Acquietancia per xlii homines. Quod forinceci exigantur in comitatibus de quibus sunt* [cf. **524** no. 80].
> 1. Several of the above lists of mainpernors are incomplete.

PLEAS OF THE CROWN 2 EDWARD I [1273–4]

246. In the same year, Gregory de Roqesley being chamberlain and Henry de Coventre and Nicholas de Wynton' being sheriffs; John Coubely and Richard Wert were with others on a ship at the wharf of Laurence Hardel,[1] loading it with wine, when a quarrel broke out among them; Stephen le Esert came up to strike John and John seeing this fell out of the ship into the water in avoiding the blow and was drowned. Stephen was afterwards arrested and delivered by jury before John de Cobham at Neugate, so nothing from him. Laurence de Amewell was attached because he was on the ship at the time, but he does not come and is not suspected. He was attached by Richard de Ware and Henry de Ware. So they are all in mercy. Because the sheriffs did not attach William Skinnere of Ware and the others who were on the ship and because the chamberlain made no mention of their names in his roll, to judgment on the chamberlain and sheriffs. All the neighbours come and are not suspected, so they are quit. Afterwards the mayor and aldermen testify that Richard Werry [sic] was arrested and detained in prison at Neugate and afterwards released publicly by royal writ to Simon le Clerk 'bereman', [Edmund]† de Suffolk vintner, Walter de [Gloucestre],† Walter le Pender, Robert de Rotherhethe, Henry le Wowere 'bereman', Roger le [Seler],† Geoffrey le Weringe, Robert de Ware, Solomon le Juvin, Adam Spendelove 'bereman' and William [Barber servant]† of John Adrian to have him here on the first day and they did not have him. So they are in mercy. Richard comes and is not suspected, so he is quit. [cf. **565**]

> † Words supplied from **565**; plea roll much faded.
> 1. ? In Vintry ward (cf. E. Ekwall, *Street-names of the City of London* (1954), 138–9 under Hardeleslane).

247. [m. 13d] Christine de London while drawing water from the bottom of a vat (*in fundendo aquam in quadam cuva*) fell into the vat and died soon

The Plea Roll

afterwards. Value of the vat *2s.* (*deodandum*) for which the sheriffs are to answer. All the neighbours come and are not suspected, so they are quit. No one else is suspected.[1] Judgment: *misadventure*.

1. *Ideo inde quieti. Nullus alius inde malecreditur.* interlined.

248. Robert son of Roger fell from a ship into the Thames and was drowned. Value of the ship **20s.* (*deodandum*) for which the sheriffs are to answer. No one else is suspected. Judgment: *misadventure*.

249. Miles le Coureur killed Henry de Kent in the ward of Henry de Coventre [Vintry ward]. He was at once arrested for the death and taken to Neugate, where before John de Cobham he was released to Nicholas le Coureur, Thomas de Norwich, William Knith, John de Cruce Roes, Geoffrey le Botoner, Henry le Crepiner, John de Grey, John Goldrik, John Lucas, Richard le Bukeler, Abraham le Traiere and Gilbert le Coureur to have him here on the first day and they did not have him. So they are all in *mercy*. Miles comes and, asked how he wishes to clear himself, for good or ill puts himself upon the verdict of forty-two men from the three aldermanries nearest to the place where the incident occurred; sworn before the justices to tell the truth, they say on their oath that he is not guilty of the death and was not present when Henry was killed, so he is *quit*. (*Acquietacio per xlii.*) Asked who did kill Henry, they say it was John de la Marche, so *let him be exacted and outlawed.*[1] No chattels. Asked also at whose instigation Miles was arrested and charged with the death, they say that it was at the instigation of Roger le Petite, servant of Henry de Coventre, who accused him out of hatred, so *let him be arrested*. (*Capiatur de abetto*.) John de Cobham put on record that the pledges undertook to produce Miles at the king's will. Miles comes now to stand to right, so it is adjudged that his pledges are quit of amercement. [cf. **566**]

Nota 81. De plegiis amerciatis quia non habuerunt primo die itineris [cf. **524** no. 81].
1. See **238** n. 2.

250. John le Gaunter and his wife Agnes beat Isabel widow of Geoffrey le Sachier in the ward of Walter le Poter [Cornhill ward]. Isabel escaped from them, but afterwards at nightfall John went to her house and killed her with a knife. He at once returned home, took all his goods and fled with his wife Agnes. He is suspected, so *let him be exacted and outlawed.*[1] No chattels, but he was harboured in the ward outside frankpledge, so the alderman and the whole ward are in **mercy* (*pro franco plegio*). The mayor and aldermen, asked whether Agnes was an accomplice in the death, say that she was, so *let her be exacted and waived.*[2] All the neighbours come except Robert de Kydemenstre and he is not suspected. He was attached by William le Engleis and Walter de Welles. So they are all in **mercy*. Afterwards it is testified that John was in the frankpledge of Humphrey le Tailur and John Cristemes. So they are in **mercy*, and nothing from the ward. [cf. **567**]

1. & 2. See **238** n. 2.

251. A boy called Bartholomew fell from a boat into the Thames and was drowned. Value of the boat 2s. (*deodandum*) for which the sheriffs are to answer. No one else is suspected. Judgment: *misadventure*.

252. William de Boys killed William le Clerk in Bradestrate. He at once fled and is suspected, so *let him be exacted and outlawed* according to the custom of the City.[1] No chattels, but he was harboured in the ward of Anketin de Auverne [Farringdon ward], so the alderman and the whole ward are in **mercy*. Nicholas de Goreham 'fruter' and John le Cordwaner, two neighbours, do not come and are not suspected. Nicholas was attached by Andrew le Barbur and Michael le Tailur, John by James the Cook and Richard le Barbur. So they are in **mercy*. [cf. **568**]

1. See **238** n. 2.

253. Peter de Perone, a lunatic (*lunaticus*), fell out of a window in a house in the ward of Douegate and died. Sauncelina, who was in the house at the time, was attached, but does not come and is not suspected. She was attached by Walter de la Forde and Adam de Walsingham. So they are in **mercy*. All the neighbours come except William de Mare 'gaunter' and he is not suspected. He was attached by Ellis Shadde and Robert de Horsham 'boghyer'. So they are in **mercy*. No one else is suspected. Judgment: *misadventure*. [cf. **569**]

PLEAS OF THE CROWN 3 EDWARD I [1274–5]

254. In the same year, the same being chamberlain and Luke de Batencurt, for whom no one answers, and Henry de Frouwyk, who answers now, being sheriffs; Henry de Suffolk fell from a step in the house of Luke de Batencurt and died. Value of the step $\frac{1}{2}$ mark (*deodandum*) for which Henry de Frouwyk is to answer. Guillot le Moler, who was in the house at the time, was attached, but does not come and is not suspected. He was attached by Hubert de Arraz and Ralph de Rumford. So they are in **mercy*. All the neighbours come and are not suspected. No one else is suspected. Judgment: *misadventure*. [cf. **570**]

255. Adam de Ramesey, Roger Aledrawere, Motekin de Sussex and William le Careter, servants of Adam de Brok, canon of St. Paul's London, killed his cook Simon in Adam's house within the churchyard of St. Paul's. They at once fled and are suspected, so *let them be exacted and outlawed* according to the custom of the City.[1] No chattels, and they were not in frankpledge because they were living within the precincts (*sanctuarium*) of the church. All the neighbours come and are not suspected, so they are quit.

1. See **238** n. 2.

256. Richard de Lamenesse bailiff with his servant Richard, William le Bret, Geoffrey le Taverner, John de Horsepol, Walter le Taverner, John le Taverner and William Shepesheved went to the house of Emma Louel in the ward of Nicholas de Winton' [Langbourn ward], to arrest some thieves who were being harboured there, as they thought. They entered the house and found no one there except Emma and her maid-servants, but John de Horsepol and William le Bret went out of the house and in the courtyard they found Richard de Veer, chaplain, hiding in a gutter (stillicidio); they at once assaulted and wounded him, so that he died in the third week after. So the sheriff is ordered to arrest them. Afterwards Richard de Laymenes, his servant Richard, William le Bret, John de Horsepol and William Shepesheved were arrested and they come now. Asked how they wish to clear themselves, John de Horsepol says that he was previously arrested for the death and delivered by men from the three wards (wardis) nearest to the place where the incident occurred before John de Cobham at Neugate. John de Cobham is present and puts this on record from his rolls, so let him be quit. Richard and the others, except William le Bret, deny the charge and for good or ill put themselves upon the verdict of forty-two men from the three aldermanries nearest to the place; sworn before the justices, they say on their oath that they are not guilty of the death, so they are *quit*. William le Bret says that he is a clerk and is not bound to answer here. Thereupon Richard de Berwes, proctor of the bishop of London, comes and claims him as a clerk; but that it may be known [for what he is to be handed over], let the truth be ascertained by the forty-two men; they say he is not guilty of the death, so he is *quit*. Asked who killed Richard, they say it was Geoffrey le Taverner, who has now absconded and is suspected, so *let him be exacted and outlawed* according to the custom of the City.¹ No chattels.

Nota 82. *De quodam ballivo Civitatis et aliis acquietatis per xlii homines trium wardarum* [cf. 524 no. 82].
1. See 238 n. 2.

257. Andrew le Sarazin, who was suffering from a fever, consulted Master John de Hexham and Master Semann his brother, doctors (medics), that they might cure him; John sent Master William de Crek to give him pills (pilas) and Andrew at once ordered his valet Richard de Langeley to look after them. Later Andrew and Richard his valet ate such a quantity of the pills that they died soon after. Master William de Crek comes and the mayor and aldermen say in the faith in which they are bound to the king that they do not suspect him of the death, so he is *quit*. Masters John and Semann were arrested and imprisoned at Neugate; John is now dead, but Semann is living in the City and it is not known how he was delivered from prison, so to judgment on the sheriffs for the *escape*. The sheriff is ordered *to arrest him*. Simon Malon [sic], Bartholomew de Raban, Otto de Gask, Henry Fos . . . , Geoffrey servant of Simon Malur [sic], Geoffrey servant of Otto, John the Cook and Nicholas Page were attached because they were present in the house when Andrew and Richard died, but they do not come and are not suspected. They were attached by Thomas le Taillur, John de Shordiche, William de Enefeud, Ralph de Araz, Ranulph de Hexham, David le Escot and John le Taillur. So they are all in **mercy*. All the neighbours come and are not suspected, so they are *quit*. Afterwards Semann comes and for good or ill puts himself upon the verdict of the mayor and citizens. Because the suspicion is slight, this is granted to him by licence of the justices. The mayor and aldermen say in the faith in which they are bound to the king that he is not guilty of the death, so he is *quit*. Asked in whose custody he

The Plea Roll

was when he was previously arrested for the death, Semann says that Luke de Batencurt sheriff arrested and imprisoned him, then took ½ mark from him and allowed him to go. The mayor and aldermen testify to this, so *to judgment* on Luke. Henry de Frowyk is quit of the escape. [cf. **571**]

258. Geoffrey Whiting and his wife Alice came out of a tavern together and, a quarrel arising between them, Geoffrey suffocated Alice. He at once fled and is suspected, so *let him be exacted and outlawed* according to the custom of the City.[1] Chattels *3s.* for which the sheriffs are to answer. In addition he had *100s.* which Ponce de Mora owed to him. So John Horn and Ralph le Blunt sheriffs are ordered to raise that sum from Ponce's lands and chattels and to answer for it to the king. He was harboured in the ward of Henry de Coventre [Vintry ward] outside frankpledge, so the alderman and the whole ward are in *mercy. Isabel la Frauncis, who was attached for the death, comes and is not suspected, so she is *quit*. All the neighbours come except Peter le Cotiler and he is not suspected. He was attached by John de Castello and Leo the Clerk. So they are in mercy. Afterwards [m. 14] the mayor and aldermen testify that Geoffrey was in the frankpledge of Walter de Abeton and Robert le Messager, so the frankpledges are in *mercy* and the ward is quit of amercement for the harbouring. [cf. **267, 572**]

1. See **238** n. 2.

259. William Sipring was trying to drag a ship into the Thames when the rope by which he was dragging it broke and he fell into the water and was drowned. Value of the ship **6s. 3d.* (*deodandum*) for which the sheriffs are to answer. Robert le Taillur, a neighbour, does not come. He was attached by Austin le Taillur and Michael the Tailor. So they are all in *mercy. No one else is suspected. Judgment: *misadventure*. [cf. **574**]

260. Peter de Burdeus servant of Reymund de Burdeus, killed John de Gaunt 'eskirmesur' with a knife in the house of Robert le Mareschall. He at once fled to the church of St. Paul's London, but later escaped from the church and has now absconded; he is suspected, so *let him be exacted and outlawed* according to the custom of the City.[1] No chattels, but he was in the mainpast of Reymund. So he is in *mercy. All the neighbours come and are not suspected, so they are *quit*. Robert le Mareschall, Hugh le Orfevere, Gilbert Trille, Richard Bonaventure, John Viel, Richard his brother, and Ralph de Balesham were attached because they were present, come and are not suspected, so they are quit. Ismania wife of Robert le Mareschall and Master Thomas le Surigien were also present at the time, but do not come and are not suspected. They were attached by Henry de Roff, Thomas Fyntard, Adam le Barbur, James the Cook, Michael le Taillur and Nicholas de Gatham. So they are in *mercy. [cf. **573**]

1. See **238** n. 2.

261. Robert le Gras and his wife Isabel, and John de Benteley and his wife Isabel appealed Richard Taillehaste that on Saturday before Christmas 2 Edward I [23 Dec. 1273] he went to Robert and Isabel's house in Wodestrate, broke down the door and entered; he beat and ill-treated the two Isabels whom he found inside so that as a result of the beating they both afterwards gave birth to still-born boys, and stole a silver brooch worth ½ mark from Isabel wife of John; that he did this wickedly and feloniously they offer [to prove]. Richard comes and denies the death, robbery and everything. He says that previously when they were at the husting the appellors made no mention of the robbery and did not appeal him in the proper form, but only made a simple plaint; so he seeks judgment whether he is bound to answer their appeal. This having been allowed, it is adjudged that the appeal be null. Robert and all the others are to be committed to *gaol* for a false appeal. To preserve the king's peace let the truth be ascertained by jury. Richard, asked how he wishes to clear himself, says that he is a clerk. Thereupon Richard de Berwes, minor canon of St. Paul's London, and by letters of the bishop of London etc. comes and claims him as a clerk; but that it may be known for what he is to be handed over, let the truth be ascertained by the neighbourhood. Forty-two men from the three nearest aldermanries, sworn before the justices, say on their oath that he is not guilty of death, robbery or any other crime, so he is *quit*.

 Nota 83. De appello in hustengo facto et postea quassato coram justiciariis. Clericus ad sectam regis acquietatus per xlii [cf. **524** no. 83].

262. Alexander de Bestenore of Buckinghamshire took sanctuary in the church of St. Botolph without Aldresgate, William de Fremingham in the church of St. Giles without Cripelgate and Margaret de Wengham in the church of St. Michael Bassieshawe. They confessed that they had burgled houses, stolen horses and committed other thefts and *abjured the realm* before the chamberlain and sheriffs. Alexander's chattels **1 mark* for which the sheriffs are to answer. The others had no chattels and were not in frankpledge because they were strangers. [cf. **574**]

263. Richard Scot of Northumberland, John Ismongere of Fremingham and Richard le Clerk of Winchester broke out of Neugate prison where they were imprisoned for theft and fled to the church of the Friars Minor London. They confessed that they had broken out of prison and *abjured the realm* before the chamberlain and sheriffs, so to judgment on the sheriffs for the *escape*. No chattels because they were strangers. [cf. **575**]

264. John le Jovene 'weder' was found killed in his house in the parish of St. Mary Abechirche. Robert de Paris tailor, William de Derbi and Alan de Hakeny were accused of the death and arrested. They come and deny the death and everything and put themselves upon the verdict of forty-two men from the three aldermanries nearest to the place where the death occurred, because they are strangers and not of the liberty of the City. These men, sworn before the justices to tell the truth, say on their oath that none of them is guilty of the death, so they are *quit*. The mayor and aldermen are asked who killed John and say in the faith in which they are bound to the king that Robert de Bannebury, Walter Cadaz, Roger de Asseborne and Geoffrey clerk of the church of St. James Graschirche[1] encountered John in the ward of Thomas de Basingge [Candlewick ward] and beat and wounded him so that he died. Robert, Walter and Roger at once fled and are sus-

The Plea Roll

pected, so *let them be exacted and outlawed* according to the custom of the City.² Walter Cadaz' chattels *16d.* for which the sheriffs are to answer. The others had no chattels. Geoffrey the Clerk took sanctuary in the church, but comes now in the king's peace to stand to right before the justices. Asked how he wishes to clear himself of the death he says that he is a clerk and is not bound to answer here. Thereupon Richard de Herwes minor canon of London comes and claims him as a clerk by letters of the bishop of London testifying that the bishop entrusted him his authority to claim clergy. But that it may be known for what he is to be handed over, let the truth be ascertained by the forty-two men; the jury say on their oath that he is guilty, so as such *let him be handed over to the bishop.* No chattels. Hugh de Gloucester, Godfrey le Barber, Robert atte Wodecote and Robert le Weder were present when the incident occurred, but are not suspected, so they are quit. All the neighbours come and are not suspected, so they are all quit. Afterwards Robert de Bannebyr', who was arrested for the death, comes and denies the death and everything and puts himself for good or ill on the verdict of forty-two men from the three aldermanries nearest to the place where the incident occurred, because he is a stranger and not of the liberty of the City; these men, sworn before the justices to tell the truth, say on their oath that he is not guilty of the death nor of any crime, so he is *quit*. Nothing from his outlawry. [cf. **576**]

Nota 84. De extraneis acquietatis per xlii. Quod maior et aldermanni dicent quis occidit mortuum. De clerico convicto per xlii et liberato episcopo. De extraneo acquietato per xlii [cf. **524** no. 84].
1. ? St. James Garlickhithe.
2. See **238** n. 2.

265. Abraham le Treyer and his wife Brunamia complain that on Monday before the feast of the Nativity of Mary 3 Edward I [2 Sep. 1275] Maud de Stanes went to their house in the parish of St. Michael Bassinggeshawe and against the peace etc. beat, wounded and ill-treated Brunamia, so that she was maimed; whence they say that they have suffered damage and loss to the value etc. and they produce witnesses. Maud comes and denies the force and injury. She strongly denies that she ever beat or maimed Brunamia as she is accused and puts herself upon the verdict of the aldermen who in the faith in which they are bound to the king testify to this. So it is adjudged that Maud is quit and Abraham and Brunamia be committed to gaol; but they are pardoned at the instance of John de Cobeham.

Nota 85. Querela de transgressione [cf. **524** no. 85].

266. Walter son of Adam le Huyrer appealed in the husting Martin Horn of wounds and battery. He does not come or prosecute his appeal, so *let him be arrested* and his pledges to prosecute are in **mercy*, viz. Robert le Cordwaner and Robert brother of Walter. Martin comes now. So let the truth be ascertained by the mayor and aldermen; they say in the faith in which they are bound to the king [blank]. He was previously arrested and released to John of St. Albans, Philip the Tawyer, Adam de Ismongerelane, Robert the Cook, Alan le Barbur and Robert le Burser to have him here on the first day and they did not have him. So they are in **mercy*. [cf. **576**]

The Plea Roll

267. John de Calabre 'bereman' appealed in the husting Geoffrey Whyting of wounds and battery. He does not come, so *let him be arrested* and his pledges to prosecute are in *mercy*, viz. Richard Rose and Alexander Codeford. Geoffrey does not come. He was attached by Peter Guillame, Martin le Criur, Walter Saule and Richard Pighe. So they are all in **mercy*. To preserve the king's peace let the truth be ascertained by the mayor and citizens; they say in the faith in which they are bound to the king [blank]. [cf. **258, 577**]

268. Alice daughter of Ralph of New Place (de Novo Loco) *appealed in the husting* Maud de Kent of wounds and battery. She does not come, so let her be arrested and her pledges to prosecute are in mercy, viz. Walter Winter and Alan le Mazon. Maud does not come and was not attached, so to judgment on the sheriffs.

269. Adam le Burser was killed in the parish of St. Botolph without Aldresgate. William de Beverle was arrested for the death and comes now. Thereupon John de Cobeham, justice, puts on record that William was previously convicted by jury before him at Neugate of killing Adam in self-defence because he could not otherwise avoid his own death, for which he was committed to prison until he should obtain the king's grace. So let him be kept in custody until the king shall make known his will. The four neighbours come and are not suspected, so they are quit.

   Nota 86. De quodam deliberato coram justiciariis itinerantibus per recordum justiciarii de Neugate [cf. **524** no. 86].

Pleas of the Crown 4 Edward I [1275–6][1]

270. In the same year, Gregory de Roqeley being chamberlain and John Horn and Ralph le Blunt being sheriffs; Robert Scot 'bereman' was crushed to death while carrying a load of lead. Value of the lead 2s. for which the sheriffs are to answer. No one is suspected. Judgment: *misadventure*.

   1. For the coroner's roll covering the later part of 4 Edward I (from March), see *C. Letter-Book B*, 256–64.

271. [m. 14d] Isabel widow of John Picot appealed in the husting[1] John de Arundel of the death of her husband John. She comes and prosecutes her appeal, but John does not come. So Isabel is told to go to the husting and prosecute him there until he be outlawed according to the law and custom of the City. Thereupon it is testified that Henry le Taverner and Robert Hodin were at the time crossing the road where the incident occurred and the mayor and aldermen in no way suspect them, so nothing from them. John de Oxford, a neighbour, does not come and is not suspected. He was attached by Richard de Export and John Wyther. So they are in **mercy*. [cf. **578**]

   Nota 87. Appellum in hustengo. Et quia appellatus non venit coram justiciariis, ideo appellans redeat ad hustengum quosque etc. [cf. **524** no. 87].
   1. Husting Common Pleas Roll 4, m. 1d., Nov. 1275.

The Plea Roll

272. Wyot the Clerk appealed in the husting Richard de Blida 'seler' of wounds and battery. He does not come, so *let him be arrested* and his pledges to prosecute are in mercy, viz. Walter Wysman and John Heron 'mercer'. Richard comes now. So let the truth be ascertained by the mayor and citizens; they say in the faith in which they are bound to the king that he is not guilty of the wounds and beating and the parties are not agreed. So he is *quit*. He was previously arrested and released to William de Blida goldsmith, John de Paris 'seler', Ralph de Balesham 'seler', Robert de la More 'lorimer', Richard le Paumer, 'seler', Robert Pecche 'seler', Robert de Assendone 'seler', Richard de Strata 'seler', Richard Joce 'seler', Robert le Chaumberlein, John de Westle and Richard de Balesham to have him here on the first day and they did not have him. So they are all in *mercy. [cf. **579**]

> Nota 88. Appellum in hustengo . . . [see **273** n].

273. John le Plomer appealed in the husting Master Robert le Fizicion le Petit and his son Robert of wounds and battery. He does not come, so let him be arrested and his pledges to prosecute are in *mercy, viz. John Attestrande and Henry Aspele. Robert and Robert do not come. They were attached by Hugh de Byflete tawyer, John de Reyley tawyer, Geoffrey Frosch 'pessoner', Richard de Bristoll, John de Derbi tawyer, Robert de Totenham, Robert Passelewe, Gilbert le Tor, Gilbert de Pelham, Peter de Terringg and Roger de Oxford tawyer. So they are all in mercy. Let the truth be ascertained by the mayor and citizens; they say in the faith in which they are bound to the king that the parties are agreed. [cf. **580**]

> Nota [**88**] Appellum in hustengo de plagis et verberatura [cf. **524** no. 88].

274. Maud la Russe *appealed in the husting* Alice de Kent of wounds and battery. She does not come, so *let her be arrested* and her pledges to prosecute are in mercy. She has not found pledges except by faith. Alice does not come. She was attached by John le Barbur by Neugate, Richard the Cook of Fridaystrete, Gerard Beynin, William de Wycombe, Matthew de Lincoln and Richard de Herwes (*liberatur episcopo*).[1] So they are all in *mercy. Let the truth be ascertained by the mayor and citizens; they say [blank]. [cf. **581**]

> 1. Apposed to **273** but perhaps belonging here (cf. **264**).

275. William de Dunhache is accused of the death of Alexander le King killed at Retherhethe; Maurice Gorel and his wife Maud of the theft of eggs, hens and capons; Adam de Say of stealing corn and other thefts; William Crete of the theft of seven sheep; John son of Robert of the Bridge of stealing a sheep and other thefts and Agnes daughter of Thomas Attehill of burning the house of William Hithe. They come and deny the death, theft, burning and everything and for good or ill put themselves upon the verdict of twelve men from the neighbourhood of Retherhethe and Enefeud where the thefts took place and this is granted to them because they are strangers. The jury say on their oath that they are not guilty of any crime, so they are quit.

> Nota 89. Forinceci acquietati per forcincecos [cf. **524** no. 89].

The Plea Roll

276. Alexander Fraunkelein is accused of the theft of a cow which belonged to Robert Cristemeson of Northale and a horse belonging to Thomas Hanche; Alexander de Langeley of the theft of two bushels of wheat; Robert le Suur of Suthwerk and Agnes Atteknol of the death of Henry le Baud; and Adam Scot of the theft of a horse. They come and deny the theft, death and everything and for good or ill put themselves upon the neighbouring wards and the neighbourhood who say that none of them except Alexander le Fraunkelein is guilty of any crime, so [let] Alexander [be hanged] (*suspensus*) and all the others are *quit*. Chattels *½ *mark* for which the sheriffs are to answer. [cf. **582**]

277. Stephen de Burton and William de Norfolk, approvers, come and withdraw from their appeal and confess that they are thieves. So [let them be hanged] (*suspensi*). No chattels.

278. Philip le Taillur accused of robbery of and receiving of horses belonging to John de Grey and William le Latimer, comes and denies that he was involved in the robbery, but freely admits that he had one of the horses in his keeping for the use of John and that he afterwards returned it to John and gave him satisfaction for it, as appears from a letter written in John's name which Philip produces and which fully testifies to this. He puts himself upon the verdict of the mayor and aldermen that he was not involved in the robbery and never committed or caused to be committed any trespass, damage, trouble, loss or grievance against John or William or any of their household. The mayor and aldermen say on the oath which they made to the king and in the faith in which they are bound to him that Philip is in no way guilty and that the horse did not come into his hands of his own volition, so he is *quit*. [cf. **146, 287–8**]

Nota 90. Acquietatus per maiorem et aldermannos [cf. **524** no. 90].

279. The jurors of the hundred of Edelmeton presented before the itinerant justices in Middlesex in 2 Edward I [1273–4] that Adam servant of Henry de Eure and Geoffrey servant of Stephen de Ponte killed Geoffrey Swomld in the vill of Enefeud in the time of King Henry when they were both living in the City with their masters Henry and Stephen; the sheriff of London was therefore ordered to arrest both masters and servants. So Henry and Stephen were arrested for the harbouring of Adam and Geoffrey and appeared before the justices in Middlesex. Thereupon the mayor and citizens of London came and said that they were of the liberty of the City and were not bound to answer there outside it and they claimed them for their liberty. So they were allowed by the justices to find pledges until the coming of the justices here. Henry and Stephen come, but because the incident occurred in the time of King Henry and the justices do not wish to proceed in this case without consulting the present king, it is adjudged that they should find pledges to stand to right at the king's will. They found pledges, viz. Edmund Horn, Nicholas Horn, John Lorenz, Henry Bole, Henry de Greneford, Thomas the Goldsmith of the Bridge, Walter le Blund, Robert de Garscherch, Robert le Burser, Gilbert de Colecestre 'taverner', Stephen Pikeman and John Jovene, but because Stephen did not appear on the first day the pledges who mainperned him before the itinerant justices in Middlesex are in *mercy*, viz. William de Storteford 'gaunter', Edmund Horn 'feroun', Roger de Ponte 'feroun', William Amis 'pessoner', Aylwin de Ponte 'feroun', William de Essex 'cornur', John de Depe, Bartholomew de Capella 'gaunter', John Hurel 'feroun', Miles de Oysterhull, Daniel de Ponte 'gaunter' and Herman le Estreis. [cf. 583]

> *Nota 91. De civibus dismissis per manucapcionem, qui attachiati fuerunt coram justiciariis itinerantibus in comitatu Midd' pro morte hominis* [cf. **524** no. 91].

280. Richard Attehale and his brother Walter were accused of burning down the house of John de Bow of Totenhale. Thereupon they were arrested during the last eyre of Middlesex and the mayor and citizens of London appeared before the itinerant justices and said that Richard and Walter were of the liberty of the City of London and were not bound to answer on any account outside the liberty. So they were released by the justices to the mayor and citizens to have them here. Richard and Walter do not come and the mayor and citizens, asked what became of them, say they were handed over to Walter de Saumford then sheriff of Middlesex,[1] who does not answer for them now, so to judgment on Walter [de Saumford] for the *escapes*. Richard and Walter [his brother] have now absconded. [cf. **588**]

> *Nota 92. De civibus London' liberatis maiori et civibus per plegios (? licet) factum esset forincecum* [cf. **524** no. 92].
> 1. So designated in **588**. Cf. **522** and *C.C.R. 1272–9*, 423.

281. Osbert le Furbur accused of the death of his wife Beatrice comes and denies the death and everything and for good or ill puts himself upon the verdict of the mayor and aldermen. Because he is a stranger and not of the liberty of the City this is granted to him. They say in the faith in which they are bound to the king that he is not guilty, so he is *quit*.

282. James de Stoke clerk, accused of breaking open a box in the church of St. Paul's London, comes and denies the theft and everything. He says he is a clerk and is not bound to answer here. Thereupon Richard de Herewes comes and claims him as a clerk by letters of the bishop of London testifying that the bishop entrusted to him his authority to claim clergy. So he is handed over to him, but so that it may be known for what he is to be handed over, let the truth be ascertained by the mayor and aldermen; they say in the faith in which they are bound to the king that he is not guilty, so he is quit and as such *let him be handed over to the bishop*.

> *Nota 92* [sic; no text; cf. **524** no. 92].

283. In the year 4 Edward I [1275–6], Gregory de Rokesle being chamberlain and John Horn and Ralph le Blunt sheriffs; Roger de Farenbergh took sanctuary in the church of St. Thomas on London Bridge, confessed that he was a thief and *abjured* the realm before the chamberlain and sheriffs. No chattels.

284. Adam Scot is accused of the theft of a horse; Thomas son of William Mus of Norhamton and Isabel de Norhamton of the theft of a silver goblet

The Plea Roll

(cipho); Henry Fraunkelein of harbouring thieves; Thomas [Shap]† of the theft of a silver goblet; Edith de Brichull of clipping coins; Henry de Lynnhull[1] of Staffordshire was arrested with three surcoats of burel (burello) stolen from a (? suit); Thomas de (? Gandone) is accused of the death of Ralph Testard; John Bonvalet of many thefts; and Denise Lovecote of harbouring Hugh de Caldewell approver.[2] They come and deny the theft, death, harbouring and everything and for good or ill put themselves upon the verdict of the aldermen and neighbourhood; who say on the oath they made to the king and in the faith in which they are bound to him that none of them is guilty of any crime except Henry de Lynnhill and John Bonvalet. So let Henry and John be [hanged] and the others are quit. Henry's chattels 5s. and John no chattels. Afterwards the mayor and aldermen testify that Denise Lovecote was previously arrested and released to Edmund [Pecok],† Walter [le Poleter],† William Slich, William de Hertford goldsmith, William de Wautham 'corder', Geoffrey le Feverer, [John]† Tanur, Nicholas le Chandeler, Walter Chubbe, Gamelin Canon and John le Seriaunt[3] to have her here on the first day and they did not have her. So they are in mercy. [cf. **584–5**]

† Names supplied from **584**; membrane much faded.
1. Huvill in **585**.
2. Cf. **234**.
3. An additional name in **584**.

285. [m. 15] Richard le Vineter of la Bernette, accused of cutting off the hand of Walter le Hewe near la Bernette in Middlesex so that he died, comes and denies the death and everything and for good or ill puts himself upon the verdict of twelve jurors from the neighbourhood of la Bernette where the incident occurred. They say on their oath that he is not guilty, so he is *quit*.

286. Holdin le Taillur was accused of harbouring thieves, so the bailiffs of the City went to arrest him. He at once fled and absconded and has now returned and been arrested. He comes and denies the harbouring and everything and for good or ill puts himself upon the verdict of the aldermen and neighbourhood who say in the faith in which they are bound to the king that he is not guilty; so he is *quit*, but he previously fled, so his chattels are to be confiscated for the flight. Chattels *20s.* for which Luke de Batencurt and Henry de Frouwyk are to answer. [cf. **586**]

287. Ives le Longe 'draper', William le Flaoner, Robert le Stor, Adam de Ismongerelane, Richard de Assewy 'brokur', Nicholas de Brente and John de Coventre are accused of robbery of horses belonging to John de Grey and to the king at Cornhulle and robbery committed in Jewry in 47 Henry III [1262–3]. They come and deny the robbery and everything and for good or ill put themselves upon the verdict of the aldermen and neighbourhood, who say in the faith in which they are bound to the king that they are not guilty of any crime except in time of war (nisi tempore guerre). So they are *quit* as regards life and limb, but are to be committed to *gaol*. Afterwards

The Plea Roll

William le Flaoner came and makes fine of *40s. on the pledges of Robert de Norwich and Thomas le Flaoner.¹ [cf. **587, 146, 278, 288**]

>Nota 94 [also apposed to **286** and **288–9** but without text]. *De quibusdam rettatis de felonia et acquietatis. Acquietati per veredictum aldermannorum et visneti.*²
>1. Cf. the list of those proscribed in 1269 (*Lib. Ant. Leg.*, 120–1).
>2. This sentence is written in large letters between **286** and **287**. A line in the margin erroneously implies that it relates to **285–90** inclusive.

288. Philip le Bret, Richard le Vilein, William de Blye, Stephen de Goteley, Roger le Avener, John le Staumpeur, Richard Dragon, Osbert le Poleter, Henry le Rous, Roger le Chaundeler, Michael le Oynter, Reginald Pointel, John de Elilaund, Martin le Bokeler, Ranulf Lure, Robert de Waldegrave, William de Manhale, Thomas de Estchep, William Egrith and Nicholas le Convers are accused of robbery of horses belonging to John de Grey and to the king at Cornhull and of robbery committed in Jewry in 47 Henry III [1262–3] and other robberies in time of peace; they come and deny the robbery and everything and for good or ill put themselves upon the verdict of the aldermen and neighbourhood, who say in the faith in which they are bound to the king that they are not guilty of any crime, so they are *quit*.

289. It is established by the verdict of the mayor and aldermen upon which Henry de Coventre put himself that at the time when he was sheriff he arrested Nicholas de Staunford, who was accused of the theft of money and goods from Ralph le Butiller clerk and Richard de Staunford, and afterwards committed him to William le Bowyer and Guillot servant of Richard de Lamenes, who allowed him to go free. To judgment on Henry, William and Guillot for the *escape*. Henry, asked if he harboured William and Guillot after the event and if any goods seized with Nicholas remained in his keeping, says no, and puts himself upon the verdict of the mayor and aldermen who say in the faith in which they are bound to the king that Nicholas had no chattels in his house, nor did any remain with him, but in truth they say that Henry harboured Guillot in his house for some time after the event, so *to judgment* for the harbouring. [cf. **589**]

290. Of Stephen de Edeworthe concerning the chattels of Robert Pointell 40s. (*Bedford*). [cf. **125, 590**]

291. Charter of Guy de Brusseles to Philip le Taillur.
'I Guy de Brusseles son and heir of Walter de Brusseles formerly citizen of London have given to Philip le Taillur citizen of the same all the lands and tenements with appurtenances which fell to me by inheritance on the death of my father Walter in the parish of St. Nicholas Shambles London in St. Nicholas and Pentecostelanes, together with 50s. annual quit rent in the same parish, namely 40s. from the tenement held by John King and 10s. from the tenement held by Denis de Benchesham, viz. whatever he holds or ought to hold in the parish, in lands, buildings of wood and stone, rents, etc., except the tenement held by Walter Carbonel in Pentecostelane, for the annual rent of a clove payable at Easter and the service due to the chief lords of the fee. I Guy and my heirs and assigns warrant the same in

The Plea Roll

perpetuity to Philip his heirs and successors against all men and women, Christians and Jews; for which gift, grant, warranty, quittance and in confirmation of the charter Philip has given me £100 as gersum. Witnesses: Gregory de Roqele, mayor of London.' He granted further that the alderman of the place might take the aforesaid tenements into the king's hand.

292. The following have sold wines contrary to the assize: Walter de England, Henry de Coventre, Ellis de Conducto [sic], Gilbert de Duntone, John de Staunford, Ralph de Suffolk, Henry de St. Osyth, Alan de Suffolk, John Hardel, Richard de St. Botolph, Robert the Scot, Richard de Kyngestone, John de Cestrehunte, Osbert de Suffolk, John le Taillur, Peter de Gysors, Thomas de Coumbe, Simon de Farnham, Bruin de Gysorc, Reginald de Suffolk, Emma la Barbere, Christine Renerii, John Stacy, Eustace le Taverner, Nicholas de Westone, Rustikel Thedald, Joce the king's purveyor (emptor regis), William Warage, John son of Saer, William de la Cornere, William de Portesmuth, William Hewe, James the Taverner, John Fuatard taverner, Reginald le Chaundeler, Adam Neverathom, Robert de Reding, Henry de Hereford, Roger de Coventre, John de Depe, William de Beille, Thomas de Conductu the elder, John Wade, Richard Deusour, Richard de la Bernette, Richard Bole, John de Northwode, John Doget, Hubelin de Arraz, Robert le Treyer, John Hache, Adam de Blakeny, Thomas de Carron, Wolmar de Essex, William Doget, Richard Cortois, Simon de Seint Liz, Thomas le Barber, Robert de Fridaiestrate, Richard de Neuwerk, Andrew le Bell, Ellen de Flete, Agnes de Wylehale, Thomas de Conductu the younger, Fulk the Taverner, James de Treys, Reginald de Lauvare, Arnold de Depe, Adam le Feroun, Eleanor de Conductu, Richard de Bedeford, Robert Russel, Roger Piggesflesh, Roger le Estmor, John Skyp, Robert de Suffolk, John de Wodeham, Roger de Garschirche, Bartholomew de Capella 'gaunter', Beatrice de Hakeford, Richard servant of Avice Hardel, Philip le Traour, John de Brilond, Deudatus Gwillam, Donelin Junte, William Russell and Robert de Dorset. So they are all in *mercy. [cf. **527, 529**]

293. Charter of Master Thomas of Pyvelesdon.[1]
'Edward by the grace of God; at the instance of R[obert Kilwardby] archbishop of Canterbury we have pardoned Master Thomas de Pywelesdon all displeasure and rancour conceived against him by reason of trespasses allegedly committed by him against our father King Henry and us and others of our faithful subjects during the recent disturbances; and we have admitted him to our grace and peace; he is not to be impleaded, molested in any way or injured on account of any such trespasses on condition that henceforth he conduct himself well and faithfully towards us and our heirs; at Westminster, 10 May 4 Edward II [1276].'[2] So he is granted firm peace.

[*Nota*] 95. [No entry, cf. **524** no. 95].
1. Among those proscribed in 1269 (*Lib. Ant. Leg.* 120–1).
2. *C.P.R. 1272–81*, 140. For an earlier pardon see **476**.

294. The following have sold cloth contrary to the assize: John Adrian the elder, John Adrian the younger, John Neuman, William de Northawe,

The Plea Roll

Anketin de Brettevill, Roger de Derbi, Reginald de Frouwyk, Robert Camayle, Stephen de Cornhull, Robert de Linton, William Bukerell, Reginald Canon, Walter Everard, John de Wylehale, Richard his brother, John Cole, Peter de Edelmeton, Richard Eswy, William de Hadestok, William of Winton', Geoffrey de Geddingges, Roger Beynin, William de Geddingges, John de Waltham, Thomas son of Thomas the younger, John Racolf, Thomas Bath, Robert de Arraz, John Heron 'peuerer', William de Beck, William de Betoyne, Rusticall Thedal, Deodatus Willame, Richard de Ewell, Robert Curteys, Ingram de Betoyne, William Heron, William le Hurer, Roger Piggesfles, William de Boys, Richard de Abindon, Boydin de Gaunt, Copin Trossin, John de Armenters, Thomas Beuvin, Thomas de Reynham, John de Brylord, John de Nichole, Adam de Blakeney, Robert de Acre of London, Richard de Arraz of Lincoln, Thomas de Melkestrete, William de Staunford the younger, Geoffrey le Taillur by St. Martin le Grand, Hugh le Taillur of Lincolnshire, Robert de Kydermenstre, William de Wouburne, William de Lewes, William le Tundur, Belin Pe de Argent, Nicholas Cauntyng, Walter Pe Dargent, Walter his son, Walter de Gowys, Hugh Loger, Peter de Cambray, Philip de Benekuk, John his brother, Jakes de la Barbere, Gerard de Heyrin, Nicholas de Wyrenale, Gerard le Carpenter, Cristelot Bel, Ingram Falconel, William Tuddehors, Bernard Pilate, Baude de Sovenaunt, John Bonebroke, [Rykewin]† de Douwai, Gerard de Staleward, Thomas his brother, John de Plankes, Wiz de Plankes, Gerard de Flos, Jake de Landa, Amaury de Castello, Bernard de Lyons, [Jomes]† Purteus, Gerard Bonfrani, Nicholas de Scaylon, Nicholas de Loberg, Terry Baudan, John le Clerk of Sevenhaunt, Baude de Midi, Nicholas [Curte, Gerardinus de la Vile],† Ingram Alein, Walter Musard, Lambert de la Potente, Alexander his son, Jakes [de Fresang, William de St. Amand],† Waubert de Pikete, Gamelin le Vilein, Thomas Pikete, Giles de Araz, [John de Furfeles, Sewel]† Pammoyle, Giles son of Baldwin son of Gerard, Godfrey son of Odeken, Gilbert ... , [John le Parchemener, Godfrey le Parchenerius].† [cf. **663–4**]

† Names supplied from **469, 663–4**; plea roll faded.

[m. 15d] RESPONSES TO THE ARTICLES [OF THE EYRE][1]
295. Of those who are in the king's mercy and have not been amerced, they say that the dean and chapter of St. Martin's London and Deodatus Gwilam were in the king's mercy for trespasses of purpresture in the last eyre and have not been amerced.

1. For a comparison of the articles of 1276 with those of 1244 see Introduction (Appendix A).

296. Of those who maliciously demolished or burned down the houses of others within the liberty of the City against the peace,[1] they say that Brian de Gowiz and William de Ferrers,[2] with others of their men, at the time when the earl of Gloucester and Hertford occupied the City of London, overthrew the houses of Solomon le Blund and Master Elias, Jews; they destroyed part of the timber and carried off the rest to the Tower of London to build barricades there; Brian and William and the Jews have reached

The Plea Roll

agreement without the king's licence, so to judgment on the Jews.[3] Thomas de Pylewesden, Stephen Bukerel, Michael Tovi the younger[4] with others overthrew the houses of Thomas de Basingges in Aldermannebury. Richard de Ware draper burned a great part of Cheap the day before the battle of Lewes, and obstructed the men bringing water to put out the fire when the great combustion occurred.

1. Cf. *London Eyre, 1244*, nos. 11, 273.
2. Cf. *Lib. Ant. Leg.*, 92.
3. Receipt Roll 6 Edward I (E 401/88, m. 5) records: *De Isaac filio Elye le Evesk 50s. de fine*; see also **551**.
4. *Lib. Ant. Leg.*, 79, 120–1.

297. Of boys and girls and ladies who are or ought to be in the king's wardship, they say they know nothing.

298. Of abbeys, priories and hospitals which are or ought to be advowsons of the king, they say that the priories of Holy Trinity London and St. Bartholomew London are advowsons of the king.

299. Of churches,[1] they say that the church of St. Paul's London and the deanery of St. Martin le Grand and the deanery of St. Peter in the Bailey are in the king's gift, and also the chapel of the Blessed Mary in Jewry. They say that the church of St. Magnus the Martyr is worth £15 yearly and Master Geoffrey de la Wade now holds it by the grant of the prior of Bermundeseie and the abbot of Westminster to whom King Henry conferred the advowson by his charter[2] as appears in the roll of the penultimate eyre. St. Andrew Huberd, worth 50s. yearly, was given to John de Ramesey by John Sperling. All Hallows Fancherche was given to John clerk of Adam de Strattone by the prior of Holy Trinity.[3] St. Michael in Cheap, worth 40s. yearly, was given to William le Affeite by the dean and chapter of St. Paul's London. St. Audoen, which is worth little, is in the gift of William Giffard. St. Peter upon Thames is worth 50s. yearly and is in the gift of the dean and chapter of St. Paul's London. St. Alphege is worth 40s. yearly and is in the gift of the dean and chapter of St. Martin's. All Hallows upon the Wall is worth £18 yearly and is in the gift of the prior of Holy Trinity London.[4] St. Augustine upon the Wall, worth 20s. yearly, is held by the same prior.[5] All these churches, so it seems to them, should be in the king's gift, unless the claimants have a warrant. So the sheriff is ordered to cause them to appear. Because they make no mention of the church of St. Augustine,[6] the mayor and the whole City are in *mercy*.

1. Cf. *London Eyre, 1244*, nos. 199, 276.
2. *C.P.R. 1232–47*, 82, 21 Nov. 1234.
3. Cf. *Cartulary of Holy Trinity Aldgate*, ed. G. A. J. Hodgett (London Record Society, 1971), no. 109.
4. Cf. *ibid.* nos. 779–81.
5. Cf. *ibid.* no. 789.
6. ? St. Augustine Watling Street; but the dean and chapter of St. Paul's were patrons (*Valuation of Norwich*, ed. W. E. Lunt (Oxford, 1926), 332) unless it was temporarily in the king's hand. Alternatively, the mayor and aldermen may have omitted St. Augustine upon the Wall (Papey) from their answer although this is not suggested by the text.

The Plea Roll

300. Of serjeanties,[1] they say that Hugh son of Otto holds a rent of 45s. in the City of London by the serjeanty of engraving the die of the king's money. They say also that there is a messuage in Garscherch street held of the king; John Lerenz holds it from the king by the serjeanty of providing the coal for making the king's crown and regalia and receives 60s. 10d. yearly for finding the coal; but they believe that this is enrolled otherwise at the king's exchequer. Fulk Peisorer holds the serjeanty of Fleet gaol with the Porsoke,[2] which is worth £18 yearly. A messuage in Thames street is in the serjeanty of the king and Walter Hervi now holds it by the serjeanty of rendering to the king yearly a helmet,[3] and it is not known by what warrant. So the sheriff is ordered to cause them to appear. Afterwards Walter Hervi comes and says that the messuage belonged to William de St. Ermine[4] by the king's gift, and that William enfeoffed him and his wife Isabel of the messuage to hold for himself and his heirs in perpetuity, rendering to William and his heirs 1d. yearly and to the king's exchequer 1 mark for all services. The king afterwards confirmed the enfeoffment and Walter proffers William's charter and the king's charter which testify to this, so he is without day.

1. Cf. *London Eyre, 1244*, nos. 198, 275, 318–21.
2. i.e. the soke of the Fleet (M. B. Honeybourne, 'The Fleet and its neighbourhood in early and medieval times', *London Topographical Record*, xix (1947), 32–8).
3. For the service rent by a helmet, see *London Eyre, 1244*, nos. 217, 302.
4. *Lib. Ant. Leg.*, 38.

301. Of those who took money from those who entertained strangers contrary to the provision made in the last eyre, they say they know nothing.

302. Of bailiffs who took bribes from anyone so that they could sell cloths contrary to the assize, they know nothing.

303. Of those who took bribes from the wine-sellers so that they could sell mixed or putrid wine and of those who mixed the wine, they know nothing.

304. Of treasure-trove, they know nothing.

305. Of sheriffs and other bailiffs who held pleas of the crown within the boundaries of the City without warrant, they know nothing.

306. Of Christian usurers alive and dead, who they were and what chattels they had, both moveable and immoveable, they say that Nicholas le Convers and Hugh de Gysorz, living Christians, were indicted before Brother Stephen de Fuleburne who was appointed for this purpose on the order of the king. They come and Nicholas proffers a charter[1] of the king pardoning of his special grace Nicholas le Convers citizen of London the trespass of extortion, usury and communication with usurers imputed to him and granting him firm peace; he is given authority henceforth to trade in (*negociandi*) goods and chattels in the realm, so that he is not to be oppressed by the king, his justices or bailiffs on account of this trespass, provided that he conducts himself well and faithfully henceforth. So he is *quit*. Hugh for good or ill puts himself upon the verdict of the mayor and

The Plea Roll

aldermen who say in the faith in which they are bound to the king that he is not guilty. So he is quit.

1. *C.P.R. 1272–81*, 73, 3 Dec. 1274. See also *C.C.R. 1272–9*, 107.

307. Of Christians who receive the goods of Jews either in charters or in money, pledges and otherwise, they know nothing.

308. Of Jews who have inflicted cruelty on Christian boys they say that two boys were found killed by Jews, as appears in the roll of the chamberlain and sheriffs. [cf. **551**]

309. Of coiners and clippers of coin, they say that William Fot goldsmith was arrested for clipping coin and was hanged.[1] Chattels 27 marks which Hugh son of Otto received. He had a house, year and waste worth 40s. [blank]; issues of the intervening period [blank]. Afterwards the king ordered that Hugh pay the money into King Henry's wardrobe[2] as by his writ. So nothing. (*Inquiratur*.)

1. Cf. **341**.
2. For another instance of such a payment see **474**.

310. Of the chattels of aliens, [and] who has them, they say that at present they know nothing. So they are told to enquire further. Afterwards they know nothing.

311. Of the king's mint and exchange, who made exchange or mintage without [leave of] the king or his bailiffs, they say they know nothing.

312. Of fugitive malefactors or burglars who are outlawed and their harbourers and those who fled and returned without warrant and their chattels, they say that Robert le Petit[1] who lived in St. Clement's Lane harboured an unknown thief who was hanged at Canterbury and now Robert himself is dead. (*Inquiratur*.)

1. Cf. **341**.

313. Of bribes taken for sending away corn and other chattels lest they be taken, they say they know nothing.

314. Of new customs levied in the City, they say they know nothing.

315. Of those who are harboured in the City and go out with bows and arrows, greyhounds or other dogs to commit trespasses in forests, parks and fishponds belonging to the king or others and of their harbourers, they know nothing.

316. Of the escape of thieves, they say that John de Frome,[1] during the shrievalty of Robert de Linton and William Essewy mercer, escaped from the prison of Neugate. So to judgment on the sheriffs for the *escape*. Likewise Roger de Clere was convicted before the justices and handed over to the bishop of Lincoln and by licence of the sheriffs he was imprisoned at

The Plea Roll

Neugate, during the shrievalty of John de Norhamton and Richard Picard; he broke out of prison and escaped with four others whose names are unknown and who were imprisoned there by the sheriffs. So to judgment on the sheriffs for the *escape*, but because Roger was not imprisoned in the custody of the sheriffs, they are quit of his escape. Likewise Roger Drinkwater and another twelve whose names are unknown, during the shrievalty of Henry de Frouwyk and Luke de Batencurt, escaped from the prison of Neugate. Henry Walemund sheriff imprisoned Roger Lythfot in his house on suspicion of theft and he escaped from his custody. So to judgment on them for the *escapes*. John Frome, Roger Drinkwater and [Roger] Lythfot have absconded and are suspected, so *let them be exacted and outlawed* according to the custom of the City. Nothing is known of chattels. So to judgment on the sheriffs for the amercements and chattels. Of the names of those who escaped ... Arnald Petri, during the shrievalty of Henry de Coventre and Adam de Bruning, broke out of the prison of Neugate and took sanctuary in the church of the Friars Minor and abjured the realm. No chattels. So to judgment for ... Likewise Thomas de Barton during the same shrievalty was being pursued by some men and took sanctuary in the church of Aldermannechirche and he afterwards absconded from the church and is suspected, so *let him be exacted and outlawed* according to the custom of the City. Chattels £4 10s. 8d. for which the sheriffs are to answer; since they concealed the chattels in their roll they are in *mercy*. [cf. **591**]

    1. Cf. *Lib. Ant. Leg.*, 22 and several writs concerning John Frome and Alan de Shoreditch, *C.R. 1254–6*, 145, 202–3, 438. See also R. B. Pugh, *Imprisonment in medieval England* (1968), 130, 135, 232, 252.

317. [m. 16] Of gaols delivered without warrant of the king or his justices in time of peace, they know nothing.

318. Of those imprisoned at the will of bailiffs without reasonable cause, they know nothing.

319. Of damages and prises taken from strangers by whom it was done and when and where and by whose authority (in cuius potestate) and of what things, they know nothing.

320. Of bailiffs and others who took prises in the name of the king for the use of themselves or others which did not come into the king's hand, they know nothing.

321. As to whether the provisions made by the justices of the last eyre[1] at the Tower of London concerning the making of attachments both in pleas of the crown and in assizes of novel disseisin and others are well kept, they say that the chamberlain and sheriffs answer for this and they know nothing further.

    1. Possibly repeating the provisions of 1244 (*London Eyre, 1244*, nos. 242–3).

322. As to whether any large sum of money was collected at the entrances and exits of the gates of the City of London, for the repair of the walls of

The Plea Roll

the City and other operations in the City and whether any money was collected as tax in the City by the mayor, sheriffs and aldermen or others who took money and what became of the money, they say they know nothing.

323. As to whether any tallage was levied whereby the poor were burdened and the rich exempt, they know nothing.

324. Of sheriffs and other bailiffs who have taken money from those accused of homicide that they might be released by pledges, when they should not have been released without the king's command, they say that the sheriffs can release by pledges all those who are of the liberty of the City until the arrival of the justices, of whatever felony (latrocinio) they are accused; on condition that each pledge is able to answer to the king for 100s.[1]

Nota 96 [no text; cf. **524** no. 96].
1. Cf. 76.

325. Of bailiffs who take fees from both sides (ambidextris), they know nothing.

326. Of sheriffs and other bailiffs who have imprisoned those who were accused of theft by indictment and detained them until they received payment from them, they know nothing.

327. Of sheriffs and other bailiffs who took money twice for one amercement, they know nothing.

328. Of those who distrain a man to pay more than the sum in which he was amerced, they know nothing.

329. Of those who distrain several people having one name, they know nothing.

330. Of those who undertook to have a man before the justices and did not have him on the first day, they say that at present they know nothing but will inquire further.

331. Of those who made extracts (extraxerunt) of the king's writs, they know nothing.

332. Of money taken for the default of those who do not come on the sheriffs' summons, who took it and how much, they know nothing.

333. Of money taken from those who have been excommunicated, they know nothing.

334. Of broken bridges, they know nothing.

The Plea Roll

335. Of felons hanged and condemned elsewhere than before the justices in eyre (ad omnia placita), nothing.

336. Of the chattels of Jews who have been killed, nothing.

337. Of those who do not permit the king's bailiffs to enter their lands to serve summonses, nothing.

338. Of bailiffs who have taken money for removing recognitors (recognicionibus), nothing.

339. Of those who fish with keddles and fishtraps, nothing.

340. Of those who were summoned and did not come[1] on the first day, they say that the following did not come on the first day: the abbot of Newenham, Robert earl of Ferar, the prior of Simplingham, the dean and chapter of Cycestre, the abbot of Kirkestede, Henry de Audeley, John de Colecestre chaplain, the abbot of Westminster, Eudes la Zouche, Reginald de Grey, Roger de Clifford the elder, Master William de la Corner, the prior of Coventre, Maud widow of Robert Walraund, William de Valence, the abbot of St. Edmunds, the prior of Thefford, Philip Marmion, Roger Loveday, the prior of Ware, the master of the Knights Templar in England, Ralph Dongon, the dean of St. Martin's London, Juliana widow of Thomas de la Forde, Robert [? son of] Fulk, Bartholomew de Brianzon, James de St. Victor, the abbot of Stratford, John de Vallibus, the abbot of Shrewsbury. So they are in *mercy. [cf. **526, 528**]
    1. *et non venerunt* interlined.

341. Of escheats, they say that John le Cofrer holds a messuage in the ward of Cheap which belonged to William le Fot goldsmith, who was convicted and hanged for felony,[1] worth 40s. yearly; John de Mundene holds a tenement in Aledemannebury which belonged to Robert de Cambridge who was convicted of felony at Canterbury,[2] worth 20s. yearly. Thereupon John le Cofrer comes and says that he holds the messuage of William de Faukeham[3] to whom it was given by King Henry. He proffers a royal charter testifying that the king gave him all the houses with appurtenances in the City of London which belonged to William and which were his escheat by reason of the felony which William committed and for which he was hanged, to have and to hold for himself and his heirs in perpetuity, saving the right of anyone in performing the due and accustomed services. Likewise John de Mundene comes and says that he holds the tenement from Henry de Otington clerk, to whom it was given by King Henry as his escheat, for Henry and his heirs to have and hold in perpetuity from the chief lords of the fee, and rendering the due and accustomed services. So they are to have their seisin.
    1. Cf. **309**.
    2. Cf. **312**.
    3. A marshal of the king's household (*C.P.R. 1266–72*, 586).

342. Of purprestures,[1] they say that the Friars Preachers have obstructed two lanes in the ward of Anketin de Auverne [Farringdon ward] to the nuisance. Afterwards the prior and friars come and proffer charters[2] of King Henry testifying that the king granted them the lanes for the enlargement of their courtyard; on condition that the well called Showell which is in the upper end of the one of the lanes should remain unobstructed, so that the neighbourhood of the City and suburb should have recourse to the well to draw water, when it is necessary.

> 1. No attempt has been made to identify the wards in which purprestures (**342–467**) occurred unless the name of the alderman of the ward is given. However, with the obvious exception of **342–5**, it would appear that purprestures for a particular ward were grouped together, e.g. Farringdon (**346–54**), Bread Street (**355–64**), Bishopsgate (**?385–?391**), Cripplegate (**434–42**), Queenhithe (**457–9**). There is no evidence that the justices perambulated the City as they had in 1246 (*London Eyre, 1244*, nos. 349–486; C. N. L. Brooke and G. Keir, *London, 800–1216* (1975), 163–6).
> 2. *C.P.R. 1258–66*, 225, 23 June 1262.

343. They say that the prioress of St. Helen's obstructed a lane in the ward of Philip le Taillur [Bishopsgate ward] to the nuisance. The prioress proffers a charter[1] of King Henry testifying that the king granted to her and to the nuns of St. Helen's permission to enclose the lane in London which lies between their lands on either side and to hold it closed in perpetuity.

> 1. *C.P.R. 1247–58*, 38, 24 Mar. 1249.

344. They say that the canons of St. Paul's London obstructed a lane in Dycereslane opposite [the convent] of the Friars Minor in the ward of Anketin de Auverne [Farringdon ward] to the nuisance. The canons proffer a charter[1] of King Henry testifying that the king granted to Master Robert de Barton formerly precentor[2] of St. Paul's permission to enclose the lane and keep it closed, provided that there should be a gate with locks at each end of the lane to allow free entrance and exit by the gates in case of fire and other mishaps which frequently occur in the City.

> 1. *C.P.R. 1247–58*, 166, 25 Nov. 1252; cf. Historical MSS. Commission, *9th Report*, Appendix (1883), 10, nos. 486, 507.
> 2. 1245 x 6– 1257; subsequently dean (J. Le Neve, *Fasti Ecclesiae Anglicanae, 1066–1300*, i. St. Paul's, ed. D. E. Greenway (1968), 24).

345. They say that the prior of Holy Trinity London obstructed a path (*viam*) between the priory and the City Wall which was formerly used by horsemen, pedestrians and carts. So the sheriff is ordered to cause the prior to appear. Afterwards the prior comes and proffers a charter[1] of King Henry [I], ancestor of the present king, granting to Norman, then prior, and the canons of Holy Trinity London permission to enclose by a wall the road between their church and conventual buildings and the City Wall, on either side up to the wall, and to hold it peacefully; the road which used to be there is now to run in front of the church on the other side; which grant was made for the souls of the king's mother and father, predecessors and successors, for his salvation and the state of the realm. Thereupon the mayor and aldermen testify that the road was obstructed as at present from the time of the said grant until the last disturbance which took place in the kingdom between King Henry and his barons, when certain enemies of the prior reopened it. The prior says that immediately after the disturbance

The Plea Roll

King Henry ordered the wardens of the City, by a writ which is enrolled on the Chancery rolls[2] to permit the prior to obstruct the road and repair and restore the other features of the close as they used to be before the disturbance, and puts himself upon the record of the Chancery rolls. Afterwards the Chancery rolls are searched and the following enrolment is found: 'Henry [III] to John Walerand and John de la Linde, wardens of the City of London; since the beautiful house of the priory of Holy Trinity London and other features of the close of the priory near the City Wall, were ruined and overthrown at the time of the disturbance in our realm, to the grievous loss of the priory, we, being especially concerned for the well-being and protection of the place, as we are indebted to it, order the wardens to permit the prior to rebuild the tenement and houses of the priory and repair and restore the other features of the close as they used to be before the disturbance. To the barons of the Exchequer; since at the time of the disturbance in our realm the prior and convent of Holy Trinity London sustained many losses and grievances and the loss of liberties granted to them by us and our predecessors, we, wishing to provide for their protection, have granted that they be restored to all their liberties and henceforth have free enjoyment of them; therefore we command you to allow this to be done and to maintain those liberties; at Westminster 11 February 50 Henry III [1266].' So it is adjudged that the prior is without day.

1. *Cartulary of Holy Trinity Aldgate*, ed. G. A. J. Hodgett (London Record Society, vii, 1971), no. 12 and n for further references.
2. *C.R. 1264–8*, 235–6.

346. They say that Gwiot the Clerk built a wall 38 feet long in the ward of Anketin de Auverne [Farringdon ward]. [cf. **726**]

347. Reginald le Chaundeler built a step and two staples (stapella) to the nuisance of the king's highway in the same ward. [cf. **736**]

348. The dean and chapter of St. Martin le Grand London built a pentice too low in the same ward.

349. The prioress of Cesterhunte built a solar overhanging more than it should have done.

350. Likewise Ellis de Hertford built two solars overhanging more than they should have done. [cf. **727**]

351. Stephen le Cordwaner built a pentice too low to the nuisance of the king's highway. [cf. **728**]

352. Michael de St. Edmunds, who has died, built a solar and a porch (porticum) which Master [m. 16d] Godewin now holds in the same state. [cf. **729**]

353. Robert de Dorset built a palisade (palacium) over the king's highway to the nuisance. [cf. **730**]

The Plea Roll

354. Thomas le Messager rebuilt a pentice to the nuisance in the same ward. [cf. **730**]

355. William de Kent built a pentice in the ward of William de Durham [Bread Street ward] too low and extending over the king's highway.

356. William Buntyng, who has died, made two steps of a cellar, too much to the nuisance of the king's highway in the same ward.

357. Gilbert de Clare earl of Gloucester and Hertford made a gutter (gutteram) through the middle of his kitchen, so that many people were offended by the stench (putredinem). So it is adjudged that the gutter should be closed in at the earl's expense, insofar as it is a nuisance.

358. Reginald de Fridaistrete made a step to a solar which extends too far over the king's highway. [cf. **732**]

359. Stephen de Harewe holds a step which John de Wyndes', who has died, made to the nuisance. [cf. **732**]

360. Bartholomew le Espicer, who has died, made a pentice which extends too far over the king's highway. [cf. ?**733**]

361. Floria Viel holds a pentice built by her former husband William which is to the nuisance. [cf. **734**]

362. Roger Hervi made a pentice to the nuisance of pedestrians and horsemen. [cf. **735**]

363. The master of the hospital of St. Bartholomew and John le Paumer, who has died, made two pentices in the ward of William de Durham [Bread Street ward]. [cf. **737**]

364. Edmund le Heymonger, who has died, made three solars to the nuisance, which Richard de Havering holds and rents from year to year.

365. They say that in the ward of Billinggesgate William Samuel, who has died, made a pentice to the nuisance, which Walter le Chaloner holds in the same state. [cf. **738**]

366. Ralph Sperling, who has died, made a wall of [blank] length on the king's highway and Simon the Baker now holds it in the same state. [cf. **738**]

367. John Sperling, who has died, made a wall in the same way which his son John now holds in the same state. [cf. **738**]

368. Richard de Derbey built a solar to the nuisance which Robert de Storteford now holds. [cf. **739**]

369. William de Arraz made a solar to the nuisance. [cf. **739**]

The Plea Roll

370. John de Honilane, who has died, made a solar too low which Robert de Linton now holds in the same state. [cf. **739**]

371. Robert Albin holds a solar and a pentice which are to the nuisance and which Ingolph le Pestour constructed. [cf. **740**]

372. Richard de Watford placed a beam (fecit trabem) and a pentice on the king's highway to the nuisance. [cf. **741**]

373. The prioress of Haliwell constructed a solar to the nuisance.

374. Robert le Burser constructed a solar which Robert Sevehod holds to the nuisance. [cf. **742**]

375. Reginald the Goldsmith built a shop to the nuisance. [cf. **743**]

376. Robert de Coringham caused his beams (trabes) to be placed on the highway to the nuisance. [cf. **743**]

377. William de Laufare made two solars much too low to the nuisance. [cf. **744**]

378. Peter the Fisherman holds a pentice which the prioress of Haliwell constructed to the nuisance.

379. Roger le Taillur, who has died, made a pentice which Laurence le Poter holds in the same state to the nuisance. [cf. **745**]

380. Peter de Gysors made (? a solar) which Robert the Tailor now holds. [cf. **746**]

381. John le Brevetour made a solar to the nuisance.

382. Master Leodegar made a solar to the nuisance.

383. Germain le Pessoner holds a solar in fee which the prior of Holy Trinity constructed to the nuisance. [cf. **746**]

384. Likewise Michael de Kemefingg constructed a solar which John Wyttefiz now holds to the nuisance.

385. Nicholas de Bysshopesgate, who has died, made a pentice which Isabel de Wodeford holds.

386. William de Mesendene, who has died, made a solar to the nuisance, which is now in the hand of the prior of the New Hospital. [cf. **748**]

387. Laurence de Maneli, who has died, made a pentice which the abbot of Shrewsbury (Salop) now holds. [cf. **749**]

388. Roger de Leukenor made two pentices which are to the nuisance. [cf. **750**]

389. Roger de Grey likewise made a pentice.

390. The prioress of St. Helen's made a pentice.

391. John de Bysshopesgate, John Walemyn and John son of Alan made their beams (trabes) to the nuisance. [cf. **751**]

392. Peter le Lymbernere, Hamund the Tiler (Tegulator), Walter Daniel, Ellis le Furmager and John de Cruce made purprestures before the doors of their houses by the appropriation of earth which had been carried away from a dike (fossato).

393. Bennet de Ageney[1] rebuilt a step and a pentice. [cf. **752**]
   1. ? *Recte* Hackney.

394. William le Rus made two dikes and planted trees upon them to the nuisance in the Porsoke of Holy Trinity. [cf. **753**]

395. John le Poter rebuilt a porch. [cf. **754**]

396. William de Boxford holds a solar which Hugh de Ive, who has died, made to the nuisance. [cf. **754**]

397. Aylbred le Tornur has a pentice. [cf. **755**]

398. Loveyn[1] le Turnur likewise has a window. [cf. **755**]
   1. *Recte* Lovekyn.

399. One Hugh [? de Clopham] likewise constructed one. [cf. ?**767**]

400. Avice de Hundesdych has two solars which her husband Richard made to the nuisance. [cf. **756**]

401. Edmund earl of Cornwall has a solar which Roger de Suffolk built to the nuisance. [cf. **757**]

402. Richard Poterel has a solar made by Hubert de Dakenes, who has died. [cf. **758**]

403. Edward le Blund made a pentice which William his son now holds to the nuisance.

404. William le Chaundeler made a solar. [cf. **759**]

405. Philip de Norhamton 'poleter' made a pentice to the nuisance. [cf. **759**]

The Plea Roll

406. Roger de Bliburg made a pentice which Ralph le Mazon holds to the nuisance. [cf. **760**]

407. Richard de Abindon made a pentice. [cf. **760**]

408. Richard Dygon made a solar. [cf. **761**]

409. Robert the Clerk obstructed a lane of St. Martin Orgar to the greatest nuisance.

410. Adam Molling for a tenement built to the nuisance. [cf. **762**]

411. Arnald Bogays made a pentice. [cf. **673**]

412. William Skileman holds a pentice which Roger Hardel holds [sic] to the nuisance. [cf. **764**]

413. Henry de Grenford likewise holds a pentice constructed by Roger Wilekin who has died.

414. William Page constructed a pentice. [cf. **764**]

415. Master Adam de Cant' a pentice.

416. Ralph de Cestre made a pentice. [cf. **765**]

417. Robert de Assendene occupied a plot on the king's highway and built a house which Gilbert Sperling holds.

418. Jordan Pigo' made a solar. [cf. **766**]

419. Adam le Chapeler made a pentice which Michael Poter holds. [cf. **766**]

420. Ellis le Mariner made a pentice. [cf. **766**]

421. Edmund Pentecost, who has died, made a solar which Edmund Horn holds to the nuisance.

422. William Carpenter, who has died, made a solar which Gunnilde Beaumond holds. [cf. **767**]

423. Ralph de Beaumond, who has died, made a solar which Richard Sharp holds to the nuisance. [cf. **767**]

424. Robert de Waunton[1] made a solar. [cf. **768**]
   1. *Recte* Waltham.

425. Nicholas Horn a solar. [cf. **769**]

426. Henry de Carpenton one.

427. Alice de Exemie holds a gutter (stillicidium) which Robert de Graschirche made. [cf. 770]

428. Geoffrey de Basingge made a gutter near his privy (cloacam) which the heir of Hugh de Eston holds to the nuisance.

429. Herman le Estreis made a gutter to the nuisance.

430. John Saher a step.

431. The abbot of St. Albans for a pentice.

432. Master Ralph Crapsy made a pentice. [cf. 772]

433. And Hugh de Wyndes'. [cf. 773]

434. And likewise the commonalty of London built a house in the ward of Henry de Frouwyk [Cripplegate ward] to the greatest nuisance.

435. John Derkin made three steps which Thomas de Clare holds to the nuisance.

436. Aaron de la Rye, a Jew, made four steps. [cf. 775]

437. Ascelina de la Boche planted a vine near her house to the nuisance.

438. Hugh Gratefyg obstructed a well to the nuisance.[1]

[1]. In a Cripplegate presentment of 1279 renewed complaint was made that Hugh Gratefige had obstructed 'Everardeswelle' (M. Weinbaum, *London unter Eduard I. und II.*, ii (Stuttgart, 1933), 154).

439. Robert le Wodemanger made a pentice. [cf. 776]

440. William son of Richard, who has died, two pentices which his wife Amice now holds in the same state. [cf. 776]

441. Roger de Bradele made a pentice.

442. Philip de Eye obstructed a path (viam) in Hoggenelane running through the middle of his courtyard which used to be public (communis).

443. They say that a lane has been obstructed with dung between the old Fish Market and Castle Baynard.

444. William Yeregesse made a solar which Robert de Paris holds.

445. Richard le Taillur, who has died, made a solar which William de Assendene holds.

446. Aaron Crispin, a Jew, made a step on the king's highway. [cf. 777]

The Plea Roll

447. Copin Troye holds a solar made by Osbert Presbyter, who has died. [cf. **778**]

448. The abbot of St. Albans made two solars and one solar which Walter Bending holds to the nuisance.

449. Walter de Merdene a solar. [cf. **779**]

450. Hugh le Lou a solar. [cf. **780**]

451. William de Middelton a pentice.

452. Robert Gratefyge a solar which Athelard the Clerk holds.

453. Thomas the Chaplain, who has died, made a solar which Walter de Foleham holds.

454. Emma la Rus made a solar which the prior of Wenloke now holds to the nuisance. [cf. **781**]

455. William le Mareschall built his beams (trabes) to the nuisance.

456. Likewise the Earl Marshal made four privies (cloacas) next to his house to the nuisance.

457. Robert Blaket, who has died, built a house on the king's highway next to the church of St. Michael Queenhithe (de Ripa) to the nuisance.

458. Stephen de Cornhull made windows for his cellar facing the king's highway. [cf. **782**]

459. Godfrey de Norhamton, who has died, obstructed a public path in the ward of Simon of Hadestok [Queenhithe ward].

460. John de Norhamton made a step to the nuisance. [cf. **783**]

461. John de Stypenhethe made a step before the door of his tavern to the nuisance. [cf. **784**]

462. John le Taillur made a step. [cf. **784**]

463. Joan widow of Martin le Arbeleter made a gutter (gutteram).

464. Thomas le Mareschal 'vineter' built four shops near the Conduit. [cf. **785**]

465. William de Chavente made a pentice.

466. Robert Hautein a step to the nuisance. [cf. **774**]

The Plea Roll

467. So they are all in *mercy*. The sheriff is ordered to remove the purprestures and restore them to their former state at the expense etc.

> [*Nota*, ? unnumbered] . . . *purpresturis* . . . *mendis* . . . *et* . . . *ad custum* etc. [much faded].

468. Of measures, they say that Walter Hervi, when alderman of this City, sealed two false quart measures which are here before the justices; they were found in the possession of Robert Sevenhode and his wife Emma and seized by Henry le Waleis then mayor and Henry de Coventre sheriff. So the sheriff was ordered to cause Walter, Robert and Emma to appear. Afterwards Walter comes and admits that the measures were sealed with his seal, but says that his seal was in the keeping of Ralph the Serjeant and Henry le Wympler, custodians of the ward of Cheap; so he says that the measures were sealed by the custodians and not by him and he is prepared to verify this as the court shall adjudge. It is testified that the measures had formerly been presented as false before the treasurer and barons of the exchequer and Walter there admitted that they were sealed with his seal, so that on his admission the barons put the measures in safe keeping to produce them here under Walter's seal. Walter says that he never made this admission before the barons and puts himself upon the record of the exchequer. So he is given a day to appear before the king at the next parliament. Nevertheless Ralph de Touvy parmenter, Alan de Castello, Peter de Winton', Ralph de Bromle, Robert Otes, Thomas de Mimmes, Godfrey le Formager, Henry le Bole, Robert de Linton, Richard le Paumer, John Wade and Roger Herevy undertook to have him here at the said term. Meanwhile the measures are to be given up to Adam de Stratton under the seal of the justices. Afterwards Henry le Wimpler and Robert Sevenehode appeared and found pledges to appear before the king at the said term; Henry's pledges, Robert Hauteyn, William de Paris, Edward Sevenhode, William de Kent, John Richemund, Henry de Farnham, Robert le Lung 'mercer', John de Hakeborn 'mercer', Roger de Amyas, William Blundel 'braeler', Walter Blundel 'braeler' and John de Berkyng 'correor'; Robert's pledges, Guillot de Paris, John le Coffrer, Robert Sevenhode the younger, Stephen le Chapeler, Thomas le Paternoster, Edward de Cerne 'mercer', Walter Sevenhod, Richard de Mimmes 'bukeler', William le Paternoster, Theywyn de Wynchelse, William de Paris, Robert le Wyt [blank]. [cf. **724**]

469. Of cloths sold contrary to the assize, they say that John Adrian the elder [blank]. [cf. **294**]

470. [m. 17][1] The king has sent to Master Roger de Seyton and his fellow justices his writ in these words: 'Edward [I] to Master Roger de Seyton and his fellow justices; whereas Maud Attelowe has long been engaged in a suit by our writ against Isabel Harang in the husting before the mayor and sheriffs of London concerning one messuage with appurtenances in the suburb of London; the action has been too long delayed because Isabel vouched to warranty a boy who was under age; since we have summoned the eyre at the Tower on the morrow of the Purification [3 Feb.], and have ordered the mayor and sheriffs to produce the record and proceedings of the action with the original writ and all other relevant documents on a set day and to fix the same day for the parties to appear before you in the action so that there should be a just process; we order you to bring to a conclusion the record and proceedings of the action received from the mayor and sheriffs and carefully inspected by them; at Winchester, 25 January 4 Edward I [1276].'

Thereupon the mayor and citizens come and say that they are not bound to answer before the justices in eyre at the Tower of London about any tenement which is within the liberty of the City unless the party impleaded vouches to warranty someone living outside the City. They say also that they can make no record while the justices are sitting at the Tower. Because it is found by inspection of the rolls of the last eyre that the mayor and citizens gave a like answer in a similar case, Maud is told to return to the husting after the eyre.

> Nota 97. *Quod justiciarii itinerantes non tenebunt placita in itinere de tenementis in London* [cf. **524** no. 97].
> [In a different hand] *Quod de tenementis in Civitate non deberent respondere coram justiciariis itinerantibus nec recordum fecerent dum justiciarii sedent.*
> 1. *Seyton* at head of membrane.

471. The jury upon which John de Elylaund plaintiff and Master Nicholas Curteney have put themselves find as follows: a quarrel broke out between John and Nicholas on Friday after the Purification [7 Feb.], after the summons of the eyre, in Smythfeld market, and Nicholas took out his knife intending to strike John in the throat; John interposed his hand and Nicholas wounded him in the hand with the knife. Therefore it is adjudged that Nicholas be taken into custody for a trespass committed after the summons of the eyre and against the peace; he is to satisfy John for his *damages* which are assessed at 5s. Afterwards Nicholas comes and makes fine of *2 marks* on the pledges of Hugh de Kendale and William de Birley. [cf. **488, 706**]

> Nota 98. *Quod justiciarii itinerantes tenebunt placita de transgressionibus* [*et recordum*] *facerent dum sedent* [cf. **524** no. 98].

472. Eleanor queen of England, the king's mother, vouched to warranty by the Friars of the Penitence of Jesus Christ, appoints in her place Nicholas son of Henry against John Duraunt on a plea of land. [cf. **485, 514**]

473. The king has ordered Master Roger de Seyton[1] to enquire by a jury whether the loss of an ear by John son of William de Bosco citizen of London happened by accident through the bite of a horse in his father's stable which took his right ear completely away from his head, or by his own fault; and to send to the inquisition to him. The inquisition was held by Walter Box, Robert Otes, Peter Miles, Richard de Habindon, John Seyer, Simon de Gandauo, Robert de Rokeslee, Robert Hayron, Peter Cosin, Robert de Mars, Walter la Forde, John de la Wyllesende; they say on their oath that the loss of John's ear was an accident and not his fault. So let the inquisition be sent to the king with the writ patent.

1. *C.P.R. 1272–81*, 174, 13 Jan. 1276; see also *ibid.*, 144, 27 May 1276.

The Plea Roll

474. William Boxe of London was summoned to answer Christine widow of Robert le Carpenter on a plea that he render her 56s. which he owes her and unjustly withholds. She claims that she sold William six quarters of wheat for 56s. in 54 Henry III [1269–70], to be paid at the following Christmas and complains that William withholds the money and refuses to render it to her, whence she says she has suffered damage and loss to the value of 50s. She brings suit and likewise produces the tally for the debt. William comes and denies force. He acknowledges the tally and agrees that he received the wheat for the said price, but says that at the time he took the wheat he was the king's purveyor and took it for the king's use and gave it up to the king's wardrobe. He had the wheat and the price enrolled on the roll of the wardrobe and he himself has so far received nothing. He puts himself upon the record of the rolls of the wardrobe. He seeks a day to certify the justices thereon and is given Wednesday in the second week of Lent [4 Mar. 1276].

475. Robert de Araz and Stephen de Munden have acknowledged that they owe the king 4 marks which they will pay in fifteen days from Easter [19 Apr. 1276]. If they do not do so, they grant that the sheriffs are to levy it from their lands and chattels. (*London recognicio.*)

476. 'Edward by the grace of God; at the instance of Robert [Kilwardby] archbishop of Canterbury we have pardoned Master Thomas de Pyvelesdon all displeasure and rancour conceived against him by reason of the trespasses allegedly committed against us at the time of the late disturbances and have admitted him to our grace and peace on condition that henceforth he conduct himself well and faithfully towards us and our heirs; at Westminster, 5 June 3 Edward I [1275].' (*Carta magistri Thome de Pevelesdon.*)[1]

1. *C.P.R. 1272–81*, 94, 7 June 1275. For a later pardon see **293**.

477. Alice widow of Gilbert de Preston sued the prior of Holy Trinity in the husting for the third part of one messuage and one curtilage with appurtenances in London as her dower. The prior came to the husting and vouched to warranty Laurence de Preston who is not of the liberty of the City, but lives in Northamptonshire. So the plea was respited according to the custom of the City. The prior comes now and vouches Laurence to warranty; he is to have him before the justices at Westminster in fifteen days from Easter [19 Apr. 1276] with the aid of the court because he is a stranger. Let him be summoned in Northamptonshire.

Nota 99. De forinseco vocato ad warantum in hustengo et adiornato coram justiciariis itinerantibus et postea coram justiciariis apud Westmonasterium [Much faded. Cf. **524** no. 99].

478. Gilbert de Oxford and his wife Alice sued Stephen le Saltere and his wife Felice in the husting for one messuage with appurtenances in London as Alice's dower. Stephen and Felice appeared in the husting and vouched to warranty Henry son of Peter Everard of Cippenham, who is not of the liberty of the City, but lives outside in Buckinghamshire, so that the plea was respited according to the custom of the City. Stephen and Felice come

The Plea Roll

now and vouch Henry to warranty; they are to have him before the justices at Westminster in fifteen days from Easter [19 Apr. 1276] with the aid of the court. *Let him be summoned in Buckinghamshire.*

[*Nota* unnumbered]. *Consimili placito.*

479. Remember that Ralph Hodding clerk [has been] handed over to the bishop of London to answer before the justices.

480. Roger de Tovi appoints Richard de Saham clerk or Adam le Garzon [his attorney] against Henry de Sobyre on a plea of custom and services. (*London'*.) [cf. **483, 489**]

481. Thomas de Clare has acknowledged that he has given to Stephen de Cornhull all that messuage which he had in the parish of St. Mary Bothaw by his charter in these words: 'We Thomas de Clare knight have given to Stephen de Cornhull citizen and draper of London all that messuage with all buildings, rents, liberties and appurtenances in the parish of St. Mary Bothawe which we had of the grant of Edmund of Almain (Alemanni), earl of Cornwall, our brother, to have and hold by him and his heirs or anyone to whom he shall give, bequeath, sell or assign it in perpetuity, rendering yearly at Michaelmas one penny and the service due to the chief lords of the fee; and we undertake to warrant the same to him, his heirs and assigns against all men in perpetuity. Witnesses: Gregory de Rokesle then mayor of the city of London and alderman of the ward [of Dowgate], Ralph le Blund and John Horn then sheriffs of London, Richard de Affron, Henry de Cokington, Nicholas Cyphywast, knights, Henry le Waleys, John Adrian, William de Durham, Nicholas de Winchester, Reginald de Suffolk, Philip le Tayllour, Richard de Wilehale, Henry de Hereford, William de Rokeslee, Peter Cosin, Simon de Gaunt, William de Bosco, Anketin de Botevil, Robert de Linton, William Bigod clerk, and others [1275-6]. (*London. Carta Stephani de Cornhell per Thomam de [Clare] militem.*)

482. [m. 17d] Joan widow of John son of Saer sued Henry le Waleys in the husting for the third part of a messuage with appurtenances in London as her dower. Henry appeared in the husting and vouched to warranty Thomas de Warpenbur' who is not of the liberty of the City, but lives outside in Warwickshire. So the plea was respited according to the custom of the City. Henry comes now and vouches Thomas to warranty. They are to have him here on Monday in the third week of Lent [9 Mar. 1276] with the aid of the court. Let him be summoned in *Warwickshire*.

[*Nota* unnumbered]. *De forinsico vocato ad warantum in hustengo* [cf. **477**n].

483. Henry de Shobyr was summoned to answer Roger de Tovy on a plea that according to the custom of the City he do all the services due from his free tenement in London which he holds of Roger, as in arrears of rent and other things; he complains that whereas Henry holds of him a messuage with appurtenances in the City by the service of 2 marks a year for every service, and Roger was seised of the service by Henry's hand until ten years

The Plea Roll

ago, Henry has refused to do him the service. Wherefore he says that for default of service the messuage should be gavelet; he also says that he has suffered loss and damage to the value of £20 and brings suit. Henry comes and denies force and injury; he acknowledges that he holds the messuage from Roger for the said service, but he says that he is not in arrears and he is prepared to prove this as the court shall adjudge. Thereupon the mayor and citizens of London come and say that this plea of customs and services should not be pleaded or terminated here or anywhere but in the husting. Because Henry freely answered the writ, the mayor and citizens agree that the plea should proceed here, saving [their right]. So the sheriff is ordered to produce on the morrow twelve [men]. Afterwards the parties agreed as appears on the following roll. [cf. **480, 489**]

> [Nota] 100. Quod breve de consuetudine et serviciis non debet placitari coram justiciariis nec alibi quam in hustengo [Drawing of a face in margin. Cf. **524** no. 100].

484. Clarice widow of John de Lynde claims against the master of the house of St. Thomas of Acon her reasonable dower due to her from the free tenement which belonged to her husband in London, from which she has nothing. Thereupon the mayor and bailiffs come and say that this writ of dower should not be pleaded here unless it had previously been initiated in the husting and then the plea had been respited until the eyre of the justices because the tenant had vouched to warranty someone who was not of the liberty of the City. They ask that the plea should not proceed here and they proffer a royal writ in these words: 'Edward to his justices in eyre at the Tower of London; after consultation and discussion of the content of your letters to us concerning ambiguities relating to customs and liberties of the City of London during the present eyre; we order you to allow the citizens to enjoy the rights granted by the charter of our father Henry when he admitted them to his grace and favour and renounced the anger conceived against them at the time of the disturbance in the realm; to allow them to enjoy the liberties and customs contained in that charter; to deal with them favourably and with justice and to be guided by Ralph de Hengham[1] whom we send to you with fuller instructions on these matters, and to proceed according to his counsel; at Poulton, 14 February 4 Edward I [1276]'. Thereupon Ralph de Hengham comes and says that it was ordained before the king and the whole council that the citizens should have the liberties contained in the charter, and should neither plead nor be impleaded concerning tenures and tenements belonging to them within the City in this eyre by any writ unless the writ had been initiated in the husting and then transferred here because the tenant vouched to warranty someone who was not of the liberty of the City; and that the action should proceed in this eyre as was the custom in other eyres. So Clarice is told to go to the husting and sue there. [cf. **720**]

> Nota 101. Consuetudo recordata quod justiciarii non debent tenere placita terra coram eis in itinere.[2] Breve regis directum justiciariis ut cives possint gaudere libertatibus suis [cf. **524** no. 101].
>
> 1. On Hengham's position as a member of the king's council see *Radulphi de Hengham Summae*, ed. W. H. Dunham (Cambridge Studies in English Legal History, 1932), p. lii.
> 2. *Consuetudo recordata* repeated; the remainder of this sentence is in a different hand.

The Plea Roll

485. John Duraunt sued the prior of the Friars of the Penitence of Jesus Christ of London in the husting for two messuages with appurtenances in London as his right by writ of right patent. The prior appeared in the husting and vouched to warranty Eleanor the queen-mother, who is not of the liberty of the City, but lives outside in Surrey, so that the plea was respited according to the custom of the City because she was a stranger. The prior comes and vouches Eleanor to warranty, to have her here on Monday in the third week of Lent [9 Mar. 1276] with the aid of the court. Let her be summoned in *Surrey*. [cf. **472, 514**]

> [*Nota* unnumbered]. *De regina Anglie vocata ad warrantum in hustengo tanquam forinseca.*

486. Roger de Hampton clerk has acknowledged that he owes Ellis Tolosan clerk one surcoat worth 1 mark, payable to Ellis at Easter next. If he does not do so, he grants that the sheriffs of London are to levy it from his lands and chattels. (*London'. Recognicio.*)

487. Deodatus the queen's servant[1] complains of Geoffrey de Rothingg and Robert de Esture that on Saturday before the feast of St. Margaret 47 Henry III [14 July 1263] they came with force and arms to Deodatus' house in London where the queen had in store cloths and gold, cloths of silk and Flemish cloths of various colours, silver flagons, gold and silver cups, silver dishes, rubies, emeralds and other precious stones, and many other jewels, to the value of £600; they took and carried off these cloths, stones and jewels against the peace, whence Deodatus says that he has suffered loss and damage to the value etc. and now he brings suit. Geoffrey and Robert come and deny force and injury. They deny that they went to Deodatus' house and took away the goods as he accuses them. They put themselves upon the verdict of the mayor and aldermen who say in the faith in which they are bound to the king that they never went to Deodatus' house or took away the goods. Therefore it is adjudged that Geoffrey and Robert be quit and Deodatus in *mercy. [cf. **707**]

> [*Nota*] 102. *Querela de transgressione terminata per sacramentum maioris et aldermannorum* [cf. **524** no. 102].
> 1. For the unpopularity of the servants of Eleanor of Provence, see Tout, *Chapters*, v, 236. Deodatus may have secured a late pardon (*C.C.R. 1272–9*, 408) if *Detaiutus* is a misreading of *Deodatus*.

488. Master Nicholas de Curtenay complains of John de Elilaund that one Friday this year at Smethefeud fair he sold him a blind horse, which he declared was able to see well; afterwards it was agreed between them that Nicholas should keep the horse in his house for the whole night and if he was not pleased with it he would then give it back. On the following day Nicholas returned the horse to John, but he refused to take it back, whence Nicholas says that he has suffered loss and damage to the value of 100s. and he brings suit. John comes and denies force and injury. He acknowledges that he sold Nicholas the horse, but says that it was not completely blind, and only had defective vision (*defectum visus*); it was agreed between them that Nicholas should keep the horse for the whole night and, if he was not pleased with it, he would send it back the following day. He says that Nicholas did not send the horse back on that day, but he kept it for a month and then brought it back at the end of the month. He is prepared to prove this as the court adjudges. Nicholas says that proof of this covenant and likewise of the offer of the horse on the following day belongs elsewhere according to the custom of the City. He produces two witnesses who were present when he returned the horse to John on the day after the said Friday, viz. John de Ba . . . chaplain and Edmund Joun. Thereupon the mayor and aldermen are asked whether according to the custom of the City John should clear himself by jury or twelve-handed, or Nicholas by two witnesses; they say in the faith in which they are bound to the king that in covenants and debts of this kind contracted in the City the demandant is nearer to prove his word (propinquior ad probandum dictum suum) and assertion by two witnesses than the defendant to defend himself by jury or by law. John says that although according to the custom of the City Nicholas should verify and prove his word by witnesses, the witnesses produced are not suitable or acceptable because one of them is a clerk and it is the custom of the City that no clerk should be received to make any proof or deraignment unless to produce a will (nisi ad testamentum perhibendum). Because the mayor and barons put on record and bear witness to this and likewise because since he formerly produced unsuitable witnesses to offer proof and cannot change them or produce others in their place, it is adjudged that John be without day and Nicholas in *mercy for a false claim. [cf. **471, 708**]

Nota 103. Querela de convencione.
In a different hand: *Nota de testibus productis per petentes contra defensionem defendensium* [sic]. *Consuetudo recordata* [Drawing of two faces (? representing the witnesses). Cf. **524** no. 103].

489. (*London*) Memorandum of a covenant made on the day of St. Peter's Chair 4 Edward I [22 Feb. 1276] at the Tower of London before Master Roger de Seyton and his colleagues between Roger de Thovy plaintiff and Henry de Schobir' deforciant for rightful services, which Roger demands from Henry for the free tenement which he holds of him in London: namely 20 marks of silver as arrears of an annual rent of 2 marks from one messuage with appurtenances which Henry holds of him in the parish of St. Augustine in the soke of Thovy. Henry acknowledges that he owes the annual rent of 2 marks payable at two terms of the year, half at Easter and the other half at the quindene of Michaelmas next, 5 marks, and at the octave of Hilary 5 marks, and at the quindene of Easter 5 marks.[1] Henry grants for himself and his heirs that unless the money is paid at the prescribed terms the sheriffs of London and Surrey are to levy the rent from his lands and chattels and give them without delay to Roger or his heirs. Further he grants for himself and his heirs that if they are in default of payment at any of the terms, Roger and his heirs are to be allowed to enter the tenement and hold it peacefully without regard to the claim of Henry or his heirs in perpetuity. Henry also grants for himself and his heirs in perpetuity that if they or others shall default in the payment of the annual rent of 2 marks at any term and this is proved by the testimony of two neighbours from the soke or ward in which the tenement is situated together with that of Roger or his bailiff or

The Plea Roll

attorney in the next husting after the expiry of the term, then the tenement with appurtenances shall be forfeit without further delay and without other burden of proof to Roger and his heirs as shortforth[2] to hold peacefully in his demesne quit of the claim of Henry and his heirs in perpetuity. Be it known that it will not be permitted for Henry or his heirs or assigns to lay waste or destroy the houses built on the tenement so that the annual rent cannot be levied and paid in full and so that the tenement with buildings cannot remain intact for Roger or his heirs if by chance it should be forfeit as was stated. In addition Henry grants under the said penalty that his wife Alice should appear in the next husting after Easter and there according to the custom of the City renounce any right in the tenement by reason of heredity or other feoffment hitherto contracted as is more fully contained in a deed drawn up between them. (*Concordia irrotulata.*) [cf. **480, 483**]

1. The text appears to be garbled concerning the terms of payment for the arrears.
2. Or 'forshort' (cf. *London Eyre, 1244*, no. 233).

490. [m. 18] William Heyron has acknowledged that he owes Master Roger de Seyton £28 of which he is to pay half at Whitsun and the other half at Martinmas. If he does not do so, he grants that the sheriff is to obtain satisfaction from his lands and chattels. (*Northumbria. Ebor'. Recognicio.*)

491. Robert le Ringerer complains of Martin le Criour and Walter Hervy that on Walter's orders Martin went to his house at Flete, entered it by force, and took and carried off his goods and chattels, namely a brooch (firmaculum) and about 300 rings of latten. Afterwards Martin made him renounce his office before Walter, whence he says that he has suffered loss and damage to the value of £40 and he brings suit. Walter and Martin come and deny force and injury. Walter acknowledges that he sent Martin to Robert's house, but says that at the time he was mayor of the City and certain goldsmiths of London had complained that Robert made brooches and rings of latten and set in them precious stones, such as sapphires and other stones, which is against the law and custom of the City and the defence of the realm; because of this he made Robert appear before him and the aldermen in la Gildhall and there by judgment of the court he made him swear that he would not put precious stones in such brooches and rings. He puts himself upon the mayor and aldermen who in the faith in which they are bound to the king testify to this. So Walter is without day and Robert is in *mercy.

[*Nota*] 104. *Querela de transgressione* [cf. **524** no. 104].

492. Memorandum of a covenant made in 4 Edward I [1275–6] between Agnes daughter of Thomas son of William on the one part and William de Burinton clerk on the other; William grants for himself and his heirs that if Agnes shall pay him 90 marks at the octave of St. John the Baptist next, then she shall have restored to her the manor of Thrafferston with which she enfeoffed him, entirely quit of William and his heirs or assigns in perpetuity. If Agnes shall default in the payment of the money on the said day and place [sic], then the enfeoffment shall stand ratified in perpetuity and William shall be obliged to pay Agnes 60 marks immediately without fraud or deceit. If Agnes shall make payment in the said form, then William is to procure the annulment of all enrolments on the rolls of the justices of the Bench concerning the feoffment. (*Scriptum. q'... Northumbria.*) [cf. **497**]

[*Nota*] 105. *Recognicio condicionalis super quamdam convencionem* [cf. **524** no. 105].

493. Henry le Waleys complains of John de St. Helens that when Henry had a ship in the harbour of Waymue in Dorset with a cargo of hides in the custody of his yeoman (valettus) Geoffrey, to the value of 410 marks, John went there with other men unknown on Monday before Ascension 51 Henry III [23 May 1267] with force and arms and took and carried off the goods that were in Geoffrey's custody against the peace; whence he says he has suffered loss and damage to the value of £300 and brings suit.

John comes and says that at the time when this *trespass* was supposed to have been committed he was of the household of Gilbert earl of Gloucester and Hertford and in his friendship; the earl was then in the City of London and King Henry pardoned him all trespasses by him and his wherever committed.[1] So he says he is not bound to answer here and if that does not suffice he will answer more fully. Afterwards on that day John comes and says that he went to the earl who at the time was in Wales and that the earl did not have with him the instruments and writings concerning the pardon which protected him and allowed benefit to the earl and his following. He denies force and injury. He denies that he ever carried off the goods and chattels on the said date as alleged and puts himself upon the jury of the place where the trespass was said to have been committed. Henry [does] likewise. So the sheriff of *Dorset* is ordered to produce before the justices at St. Martin le Grand London on the morrow of the Ascension [15 May 1276] twelve [men]. Afterwards on that day the jury were respited until the octave of Michaelmas at Westminster for default of the jury because no one came. So the sheriff is to have the bodies at the same term, and also as many from the town of Waymue and the neighbourhood of the town.[2]

They are given a day on Monday in the third week of Lent [1 Mar. 1277] and Robert de Bryton of Buckinghamshire and Walter de Hocking of Essex are pledged[3] to have John here at the said term; and he appoints Ellis le Taylour his attorney.[4]

[*Nota*] 106. *De placito forinceco placitato coram justiciariis itinerantibus* [cf. **524** no. 106].
1. For similar pardons see *C.P.R. 1266–72*, 315, 378.
2. Considerable blank space between paragraphs.
3. Cf. **498**.
4. For the continuation of this plea, see CP 40/17 m. 67.

494. An assize comes in the husting to declare whether Henry Attelethe, father of Amice wife of Henry le Sawyere, was seised in his demesne as of fee of a messuage with appurtenances in London on the day on which [he died] and whether Amice is the next heir. The messuage is held by Thomas le Porer who previously appeared in the husting and vouched to warranty Reginald de Rothinges who is not of the liberty of the City but a stranger, so that the plea was respited according to the custom of the City. Thomas comes and the parties are agreed. The agreement is that Thomas acknowledges that the messuage belongs to Amice and he has restored it to her. So let her have seisin. And for this Henry and Amice give Thomas a silver mark.

[*Nota*] 107. *Quoddam placitum mortis antecessoris de quodam forinceco ad warantum in hustengo* [cf. **524** no. 107].

495. John de Cameys and his wife Margery (Margeria) by Margery's attorney complain of Robert del Ostre and his wife Rose that whereas they hold of them one messuage with appurtenances in London in the ward of Walter le Poter [Cornhill ward] by the service of rendering John and Margery (Margarie) 4 marks yearly and providing them with free hospitality in the house whenever they were in London; John de Gatesdene,[1] Margery's father, whose heir she is, was seised of this service and hospitality as of fee and right for the whole of his life and after his death John and Margery were in peaceful seisin until after the summons of the eyre, Robert and Rose prevented them from enjoying the hospitality as previously; whence he says he has suffered loss and damage to the value of £10 and he brings suit. Robert and Rose come and deny force and injury. They acknowledge that they hold the messuage of John and Margery for the service of 4 marks and that they were given hospitality there, as were other strangers, by their generosity (pro suo dando), not by fee and right but by Robert and Rose's own free will. They put themselves upon the ward and John and Margery [do] likewise. The jury say on the oath that they made to the king and in the faith in which they are bound to him that John de Gatesdene, father of Margery, whose heir she is, enfeoffed William de Wateford of the messuage by the service of 4 marks yearly and providing suitable hospitality for himself, his heirs and his free household whenever it happened that they came to the town. He was seised of this for all his life and after his death Hawise de Nevill his widow was in seisin and after her death John and Margery until Robert and Rose refused them hospitality. So it is adjudged that John and Margery recover their right to hospitality and Robert and Rose are in *mercy. Afterwards John and Margery come and complain that they are unable to receive hospitality as was adjudged. Thereupon Robert and Rose come and proffer a charter of gift and the granting of hospitality, as appears on the following roll. [cf. **501, 719**]

[*Nota*] 108. *Quoddam placitum de convencione super impedimento hospicii cuiusdam magnatis in London* [cf. **524** no. 108].
1. Keeper of the wardrobe of Eleanor of Provence.

496. Miles le Coureur complains of Henry de Coventre that while sheriff of the City he maliciously accused him of homicide and imprisoned him in Newgate taking from him two pieces of leather (coreor) worth 5s. and a brass pot worth 2s.; he kept him in prison until by judgment of the court and the verdict of a jury he was acquitted of the death; whence he says that he has suffered damage and loss to the value of 100s. and he brings suit. Henry comes and denies force and injury. He acknowledges that Miles was arrested and imprisoned but says this was on the indictment of the neighbourhood and because Miles made an agreement (finem) with a certain William then keeper of the prison under Henry, for 4s. to have 'suete de prison'[1] and Miles pledged the brass pot for the 4s.; Henry denies taking the other chattels. He puts himself upon the nearest wards who say in the faith in which they are bound to the king that Henry did take the chattels and Miles after he was released from prison by judgment of the court did claim the chattels from Henry, who until now has refused to return them to him. Because Henry admits that William his underbailiff took the 4s. from Miles for 'suete de prison' which is against the law and custom of the realm and the City, it is adjudged that Miles should recover the chattels. Henry is to be committed to *gaol and is ordered to give satisfaction to Miles for his damages which are assessed at [blank]. [cf. **249**]

[Nota] 109. . . . *placitum de inprisonamento* [cf. **524** no. 109].
1. An amenity or alleviation of imprisonment (R. E. Latham, 'Minor enigmas from medieval records, 2nd series', *English Historical Review*, lxxvi (1961), 633–6).

497. William de Burinton acknowledges that he owes Agnes daughter of Thomas £20 which he is to pay her at Easter this year. If he does not do so, he grants that the sheriff is to levy it from his lands and chattels. Afterwards Agnes comes and acknowledges that William has given her satisfaction for the money. (*Northumbria. Recognicio.*) [cf. **492**]

498. Margery de Canterbury wife of Master William de Werblynton acknowledges that she received from Roger de Nasinger a chest with all its contents which William before his journey to the Roman curia had given into Roger's custody, as is contained more fully in a document drawn up between them. She is given a day on Monday in the third week of Lent [9 Mar. 1276] and Robert de Bryton of Buckinghamshire and Walter de Hocking of Essex[1] are pledged to have John [sic] here at the same time.

1. Cf. **493**.

499. Richard de Ashwy complains of Henry le Waleys, Henry his son, Joan daughter of William de Haddestok, John the Clerk, Michael de St. Albans and Nicholas Bate that whereas he was seised of 20s. rent with appurtenances in the parish of St. Michael Bassinghawe after the death of Hawise, who held it for life by the gift of her mother Joan, whose heir he is, and he has for a long time had peaceful possession of it, Henry and the others unjustly ejected him after the summons of the eyre. Henry and all the others come and Henry son of Henry, and Joan answer for themselves and the others. They say that Richard was never seised of the rent and therefore could not be disseised and they ask for an enquiry. [m. 18d] Richard says that the rent was the right and perquisite of his mother Joan whose heir he is, grandmother of Henry and Joan, daughter of William, and in her last will and testament she devised it to Hawise her daughter, a nun of Berking, aunt of Henry and Joan, to hold for life, with remainder to her son Thomas, Hawise's brother, and on his death to Avice, his sister, with reversion on the deaths of Thomas and Avice to Joan and her heirs. He says that after the death of Hawise he entered on the rent as son and next heir of Joan because Hawise outlived both Thomas and Avice and he was in peaceful seisin, receiving 5s. for one term and the same rent from the tenants at the Nativity of St. John the Baptist 3 Edward I [1275] until Henry and Joan unjustly ejected him after the summons of the eyre. Henry and Joan say that Richard was never seised of the rent, but they acknowledge that it was the right and perquisite of Joan and she devised it for life to Hawise, with reversion to her son Thomas, on condition that if Thomas should die before Avice it should remain to Avice without reversion to Joan's heirs. Thomas did outlive Avice, and since according to the will the rent should not revert to the heirs of Joan but should remain with the next heirs of Thomas because Avice died in his lifetime, they immediately entered on the rent on the death of Hawise as the next heirs of Thomas and they are in seisin thereof, without Richard having anything there except only by his intrusion which he made there when distraining for the rent of 5s. while Hawise was still alive. He [i.e. Henry] seeks judgment whether he [i.e. Richard] is able to claim a jury or sue in the same. On inspection of the will it is clearly established that Joan devised the rent to Hawise for her lifetime, on condition that on her death it remain to Thomas and on his death to Avice and if Avice outlived Thomas on such terms that it should not revert to Joan's heirs on the deaths of Thomas and Avice; Henry and Joan immediately after Hawise's death entered on the rent and it is quite clear that they are the rightful and next heirs of Thomas and Avice and Richard can claim nothing under the will from the rent by any reversion as the heir of Joan and he never had any interest in the rent except only that he took the 5s. while Hawise was still alive. So it is adjudged that Richard receive nothing, but is in *mercy for a false claim. [cf. **709**]

[*Nota*] *110. Placitum de disseisina facta infra sumonicionem itineris* [cf. **524** no. 110; a further *nota* to the same effect (partly illegible) appears on m. 18d, cf. **524** no. 111].

500. Hugh de Gloucestre complains of Walter son of Ellen de Flete, John le Taverner, and John de Brokesburne that on Friday in the first week of Lent this year [28 Feb. 1276] after the summons [of the eyre] they and others seized him at Fletebrugg in the ward of Anketin de Auverne [Farringdon ward] after curfew and struck him with iron staves, swords and axes, wounding and ill-treating him, so that he barely escaped with his life, against the peace, whence he says that he has suffered loss and damage to the value of £10 and he brings suit. Walter, John and John come and deny force and injury. They deny that they ever beat Hugh on that day or committed any trespass against him, as he alleges, and put themselves upon the ward. Hugh [does] likewise. The *jury* say on the oath that they made to the king and in the faith in which they are bound to him that Walter and the others never beat Hugh or committed any offence against him. So it is adjudged that Walter and the others be without day and Hugh in *mercy. [cf. **710**]

[*Nota* unnumbered]. *Placitum de transgressione.*

501. 'I, John de Gatesdene have granted to William de Wateford draper of London and his wife Rose the whole of the capital messuage with appurtenances which I had in London in the parish of St. Michael Cornhull between the tenement which William de Westden holds from me in fee on the north, and the tenant of Geoffrey de Trye on the south, and extending in length from the king's highway to the land of Peter son of Alan on the west; viz. whatever I had there in lands and buildings of wood and stone in length and breadth and in all things without diminution, for William and Rose to have and to hold to them and their heirs, of me and my wife Hawise and my heirs and assigns in fee in perpetuity, rendering therefor yearly 4 silver marks at the four terms of the year; and performing the service due to the chief lords of the fee. I and my wife Hawise and our heirs will defend and acquit the house (managium) with all appurtenances to William, Rose and their heirs against all men in perpetuity reserving to ourselves and our household free hospitality whenever we visit London.' John and William have confirmed this chirograph with their seals that the gift should remain ratified in perpetuity.

Because on inspection of the charter John saved and reserved for himself and his heirs and his household adequate hospitality whenever he came to London, and because the king's marshals, whenever they grant hospitality, assign a hall, sufficient rooms, a pantry, buttery, stable and kitchen and all other necessary rooms, it is adjudged that John de Cameys and his wife Margery, heirs of John de Gatesdene, have in the messuage a hall, a room and such other accommodation in the easements of the house as shall be necessary. [cf. **495**]

[*Nota*] 111. *Carta Johannis de Gatesdene.*
In a different hand: *Carta irrotulata* [cf. **524** below no. 111].

502. An assize comes in the husting to declare whether Thomas son of Adam de Basinges, uncle of Henry, son of Henry le Waleys and of Joan daughter of William de Hadestok, was seised in his demesne as of fee of 2 marks rent with appurtenances in the parish of St. Andrew Holeburne on the day on which he died and whether [Henry and Joan are the next heirs]. This rent is held by Richard de Stanes goldsmith who previously came to the husting and vouched to warranty Ralph de Pelham parson of the church of St. Michael in Bassieshawe who is not of the liberty of the City, but a stranger, so that the plea was respited until the coming of the justices. Ralph comes and freely warrants Richard. He says that Henry and Joan can claim no right in the tenements by hereditary descent from Thomas because Thomas in his will proved and enrolled in the husting[1] according to the custom of the City bequeathed them to Ralph, so he seeks judgment. Henry and Joan say that Thomas could not bequeath the rent to anyone because his father Adam bequeathed it to Thomas to hold of himself and the heirs of his body and he died without issue. They say that through their guardians they sued in the husting and produced there Adam's charter of feoffment and that by judgment of the husting the will was annulled in this respect, so the rent cannot and should not remain with Ralph. Ralph cannot deny this. Therefore it is adjudged that Henry and Joan recover seisin and Ralph is in **mercy*. [cf. **517**]

[*Nota*] 112. *Quoddam placitum super assisam mortis antecessoris* [cf. **524** no. 112].
1. *C. Wills*, i, 23–4.

503. A jury comes to declare whether one messuage with appurtenances in the parish of the church of St. Michael Paternosterchirch is free alms belonging to the church, of which Bartholomew is parson, or the lay fee of

The Plea Roll

Roger le Mareshall,[1] Walter le Engleys and John de Chesthunte. Roger and the others come and say that they are not bound to answer on this writ because pleas of this kind should not be terminated[2] here unless they were initiated in the husting. Because on inspection of the rolls of the preceding eyre it is found that such pleas were not previously heard before the justices, it is adjudged that Roger and the others be without day.

Nota 113. Consuetudo allegata. Quod placitum non debet placitari in itinere nisi prius fuit in hustengo [cf. **524** no. 113].
1. *Cal. Wills*, i, 27.
2. *terminari* (*placitari* deleted).

504. William de Reygate complains of Reginald Sone and his wife Edith that they have unjustly intruded upon a messuage in the parish of St. Albans. He complains that whereas he was in seisin of it by the demise of the abbot of St. Albans, Reginald and Edith have unjustly ejected him after the summons of the eyre. Reginald and Edith come and say that William never was in seisin of it as of a free tenement so that he could be disseised thereof. They say that the abbot enfeoffed Richard la Persone, formerly husband of Edith, and Edith herself of the messuage to hold during the whole lives of Richard and Edith and on Richard's death William intruded upon the messuage and ejected Edith, so that she at once went to the abbot and made complaint (cantum fecit) to him; the abbot sent some of his men to London and restored Edith to possession and ejected William, wherefor they deny disseisin or injury and put themselves upon the ward of Henry de Frowik [Cripplegate ward]. The ward comes and testifies to this. So it is adjudged that Reginald and Edith be without day and William in *mercy for a false claim. [cf. **711**]

[*Nota 114*]. *Placitum de intrusione* [cf. **524** no. 114].

505. Henry de Greneford of Garschurstrate was attached to answer Denise la Vileyn on a plea that whereas she had demised him all her land with the houses built upon it which she had in Distaflane in the parish of St. Nicholas Coldhabbeye London for himself and his heirs to have in perpetuity, and Henry and his heirs were to provide for Denise all her necessities in food and clothing for her lifetime and on her death to bury her body honourably at their expense in the priory of the nuns of Clerkewelle; three and a half years ago Henry withdrew the necessities and refused to provide them, as had been agreed between them, whence she says that she has suffered loss and damage to the value of 10 marks. Henry comes and the parties are agreed. The agreement is that Henry shall give to Denise every year for the rest of her life 24s. for the said necessities, of which he shall render 6s. at Easter this year, 6s. at the feast of the Nativity of St. John the Baptist, 6s. at Michaelmas next and 6s. at Christmas. If he does not do so, he grants that the sheriff shall levy the sum from his lands. In addition he shall give her 40s. of which he shall pay 20s. at once and the rest at the quindene of Easter this year. And thereon he finds these pledges [blank].

[*Nota*] 115. *Concordia super quadam convencione facta inter partes de victu et vestitu inveniendis* [cf. **524** no. 115].

The Plea Roll

506. It is found by the verdict of the wards of Simon de Haddestok and Henry de Coventre [Queenhithe and Vintry wards] upon which Roger de Leges plaintiff and Hugh le Taverner have put themselves, that Hugh never beat, wounded or maltreated Roger or committed any trespass against him or caused him any trouble or damage, as Roger alleged of Hugh. So it is adjudged that Hugh be without day and Roger in *mercy for a false claim.

507. Walter de Shelfhangre[1] sheriff is in *mercy for contempt. (? 100s.) [cf. **712**]

1. Sheriff of Norfolk and Suffolk 1275–7.

[m. 19] CIVIL PLEAS (EXTRA CORONAM) CONTINUED
508. William de St. Denis 'armorer' of London complains of Walter Hervy that when William was at peace in his house in the parish of St. Pancras on Saturday after the close of Easter 51 Henry III [30 Apr. 1267] Walter, then bailiff of the City of London, went to his house and took a hauberk, a horse-trapper (coopertorium) of iron mail of Chaumbliz, a (? lance head)[1] of iron, an iron corset (corsetum), a steel hat (capellum acerenum) and a basnet (basinum) covered with white leather, worth 14 marks; he carried the goods off and kept them against the peace, whence he says that he has suffered loss and damage to the value of 100s. and brings suit. Peter le Furbur complains that on the same day Walter took an iron hat of his worth 15s. and carried it off against the peace to his loss 40s. Walter comes and acknowledges that he took the armour belonging to William and Peter on the order of John de la Lynde as his underbailiff (sub-ballivus). He says that John while he was constable of the Tower and bailiff of the City of London and the City was in the hand of the king, ordered him to take the armour to go out against some thieves whose evil intentions he feared. He says he did not take them for his own use nor did he convert them to it. He puts himself upon the ward of Cheap and William and Peter [do] likewise. The ward comes and says in the faith in which they are bound to the king that Walter did not take the armour for his own use. So it is adjudged that Walter be without day and William and Peter in *mercy for a false claim. [cf. **713**]

[*Nota*] 116. *Querela de transgressione super Walterum Hervi ballivum* [cf. **524** no. 116].
1. *lencellam.*

509. Ralph le Buryler complains of Henry de Coventre that whereas a certain Nicholas de Saumford carried off his goods in silver, money, silver cups and other valuables to the value of 30 marks and was afterwards arrested by Henry, then sheriff of London, and imprisoned in Henry's house; when Ralph came to the house and sought to have speech with Nicholas and to have restored to him the goods and chattels taken, Henry refused to allow him to talk with Nicholas and permitted Nicholas to go away against the peace, whence he says that he has suffered loss and damage to the value etc. Henry comes and acknowledges that Nicholas was arrested by him and imprisoned in his house, but he says that Ralph never came to him to ask for the goods nor to have speech with Nicholas while he was in his custody, but the goods of which he complains remained in his possession.

The Plea Roll

He puts himself upon the verdict of the mayor and aldermen, and Ralph likewise. They come and say on the oath which they made to the king and in the faith in which they are bound to him that Ralph never went to Henry to recover any goods or to have speech with Nicholas while he was in his custody and that no goods belonging to Ralph remained in his possession, so it is adjudged that Henry be without day and Ralph in *mercy for a false claim.

[Nota] 117. Querela de transgressione super Henricum de Coventre vicecomitem [cf. 524 no. 117].

510. Felice Ferebraz presented herself on the fourth day against Robert de Gotele on a plea of detinue of charters, whereon she impleads him without a writ. He does not come. The sheriff of London was ordered to attach him to be present on this day, but did nothing, and reported that he did not have lands or tenements in the City by which he could be distrained or attached. It is testified that he had sufficient lands in Kent by which he could be attached. So the sheriff of *Kent* is ordered to distrain him, and to have his body in fifteen days from Easter [19 Apr. 1276] at Westminster in the Bench.

[Nota] 118. Magna districcio retornabilis in banco [cf. 524 no. 118].

511. James de Montibus and Cecily widow of Jollan de Durham complain of Walter de Frowik that on Monday before the feast of St. Matthew the Apostle 48 Henry III [18 Feb. 1264] he and others came with force and arms to the manor of Suthhale in Great Dunmawe in Essex and seized and abducted her son Jollan, who was in her wardship until he came of age, and took and carried off a gold brooch worth 40s., a silk girdle worth 20s., eighteen silver spoons worth 18s., a horse worth 40s., six gold rings worth 20s. and 40s. in money belonging to Cecily and committed other outrages against the peace, whence they say they have suffered loss and damage to the value of £100 and they bring suit. Walter comes and denies force and injury. He denies that he ever seized Jollan from her wardship on that day or took away any goods or did any wrong to her, as she alleges of him. He puts himself upon the jury of the county of Essex where the trespass is said to have occurred and James and Cecily [do] likewise. So the sheriff of *Essex* is ordered to produce before the justices at Westminster in the Bench in fifteen days from Easter [19 Apr. 1276] twelve [men]. Let us proceed in the said form etc.

[Nota] 119. Placitum de transgressione facta in comitatu Essex placitum in itinere London' et partes postquam se posuerunt in inquisicionem adiornate fuerunt in banco ad quindenam Pasche [cf. 524 no. 119].

512. The same James and Cecily complained of Nicholas de Winton' concerning the above trespass [**511**] and now do not proceed against him. So they and their pledges to prosecute are in *mercy, viz. Richard le Woder and Roger le Corder. [cf. **714**]

513. Essoins taken at the Tower of London on Monday before mid-Lent [9 Mar. 1276] (*Essonie London'*).
 Thomas de Wapyngbyr' whom Henry le Waleys vouches to warranty

against Joan widow of John Sayer on a plea of dower by Simon de Ludgate. (*Warr'*.) [cf. **482, 515**]

514. John Duraunt claimed in the husting against the prior of the Friars of the Penitence of Jesus Christ of London as his right by writ of right patent two messuages with appurtenances in London, of which he was seised in fee and right in time of peace during the reign of King Henry, by taking all the profits therefrom and that such is his right he has offered to prove. The prior previously came to the husting and vouched to warranty Eleanor the queen mother, who is not of the liberty [of the City], so that the plea (loquela) was respited until the coming of the justices. Eleanor comes by her attorney and warrants the prior. She denies the right and seisin of John and everything. She puts herself upon an inquest of the country (inquisicionem patrie) and asks that a recognition be made according to the custom of the City as to whether she or John has the greater right in those tenements. The mayor and aldermen put on record that according to the custom of the City when anyone is impleaded by writ of right concerning a tenement in the City and puts himself upon an inquest of the country concerning his right, twenty-four men should be chosen from the neighbourhood, twelve from the ward where the tenement is situated and twelve from the two adjoining wards, six from one and six from the other. They are to be chosen at once and are to come on Wednesday. The mayor and aldermen, asked whether the jurors in this case should be sworn or not, say that in cases of gaining or losing land as in cases of homicide [the jurors] are bound to swear to tell the truth. The jurors say on their oath that Eleanor has a greater right in those tenements than John. So it is adjudged that the prior should hold the tenements in peace, quit of John and of his heirs in perpetuity. Eleanor is without day and John in *mercy for a false claim. [cf. **472, 485, 715**]

[*Nota*] *120. De placito placitato coram justiciariis itinerantibus apud Turrim racione forinseci vocati ad warrantum in hustengo. Et qualiter inquisicio debet eligi et si illi de inquisicione debeant iurare nec ne* [cf. **524** no. 120].

PLEAS OF MONDAY IN THE THIRD WEEK OF LENT [9 Mar. 1276]
515. Henry le Waleys presented himself on the fourth day against Thomas de Wapenbir' on a plea that he warrant him a third part of one messuage with appurtenances in *London* which Joan widow of John son of Saer claims as dower against him, whereof Henry vouched Thomas to warranty against her. He does not come. The sheriff of *Warwickshire* was ordered to summon him but did nothing and did not send a writ. So he, William Hamelyn,[1] is in mercy. So as previously the sheriff is ordered to summon him to appear in fifteen days from Easter at *Westminster* in the Bench. The same day has been given to Joan to appear in the Bench. [cf. **482, 513**]

1. Sheriff of Warwickshire and Leicestershire, 1275–8.

516. William Doget and his wife Isabel came before the justices here and claimed an assessment of the damages that they suffered at the time of the intrusion of Martin Horn upon a messuage with appurtenances in London, as was found by an assize held between them. Martin comes and says that the damages should not be assessed because the [plea of] intrusion was not taken according to the law and custom of the City because it was taken by Walter Hervy, then chamberlain, without the sheriff being present. Because William and Isabel acknowledge that the [plea] was taken without the sheriff and on inspection of the rolls of the last eyre it is found that assizes of this kind concerning intrusion should be taken before one sheriff at least if the other cannot be present, and before the alderman of the place where the intrusion took place,[1] it is adjudged that there be nothing for the damages and that Martin recover his seisin.

[Nota] 121. De placitis assise nove disseisine non tenendis sine vicecomite [cf. **524** no. 121].
1. Cf. *London Eyre, 1244*, no. 243.

517. [m. 19d] Richard de Ashwy executor of the will of Thomas son of Adam de Basing was attached to answer Henry le Waleys and William de Hadestok, citizens of London, guardians of Thomas' lands and heirs, on a plea that he return to them charters concerning rents of 116s. 4d. due to the heirs, which he has withheld from them to the great damage and disinheritance of the heirs. Richard comes and acknowledges that he has four of Thomas' charters, one of which he at once returns to them, but he says they should not have the others as they make mention of 3½ marks rent which Thomas bequeathed to him in his last will and of which he was seised until Henry ejected him. The guardians say that the rent was the right of Adam de Basing, Thomas' father, who bequeathed it to Thomas to hold for himself and the heirs of his body only. Because Thomas died without issue, the guardians in the name of the heirs, went to the husting where Richard with his co-executors and others to whom Thomas had bequeathed other rents wanted to prove Thomas' will, and opposed probate. Because of this objection on good grounds (certis racionibus) the will was annulled by judgment of the husting.[1] So he seeks judgment whether Richard can justly claim to retain the charters. Thereupon the mayor and aldermen come and put on record that the will was annulled before them; it is the custom of the City that if anyone shall have bequeathed (legaverit) land or rent and the will is afterwards annulled by judgment in the husting, nothing more can accrue to the legatee from such a legacy, nor need the heir of the testator proceed against the legatee in the husting to recover seisin by a judgment; on the contrary, the heir can lawfully put himself in the seisin of that legatee (in seisinam ipsius legati); just as it is not necessary when a will has been confirmed and proved in the husting for the legatee to sue the heirs of the testator if they were in seisin. Richard acknowledges that the rent at one time was Adam's and was bequeathed by Thomas to Richard and that afterwards the will was annulled in the husting. He cannot deny that the custom of the City is as stated. So it is adjudged that Richard return the charters to the guardians to be kept with the other charters in wardship until the heirs come of age. And Richard is in *mercy because he did not return them sooner. [cf. **502, 716**]

Nota 122. De placito detencionis cartarum.
Nota 123. De terris et redditibus legatis. Consuetudo allegata [With pointing hand. Cf. **524** nos. 122–3].
1. C. *Wills*, i, 23–4.

The Plea Roll

518. Robert de Rokesle gives *½ *mark* for licence to agree with Thomas de Basing[1] on a plea of trespass by the pledge of Thomas. [cf. **717**]

1. i.e. the nephew and not the deceased son of Adam de Basing.

CIVIL PLEAS CONTINUED   Seyton[1]

519. William de Hadestok and his wife Joan complain of James de Montibus that on Friday after the feast of St. Mary Magdalene 53 Henry III [26 July 1269] he went to their house in London in the ward of Simon de Hadestok [Queenhithe ward], broke down the door and entered; he broke Joan's finger and committed other outrages against her against the peace, whence they say that they have suffered loss and damage to the value of £100 and they bring suit. James comes and denies force and injury. He acknowledges that he went there with Stephen de Edesworth, constable of the Tower of London, whom the king had ordered by writ to deliver to James, Bartholomew son and heir of Jollan de Durham who should have been in his wardship. He says that he did not go with any other purpose to their house or commit any trespass against them and puts himself upon the ward and that of Henry de Coventre [Vintry ward] as those nearest. William and Joan [do] likewise. The wards come and say in the faith in which they are bound to the king that James with many others came with force and arms with a king's bailiff to Joan's house before William married her and that after he had entered the house, he closed the door and tore her dress down to the navel, threw her to the ground and raped her, breaking her finger. So it is adjudged that James be committed to *gaol* until he has satisfied William and Joan for their damages, which are assessed at 100s. by the wards. [cf. **511, 718**]

Nota 114. *Placitum de transgressione* [cf. **524** no. 114].
1. The name of the justice is written twice on this membrane.

520. Henry de Frowik presented himself on the fourth day against Maud[1] widow of Luke de Badencurt on a plea of trespass whereon he impleads her without a writ. She has not come, and has made many defaults. So the sheriff of *Essex* is ordered to distrain her by all her lands. And he is to have her body before the justices on the morrow of the Ascension [15 May 1276] at St. Martin le Grand London.

[*Nota* 125]. *Districcio magna.*
1. Cf. **182**.

521. The king has sent this writ to the justices of the eyre: 'John Maunsel, treasurer of York, formerly clerk of King Henry our father and of ourselves, had in his possession in the priory of Holy Trinity London many papal privileges and other instruments and writings touching us both in his wardrobe (garderoba) above the Walebrok, viz. in the house of Luke de Luca and his associates, among their private papers (arcana sua) and other things which they kept there at the time of the disturbances and which were dispersed by the hand of various men from the City and others; we therefore firmly enjoin you to make enquiry by the oath of good and lawful men from the aldermanries of the City by whom the truth may better be known in the presence of the treasurer (thesaurarii) of London and Reginald the Barber, formerly a member of John's household, into whose hands the aforesaid privileges and instruments concerning us came, and to induce them freely to restore them to us; we grant a full pardon and firm peace to all those who wish to confess and make amends for their trespass in taking possession of and carrying away the documents; at Kynesmeresford 10 February 4 Edward I [1276].' Four men from each aldermanry come and say in the faith in which they are bound to the king that Richard le Teyere clerk, Philip de Hastede, Edmund de Exeport with others broke open that wardrobe in Walebrok and a part of the things therein came into the hands of Thomas son of Thomas and the rest were given into the keeping of Robert de Mounpellers by Reginald le Barbur, then of John's household, by chirograph. After the death of John Maunsel, Robert handed over the goods entrusted to him by the chirograph intact to John's executor, a Friar Minor of Deulacres, who disposed of them at his discretion. After the death of Thomas son of Thomas, Hugh le Bygot came and took the goods which Thomas had in his possession, carried them off and did with them as he would. They say also that Simon son of Simon de Montefort, Grimbald Pauncefot and many others whose names are unknown, went to the priory of Holy Trinity and broke open a chest belonging to John with his secret instruments and documents and other things deposited in it. Simon took home with him only a psalter found in the chest; the rest of the contents was left to be kept in that chest under his seal. Afterwards Grimbald caused the chest with its contents to be conveyed from the priory in a long cart to the bishop of Durham's house, and he took things from it and disposed at will of the contents, and shortly afterwards he sent the chest to Richard Avel's house, and left it there without lock or seal against Richard's will. There it remained for about a quarter of a year and then Ralph Perot went to Richard's house and carried it off with everything in it, saying that he would admit readily doing so if anyone accused Richard; but what became of the chest subsequently or where it is now they do not know. Afterwards a certain John le Coffrer comes and says that he has two coffers which belonged to John Maunsell on the pledge of Hugh le Bygot and which the same Hugh gave him to be repaired.

522. Henry le Waleys and William de Durham agree that Gregory de Rokeslee mayor, John Adrian, Thomas de Basing and John Horn, aldermen, are to arrange and dispose among themselves how William is to make satisfaction to Henry for the timber of a room belonging to Thomas de Basing which has been demolished and what ought to go to him as guardian of Thomas' heirs; and likewise how William is to make him satisfaction for his prison at the time that he was sheriff of Middlesex under Henry, whereof he [William] took the perquisites and has not yet answered for them to him; provided always that power and jurisdiction on the making of this ordinance shall remain with the justices. (*Assensus ? quorundam.*)

523. The king has sent this writ to the justices: Amice daughter of Richard de Chelmereford lately impleaded on a royal writ of right Ralph Crepyn in the husting[1] of London for two messuages with appurtenances in London and Amice and Ralph put themselves upon an inquest to be held in the husting; because those by whom the inquest was made were not well enough examined, Amice was ordered by judgment of the husting to withdraw without day, to her grave loss and manifest disinheritance; therefore the king has recently commanded the justices to call the parties before them and examine this business further and to do full and speedy justice. Subsequently on Monday after the quindene of Trinity [22 June] in the husting before the justices the mayor and aldermen put on record that Amice previously sued Ralph in the husting for the two messuages by a writ of right which she claimed as her right of seisin of her property (ut ius suum de seisina sua propria) from the time of King Henry III; so Ralph came in the husting and denied Amice's right and seisin as of fee and right and put himself upon a jury of the vill (ville) [to declare] whether he or Amice had the greater right in the messuages. An inquest was made by a jury of twenty-four according to the custom of the City, who said on their oath that Ralph had the greater right, so that it was then adjudged that he should hold in peace and Amice take nothing by her writ, but be in mercy for a false claim. Now Amice and Ralph come and now Amice complains that the jury consisted of only eleven men instead of the twenty-four required by the custom and law of the City. Because the mayor and aldermen put on record that the jury consisted of twenty-four according to the custom of the City it is adjudged that Ralph be without day.

[*Nota* largely illegible.]
1. Husting Pleas of Land Roll 3 (3 Edward I), mm. 2d, 3.

524. [m. 20 Schedule of Legal Annotations]
[In a 14th-century hand. References to regnal years and membrane numbers appear in the margin but are omitted below.]

1. Quod manucaptus usque ad iter justiciariorum sit coram justiciariis primo die alioquin vicecomites amerciabuntur [cf. **6**].
2. De maiore et communitate amerciatis quia in uno itinere dedixerunt id quod prius in alio itinere concesserunt [cf. **18**].
3. Quod nullus latro qui fugit ad ecclesiam debet custodiri nec vigilari per cives [cf. **20**].
4–5. [As **21**n, **22**n (but erroneously omitting *non*).]
6. Si secta debeat fieri post latrones aut hutesium levari. Et de camerario amerciato quia nullam fecit mencionem in rotulis suis de plegiis vicinorum [cf. **24**].
7. [As **25**n.]
8. De quatuor vicinis semper attachiandis ubi aliquis interfectus fuerit per feloniam [cf. **26**].
9. De warda amerciata quia receptaverunt in eadem quemdam qui non fuit in franco plegio [cf. **29**].
10. [As **29**n.]
11. De warda amerciata quia non nominaverunt vicinos coram camerario et vicecomitibus [cf. **31**].
12. De warda amerciata quia nesciverunt qui fuerunt cum quodam qui oppressus fuit per quemdam [sic] arborem per infortunium. Et de camerario et vicecomitibus amerciatis quia male appreciaverunt deodandum [cf. **32**].
13–14, 15–16, 17. [As **37**nn, **39**nn, **41**n.]

The Plea Roll

18. Et de camerario et vicecomitibus amerciatis quia non inquisiverunt de catallis felonum [cf. **41**].
19. [As **43n**.]
20. Quod maior et aldermanni presentaverunt quod nemo tenetur respondere de evasione in Civitate [cf. **48**].
21. [As **50n**.]
22. De abiuracione recipienda per constabularium Turris et per aldermannos et vicecomites London' si camerarius absens fuit [cf. **52**].
23. [As **53n**.]
24. De warda amerciata pro falsa appreciacione deodande [sic] [cf. **54**].
25. De camerario amerciato quia non fecit appreciare deodandum. (Nota.) Et quia vicecomites obierunt, nullus respondet [cf. **59**].
26. Quod non oportet quod extranei sint in franco pleggio. Et quod vicecomites respondebunt de evasione nisi respondent ubi capti sunt deliberati [cf. **60**].
27. [As **65n**.]
28. De warda amerciata pro discordia inter presentacionem suam et rotulos camerarii [cf. **67**].
29–41. [As **70n**, **72n**, **73n**, **75n**, **76n**, **77n**, **78n**, **85n**, **87n**, **88n**, **97n**, **98n** (but omitting *et hoc patet hic*), **99n**.]
42. De warda amerciata et quibusdam amerciatis eo quod presentaverunt se vicinos et non fuerunt. [cf. **101**].
43–5. [As **102n** (but omitting *similiter*), **108n** (but omitting *et hoc patet hic*), **109n**.]
46. De tota warda amerciata pro receptamento cuiusdam qui non fuit in franco pleggio [cf. **112**].
47. De camerario et vicecomitibus amerciatis eo quod dederunt duobus abiurantibus regnum simul et semel diversos portus transeundi extra regnum [cf. **115**].
48. Quod oportet quod manucaptus pro felonia sit coram justiciariis primo die [cf. **116**].
49–50. [As **117n**, **119n**.]
51. De tota warda amerciata pro franco pleggio [cf. **120**].
52. [As **122n**.]
53. Missing from list, cf. **127**].
54. De cyrographo faciendo inter vicecomites de prisonibus tempore recessus eorum de balliva sua et de vicinis non attachiandis scilicet unumquemque per alium [cf. **134**].
55, 56–7, 58. [As **138n**, **140nn**, **141n**.]
59. De casu Michaelis Thovy per veredictum maioris et aldermannorum [cf. **146**].
60. De appello de mahemio quassato per varias proposiciones contra appellum factas . . . per xii homines de warda et non per maiorem et aldermannos . . . missum per manucapcionem [cf. **147**].
61–9. [Mainly illegible, cf. **149n**, **152n**, **154n**, **176n**, **177n**, **183n**, **187n**, **194n** (**197n** or **198n**), **203n**.]
70. [m. 20d] . . . secum per unum annum et amplius postquam idem rettatus interfecerit hominem cat . . . [cf. **205**].
71. De carta regis Henrici pro pace facta Laurencio Duket [cf. **207**].
72. Quod manucapti pro morte hominis usque ad iter justiciariorum non possunt se acquietare per veredictum aldermannorum et visneti ibidem ut dicitur ibi et postea invenies contrarium. Qualiter magna lex debeat fieri ibidem. Quod omnes manucapti ad iter justiciariorum veniant primo die itineris [cf. **209**].
73. Quod non oportet quod extraneus, scilicet pepoudrous vel aliquis de familia alicuius magnatis sit in franco pleggio [cf. **214**].

The Plea Roll

74–6. [As **214**n, **219**n, **221**n (*de Arcubus London'*).]
77. De quodam Adam de Ware capto pro morte Reginaldi Tropynel tradito in ballium per libertatem Civitatis [cf. **228**].
78. De fugientibus a Civitate pro felonia attachiandis cum proximo redierint [cf. **230**].
79. Quod extraneus se debet acquietare de morte hominis per xlii homines de tribus wardis [cf. **233**].
80. De appello faciendo in hustengo. Et quod extraneus se acquietabit per xlii homines de tribus wardis ut supra. Et quod extranei debent exigi et utlagari in comitatibus de quibus sunt [cf. **245**].
81. De pleggiis amerciatis quia non habuerunt quem manuceperunt primo die itineris. Item de pleggiis eodem modo. Et de quodam fornicato acquietato per sacramentum xlii hominum [cf. **249**].
82. [As **256**n.]
83. De appello facto in hustengo et postea quassato coram justiciariis. Et de appellato postea acquietato per xlii homines [cf. **261**].
84. De extraneis acquietatis per xlii homines. Et quod oportet quod maior et aldermanni dicent quis [occidit] mortuum. Et de clerico convicto per xlii homines de tribus wardis et liberato episcopo. Et de extraneo acquietato per xlii homines etc. [cf. **264**].
85. De querela de transgressione ubi pars tunc querelatus se posuit super veredictum aldermannorum [cf. **265**].
86–7. [As **269**n, **271**n.]
88. De appello in hustengo de plagis et verberatura [cf. **272–3**].
89. De forinsecis acquietatis in itinere per forincecos [cf. **275**].
90. De Philippo le Taylour rettato de roberia acquietato per maiorem et aldermannos [cf. **278**].
91. [As **279**n.]
92. De civibus London' liberatis maiori et civibus per pleggios per justiciarios itinerantes in comitatu Midd' licet factum esset forincecum [cf. **280**]. De Jacobo de Stokes clerico rettato de latrocinio et acquietato per maiorem et aldermannos et liberato episcopo [cf. **282**].
93. De Adam Scott et aliis forincesis acquietatis per veredictum aldermannorum et visneti [cf. **284**].
94. De quibusdam rettatis dc felonia et acquietatis [cf. **287**].
95. Carta magistri Thome de Pyvelesden [cf. **293**].
96. Quod vicecomites possunt dimittere omnes illos qui sunt de libertate Civitatis per plevinam usque ad adventum justiciariorum de quocumque latrocinio rettati fuerint [cf. **324**].
    Quoddam placitum de transgressione [deleted].
    Quoddam placitum de debito [deleted].
97. Quod justiciarii itinerantes non tenebunt placita in itinere de tenementis in London' [cf. **470**].
98. Quod justiciarii itinerantes tenebunt placita de transgressionibus [cf. **471**]. Item quoddam placitum de debito [cf. **474**].
    Item alius processus de eadem materia [deleted].
99. [As **477**n; cf. **478**, **482**].
    Quoddam placitum de convencione et de testibus (vocatis et productis in curia et quales *deleted*) debeant esse (testes ad probandum *deleted*) [cf. no. 103].
100. Quoddam placitum de rectis serviciis in quo maior allegavit quod justiciarii huiusmodi placita tenere non debent [cf. **483**].
101. Consuetudo (probata *deleted*) recordata quod justiciarii non debent tenere placita terre coram eis in itinere, et hoc per breve regis [cf. **484**].

The Plea Roll

Quedam placita de tenementis in Civitate adiornata de itinere usque in bancum [deleted].
Carta Stephani de Cornhull irrotulata in itinere per Thomam de Clare militem [deleted. Cf. **481**].
De quodam extraneo vocato ad warantum [deleted. Cf. ?**485**].

102. Quoddam placitum de transgressione terminatum per sacramentum maioris et aldermannorum [cf. **487**].
De quodam forinceco vocato ad warantum [deleted].
Quedam concordia irrotulata in rotulis justiciariorum [deleted. Cf. **489**].
Quoddam placitum transgressionis placitatum coram justiciariis [deleted].
Item aliud placitum placitatum ibidem [deleted].
103. Querela de convencione et testibus vocatis et productis in curia et quales debent esse testes ad probandum [cf. **488**].
104–6. [As **491**n, **492**n, **493**n (omitting *itinerantibus*).]
107. Quoddam placitum mortis antecessoris de quodam forinseco vocato ad warantum [cf. **494**].
108. [As **495**n.]
109. Quoddam placitum de imprisonamento [cf. **496**].
110. Placitum de disseisina facta infra sumonicionem itineris [cf. **499**].
111. Adhuc de placito assise nove disseisine unde placitum incipit inferius [cf. **499**].
Item quoddam placitum de tenementis [deleted].
Item quedam carta irrotulata Johannis de Gatesden [deleted. Cf. **501**].
112. [As **502**n.]
113. Quod placitum non debet terminari in itinere nisi prius fuit in hustengo [cf. **503**].
114–16. [As **504**n, **505**n, **508**n.]
117. Item querela de transgressione super Henricum de Coventre vicecomitem (qui se purgavit per maiorem et aldermannos *in a different hand*) [cf. **509**].
118–19. [As **510**n, **511**n.]
120. De placito placitato coram justiciariis itinerantibus apud Turrim racione forinseci vocati ad warantum in hustengo [cf. **514**].
121. De placito nove disseisine non tenendo sine vicecomite. Et qualiter inquirentes debent eligi et si illi de inquisicione debeant iurare necne [cf. **516**].
122, 113 [recte 123], 114 [recte 124], [125]. [As **517**nn, **519**n, **520**n.]
115 [sic]. Recordum maioris et aldermannorum factum in hustengo de custodibus qui non venerunt in itinere justiciariorum [cf. ?**523**].
116 [sic]. Concordia facta coram justiciariis itinerantibus de tenementis . . . in hustengo.
117 [sic]. Placita coram justiciariis itinerantibus de arreragiis annui (?redditus).
Nota quod annum et vastum debent placitari in itinere.

THE ESTREAT
(THE EXCHEQUER SUMMONS)
(Corporation of London Records Office, Misc. Roll BB)

525. [m. 1] Edwardus dei gratia rex Anglie, dominus Hibernie et dux Aquitanie vicecomiti London salutem. Vide sicut te ipsum et omnia tua diligis quod solvas ad scaccarium nostrum apud Westmonasterium in crastino Sancti Michaelis et habeas ibi tecum medietatem omnium debitorum subscriptorum et aliam medietatem in crastino clause Pasche.

De finibus et amerciamentis de itinere Rogeri de Seython et sociorum suorum justiciariorum itinerancium apud Turrim London anno rengni nostri quarti, videlicet[1]

1. Completed in **786**, 14 June 1276. On the dorse of m. 1: *E 86 li. 14d. ob.*

DEFAULTS[1]

526. *Breve di. m. per tall' vicecomitat' de residuo* + *De abbate de Newenham 1m. pro defalta.[2]
Breve + De priore de Simpringham 100s. pro eodem.
Breve + *De abbate de Kirkstede 6m.
Vicecomitat' allocetur + De Johanne de Colecestre capellano 2m.
Breve[3] *T.* + De priore de Coventre 4m.
+ De Matilde que fuit uxor Roberti Walrand 40s.
... *m. 6d.* + De priore de Theford 6m.
T. per tall' penes se + De priore de Ware 40s.[4]
+ De magistro Milicie Templi in Anglia 10 li.
Breve[5] + *De decano et capitulo Sancti Martini London' 100s.
T. + *De Juliana que fuit uxor Thome de la Forde di. m.[6]
Breve[7] + De Bartholomeo de Brianson 1m.
Alibi per Nicholaum de Castello[8] + De Jacobo de Sancto Victore ⟨*modo clericus de Hengeham*⟩ di. m. [cf. **340**].

1. Cf. **340**. The abbot of Westminster was excused from the common summons of the eyre, 29 Nov. 1275 (*C.C.R. 1272–9*, 262, 324).
2. Paid Easter 1278 (E 401/88 m. 8).
3. Respite Easter 1278 (E 159/51 m. 8d).
4. Paid Easter 1280 (E 401/95 m. 4).
5. Order to Exchequer to acquit, 25 Nov. 1277 (*C.C.R. 1272–9*, 432).
6. Paid Easter 1278 (E 401/88 m. 6).
7. Order to Exchequer to acquit, 5 June 1277 (E 368/50 m. 6; *C.C.R. 1272–9*, 392).
8. Exchequer clerk (E 368/53 m. 4; *Calendar of Liberate Rolls, 1267–72, passim*).

ASSIZE OF WINE[1]

527. *T. tall' per tall'* *De Waltero le Engleys 20s. pro vinis venditis contra assisam.[2]
T. tall' per tall' *De Elya de Conductu 20s. pro eodem.
T. tall' per tall' *De Gilberto de Dunton 20s.[3]
Breve De Hugone de Dunton[4] 20s.

The Estreat (The Exchequer Summons)

T. per tall' *De Johanne de Stanford di. m.
T. per tall' *De Radulfo de Suffolk di. m.
T. per tall' . *De Henrico de Sancta Ositha 1m.[5]
T. per tall' *De Alano de Suffolk di. m.
T. per tall' *De Johanne Herdel de Normaund 1m.[6]
T. per tall' *De Ricardo de Sancto Botulfo di. m.
T. per tall' *De Roberto Scotico 20s.
T. per tall' ponit X *De Ricardo de Kingeston 1m.[7]
T. Radulfus per tall' *De Johanne de Cestrehunte 40s.[8]
T. per tall' *De Osberto de Suffolk di. m.
Pars Radulfus per tall' *De Johanne le Taylur 40d.
T. per tall' *De Petro de Gisors di. m.
T. per tall' *De Rogero le Barbur 20s.
T. per tall' *De Thoma de Coumbe di. m.
T. Radulfus per tall' . *De Roberto le Treyer 40s.[9]
T. per tall' *De Simone de Farnham 40d.
T. per tall' *De Bruyno de Gisorz di. m.
Att' per breve[10] De Reginaldo de Suffolk 40s.
T. per tall' *De Emma la Barbere 1m.
T. *De Christiano Reyner[11] 40d.
T. R. le Fevre *De Johanne Stacy di. m.
T. Arraz *De Nicholao de Weston 40d.[12]
(? *Att'*) De Rustikello Thedal 5m.
Breve de respectu [13] De Joceo le Acatur le Rey 2m.
T. *De Willelmo Warrache di. m.[14]
T. per Radulfum 2 . *De Eustachio le Taverner 40d.
T. per tall' *De Johanne filio Saeri 40d.
Nichil mortuus nuper . De Willelmo de la Cornere 40d.[15]
T. 2 De Willelmo de Portesmuth 40d.[16]
T. per tall' *De Willelmo Hewe di. m.
T. Radulfus *De Johanne Fuatard 40d.[17]
T. per tall' *De Reginaldo le Chaundeler 40s.
(? *Breve*) De Ada Neveratham di. m.
T. *De Roberto de Redingges di. m.[18]
T. per tall' *De Henrico de Hereford 40s.[19]
T. per tall' *De Rogero de Coventre di. m.
T. Radulfus per tall' *De Johanne de Dere[20] 1m.
T. per tall' *De Willelmo de Beverlaco di. m.
Pars 40d. per tall' T. 2 . De Thoma de Conductu Maiore di. m.[21]
T. per tall' *De Johanne Wade 20s.
T. per tall' *De Johanne Skyp 1m.
Pauper . De Ricardo de la Barnete 40d.
Pauper De Jacobo Pele[22] di. m.
T. per tall' *De Johanne de Northwode di. m.
T. Radulfus per tall' *De Johanne Doket 20s.
Nota + De Hubeleto de Arraz di. m.
T. . *De Ada de Blakenye di. m.[23]
(? *Episcopo pro*) *sok' Midd'* De Thoma de Karroun di. m.
T. per tall' . *De Wolmaro de Essex 1m.[24]
T. Radulfus Fevere sine tall' *De Willelmo Doget 40d.
T. per tall' *De Faukes le Taverner 20s.
T. Radulfus . *De Ricardo Curteys 40d.
T. per tall' *De Simone de Sancto Lycio 40d.
T. per tall' *De Thoma le Barber 40d.

The Estreat (The Exchequer Summons)

T. per tall' *De Roberto de Fridaistrete 40d.
T. per tall' *De Ricardo de Newerk 40d.[25]
T. per tall' *De Andrea le Bel et Elena uxore eius 40d.[26]
T. per tall' *De Angnete de Wylehale 40d.[27]
T. per duas tallias *De Thoma de Conductu Minore 20s.[28]
T. per tall' *De Rogero le Estmor di. m.[29]
T. . *De Jacobo le Treys 40d.[30]
T. per tall' *De Reginaldo de Laufare 20s.[31]
T. vicecomitatus oneratur de 20s. De Arnaldo de Depe ⟨*Rogerus clericus res'*⟩ 20s.[32]
T. per tall' *De Ada le Ferur et Elyenora[33] uxore eius di. m.
T. Radulfus per tall' . *De Ricardo de Bedford 1m.
T. 2 . . De Roberto Russel 40d.[34]
T. per tall' *De Rogero Piggesflech di. m.[35]
T. tall' . *De Roberto de Suffolk 1m.[36]
T. per tall' . *De Johanne de Wodeham di. m.[37]
T. Radulfus per tall' . *De Rogero de Garskirke di. m.
T. Radulfus per tall' . *De Bartholomeo de Capella gaunter di. m.
Ignota De Beatrice Aleford[38] 40d.
Nichil hic quia inferius De Ricardo qui fuit cum Avicia Hardel 40d. *R. le Fevere.*
T. Radulfus per tall' . *De Philippo le Treur 40d.
. De Johanne de Brylaund 40s.
Breve de perdonacione[39] De Deotato Willame 40s.
Per De Willelmo Russel di. m.
Arraz *De Roberto de Dorset di. m.
T. per tall' . *De Donelino Jointe 20s.[40]
T. per tall' *De Stephano Hauteyn[41] di. m.[42]
Pauper obiit De Nicholao Greygrom 40d.
2 De Roberto de Clopton di. m.
T. Ro 2 De Roberto Heyron 40d.[43]
T. *De Willelmo le Whyte 40d.[44]
De Martino le Arblaster 20s.
T. per tall' *De Gilberto le Armurer 40d.[45]
T. R. le Fevere . *De Germano Clerico extra Alegate 40d.
T. (? ex . . . arer') 2 De Willelmo de Hereford di. m.[46]
Fugit nec aliquid habet De Roberto de Gysorz di. m.
T. Radulfus . *De Gilberto de Colescestre 40d.
T. Ro 2 De Willelmo de Dunton 40d.
T. per tall' *De Katerina de (? Neverethome) di. m.[47]
Atterm' . De Montere Bonnemi 1m.
[m. 2] *T. per tall'* *De Giles de Garskirke 40d.
Suwerk *De Ada de Ironmongereslane 40d.

1. Cf. **292** where the following additional names appear: Ricardus Deusour, Johannes Hache and Jacobus Tavernarius. But note the large number of names cited in **527**, and not mentioned in **292** (see below nn. 4, 41).
2. Paid Hilary 1277 (E 401/82 m. 1).
3. Paid Hilary 1277 (E 401/82 m. 7) and Hilary 1281 (E 401/97 m. 9).
4. Not in **292**. Respite Hilary 1278 (E 368/51 m. 7d; cf. **693**); paid 14 Edward I (E 372/131 m. 5d).
5. Paid Hilary 1277 (E 401/82 m. 8).
6. Paid Easter 1278 (E 401/88 m. 8).
7–8. Paid Hilary 1277 (E 401/82 m. 8).
9. Paid Michaelmas 1280 (E 401/97 m. 9).
10. Cf. **624**, **757**.
11. *Christina Renerii* (**292**).
12. Paid Easter 1278 (E 401/88 m. 7).

The Estreat (The Exchequer Summons)

13. Cf. **560**.
14. Paid Easter 1278 (E 401/88 m. 8).
15. Removed to Pipe Roll 14 Edward I (E 372/131 m. 6).
16. Paid Easter 1280 (E 401/95 m. 7).
17–18. Paid Easter 1278 (E 401/88 mm. 7, 8).
19. Paid Easter 1277 (E 401/84 m. 4).
20. *Depe* (**292**).
21. Paid Hilary 1277 (E 401/82 m. 7) and Easter 1278 (E 401/88 m. 7).
22. *Ricardus Bole* (**292**).
23–4. Paid Easter 1277 (E 401/84 m. 3).
25–7. Paid Easter 1277 (E 401/83 m. 1).
28. Paid Easter 1277 (E 401/84 m. 6).
29. Paid Easter 1277 (E 401/83 m. 1).
30. Paid Easter 1278 (E 401/88 m. 7).
31. *Lanare* (**292**). Paid Easter 1277 (E 401/83 m. 1).
32. Paid Easter 1277 (E 401/83 m. 1); removed to Pipe Roll 7 Edward I (E 372/123 m. 9).
33. *Elinora de Conductu* (**292**).
34. Part paid Easter 1280 (E 401/95 m. 8).
35. Paid Easter 1277 (E 401/83 m. 1).
36. Paid Hilary 1277 (E 401/82 m. 7) and Easter 1278 (E 401/88 m. 8).
37. Paid Easter 1277 (E 401/83 m. 1).
38. *Hakeford* (**292**).
39. Pardon Hilary 1278 (E 159/51 m. 3d, cf. **663**). See also **487, 707** and for total debt *C.C.R. 1272–9*, 408.
40. Paid Easter 1277 (E 401/83 m. 1).
41. This and the names which follow in **527** are not in **292**.
42. Paid Easter 1277 (E 401/83 m. 1).
43. Paid Easter 1282 (E 401/101 m. 8).
44. Paid Easter 1278 (E 401/88 m. 7).
45. Paid Easter 1277 (E 401/83 m. 1).
46. Paid Easter 1280 (E 401/95 m. 7).
47. Paid Easter 1277 (E 401/83 m. 1).

Default

528. T. per tall' X quia male purperta *De Roberto Fulcone di. m. pro defalta.[1] [cf. **340, 526**]

1. Paid Easter 1277 (E 401/83 m. 1).

Assize of Wine

529. (*In respectu*) per breve[1] *De Henrico de Coventre 5m. pro vino vendito contra assisam. [cf. **292, 527**]

1. Writ to the barons of the Exchequer, 13 May 1277, to acquit Henry of £57 16s. 8d. of £97 16s. 8d. exacted for escapes and other causes [**585, 589, 591**] and to atterm the remaining £40 (E 368/50 m. 6; *C.C.R. 1272–9*, 385). Order (attached), 14 June 1277, to the sheriffs of London to same effect. The Pipe Roll of 7 Edward I (E 372/123 m. 9) enters the original debt and the acquitted sum and records his paying £10 10s. *de pluribus debitis*.

Amercements, 1252–3

530. *Ignotus* De Ricardo de Kynggeford di. m. quia non habuit. [cf. **15**]

531. *Superplus* De Willelmo de Dunelm vicecomite 5m. pro pluribus transgressionibus.
De eodem Willelmo et Thoma Wyburn vicecomitibus de catallis Arnati de Garsie fugitivi 3s. [cf. **29**]

The Estreat (The Exchequer Summons)

532. *T. Araz* *De Henrico de Wymbeldon quia non venit et Willelmo Aubyn pro plegio eiusdem 10s. *Unde Henricus 40d. solvit Araz.*
Obiit pauper De Willelmo Louesham 40d. quia non venit. [cf. **32**]

AMERCEMENTS, 1253–4

533. *Rob' de Castello breve ad scaccarium*[1] *De Johanne de Norht' vicecomite 20 li. pro evasione Radulfi le Parmenter.
Pars 10s. De Radulfo le Parmenter 20s. pro habenda inquisicione.
(? . . . *ethefeld*) *levar' apud Flet'* Ø De Johanne le Milneward tanner vicino quia non venit; Nicholao Hund et Willelmo Hugge 10s. pro plegio eiusdem.
Breve pro Johanne prius scaccario De Ricardo Pikard et Johanne de Norht' vicecomitibus de catallis Ricardi Fokkelappe fugitivi 2s.
*De eodem Johanne 100s. pro transgressionibus. [cf. **37**]

> 1. Writ to barons of the Exchequer, 12 May 1277, acquitting John de Northampton of £30 of the £60 exacted for escapes while he was sheriff (E 368/50 m. 6; *C.C.R. 1272–9*, 385). See also *C.P.R. 1272–81*, 202. Remaining debt removed to Pipe Roll 7 Edward I (E 372/123 m. 9): 'De amerciamentis coram magistro R. de Seiton, Johannes de Norht' reddit compotum de 65 li. pro pluribus evasionibus sicut continetur ibidem et di. m. pro transgressionibus purpresture [cf. **460, 783**]. In thesauro 30 li. per breve regis adhuc inter communia anni quinti. Et debet 35 li. et di. m.'

534. De eisdem Ricardo et Johanne vicecomitibus de catallis Radulfi de Worthstede suspensi 4s.
Ignotus De Alecok de Whiteby quia non venit; Thoma le Paternoster ⟨*obiit pauper*⟩ di. m. pro plegio eiusdem. [cf. **41**]

535. *T.* *De Johanne de Stebenheth seniore vicino et plegiis suis 1m. quia non venit. [cf. **43**]

536. De Thoma de Morton vicino quia non venit; Ricardo le Tuler ⟨*obiit pauper*⟩ et Waltero Frebodi ⟨*ignotus*⟩ di. m. pro plegio eiusdem.
Obiit pauper De Henrico le Tuler vicino quia non venit; Johanne de Waldegrave ⟨*nullus talis*⟩ et Ricardo Frere ⟨*obiit ante iter*⟩ di. m. pro plegio eiusdem. [cf. **45**]

AMERCEMENTS, SEP. 1254–FEB. 1255

537. *R. de Linton distr' est per 2 ciph. de maiore unum cum al'* (? *sine ped'*) De Willelmo Essewy et Roberto de Lynton vicecomitibus de catallis Thome de Halestede fugitivi 10s.
Calumpnia catall' De eodem Roberto di. m. pro pluribus transgressionibus.[1] *Linton.*[2] [cf. **50**]

> 1. Paid Easter 1278 (E 401/88 m. 8).
> 2. With pointing hand.

538. De eisdem Willelmo et Roberto vicecomitibus de catallis Roberti de Pontefracto fugitivi 6m. [cf. **51**]

AMERCEMENTS, FEB.–SEP. 1255

539. *In pace H. per scaccarium in respectu* De Stephano de Oystregate et Henrico Walmond quondam vicecomitibus pro evasione Willelmi Longman, Radulfi Longman et Henrici Smyth fugitivorum 60 li.
In calumpnia De eisdem vicecomitibus de catallis eorundem 26s. [cf. **60**]

The Estreat (The Exchequer Summons)

540. *Per breve* De eisdem vicecomitibus pro evasione Willelmi Cryol fugitivi 20 li. [cf. **62**]

AMERCEMENTS, SEP. 1269–JULY 1270

541. *Calumpnia* De Thoma de Basingg et Roberto de Cornhull vicecomitibus[1] de catallis Thome garcionis Roberti Walrand fugitivi 4s. [cf. **214, 655**]

  1. Both sheriffs were granted a respite Trinity 1277 (E 368/50 m. 6).

542. *2* De eisdem vicecomitibus de catallis Guyloti le Paternoster et Lucie uxoris eius fugitivorum 2s. [cf. **215**]

543. *W. Plastrer 40d. T.* (? *post*) *resp' batillar'* De Rogero de Chesewyk, Ada le Boter ⟨*obiit pauper ante iter*⟩ vicinis quia non veniunt; Willelmo le Plastrer, Simone le Plastrer, Willelmo de Wautham et Johanne le Devenays ⟨*ignotus*⟩ di. m. pro plegio eorundem. [cf. **217**]

544. (**Superplus*) *calumpnia* De Thoma de Basingg et Roberto de Cornhull vicecomitibus de catallis Johannis Russel confiscatis 20s. pro fuga.
T. per duas tallias de Matheo et Johanne di. m. Radulfus 2 De Roberto de Lavenham vicino quia non venit; Matheo le Chaundeler et Johanne le Barber 10s. pro plegio eiusdem. [cf. **218**]

545. *T. Radulfus per talliam* *De Jacobo Angelaunt de Pistoria 100s. quia non habuit quem plegiavit.[1] [cf. **219**]

  1. Paid Easter 1277 (E 401/84 m. 8).

AMERCEMENT, JULY–SEP. 1270

546. *T.* *De Waltero le Poter 5m. quia non fecit inquisicionem.[1] [cf. **220**]

  1. Paid Easter 1278 (E 401/88 m. 1).

AMERCEMENTS, 1270–1

547. *De Stephano de Cornhull vicino 20s. quia non venit.[1]
Pars per tall' 10s. 2 Ø De Anketino de Betteuil 20s. pro plegio eiusdem.[2]
Pauper De Roberto Camayl 1m. pro eodem. [cf. **221**]

  1. Writ of respite (attached), 10 May 1277, to sheriffs of London concerning a total debt of £23 (i.e. including fines arising from **663** and **782**). Acquittance Michaelmas 1277 (E 159/51 m 1d).
  2. Paid Easter 1278 (E 401/88 m. 1).

548. *T. Radulfus per tall'* + *De Roberto de Hakeney cuteler di. m. quia non venit.[1]
T. Radulfus per tall' + *De Radulfo le Paumer cuteler 1m. pro plegio eiusdem.[2]
T. Radulfus per tall' + *De Salomone le Cuteler 40d. pro eodem.[3]
Obiit pauper + De Johanne de Mymmes di. m.
Vad' Arraz 2 + De Johanne le Marbrer 40d.
Obiit pauper De Nicholao May coureor 40d.
T. Radulfus per tall' + *De Ada le Chaundeler di. m.
T. Radulfus per tall' + *De Stephano le Feron de Conductu di. m.[4]
T. + *De Gyloto le Rus cordwaner di. m.[5]

The Estreat (The Exchequer Summons)

In respectu per preceptum scaccarii usque ad festum Sancti Michaelis[6] 2 De Willelmo Bonafaunt seler 40d.
T. + *De Edwardo le Mercer 40d.[7] [cf. **222**]

    1–4. Paid Easter 1277 (E 401/84 m. 3).
    5. Paid Easter 1278 (E 401/88 m. 7).
    6. Michaelmas 1277 (E 368/51 m. 7d).
    7. Paid Easter 1278 (E 401/88 m. 7).

549. *In calumpnia* De Gregorio de Rokesle et Henrico le Waleys vicecomitibus de catallis Petri de la Mote fugitivi 2s.
Obiit pauper De Henrico de Suffolk vicino 40d. quia non venit. [cf. **223**]

550. *Nichil* [*in ballio*] De magistro Boneto clerico regis 40s. pro fuga Willelmi servientis sui qui fugit; in manupastu. [cf. **226**]
T. *De Johanne Prudford Keu[1] 40d. quia non habet quem plegiavit.

    1. Not in plea roll.

551. T. *nr' Turrim* *De communitate Judeorum Anglie de fine 1,000 li. pro pluribus transgressionibus.[1]

    1. Unrelated to the amercements of 1270–1 and not arising from **296** or **308**; perhaps part of a larger fine (*C.C.R. 1272–9*, 265, 271–4, 298, 306; *C.F.R. 1272–1307*, 66–7).

552. *Midd' Episcopo ignotus* De Roberto filio Petri de Stebenheth 40d. quia non venit primo die.
De Willelmo Godwyne de Hendon, Willelmo Spileman fratre eius, Johanne Spendelove, Rogero[1] Edwyne, Radulfo Swthingg, Johanne Strip, Johanne Whitsone, Willelmo Bagel, Hugone le Porcher, Johanne de Hese, Waltero de Clive, Hugone de Cruce et Henrico Fige 20s. pro plegio eiusdem. [cf. **227**][2]

    1. *Reginaldus* (**227**).
    2. Considerable variation in the spelling of names.

Amercements, 1271–2

553. R. *Wal 40d. Ro clerici res'* 2 De Ricardo Waleden vicino quia non venit; Ricardo le Cupere ⟨*obiit pauper ante iter*⟩ et Galfrido le Forbor di. m. + pro plegio ciusdem. [cf. **228**]

554. *In calumpnia* Ø De Johanne de Buddel et Ricardo de Parys vicecomitibus de catallis Galfridi le Marescal fugitivi 20s.[1] [cf. **231**]

    1. Payment in excess of this sum *pro transgressionibus* Easter 1278 (E 401/88 m. 7).

555. *Breve in scaccario de quietancia pro Ricardo*[1] *De eisdem vicecomitibus pro evasione Roberti de Hadestok, Johanne Porteroye [sic], Matildis la White et Juliane de Wynthon fugitivorum 80 li. [cf. **230**]

    1. Both sheriffs (one of them now deceased) were acquitted of this and other debts 20 July 1276 (E 368/50 m. 1). Commissioners of oyer and terminer, appointed 8 July 1276, heard their case in the husting (*C.P.R. 1272–81*, 179).

556. T. *Radulfus* *De Jacobo Bonacours vicino quia non venit; Thoma Purte et Nicholao le Taverner di. m. pro plegio eiusdem. [cf. **232**]

Amercements, 1272–3

557. *Calumpnia* Ø De Johanne Horn vicecomite de catallis Hugonis Caldewell fugitivi 18s.[1]

The Estreat (The Exchequer Summons)

De eodem de catallis eiusdem di. m. [cf. **234**]

    1. *28s.* (**234**).

558. *De Constancia ⟨ignota⟩ que fuit uxor Willelmi Tuk quia non venit; Willelmo Fucher et Mauricio de Sandwyce ⟨ignotus⟩ di. m. pro plegio eiusdem. [cf. **235**]

559. *T. per tall' et denarios* Ø *De Willelmo le Teler ⟨40d.⟩ bracerio quia non venit; Roberto de Malling et Thoma le Barber ⟨40d.⟩ di. m. pro plegio eiusdem.

T. precip' levar' fac' Ø De Elya de Rokele quia non venit; Roberto le Escot et Matheo de Carun 1m. pro plegio eiusdem *unde Elya 20d.*

Midd' De Thoma Carun[1] pro se et plegiis suis di. m. quia non venit. [cf. **237**]

    1. *Baron* (**237**).

560. *Ignotus* De Johanne fratre Petri de Stonhale 40d. quia non venit.

Breve de respectu prius[1] Ø De Joceo le Acatour 1m. pro plegio eiusdem.

T. Ø *De Willelmo de Enefeud 40d. pro eodem. [cf. **239**]

    1. Cf. **527**.

561. *T. 2* *De Ricardo de Sancto Botulfo vicino 40d. quia non venit.

Pars pro Henrico per denarios T. pro Roberto per denarios et tall' De Henrico le Wympeler ⟨8s. 4d.⟩ et Roberto Gratefige ⟨8s. 4d. *per denarios et per tall'* 20d.⟩ 20s. pro plegio eiusdem.[1] [cf. **241**]

    1. Part paid for Robert Gratefige, Easter 1278 (E 401/88 m. 7).

562. *Pars pro Elya* De Huberto le Taylur[1] ⟨mendic'⟩ vicino quia non venit; Stephano de Suffolk pistore, Ricardo le Fevere ⟨*obiit pauper ante iter*⟩ pro plegio eiusdem. Elya Pikard ⟨20d.⟩ et Johanne le Wyntere ⟨ignotus⟩ vicinis di. m. quia non veniunt. [cf. **240, 244**]

    1. As Hubert le Taylur was a neighbour in two pleas (**240, 244**) the exchequer clerk entered all the neighbours together.

563. *Pars pro Willelmo* De Willelmo le Breware ⟨40d.⟩, Willelmo de Suffolk, Ricardo de Scotewy, Nicholao de Oxonia, Hugone le Brewere et Johanne le Taylur di. m. pro plegio eiusdem. [cf. **244**]

564. *Episcopo.*[1] *Totus iste passus vacat a Willelmo de Haringore usque Nicholaum de Winton in summonicione de anno septimo. Memorandum quod vicecomites oneratur de 5 solidis pro priorissa sanctimonialium de Cestrehunt. Recept' Radulfi 15 li. 16s. 6d. in denariis. Memorandum quod Radulfus acquietavit vicecomitatu residum de 8s. 8d. Item de 40s. 10d. de quibus idem Radulfus talliam fieri fecit adhuc alloc'. Memorandum quod Radulfus fecit allocari Roberto de Arraz 13 li. 11s. 8d. de pecunia retenta de itinere Midd. Et sic ret' plus quam fecit allocari 40s. 10d. Et remanent de superplus 63s. 4d. videlicet de predicta priorissa 5m., de W.[2] le Walerand di. m.*[3]

[For Robert Randolf][4] De Willelmo de Haringey de Hakeney, Roberto Marchaunt de eadem di. m. quia non habuerunt Robertum Randolf primo die quem plegiaverunt. De Johanne Goldston, Roberto de Sakewell de Hakeneye di. m. pro eodem. De Henrico Atelane de Schoredich et Ricardo Clerico de Hakeney di. m. De Johanne de Aston de Hakeneye, Johanne Pede de eadem di. m. De Ricardo Aylward de Hakeneye, Ricardo le Veer de eadem di. m. De Roberto le Rus de eadem, Johanne le Stor de Stebbenheth di. m.

[For William Turgis] De Willelmo le Ver de Hakeneye, Willelmo Charle de

The Estreat (The Exchequer Summons)

eadem, Henrico le Schoueler de eadem et Johanne le Ver de eadem 1m. quia non habuerunt Willelmum Turgis primo die quem plegiaverunt. De Thoma le Freman de Hakeneye, Ricardo le Woder de Stebbenheth, Ricardo le Schapman de Hakeneye et Willelmo Bissop 1m. De Laurencio Mauntel de Haliwell, Johanne Atenhok, Willelmo le Fevere et Warino Grosyle 1m.

[For Richard de Hoke] De Willelmo Atemere de Hakeneye, Johanne Atenhegge de eadem, Edmundo Kyse de Stebenheth et Willelmo Ategrove de Hakeney 1m. pro eodem. De Roberto Rog', Warino Selketop, Ricardo Leuys et Adineto Merk 1m. De Ricardo le Canon de Hakeney, Ricardo Pye de eadem, Ricardo Gilbert de eadem et Willelmo Warin 1m.

[For Robert de Hull] De Willelmo Brouning, Ricardo filio Roberti de Hakeney, Alano filio Philippi de eadem, Willelmo Atebrok 1m. quia non habuerunt Robertum de Hull quem plegiaverunt. De Rogero Brouning de Stebbenheth, Roberto Atewell de eadem, Waltero[5] Atemerk et Ricardo Atenhull 1m. De Ricardo filio Petri de eadem, Warino Attestile, Willelmo Goding et Waltero Atemere de Hakeney 1m.[6]

[For Robert Swayn] De Ada de Caldelond de Stebbenheth, Ricardo Atepirie de Iseldon, Willelmo Pyg de Hakeneye et Roberto Coleman 1m. quia non habuerunt Robertum Swayn primo die quem plegiaverunt. De Osberto Atewell de Hakeneye, Ricardo Osbern de eadem, Johanne Atenasse de eadem et Ricardo Patrik 1m. De Johanne Selketop de Hakeney, Waltero le Wodeward, Willelmo Aston et Ricardo Swayn 1m.[7]

[For William Tuler] *Der' s. p.* De Brouningo Mauntel de Schordich, Ricardo Mauntel de eadem, Johanne le Pyl de eadem et Willelmo Wranghorn de eadem 1m. quia non habuerunt Willelmum Tuler.[8] De Ricardo Atewell, Reginaldo Alvene, Roberto Nichol et Godefrido le Tuler 1m. De Paulino Herion de Schordich, Ada Herion de eadem, Daniel le Tuler et Herione de Hoxston 1m.

[For Robert Prituse] De Roberto Ateponde de Hakeney, Henrico le Nas de Stebbenheth, Ricardo le Veyr de Hakeneye, Reginaldo Newman 1m. quia non habuerunt Robertum Pretewse quem plegiaverunt. [m. 3] De Alano Dusse, Willelmo Brid, Salomone Ateclive de Stebbenheth et Ricardo Arthur de Hakeneye 1m. De Johanne Godingg de Stebbenheth, Hugone Goding de eadem, Johanne filio Roberti de Edelmeton et Johanne le Sender de Stebbenheth 1m. [cf. **245**]

1. Repeated several times.
2. ? Recte *J.*
3. These irregularly spaced annotations are presumably the work of the London sheriffs of 7 Edward I.
4. The names of the mainpernors are printed in seven paragraphs, and for ease of reference, the name of the person mainprized is supplied in square brackets at the beginning of each paragraph.
5. *Roberto* (**245**).
6. Walter Atemere not in **245**.
7. William Aston and Richard Swayn not in **245**.
8. Membrane damaged at this point.

Amercements, 1273–4

565. (? *Sumoneatur*) *apud Hertford* 40d. *pro Henrico unde E.*[1] *respondebit* De Laurencio de Amewell di. m. quia non venit; Ricardo de Ware et Henrico de Ware pro plegio eiusdem.

2 De Nicholao de Wynthon vicecomite 20s. pro pluribus transgressionibus.[2]

Per breve[3] *De Henrico de Coventre 10 li. pro eodem.

Pauperes[4] De Simone le Clerc bereman 100s. quia non habuit Ricardum Werry quem plegiavit.

Pars De Edmundo ⟨40d.⟩ de Suffolk vinetario 100s. pro eodem.

The Estreat (The Exchequer Summons)

Pars ⟨*De Willelmo le* ...⟩[5]
De Waltero de Glouc' 100s.
De Waltero le Pendere 100s.
De Roberto de Retherh' 100s.
De Henrico le Wowere bereman 100s.
De Rogero le Seler 100s.
De Roberto de Ware 100s.
De Salomone le Jonior 100s.
De Ada Spendelove bereman 100s.
Pars De Willelmo Barber serviente Johannis Adrian ⟨*di. m.*⟩ 20s. de eodem. (? *pleg' de alquand' vic' s'*). [cf. **246**]

1. Presumably Walter de Essex, sheriff.
2. Respite Trinity 1277 (E 368/50 m. 6).
3. Cf. **529**.
4. Referring to Simon le Clerc and the subsequent debtors in **565**.
5. The line has been erased.

566. *Ignotus* De Rogero le Petit serviente Henrici de Coventre 20s. pro transgressione. *Johanne Painasset, Philippo Fre* ... [cf. **249**]

567. *Pars per breve*[1]. *De Roberto de Kedermenstre quia non venit; Willelmo le Engleys et Waltero Welles di. m. pro plegio eiusdem.[2]
Pauperes De Humfrido le Taylur[3] et Johanne ⟨? *nullus*⟩ Cristemes di. m. pro fuga Johannis le Gaunter. [cf. **250**]

1. Writ (attached), 12 July 1277, to the sheriffs of London, informing them of Robert's payment and ordering them to return any distraints.
2. Robert's share paid Easter 1277 (E 401/84 m. 7).
3. Paid Easter 1280 (E 401/95 m. 2).

568. *T.* *De Nicholao de Gorham fruter vicino quia non venit; Andrea le Barbere et Michaele le Taylur ⟨*pauper*⟩ di. m. pro plegio eiusdem. [cf. **252**]

569. *Vad' pars pro Waltero 5s. per tall'* De Waltero de la Forde et Ada de Walsingham ⟨*obiit pauper ante iter*⟩ di. m. quia non habent Sauncelinam[1] quam plegiaverunt. *unde Adam 20d.*
De Willelmo de Mare gaunter vicino quia non venit; Elya Sadde ⟨*obiit pauper*⟩ et Roberto de Horsam ⟨*submersit; obiit pauper*⟩ di. m. pro plegio eiusdem. [cf. **253**]

1. *Sauncelinam* supplied from **253**.

Amercements, 1274–5

570. *Pauper* Ø De Gyloto le Moler quia non venit; Huberto de Arraz et Radulfo de Ryngefeld[1] pro plegio eiusdem 1m. *unde Hubertus 10s.* [cf. **254**]

1. *Rumford* (**254**).

571. *Nichil [in ballio]* De Luca de Batencort vicecomite 20 li. pro evasione magistri Semanni.
Ultra mare De Odyno de Gare,[1] Galfrido serviente suo 5m. quia non venit.
T. Ø De Willelmo de Enefeud et Radulfo de Arraz[2] di. m. pro plegio eiusdem.
De Ranulfo de Hexham aurifabro ⟨*ignotus*⟩, David le Escot ⟨*obiit pauper*⟩ di. m. pro eodem.
. De Johanne le Taylur 40d. pro eodem. [cf. **257**]

1. *Oto de Gask* (**257**).
2. Paid 12 Edward I (E 372/130 m. 1).

The Estreat (The Exchequer Summons)

572. *Calumpnia* De Luca de Batencourt et Henrico de Frowyk vicecomitibus de catallis Galfridi Whytyng 3s.
De eodem Luca 100s. de catallis eiusdem.
Pauperes De Petro le Cotiler vicino ⟨*obiit pauper*⟩ quia non venit; Johanne de Castello ⟨*potarius apud Turrim*⟩ et Leone Clerico di. m. pro plegio eiusdem. [cf. **258**]

573. *Breve de Perdonacione*[1] *De Reymundo de Bordeus 20s. pro fuga Petri garcionis sui.
T. *De Roberto le Marescal et Ismania uxore eius di. m. quia non veniunt.
Obiit pauper De magistro Thoma le Surisien di. m. pro eodem.
Pars pro Ada Ø De Henrico de Roff', Thoma Finthard ⟨*obiit pauper*⟩, Ada le Barber ⟨*2s. 2d. ob.*⟩ di. m. pro plegio eiusdem.
Ø De Jacobo Coco, Michaele le Taylur ⟨*pauper*⟩ et Nicholao de Gotham di. m. pro plegio eiusdem. [cf. **260**]
  1. Respite Michaelmas 1277 (E 159/51 m. 15).

574. *Pauperes* . De Roberto le Taylur vicino quia non venit; Michaele le Taylur et Augustino le Taylur di. m. pro plegio eiusdem. [cf. **259**]
Calumpnia De Luca de Batencort et Henrico de Frowyk vicecomitibus de catallis Alexandri de Bestenore qui abiuravit regnum 1m. [cf. **262**]

575. *Breve*[1] De eisdem vicecomitibus pro evasione Ricardi le Escot de comitatu Northumb' et Johanne le Ismongere de Fremingham et Ricardo le Clerc de Wynton' 60 li. [cf. **263**]
  1. Presumably one of the writs attached below (cf. **591** n. 3) which properly belongs here.

576. De eisdem vicecomitibus de catallis Walteri Cadaz fugitivi 16d. [cf. **264**]
De Johanne de Sancto Albano ⟨*obiit pauper*⟩, Ada de Ismongerelane ⟨*Suwerk*⟩, Roberto Coco, Alano le Barber ⟨*Alanus pauper*⟩ et Ricardo[1] le Borser 40s. quia non habuerunt quem plegiaverunt. *per pleg' Henrici vicecomitis.*
T. Ro 2 Ø De Waltero filio Ade le Hurer quia non est prosecutus appellum; Roberto le Cordwaner et Roberto fratre eiusdem Walteri di. m. pro plegio eiusdem. [cf. **266**]
  1. *Robertus* (266).

577. Ø De Johanne de Calabre quia non est prosecutus appellum; Ricardo Rose et Alexandro de Godeford[1] di. m. pro plegio eiusdem.
T. *De Petro Gwillame 20s. quia non habet Galfridum Whyting quem manucepit. [cf. **267**]
  1. *Codeford* (267).

AMERCEMENTS, 1275–6

578. *T. 2* Ø De Johanne de Oxonia vicino di. m. quia non venit.
Pars pro Ricardo Ø De Ricardo de Exepote ⟨*40d.*⟩ et Johanne Wyther ⟨*apud Guldeford*⟩ di. m. pro plegio eiusdem. [cf. **271**]

579. *T. Radulfus 2* Ø De Wyoto Clerico di. m. quia non est prosecutus appellum.
T. (? *J. addr' res*') *2* Ø De Waltero Wysman et Johanne Heron di. m. pro plegio eiusdem.
T. pars W. et R. Ø De Willelmo de Blida[1] aurifabro ⟨*26d. ob.*⟩, Johanne de Parys ⟨*40d. Ro cleric'*⟩ et Radulfo de Balesham ⟨*40d.*⟩ di. m. quia non habent quem plegiaverunt.

The Estreat (The Exchequer Summons)

*Pars pro R. de Mor*² De Roberto de la Mor lorimer ⟨40d.⟩; Ricardo le Paumer seler ⟨*pauper*⟩ et Roberto Peche ⟨*pauper*⟩ 10s. pro eodem.

Pars pro R. et R. De Roberto de Assindon seler ⟨40d.⟩, Ricardo de Strate seler ⟨40d.⟩, Ricardo Joce seler 10s. pro eodem.

Pars pro Ricardo De Roberto le Chaumberleng, Johanne de Westle et Ricardo de Balesham ⟨40d.⟩ 10s. pro eodem. [cf. **272**]

1. Paid Easter 1278 (E 401/88 m. 7).
2. Respite, with others, Trinity 1277 (E 368/50 m. 6).

580. Ø De Roberto¹ le Ploumere di. m. quia non est prosecutus appellum.

T. *De Johanne Atestronde et Henrico Appeleye di. m. pro plegio eiusdem.

T. *De Hugone de Biflete di. m. quia non habet quem plegiavit.

T. Radulfus *De Galfrido Fros piscenario di. m. pro eodem.

T. per duas tallias Ø *De Ricardo de Bristoll² et Roberto de Totenham³ di. m. pro eodem.

Hibern' Ø De Roberto Passelewe 40d. pro eodem.

T. *De Gilberto le Tor di. m. pro eodem.

T. *De Gilberto de Pelham ⟨di. m.⟩ ⁴ 1m. pro eodem.

T. *De Petro de Therringg di. m. pro eodem.

Pauper De Rogero de Oxonia cordwaner 40d. pro eodem.

Pauper Ø De Roberto le Fisicien et Roberto filio eius di. m. quia non venerunt. [cf. **273**]

1. *Johanne* (**273**).
2–4. Paid Easter 1278 (E 401/88 mm. 4, 7, 8).

581. *Pauper* Ø De Alicia de Kancia quia non venit et Johanne le Barber iuxta Newgate et Ricardo Coco de Fridaistrete di. m. pro plegio eiusdem.

Pauper De Gerardo Beynin et Willelmo de Wycombe di. m. pro plegio eiusdem.

De Matheo de Lincoln et Ricardo de Herewes di. m. pro eodem. [cf. **274**]

582. Ø De Johanne Horn et Radulfo le Blund vicecomitibus de catallis Alexandri le Fraunkeleyn ⟨*suspensus*⟩ di. m. [cf. **276**]

583. *T. Radulfus per duas tallias* *De Willelmo de Storteford gaunter, Rogero de Ponte feron di. m. quia non habent quem plegiaverunt.

T. Radulfus le Fevere *De Willelmo Amys pessoner di. m. pro eodem.

T. Radulfus per duas tallias *De Aylwyno de Ponte et Willelmo de Essex cornur di. m.

T. Radulfus per tall' *De Johanne de Depe di. m.

T. Radulfus per tall' *De Bartholomeo de Capella gaunter di. m.

T. Radulfus X *De Johanne Hurel feroun di. m.

T. Radulfus per tall' . *De Milone de Oysterhull di. m.

T. Radulfus X *De Daniele de Ponte 40d.

J. de Cobeham pars 5s. De Hermanno le Estreys 10s.¹ [cf. **279**]

1. Paid Hilary 1281 (E 401/97 m. 9).

584. *Addr' ad di. m. pro se et plegiis suis* De Edmundo Pecok et Waltero le Poletere di. m. quia non habent Dionysiam Lovecote.

De Willelmo Slych et Willelmo de Hertford di. m. pro eodem.

De Willelmo de Waltham cordwaner di. m.¹

De Johanne de Smethefeld di. m.²

De Nicholao le Chaundeler et Waltero Chobbe di. m.

De Gamelino Canon, Johanne le Cuver di. m.³

The Estreat (The Exchequer Summons)

De Johanne le Seriaunt 40d. [cf. **284**]

    1–2. Paid among *parciales* of the eyre 13 Edward I (E 372/130 m. 10d).
    3. Paid by Richard le Cuver Easter 1278 (E 401/88 m. 7). Neither John nor Richard occur in **284**.

585. *Calumpnia* Ø De Johanne Horn et Radulfo le Blund vicecomitibus de catallis Henrici de Huvill[1] suspensi 5s. [cf. **284**]

    1. *Lynnhull* (**284**).

586. De eisdem vicecomitibus de catallis Holdin le Tailur confiscatis 20s. pro fuga. [cf. **286**]

587. *Pars 20s. T. 2* De Willemo le Flaoner de fine 40s. *solvit 20s.* (? *J. addr'*) *per pl' Roberti de Norwyco et Thome le Flaoner.* [cf. **287**]

588. *Bek' Herlewyn levar' fac'* De Waltero de Saunford quondam vicecomite Midd pro evasione Ricardi Atenhal et Walteri fratris eius 10 li. [cf. **280**]

589. *Breve prius*[1] De Henrico de Coventre pro evasione Nicholai de Staunford 20 li.
De eodem Henrico pro receptamento Gyloti garcionis Ricardi de Laminesse qui consensit predicte evasioni 10 li. [cf. **289**]

    1. Cf. **529, 565**.

590. *Redd'*[1] De Stephano de Eddwrth de catallis Roberti Pointel 40s. [cf. **290**]

    1. *Bedford* (**290; 650**; among the *parciales* of the eyre 13 Edward I, E 372/130 m. 10d).

Escapes

591. *Lynton 10 li. per tall' pro Roberto* Ø *De Roberto de Lynton[1] et Willelmo de Assewy nuper vicecomitibus pro evasione Johannis de Frome 20 li. Linton.*[2]
Breve pro Johanne *De Johanne de Norh' et Ricardo Pikard vicecomitibus pro evasione quatuor sociorum Rogeri de Clere 80 li.
Breve pro Henrico ut prius *De Henrico de Frowyk et Luca de Batencort vicecomitibus pro evasione Rogeri Drinkwater et 12 sociorum suorum 260 li.[3]
Breve prius[4] *De Henrico de Coventre vicecomite pro evasione Arnaldi Petri fugitivi 20 li.
*De eodem Henrico pro evasione Thome de Barthon fugitivi 20 li.
*De eodem Henrico de catallis eiusdem 4 li. 10s.
*De eodem Henrico quia concelavit catalla illa et evasit illos 10 li. [cf. **316**]

    1. Writ (attached), 21 July 1277, to sheriffs of London, informing them of payment by Robert of £10 and ordering them to make no further demands and to return distraints.
    2. With pointing hand.
    3. Cf. **575** n. 1. Writ of respite (attached), 20 Feb. 1276, to sheriffs of London, promising further consideration after the King's return from Wales. Acquittance of £110 of a total of £160 [sic] and attermination of the remainder, 12 May 1277 (*C.C.R. 1272–9*, 385). Michaelmas 1280 given as day for final settlement in Memoranda Roll, Trinity 1280 (E 368/53 m. 7d).
    4. Cf. **529, 565, 589**.

Amercements, 1255–6

592. *Catalla calumpnia* De Matheo Bukerel et Johanne le Minur vicecomitibus de catallis Willelmi de Langeford qui abiuravit regnum 2s. [cf. **66**]

The Estreat (The Exchequer Summons)

593. *T. R.* Ø De Thoma le Waleys puleter vicino quia non venit; Radulfo de Bedford parmentario et Henrico de Staundon di. m. pro plegio eiusdem. [cf. 67]

594. *Tenementa et redditus* De Matheo Bokerel et Johanne le Minur vicecomitibus de anno et vasto terre Philippi de Glouc' di. m. [cf. 72]

Amercements, 1256–7

595. *Midd' et Essex* *De Ricardo de Ewell vicecomite 10 li. pro pluribus transgressionibus. [cf. 76]

596. *W. att'* De Willelmo Assewy et Ricardo de Ewell vicecomitibus de catallis magistri Ade de Lynton fugitivi 20m.
De eisdem vicecomitibus de anno et vasto domus eiusdem 2m.
De eisdem vicecomitibus [de] medio tempore eiusdem domus 38m.
Templ' De magistro Milicie Templi in Anglia quia cepit catalla illa sine warranto et pro receptamento predicti Ade post factum 20 li. [cf. 75]

Amercements, 1257–8

597. *Calumpnia* Ø De Thoma filio Thome et Willelmo Gratefige vicecomitibus de catallis Thome Atewode qui abiuravit regnum 1m. [cf. 79]

598. *Domus vacat* De Johanne filio et herede Henrici de Bathon et herede ⟨Mathei⟩[1] de la Mare de catallis Oliveri de Wynchels' 20m. [cf. 80]
   1. *Henr'* deleted.

599. [m. 4] *Breve de respectu*[1] De herede Mathei Bukerel vicecomitis pro evasione Johannis Wodman fugitivi 20 li.
Calumpnia De eodem vicecomite de catallis eiusdem 14d. [cf. 83]
   1. Not traced in Memoranda Rolls. The combined debt of £20 1s. 2d. removed to the Pipe Roll 13 Edward I (E 372/130 m. 10).

Amercements, 1258–9

600. *Pauper T. Ro 2* De Reginaldo le Barbour 40d. quia non habuit Johannem de Coventre quem plegiavit.
Pars per tall' 2 marc' di. T. 2 De Johanne Adrian vicecomite 5m. pro pluribus transgressionibus.
T. Ro 2 . De Petro de Gysorc' camerario di. m. pro eodem. [cf. 86–7]

601. *Calumpnia* Ø De Johanne Adrian et Roberto de Cornhull vicecomitibus de catallis Lucie la Braceresse weyvate 3s. [cf. 89]

602. *Nichil* [*in ballio*] Ø De Stephano de Smethefeld quia non venit; Thoma le Sopere et Johanne le Cordwaner di. m. pro plegio eiusdem. [cf. 91]

603. De eisdem Johanne et Roberto vicecomitibus de catallis Henrici de Wokyndon qui abiuravit regnum 5s. [cf. 92]

604. *Pars pro J. T. 2*[1] *per tres tallias Johannis de la Toure* De Petro de Flegh vicino quia non venit et Johanne de la Tour ⟨40d.⟩ pro plegio eiusdem 10s. *unde Petrus 40d.* [cf. 93]
   1. With horizontal line crossed through twice.

The Estreat (The Exchequer Summons)

605. *Pars* Ranulfus et Ricardus solverunt 4s. 7d. De Ranulfo Lyne ⟨*solvit 2s. 4d.*⟩, Ricardo Corteys ⟨*solvit 2s. 3d.*⟩ et Roberto Nicholao di. m. quia non venit.
Radulfus le Fevre pauperes De Hamone le Drawer quia non venit; Fulcone le Drawer et Henrico le Drawer di. m. pro plegio eiusdem. [cf. **99**]

Amercements, 1259–60

606. *Pauperes* De Thoma de Norht' et Willelmo le Taylur di. m. quia falso presentaverunt se vicinos. [cf. **101**]

607. T. *De Thoma Pourt pro receptamento Willelmi Knyth qui fuit de manupastu suo 40d.[1] [cf. **102**]

  1. Paid Easter 1278 (E 401/88 m. 7).

608. *W. et A. obierunt pauperes breve pro R, distr'*[1] *pro tall'* De Ricardo Amberesbire[2] vicino quia non venit. Willelmo le Chaundeler et Ada Pistore di. m. pro plegio eiusdem. [cf. **103**]

  1. Writ (attached), 28 June 1277, to sheriffs of London, informing them of Richard's full payment of 6s. 8d. and ordering them to make no further demands and to return distraints.
  2. Paid Easter 1278 (E 401/88 m. 7).

609. *Pars pro H. per tall'* Ø De Humfrido le Megucer[1] ⟨*20d.*⟩ vicino quia non venit; Willelmo le Megucer et Gilberto le Marescal di. m. pro plegio eiusdem. [cf. **105**]

  1. Paid Easter 1278 (E 401/88 m. 7).

Amercements, 1260–1

610. *Pars pro J. T. Ro 2* De Johanne ad Crucem vicino ⟨*40d.*⟩ quia non venit; Radulfo le Large et Ricardo le Cupere di. m. ⟨*unde J. 40d.*⟩ pro plegio eiusdem. [cf. **108**]

611. *Vad'* De Petro le Vineter vicino quia non venit; Gervasio de Notingham 40d. pro plegio eiusdem. [cf. **109**]

612. Ø De Johanne le Carpenter vicino quia non venit et Baldewyno de Gaunt di. m. pro plegio eiusdem. [cf. **114**]

613. *Pauper* De Matheo de Pontefracto[1] 100s. quia non habuit Arnulfum monacum de Bermund quem manucepit.
Atterm'[2] *per tall' 10s.* De Jacobo le Peuerer 100s. pro eodem. [cf. **116**]

  1. Part paid Easter 1282 (E 401/101 m. 5). Remaining charge removed to *parciales* of the eyre 13 Edward I (E 372/130 m. 10d).
  2. Instalments paid Easter 1278 (E 401/88 m. 6); Michaelmas 1280 (E 401/97 m. 10); Easter 1282 (E 401/101 m. 7).

614. *Calumpnia* De Johanne de Norht', Ricardo Picard vicecomitibus de catallis Emme uxoris Henrici le Chaloner fugitivi 12d. [cf. **117**]

615. *Breve de respectu*[1] De priore de Bermundesey pro receptamento Arnulphi monachi sui qui interfecit Ricardum Borham 10 li. [cf. **116**]

  1. Writ (attached), 8 May 1277, to sheriffs of London, granting to the prior respite until the next Parliament at Michaelmas.

The Estreat (The Exchequer Summons)

616. *T.* *De Isabella Bokerel di. m. quia non venit.
Ø De Willelmo le Corner et Willelmo de Waltham di. m. pro plegio eiusdem. [cf. **118**]

Amercements, 1261–2

617. *T.* *De Philippo le Taylur vicecomite 20s.[1] pro pluribus transgressionibus. [cf. **119**]

1. Paid Easter 1278 (E 401/88 m. 7).

618. *N.G.W. s* De Nicholao de Wygorn vicino quia non venit; Godefrido de Bromle et Willelmo le Gardiner di. m. pro plegio eiusdem. [cf. **119**]

Amercements, 1262–3

619. *Ignotus* De Ada Beney de Hakene 40d. pro transgressione. [cf. **133**]

620. *Ignotus* De Willelmo filio Ade vicino quia non venit; Rogero le Tyveler di. m. pro eodem. [cf. **134**]

621. Ø De Galfrido le Saltere, Thoma le Barbure[1] vicinis di. m. quia non ven'. [cf. **136**]

1. Paid Easter 1278 (E 401/88 m. 7).

622. *Nichil in ballio T.* 2 De Thoma Vyel di. m. pro falso appello per plegium Willelmi de Hadestok.
Pauper Ø De Roberto le Stur[1] di. m. pro transgressione. [cf. **147**]

1. *de Esture* (**147**).

Amercements, 1263–4

623. *Calumpnia* Ø De Gregorio de Rokesle et Thoma de la Forde vicecomitibus de catallis Walteri garcionis Radulfi Basset fugitivi 2s. [cf. **148**]

624. *Breve ut prius*[1] De Reginaldo de Suffolk camerario 100s. pro pluribus transgressionibus. [cf. **151**]

1. Cf. **292, 527, 757**.

625. *Pauperes obierunt* De Constantino le Broker, Ricardo le Mercer, Henrico Deubeney custodibus de Alegate pro evasione Hugonis de Staunford 20 li. [cf. **153**]

626. *Pauperes* De Johanne le Suur vicino quia non venit; Roberto de Sancto Egidio et Willelmo de Glouc' di. m. pro plegio eiusdem. [cf. **155**]

Amercements, 1264–5

627. *Pars 10s. T. duas tall'* 2 De magistro hospitalis Sancte Katerine 20s.[1] pro receptamento Thome le Gardiner.
Pauperes Ø De Johanne de Kancia girdeler vicino quia non venit; Stephano de Hundesdich et Roberto de Retherheth di. m. pro plegio eiusdem. [cf. **156**]

1. Paid Easter 1282 (E 401/101 m. 9).

The Estreat (The Exchequer Summons)

628. *Tall' vad'*[1] *In calumpnia per breve J. addr'*[2] + De Johanne filio Johannis de Gysorz 10 li.[3] quia non respondet de tempore patris sui quondam vicecomitis.[4] [cf. **19, 24, 25**][5]

1. With pointing hand.
2. Trinity 1277 John is given a day three weeks from Michaelmas 1277 to make amends and give account (E 368/53 m. 7 but no writ is cited). Cf. n. 3 below.
3. Paid Easter 1277 (E 401/83 m. 1).
4. Recte *camerarii* or perhaps *aldermanni*. The error was not perpetuated on the Memoranda or Receipt Rolls.
5. Or perhaps **159, 181** (see n. 4 above).

629. De Galfrido[1] de Hundesdich tanner di. m.[2] quia non habet quem plegiavit. [cf. **156**]

1. *Stephanus* (**156**).
2. Removed to Pipe Roll 5 Edward I (E 372/121 m. 18d).

630. *Pars pro W. T. Ro 2* De Johanne Stacy et Waltero ⟨*40d.*⟩ Bole[1] di. m. pro eodem. [cf. **157**]

1. Paid 7 Edward I (E 372/123 m. 9).

631. *Calumpnia* Ø De Johanne filio et herede Edwardi le Blund et herede Petri Aunger de catallis Henrici Russel fugitivi 18d.
Pars pro J. Ø De Waltero de Sutht' quia non venit; Johanne de Sutht' ⟨*di. m.*⟩ et Johanne de la Lade 10s. pro plegio eiusdem *unde Johannes de Sutht' solvit di. m.*
T. *De Roberto de Doveria quia non venit; Stephano le Gorger et Alano de Karl di. m. pro plegio eiusdem.
T. tall' levand' Ø *De Johanne de Godington 40d.[1] quia non habet quem plegiavit. [cf. **159**]

1. Paid Easter 1278 (E 401/88 m. 8).

632. *Calumpnia* + De Johanne filio et herede Edwardi le Blund et herede Petri Aunger vicecomitum de catallis Henrici le Hors fugitivi 10s.
+ De eisdem de catallis Ade de Pampeworth fugitivi di. m.
+ De eisdem de catallis Johannis le Botiler fugitivi 1m. [cf. **163**]

633. Ø De Johanne le Barber vicino quia non venit; Waltero de Brakel et Johanne le Paumer di. m. pro plegio eiusdem. [cf. **165**]

634. *T. per tall' et denarios* Ø *De Roberto de Fridaistrete ⟨*40d.*⟩ pro se et plegiis suis di. m.[1] quia non venit. [cf. **166**]

1. Paid Easter 1278 (E 401/88 m. 8).

635. *Ignotus* De Nicholao Portel vicino quia non venit; Hugone le Coureor et Roberto de Sancta Brigide di. m. pro plegio eiusdem. [cf. **168**]

Amercements, 1265–6

636. *Calumpnia* De Johanne Adrian et Waltero Hervy vicecomitibus de catallis Roberti filii Walteri le Carpenter qui abiuravit regnum 9s. 6d. [cf. **172**]

637. *Pars pro Henrico* De Willelmo de Bixle quia non venit; et Henrico Moneor ⟨*40d.*⟩ di. m. pro plegio eiusdem.
Ignoti De Angnete de Chendut quia non venit; Ricardo le Chapeler et Henrico Pistore di. m. pro plegio eiusdem.

The Estreat (The Exchequer Summons)

Ignoti De Ricardo de Hanningthon quia non venit; Willelmo de Haverham et Willelmo le Chapeler di. m. pro plegio eiusdem. [cf. **174**]

638. Ø De Johanne Adrian et Waltero Hervy vicecomitibus pro evasione Rogeri le Tyweler 20 li.
De eisdem vicecomitibus de catallis eiusdem 54s.
T. Ø De Reginaldo de Cantuaria vicino quia non venit; Johanne de Cantuaria cordwaner et Milone de Hibernia di. m. pro plegio eiusdem. [cf. **176**]

639. Ø De Galfrido le Fruter vicino quia non venit; Thoma le Taylur et Johanne le Peleter di. m. pro plegio eiusdem. [cf. **177**]

Amercements, 1266-7

640. Ø De herede Willelmi filii Ricardi quando vicecomitis de catallis Thome de Stocton fugitivi 18d.
Pars pro Willelmo Ø De Henrico de Kensingthon quia non venit; Galfrido de Arcubus, Willelmo de Holeborn ⟨di. m.⟩ pessoner 1m. pro plegio eiusdem. *unde Willelmus dimidiam marcam.*
Ignoti T. 2[1] De Matilde que fuit uxor Gilberti Makeheyt[2] quia non venit et Waltero le Engleys di. m. pro plegio eiusdem. [cf. **181**]
  1. With horizontal line crossed through twice.
  2. Paid Easter 1280 (E 401/95 m. 7).

641. *Pauper* De Alicia de Brakele di. m. quia non venit. [cf. **182**]

642. *Simon apud Modingham* Ø De Stephano Bonior ⟨*pauper*⟩ vicino quia non venit; Symone de Norht' et Willelmo le Callere ⟨*pauper*⟩ 5s. pro plegio eiusdem.
(? *s*) *pauper* Ø De Willelmo Reve quia non habuit Rogerum de Aunger quem manucepit 100s. *per pleg' J. Adriani et L. Batencourt vicecomitum.*
Pauper De Rogero de Mareworth 100s. pro eodem. *per plegium eorundem.*
Pauper De Henrico le Dubbur 100s. pro eodem. *per plegium eorundem.*
Obiit pauper De Petro le Hodere 100s. pro eodem. *per plegium eorundem.*
Pauper De Johanne le Deneman 100s. pro eodem. *per plegium eorundem.*
Mendicans De Jacobo de Halstede 100s. pro eodem. *per plegium eorundem.* [cf. **183**]

643. *T.* *De Osberto le Poleter vicino quia non venit; Henrico le Escot et Ricardo le Seler[1] di. m. pro plegio eiusdem. [cf. **185**]
  1. Payments for Osbert, Henry and Richard, Easter 1277 (E 401/88 m. 6).

644. *Calumpnia* Ø De Johanne Adrian et Luca de Batencort vicecomitibus de catallis Johannis filii Roberti de Eure qui abiuravit regnum 14d. [cf. **186**]
De eisdem vicecomitibus de catallis Galfridi de Beverlaco suspensi 40 li. [cf. **188**]

Amercements, 1267-8

645. *Ignotus adhuc* De Stephano le Taylur de catallis Jaketti le Taylur 5s.
De eodem Stephano quia cepit catalla illa sine waranto di. m. [cf. **189**]

646. *Calumpnia* De Waltero Hervy de catallis Johannis le Paternoster qui abiuravit regnum 22s. [cf. **194**]

The Estreat (The Exchequer Summons)

647. *Pars pro W. Hodin* De Johanne le Clerc batiler ⟨*pauper*⟩ vicino quia non venit; Waltero Hodyn ⟨2s. 2d. ob.⟩ et Willelmo Pepys di. m. pro plegio eiusdem *W. Hodyn 2s. 2d. ob.* [cf. **196**]

648. *Breve* De Johanne de Norht' vicino quia non venit et Hugone le Berman di. m. pro plegio eiusdem. [cf. **197**]

649. *T. per tall' et denarios* *De Andrea de Donstre[1] vicino quia non venit; Johanne de Berkhamstede ⟨40d.⟩ di. m. pro plegio eiusdem. [cf. **198**]

    1. Paid Easter 1278 (E 401/88 m. 8).

AMERCEMENTS, 1268–9

650. *Calumpnia*[1] De Willelmo de Dunelm et Waltero Hervy vicecomitibus de catallis Johannis de Herefeud fugitivi[2] 54s. 6d.
Redd' Bed'[3] De Stephano de Eddeworth camerarii 5m. pro contemptu. [cf. **202**]

    1. Perhaps associated with William de Durham's later step when he empowered his son to act as his attorney for his remaining debts, Trinity 1279 (E 368/52 m. 8).
    2. *Johannes de Hertfeld* was hanged (**202**).
    3. Cf. **590n**.

651. Ø De Roberto Wyberd vicino quia non venit; Roberto de Springham et Ada Picard di. m. pro plegio eiusdem. [cf. **203**]

652. Ø De Henrico Walmound quando ballivo Civitatis 20 li. pro evasione Rogeri de Coventr'. [cf. **204**]

653. *Nichil in ballio* De Hugone de Turbervil 20 li. pro receptamento Roberti le Marescal qui fuit de manupastu suo. [cf. **205**]

AMERCEMENTS, 1269–70

654. *Superplus calumpnia*[1] De Roberto filio Roberti de Cornhull et Thoma de Basingg vicecomitibus de catallis Simonis Ferol felonis de se 3s. 1d. [cf. **206**]

    1. Both annotations presumably refer to discussions at the exchequer which led to a respite, Trinity 1277 (E 368/50 m. 6).

655. *T.* *De Petro le Furbur vicino quia non venit; Thoma Payn sutore et Johanne de Borham coureor di. m. pro plegio eiusdem. [cf. **214**]

656. *J. et R. ignoti Robertus apud Combray* De Johanne Hayward vicino quia non venit; Ricardo le Paternoster et Roberto de Derby[1] di. m. pro plegio eiusdem. [cf. **212**]

    1. *Stroby* (**212**).

657. *Breve atterm'*[1] *Essex* De Galfrido de Rothinges 100s. quia non habuit Ceciliam que fuit uxor Jollani de Dunolm quam manucepit.
T. per tall' *De Henrico le Burger 20s. pro eodem.
Ignotus De Willelmo de Wynteringthon 100s.
Pauper De Roberto de Essex burel 100s.[2]
Ø De Ada le ⟨*Eye*⟩ teinturer 100s.
Pars per tall' Alloc' 1 marca (? *1. per abr'*)* *di. marc'* Ø *De Roberto de Lynton 100s. *Linton*[3]

The Estreat (*The Exchequer Summons*)

T. per tall' di. m. *De Fulcone de Sancto Edmundo 20s.[4] [cf. **209**]

1. Writ of attermination (attached), 10 May 1277, to the sheriffs of London, referring to the Fines Roll [not traced in *C.F.R.*].
2. Although Robert is here described as a pauper, his debt is removed to the Pipe Roll 7 Edward I (E 372/123 m. 9).
3. With pointing hand. Writ (attached), 21 July 1277, to the sheriffs of London, referring to an entry on the Fines Roll [not traced in *C.F.R.*]; Robert is permitted to pay 100s. for his debts in **657** and **663** and the sheriffs are ordered to cease distraint until further notice.
4. Paid Easter 1277 (E 401/84 m. 6).

658. *W. et R. obierunt pauperes G. pauper* De Willelmo le Chaloner quia non venit; Ranulfo le Chaloner et Gilberto le Chaloner di. m. pro plegio eiusdem. [cf. **210**]

659. *Superplus* Ø De Thoma de Basing vicecomite 100s. pro pluribus transgressionibus.

660. *Ignotus adhuc* De Edmundo le Orfevre vicino 40d. quia non venit. [cf. **212**]

661. [m. 5] Ø De Thoma de Basing et Roberto de Cornhull vicecomitibus de catallis Alexandri le Spigornel felonis de se 17s. 4d. [cf. **213**]

662. *Pars pro S. per tall' T. alloc'* *De Ricardo le Armurer vicino quia non venit; Johanne ⟨40d. *sine tallia*⟩ May[1] et Salomone Cotiler[2] di. m. pro plegio eiusdem. [cf. **214**]

1. Paid Easter 1277 (E 401/84 m. 4).
2. Paid Easter 1278 (E 401/88 m. 7).

Assize of Cloth

663.[1] *Tall' penes se de parte de parte 100s. T.*[2] De Johanne Adrian 10 li.[2] pro pannis venditis contra assisam.

Tall' penes se de parte 2m di. T.[2] De Johanne filio eius 5m.[3]
Pars 40d. Ø . De Johanne Norman[4] di. m.
Pars 20s. Ø . De Willelmo de Northawe 40s.[5]
T. per tallias duas *De Anketino de Breteuil 5m.[6] *solvit 50s.*
T. per tall' *De Rogero de Derby 40s.[7]
T. per tall' . *De Reginaldo de Frowyk 1m.[8]
Pauper De Roberto de Camayl di. m.
Breve de respectu ut prius[9] *De Stephano de Cornhull 20 li.
T. Ø . *De Roberto de Lynton di. m. *Linton.*[10]
T. per tall' . *De Willelmo Bokerel 5m.[11]
Episcopo T. Ro 2 De Reginaldo Canon 5m.
(? *Pars 20s.*) *Ro* Ø De Waltero Everard 40s.[12]
T. per tall' *De Johanne de Wylehal 10 li.[13]
T. per duas tallias Ø *De Ricardo fratre eius 2m.[14]
Tall' de di. m. J. addr' res' T. 2 De Johanne Cole 20s.[15]
T. per 2 tallias Ø *De Petro de Edelmeton 100s.[16]
T. per duas tallias X *De Ricardo de Essewy 2m.[17]
Ø De Willelmo de Hadestok 40s.
T. per tall' . *De Willelmo de Wynton 1m.[18]
T. per tall' . *De Galfrido de Gedding 40s.[19]
T. per tall' . *De Willelmo de Gedding 60s.[20] *solverunt 4 li.*[21]
T. per tall' . *De Johanne de Waltham 40s.[22]

The Estreat (The Exchequer Summons)

T. per tall' . *De Thoma filio Thome Junioris [sic] di. m.[23]
Pauper[24] De Johanne Racolf 1m.
Pars di. m. per tall' T. 2 De Thoma Bath 1m.[25] *di. m.*
T. per duas tallias *De Roberto de Arraz di. m.[26]
Di. m. per tall' T. 2 De Johanne Heyron peuerer 1m.[27]
T. per tall' . *De Willelmo de Bek 1m.[28]
T. per tall' *De Willelmo de Betoyne di. m.[29]
Scaccarium De Rusticallo Thedelday 10 li.
In respectu ut prius[30] Ø . De Deotato Gillelmo 20 li.
Essex[31] *De Ricardo de Ewell 10m.
Pars di. m. per tall' T. addr' res' 2 De Roberto Curteys 1m.[32] *solvit di. m.*
Ø De Ingeramo de Bettoyne 1m.[33]
Pars 20s. per tall' De Willelmo Heyron 40s.[34] *solvit di. m.*
40d. tall' 2 . De Willelmo le Hurer di. m.[35]
T. *De Rogero Piggesfles di. m.
T. Radulfus tall' *De Bordino de Gaunt 20s.
T. Ø . *De Johanne de Armenters di. m.
T. . *De Thoma Beuwyn di. m.
T. Radulfus tall' . *De Roberto de Reynham 2m.
Att' ad scaccarium . De Johanne de Brylaunde 20m.
Pars 10s. Radulfus le Fevrer addr' res' De Johanne de Nycole 20s.
T. per tall' *De Ada de Blakeney 1m.[36]
Flandr'[37] De Jakes de Fresang 100s.
⟨*De Ricardo Arraz de Lincoln 100s.*⟩[38]
T. per duas tallias *De Rogero Beynen 5m.[39]
T. per duas tallias . De Willelmo de Boys 5m.
T. per duas tallias . *De Ricardo de Abbyndon 100s.[40]
T. tall' Radulfus . *De Copyn Trossyn 40s.
T. tall' *De Thoma de Melkestrete di. m.[41]
T. De Willelmo ⟨40d.⟩ de Staunff Juniore di. m.[42] *R. de Arraz*
T. tall' . *De Galfrido le Taylur iuxta Sanctum Martinum Magnum di. m.[43]
T. tall' . *De Roberto de Kyderminstre 1m.
Vad' atterm' De Willelmo de Wouborn 1m.
Ignotus T. 2 De Willelmo de Lewes di. m.
Vad' T. 2 De Willelmo le Retoundor 1m.[44] [cf. **294**]

1. Cf. **294** in which the names occur in approximately the same order but includes Robert de Acre of London and Hugh le Tailur of Lincoln who are omitted here. For Flemish merchants included in **294** see **664**.
2–3. Paid Easter 1277 (E 401/84 mm. 2, 4). For John Adrian see also **469**.
4. *Neuman* (**294**). Paid by John le Norman, Easter 1277 (E 401/84 m. 6).
5. Paid Easter 1277 (E 401/84 m. 2).
6–8. Paid Easter 1277 (E 401/83 m. 1).
9. Cf. **547**.
10. With pointing hand. Cf. **657** n. 3.
11. Paid 16s. 8d. Easter 1277 (E 401/83 m. 1).
12. Removed to *Nova oblata* in Pipe Roll 9 Edward I (E 372/125 m. 12d) where record continues: 'de quibus Radulfus [Crepyn] clericus maioris London' debet ipsum acquietare de 20s. sicut rec' et resp' infra. Et debet Walterus 20s. Radulfus clericus maioris London' 20s. pro Waltero Everard sicut supra continetur.'
13. Paid Easter 1277 (E 401/83 m. 1).
14. Paid Easter 1277 (E 401/84 m. 7) and Easter 1278 (E 401/88 m. 8).
15. Paid Easter 1277 (E 401/84 m. 8).
16–17. Paid Easter 1277 (E 401/84 m. 2) and Easter 1278 (E 401/88 m. 2).
18–19. Paid Easter 1277 (E 401/83 m. 1).
20. Paid Easter 1277 (E 401/83 m. 1) and Easter 1278 (E 401/88 m. 8).
21. Referring to both William and Geoffrey.
22–3. Paid Easter 1277 (E 401/83 m. 1).
24. With horizontal line crossed through twice.

The Estreat (The Exchequer Summons)

25. Paid Easter 1277 (E 401/83 m. 1).
26. Paid Easter 1277 (E 401/83 m. 1) and Easter 1278 (E 401/88 m. 7).
27–9. Paid Easter 1277 (E 401/83 m. 1).
30. Cf. **487, 527, 707.**
31. Cf. **595.**
32. Paid Easter 1277 (E 401/83 m. 1).
33. Removed to Pipe Roll 14 Edward I (E 372/131 m. 6) under: 'De amerciamentis per magistrum Rogerum de Seyton. Idem vicecomites debent 1m. de Ingeramo de Wethonia pro pann' vend' contra assisam.'
34–6. Paid Easter 1277 (E 401/83 m. 1; 84 m. 3).
37. A warning that the name belongs with **664.**
38. Attermed in three instalments, 28 June 1284 (*C.F.R. 1272–1307*, 204–5).
39. Paid Easter 1278 (E 401/88 m. 7).
40. Respite Trinity 1277 (E 368/50 m. 6); paid Easter 1277 (E 401/84 m. 1) and Easter 1278 (E 401/88 m. 1).
41. Paid Easter 1277 (E 401/83 m. 1).
42. Paid Easter 1278 (E 401/88 m. 7).
43. Paid Easter 1277 (E 401/83 m. 1).
44. Not in **294**. Paid Easter 1280 (E 401/95 m. 7).

664.[1] *Breve de respectu pro Flandr'*[2] . De Nicholao Cauntingg 4m.
. De Waltero Pedeargent 10m.
. De Waltero filio eius 20s.
. De Waltero Couwyte 100s.
. De Hugone Logger 6m.
. De Petro de Caumbrey 1m.
. De Philippo de Bonebuk 40s.
. De Johanne fratre eius 40s.
. De Jakes de la Barberie 1m.
. De Gerardo de Heryn 1m.
. De Nicholao Wylernale di. m.
. De Gerardo le Carpenter 20s.
. De Cristelot Bel 20s.
. De Ingeramo Falconel 20s.
. De Willelmo Tut dehors 1m.
De Bernardo Pylat 40s.
De Baud de Sevenaunt 100s.
De Jon Bonebroke 10 li.
De Rykewyn de Dowey di. m.
De Johanne Clerico 1m.
De Lotimo de Dowey di. m.
De Gerardo Staleward 6m.
De Thoma fratre eius 6m.
T. 2 De Johanne Plankes di. m.
De Wyse de Plankes 1m.
T. *De Gerardo de Flos di. m.[3]
De Jakes de Landa 100s.
De Amarico de Castel 100s.
De Bernardo de Lynns di. m.
De Jokemes Porteous 6m.
De Gerardo Bonfreyn 6m.
De Nicholao de Scaylon di. m.
De Nicholao Loberge 2m.
De Terrico Baudan di. m.
De Johanne le Clerk de Sevenaunt di. m.
De Baud de Midi 20s.
De Nicholao Curte 20s.
De Egidio de Arraz 20s.

The Estreat (The Exchequer Summons)

De Egidio filio Baldewyny filii Jeremie di. m.
Pr' istius G. De Gerandino de la Vile 20s.
De Ingeramo Alewyn 20s.
De Waltero Musard 1m.
De Lamberto de la Potente 40s.
De Alexandro filio eius 2m.
De Willelmo de Sancto Amando di. m.
De Wamberto Piket di. m.
(? *Dover*) De Gamelino le Vilein di. m.
De Thoma Piket di. m.
De Johanne de Purfeles 40s.
De Sewallo Painmoyle 1m.
De Godefrido filio Odekin 20s.
De Johanne le Parchemener 1m.
T. *De Godefrido le Parchemener di. m.[4] [cf. **264**]

1. The names of Flemish merchants match those in **294**. For Flemish merchants omitted from **294** see **665**.
2. Writ of respite (attached), 13 May 1277, to the sheriffs of London, until the quindene of Michaelmas 1277. The writ also relates to those in **665**.
3-4. Paid Easter 1278 (E 401/88 m. 7).

665.[1] De Johanne de Stanstrate 1m.
De Johanne de Syhen 5m.
De Johanne de Ravenescote di. m.
De Ebor' Crane di. m.
De Salamone de Holebourne di. m.
De Johanne Gyrime 1m.
De Johanne de Edelyre 1m.
De Lyhussenere de Lovayne 20s.
De Ogero le Campion 40s.
[m. 6] De Abraham le Gaunt 1m.
De Baldewyno Gruyte 1m.
De Nicholao de [sic] Rous de Gaunt di. m.
De Johanne de Lo 40s.
De Petro de Lo fratre eius 20s.
De Johanne Baudri 40s.
De Hugelot Crosselin 40s.
De Lamberto le Sage 40s.
De Michaele filio Johannis Bardolf 1m.
De Johanne Halle 1m.
De Lamberto de Templo di. m.
De Terrico Baker di. m.
De Michaele de Cassele 20s.
De Abraham Gedenare di. m.
De Willelmo de Prus di. m.
De Terrico de Puys di. m.
De Johanne de Mesme di. m.
De Johanne Waterbolkere di. m.
De Baldewyno Poleyn 40s.
De Jakemo filio eius 1m.
De Johanne le Blaunker 40s.
De Arnaldo Bonin 40s.
De Johanne de Buskele 40s.
De Waltero de la Hyde 40s.

The Estreat (The Exchequer Summons)

De Lamberto de Ypre 40s.
De Henrico de Barblegen 40s.
De Fraunk Iverne 40s.
De Godefrido de Welnouth 20s.
De Gerardo Welnouth 40s.
De Johanne de Lyon 40s.
De Johanne de Nuele 20s.
Usque huc de Flandr' De Henrico de Malkse 20s.

1. The Flemish merchants in this list are not included in **294**.

666.[1] *Breve de respectu*[2]. De Luca de Luke et sociis suis 40 li.
. De Theobaldo de Luk' et sociis suis 10 li.
d . . . *hodie* . De Perruche de Plesent' et sociis suis 100s.[3]
. De Poncio Elie de Caword' 40s.
. De Petro de Sancto Petro 5m.
. De Johanne Doneden 10m.[4]
. De Willelmo Berand 10 li.[5]
. De Willelmo Fressenede 10 li.
. De Johanne Suliz 20m.
T. per tall' Ø *De Lupo de Luca 20s.[6]
Breve de respectu ut prius De Nicholao Test 100s.

1. The debtors in **666** are not included in **294**.
2. Writ of respite (attached), 15 May 1277, to the mayor and sheriffs of London, for Theobald de Luke and associates until the king's return from Wales, in respect of a total of £15. Final acquittance of £40 granted to the same, 17 Jan. 1278 (*C.C.R. 1272–9*, 437).
3. Paid Michaelmas 1280 (E 401/97 m. 2).
4. Writ of acquittance (attached), 16 Nov. 1278, to sheriffs of London.
5. At Michaelmas 1278 a day is given for the morrow (E 368/52 m. 8).
6. Paid Easter 1278 (E 401/88 m. 8).

667.[1] *Flandr'* De Eustachio de Araz di. m.
De Jakes Watelyn 40s.
De Johanne le Forner 40s.
De Willelmo Bonafaunt 100s.
De Johanne Conin 20s.
De Lamberto del Kene 1m.
De Willelmo Hert di. m.
De Henrico Skanke di. m.

1. A further list of Flemish merchants not included in **294**.

Disseisin, False Claims and Other Matters[1]

668. *Hic incipiunt disseisine Surr'* De Waltero de Molsham 40d. pro disseisina.
Pauper De Jordano le Fruter di. m. pro plegio eiusdem.

1. A number of exactions (**668–705, 722–3, 725**) are unrelated to any entry on the plea roll.

669. Ø De Johanne Durant narratore di. m. pro eodem.

670. *Pauper* De Johanne (? Anure) aurifabro di. m. pro disseisina.

671. *Pauper Memorandum pro J. de Lincoln clerico* De Galfrido le Marescal 40d. pro eodem.

672. *Turr'* De Cresse filio Gent 100s. pro eodem.

The Estreat (The Exchequer Summons)

673. Ø De magistro Ada de Cantebr' 1m. pro eodem.
T. Radulfus *De Petro de Micham di. m. pro plegio eiusdem.

674. *Vad' pauper 2* De Gilberto de Colecestre cissore di. m. pro eodem.

675. *Ignotus* De Hugone serviente Benedicti di. m. pro eodem.

676. *Obierunt pauperes* De Alano le Fevere di. m. pro eodem.
De Ricardo de Cantebr' di. m. pro eodem.

677. *T. Radulfus* *De Willelmo de Keleveden di. m. pro eodem.

678. *Ignotus* De Nicholao de Newport di. m. pro eodem.

679. *Pauper* De Stephano le Tailur di. m. pro eodem.

680. *Pauper* De Roberto Russel di. m. pro eodem.

681. *Ignotus* De Willelmo Boldhed piscatore di. m. pro eodem.

682. *Pars 10s. 2* De Thoma de Estchep 20s. pro disseisina.

683. *Pars Radulfus vic' oneratur* *De Waltero le Wodere ⟨*di. m.*⟩ 1m. pro eodem.

684. *T. Radulfus le Fevre* *De Willelmo de Laufare chaloner di. m. pro eodem.

685. *Breve in scaccario de perdonacione*[1] *De Johanne de Wautham magistro hospitalis Sancti Bartholomei 1m. pro eodem.
*De Thoma (? Hervi) fratre Milone [sic] de Waltham di. m. pro eodem.
+ *De Thoma Hed' di. m. pro plegiis eorundem.
*De Rogero Crok' di. m. pro eodem.
*De Willelmo Atehale di. m. pro eodem.
*De Waltero Pope di. m. pro eodem.
*De Willelmo Berewe di. m. pro eodem.
*De Johanne le Barbur di. m. pro eodem.
*De Johanne le Chaucer di. m. pro eodem.
*De Nicholao le Chaundeler di. m. pro eodem.
*De Willelmo Slich di. m. pro eodem.
*De Roberto le Mareschal di. m. pro eodem.
*De Henrico de Grene di. m. pro eodem.
*De Henrico de Sancto Bartholomeo di. m. pro eodem.

1. Writ of respite (attached), 13 May 1277, to the sheriffs of London (cf. *C.C.R. 1272-9*, 385, 12 May 1277). Writ to the barons of the exchequer pardoning the master and brethren, Trinity 1278 (E 159/51 m. 10d). Cf. **737.**

686. *Pauper* De Hugone Gratefige di. m. pro disseisina.
40d. per tall' De Waltero le Ferun di. m.[1] pro plegio eiusdem.

1. Part paid Easter 1277 (E 401/84 m. 3).

687. *T. per tall' penes se* De Nicholao de Wylton di. m. pro eodem.

688. *T. per duas tallias* *De Gilberto de Honilane di. m.[1] pro eodem. *40d. solvit.*

1. Paid Easter 1277 (E 401/83 m. 1) and Easter 1278 (E 401/88 m. 7).

The Estreat (The Exchequer Summons)

689. *T. tall'* *De Roberto de Woking di. m.[1] pro eodem.
   1. Paid Easter 1277 (E 401/83 m. 1 reading Bokyng).

690. *T. tall'* *De Godefrido le Cofrer di. m.[1] pro eodem.
   1. Paid Easter 1277 (E 401/83 m. 1).

691. *T. tall'* *De Willelmo de Manhale[1] di. m. pro eodem.
   1. Paid Easter 1277 (E 401/83 m. 1).

692. *T.* *De Ricardo le Poter di. m. pro eodem.

693. *Breve prius*[1] Ø De Hugone de Dunton di. m. pro eodem.
   1. Cf. **527**.

694. *Pauper* De Thoma filio Jocei di. m. pro disseisina.
Kancia De Johanne de la Burne di. m. pro plegio eiusdem.

695. De Willelmo le Rus di. m. pro eodem.

696. *Ignotus* Ø De Nicholao Herlewyn di. m. pro eodem.

697. *Ignotus* De Rogero de Honecote di. m. pro eodem.

698. *Surr'* De Willelmo de Clopton di. m. pro eodem.

699. *P. apud Hibern' W. obiit pauper* De Petro de Hakeney et Willelmo de Eboraco 1m. pro eodem.

700. *R. mendicans* Ø De Stephano le Balur et Roberto Heyrun di. m. pro plegio Ricardi del Eyt'.

701. Ø De Willelmo de Berkweye di. m.[1] pro eodem.
   1. Paid Easter 1282 (E 401/101 m. 9).

702. *Obierunt pauperes ante iter* De Gerardo Gofeir et Johanne Gofeir di. m. pro disseisina.
Mort' Essex De Johanne Hardel di. m. pro plegio eiusdem.

703. *R. obiit pauper S. mendicans levar' fac'* De Roberto Scot et Simone Turrok 1m. pro eodem.

704. *Obierunt pauperes ante iter* De Willelmo Aron et Willelmo le Marescal 1m. pro eodem.

705. *Vic' oneratur* De Roberto Gratefige et Johanne Waylaund 1m. pro eodem.

706. *Nichil in ballio* De magistro Nycholao de Curtenay de fine 2m. pro transgressione per pleg' Hugonis de Kendal et Willelmi de Birkweye. [cf. **471**]

707. *In pace per scaccarium*[1] Ø De Deotato mercatore Florencie 5m. pro falso clamio. [cf. **487**]
   1. Cf. **292, 294**.

708. *Nichil in ballio* De Nicholao de Curteney di. m. pro eodem. [cf. **488**]

The Estreat (The Exchequer Summons)

709. *Per duas tallias* *De Ricardo Assewy draper 20s.[1] pro eodem. [cf. **499**]
  1. Paid Easter 1277 (E 401/84 m. 3) and Easter 1278 (E 401/88 m. 8).

710. *Ignotus adhuc* De Hugone de Glouc' di. m. pro eodem. [cf. **500**]

711. *T. tall'* *De Willelmo de Reygate di. m.[1] pro falso clamio. [cf. **504**]
  1. Paid Easter 1277 (E 401/83 m. 1).

712. *Suffolk* De Waltero de Shelfangere vicecomite Suff' 100s. pro contemptu. [cf. **507**]

713. *T. tall'* *De Willelmo de Sancto Dionisio di. m.[1] pro falso clamio.
T. *De Petro le Forbour di. m. pro eodem. [cf. **508**]
  1. Paid Easter 1277 (E 401/83 m. 1).

714. *40d. pro Rogero R. Fevere T. Ro 2 pauper* De Ricardo le Woder, Rogero le Corder di. m. pro plegio Jacobi de Montibus. [cf. **512**]

715. Ø De Johanne Durant narratore di. m. pro falso clamio. [cf. **514**]

716. [m. 7] *T. per duas tallias* *De Ricardo Assewy executore testamenti Thome filii Ade de Basing di. m.[1] pro iniusta detencione. [cf. **517**]
  1. Paid Easter 1277 (E 401/84 m. 3) and Easter 1278 (E 401/88 m. 8).

717. *T. R. le Fevere* *De Roberto de Rokel' de fine di. m. pro licencia concordandi. [cf. **518**]

718. *Nichil in ballio* De Jacobo de Montibus di. m. pro transgressione et quia non est presens. [cf. **519**]

719. *Att' sicut inferius* Ø *De Roes de Watford di. m.[1] pro iniusta detencione. [cf. **495**]
  1. Paid Michaelmas 1277 (E 401/85 m. 1).

720. *T. tall'* *De magistro et fratribus Sancti Thome in Aconia 1m. pro eodem. [cf. **484**]

721. *Vad' T. 2* De Henrico le Wympler di. m. quia non habet quem plegiavit. [cf. **241, 561**]

722. *T.* *De Roberto de Meldeburn' di. m. pro eodem.

723. *Di. m. tall' T. Ro 2* De Johanne de Depe mercer in Sopereslane 1m.[1] pro eodem.
  1. Paid Easter 1277 (E 401/83 m. 1).

724. *T. tall'* *De Willelmo le Paternoster di. m.[1] pro eodem.
T. per tall' *De Roberto Hauteyn di. m.[2] pro eodem.
Obiit pauper De Thoma le Paternoster di. m. pro eodem. [cf. **468**]
  1. Paid Easter 1277 (E 401/83 m. 1).
  2. Paid Easter 1278 (E 401/88 m. 7).

725. *Ignotus* De Waltero de Lannes di. m. pro eodem.

The Estreat (The Exchequer Summons)

Purprestures[1]

726. *Hic purpresture T.* Ø De Gwyoto Clerico di. m. pro transgressione purpresture. [cf. **346**]
   1. Some exactions (**731, 747, 771**) are unrelated to entries on the plea roll.

727. *Tall' penes se T.* Ø *De Elia de Hertford di. m.[1] pro eodem. [cf. **350**]
   1. Paid Easter 1277 (E 401/84 m. 6).

728. *Redd'* De Stephano de Eddeworth 1m. [cf. **351**]

729. (? *Man'*) *infra Turrim* De magistro Godwyne di. m. [cf. **352**]

730. De Roberto de Dorset et Thoma le Messeger 40d. [cf. **353–4**]

731. *De Waltero le Waleys di. m.[1]
   1. Paid Easter 1278 (E 401/88 m. 7).

732. *T.* Ø *De Reginaldo de Fridaistrete et Stephano de Harewe fratre di. m. *unde Stephanus 5s.* [cf. **358–9**]

733. *T. per tall'* Ø *De Anketino de Breteuil 1m.[1] [cf. **360**]
   1. Paid Easter 1278 possibly for the deceased Bartholomew l'Espicer (E 401/83 m. 8).

734. *T.* (...) *in bonis* Ø *De Flora Viel 40d. [cf. **361**]

735. Ø De Rogero Hervy di. m. [cf. **362**]

736. *T.* Ø *De Reginaldo le Chaundeler di. m. [cf. **347**]

737. *Breve prius distr' pro br'*[1] De magistro hospitalis Sancti Bartholomei di. m. [cf. **363**]
   1. Cf. **685**.

738. *Pars pro J. et W. R. Fevere* Ø De Waltero le Chaloner ⟨2s. 2d.⟩, Simone Pistore et Johanne Sperling ⟨solvit 2s. 2d.⟩ di. m. *Simon distr' per 1 cipham* (? *de arreragiis*). [cf. **365–7**]

739. *Pars pro Willelmo per tall'* De Roberto de Storteford et Willelmo de Arraz[1] ⟨40d.⟩ et Roberto de Linton di. m. [cf. **368–70**]
   1. Paid Easter 1277 (E 401/83 m. 1).

740. *Ignotus* De Roberto Albin di. m. [cf. **371**]

741. *T. per tall'* Ø *De Ricardo de Watford di. m. [cf. **372**]

742. *T. pro W. 40d. per duas tallias de R.* Ø *De Willelmo le Cotiler[1] et Roberto Sevehod[2] di. m. [cf. **373–4**]
   1. Paid Easter 1278 (E 401/88 m. 7).
   2. Paid Easter 1277 (E 401/84 m. 6 adding *de Cornhull*).

743. *T. pro Reg' pars pro Rob'* *De Reginaldo ⟨solvit 40d. per denarios⟩ Aurifabro et Roberto ⟨solvit 40d. per denarios et 40d. per talliam⟩ de Conyngham 10s.[1] *unde Robertus di. m.* [cf. **375–6**]
   1. Paid Easter 1278 (E 401/88 m. 8).

The Estreat (The Exchequer Summons)

744. *T. Radulfus le Fevre* *De Willelmo de Laufare di. m. [cf. **377**]

745. *Ignotus*[1] De Rogero le Taylur ⟨*qui obiit*⟩ mercer 10s.
Pars 40d. per tall' De Gilberto[2] le Poter di. m. [cf. **379**]
  1. With a drawing of a bishop's mitre.
  2. *Laurentius* (379).

746. *Pars T. 2* De Roberto le Taylur ⟨*Addr'*⟩ et Germano ⟨*40d.*⟩ le Pessoner[1] di. m. [cf. **380, 383**]
  1. Paid Easter 1278 (E 401/88 m. 8).

747. *Domus vacat* De Waltero de Essex di. m.

748. *In respectu per scaccarium* De magistro Novi Hospitalis London 1m. [cf. **386**]

749. *T. Addr' 2* De abbate de Salop 1m. [cf. **387**]

750. *Domus vacat* De Rogero de Leukenore di. m. [cf. **388**]

751. Ø De Johanne de Bishopesgate di. m.
Vad. T. 2 De Johanne Wylemyn di. m. [cf. **391**]

752. *Di. m. R. le Fevere et per duas tallias res'* De Benedicto de Hakeneye 1m.[1] [cf. **393**]
  1. Paid Easter 1280 (E 401/95 m. 7).

753. *T. per duas tallias* *De Willelmo le Rus. di. m.[1] [cf. **394**]
  1. Paid Easter 1277 (E 401/83 m. 1) and Easter 1278 (E 401/88 m. 7).

754. *T. per duas tallias* De Johanne le Porter[1] et Willelmo ⟨*Addr' res'*⟩ de Boxford di. m. [cf. **395–6**]
  1. *Poter* (395).

755. *Pars 40d. per tall' Addr' res'* *De Albrhid le Torner ⟨*20d.*⟩ et Lovekino ⟨*20d.*⟩ le Turner[1] di. m. [cf. **397–8**]
  1. Paid Easter 1278 (E 401/88 m. 1).

756. *T. Radulfus* *De Alicia de Hondesdik 40d. [cf. **400**]

757. *Breve sicut prius*[1] *De Reginaldo[2] de Suffolk di. m. pro uno solio. [cf. **401**][3]
  1. Cf. **527, 624**.
  2. *Rogerus* (401).
  3. For a presentment unrecorded in the plea roll see *C.C.R. 1272–9*, 384.

758. *T. tall'* *De Ricardo Poterel[1] di. m. [cf. **402**]
  1. Paid Easter 1277 (E 401/83 m. 1).

759. *Pars 5s. pro W.* Ø De Philippo de Norht' pellipario et Willelmo le Chaundeler 1m. *unde Willelmus 10s.* [cf. **404–5**]

760. *Tall' pro R. tall' levand'* Ø De Radulfo le Mason et Ricardo de Abbendon 10s. *unde Ricardus di. m.* [cf. **406–7**]

761. *T.* *De Ricardo Dykon 40d. [cf. **408**]

The Estreat (The Exchequer Summons)

762. *T.* *De Ada Molling 40d. [cf. **410**]

763. *T.* *De Ernaldo Bogeys di. m. [cf. **411**]

764. *40d. pro Willelmo Skileman* De Willelmo Skyleman et Willelmo Page di. m. [cf. **412, 414**]

765. *T.* *De Radulfo de Cestre di. m. [cf. **416**]

766. *14d. pro Jordano T. 2 T. pro Elia* De Jordano Pygon, Michaele ⟨*22d. J. Addr'*⟩ le Poter, Ada le Chapeler et Elya ⟨*40d.*⟩ le Mariner[1] di. m. *unde Elyas 40d.* [cf. **418–20**]
    1. Paid Easter 1278 (E 401/88 m. 8).

767. *T.* *De Gonnilda Beaument, Ricardo ⟨*40d.*⟩ Charp et Hugone de Clopham 10s. [cf. **422–3, ? 399**]

768. *Vad' T. Addr' 2 1* De Roberto de Waltham 40d. [cf. **424**]

769. *T.* *De Nicholao Horn di. m. [cf. **425**]

770. *T. Radulfus* *De Alicia de Exemie 40d. [cf. **427**]

771. *T. R. de Fevere* *De Roberto de Rokesle di. m.

772. *Ignotus* De magistro Ada[1] Crapfy di. m. [cf. **432**]
    1. *Radulfus* (**432**).

773. *T.* De Hugone de Wyndes' di. m. [cf. **433**]

774. *Pars per tall' T. 2* De Roberto Hauteyn 1m.[1] [cf. **466**]
    1. Paid Easter 1278 (E 401/88 m. 8).

775. *Turr'* De Aron de la Rye judeo 100s. [cf. **436**]

776. *T. d pro Roberto tall'*[1] *Amicia alloc'* *De Roberto le Wodemongere et Amicia que fuit uxor Willelmi filii Ricardi 10s.[2] *unde Robertus 40d.* [cf. **439–40**]
    1. Deleted with cross-hatching.
    2. Paid Easter 1278 (E 401/88 m. 8).

777. *Turr'* De Aron Crespyn judeo 100s. pro transgressione purpresture. [cf. **446**]

778. *T.* *De Copyno de Troys 40d.[1] pro eodem. [cf. **447**]
    1. Paid Easter 1278 (E 401/88 m. 7).

779. *T.* *De Waltero de Berden[1] 40d. [cf. **449**]
    1. *Merdene* (**449**).

780. *T.* *De Hugone le Lou di. m. [cf. **450**]

781. *Domus vacat* De priore de Wenlock 20s. [cf. **454**]

782. *Breve ut prius*[1] De Stephano de Cornhull 40s. [cf. **458**]
    1. Cf. **547**.

The Estreat (The Exchequer Summons)

783. *In respectu* De Johanne de Norht' di. m.[1] [cf. **460**]
   1. Paid 7 Edward I (E 372/123 m. 9).

784. *T. per duas tallias* *De Johanne de Stebben'[1] et Johanne le Taylur 40d. [cf. **461–2**]
   1. Paid Easter 1278 (E 401/88 mm. 7–8).

785. De Thoma le Marescal viniter 10s. [cf. **464**]

THE SUMMONS CONCLUDED
786. Teste fratre Josep de Chauncy Thesaurario nostro apud Westmonasterium 14 die Junii anno rengni nostri quarto.

INDEX

References are to entry numbers and not pages.

Abbeys in the king's gift, 298
Abduction, alleged, 511
Aberdas, Alexander, 14
Abetment, 249
Abeton, Walter de, 258
Abingdon (Abyndon, Habindon, etc.)
   Richard de, 294, 407, 473, 663, 760
   William de, 51
Abjuration of the realm
   after confession of: burglary, 115, 262; cutting purses, 20, 65; escape from prison, ? 204, 263, 316; forgery, 11; harbouring a felon, 28; plundering, 42; receiving, 28; robbery, 52; slaying, 81, 84, 90, 97, 241; theft, 9, 20, 23, 38, 57–8, 65–6, 73, 79, 82, 92, 100, 106, 110, 112, 123, 172, 186, 242, 262, 283
   in the chamberlain's absence, 52
   ports assigned, 115
Abortion, 187; resulting from battery, 63, 76, 222, 261
Abraham, Nicholas, 201
Acatour, Joce le, king's purveyor, 239, 292, 527, 560
Accusation: false, 249; malicious, 496
Acre, Robert de, of London, 294
Adam, William son of, 134, 620
Adestok, *see* Hadstock
Adinett, king's tailor, 170
Adjournment: in a crown plea, 70; in civil pleas, 510–11, 515, 520
Adrian
   John (I), mayor & sheriff, 3–4, 86–99, 168–77, 182–92, 207, 246, 294, 469, 481, 522, 600–1, 603, 636, 638, 642, 644, 663; ward of, *see* Walbrook ward
   John (II), son of John (I), 294, 663
   Ralph, 47
Advowsons, 298–9
Affeite, William le, 299
Affron, Richard de, kt., 481
Ageney, *see* Hackney
Agnes, a woman named, 35
Agreements: in eyre, 522; none reached, 72, 85, 222, 272; reached out of court, 273, 296, 483, 494, 498, 501, 505, 518
Aguiler, Richard de, 58
Aguilon, William, justice of gaol delivery, 108

Alan
   John son of, 391
   Peter son of, 501
Albertis, Reyner, Florentine merchant, 219
Albin (Albyn, Aubyn)
   Robert, 371, 740
   William, 32, 532
Albredus, *see* Aubrey
Aldermanbury (Aldemannebury), 296, 341
Aldermen: in pleas of intrusion, 516; receive abjurations, 52
Aldersey (Alsithere), Robert son of Nicholas de, 115
Aldersgate (Aldresgate), gate, 25; street, 18; ward, 25, 32, 109, 155
Aldgate (Al(l)egate): gate, 43, 233; keepers of, 153, 625; ward, 50, 153, 219
   William de, & Alice his wife, 98
Alditha, a woman named, 43
Aldwych, Andrew de, 141
Aledrawere, Roger, 255
Aleford, *see* Hakeford
Alein (Alewyn), Ingram, 294, 664
Aliens, 310; *see also* Merchants
All Hallows Barking: Hawise, a nun of, 499
All Hallows Bread Street, church, 186
All Hallows Colemanchurch, parish, 119
All Hallows Fenchurch, *see* St. Gabriel Fenchurch
All Hallows Gracechurch, ? 219
All Hallows London Wall, church, 299
Allegate, *see* Aldgate
Allor, Beatrice, & Thomas her servant, 154
Almain, *see* Cornwall, earl of
Alms, free, 503
Alorinton, Andrea widow of John de, 221
Alsithere, *see* Aldersey
Alvene, Reginald, 245, 564
Alvernia, *see* Auvergne
Alward (Aylward), Richard, 245, 564
Amercements: analysis of, App. B; article concerning, 295; roll of, 525–786
Amesbury (Ambersbyre, etc.)
   Fulk servant of John of, 46
   Richard de, 103, 608
Amewell (Amerwell), Laurence de, 246, 565

153

Index

Amiens (Amias, Amyas, Damyas)
  Ellis the clerk of, 118
  Richard, 24
  Roger de, 468
Amis, William, 279, 583
Anagni (Anania), Master Sylvester of, 29
Anaine, Nicholas, 15
Andrew, Stephen, & John his son, 80
Anglie, *see* English
Angolam (Angulame), Bernard, 231
Anguillaunt (Angelaunt), James, of Pistoia, 219, 545
Animals, *see* Capons; Cows; Dogs; Horses; Oxen; Pigs; Sheep
Anlace, 51
Anure, John, 670
Appeals
  of: abortion, 187; battery & abortion, 222; battery, abortion & robbery, 261; homicide, 6, 72, 120, 131, 137, 149, 159, 245, 271; homicide by poison, 209; homicide & robbery, 145; rape, 85; rape & theft, 74; wounding & mayhem, 141, 147; wounds & battery, 140, 266–8, 272–4
  appellees: acquitted, 85, 140, 187, 209, 222, 261; claim clergy, 187; default, 120, 141, 267–8, 271, 273–4; pardoned, 6, 72
  appellors: default, 6, 72, 74, 85, 131, 141, 149, 159, 209, 222, 266–8, 272–4; die, 187, 245; withdraw, 145; women, 72, 74, 85, 120, 131, 137, 145, 149, 187, 245, 261, 268, 271, 274
  in the county, 131
  parties agree in, 273
  pledges by faith in, 6, 72, 274
  quashed, 140, 147, 261
  remitted to the husting, 120, 271
Appeleye, *see* Aspele
Approvers, 284; appeal of, 277
Arbeleter (Arblaster)
  Joan widow of Martin, 463
  Martin le, 527
Arbitration, 522
Archery, 61
Arcubus, de, *see* Bow
Armenters, John de, 294, 663
Armour, 234, 508
Armourer (Armurer), 508
  Gilbert le, 527
  Richard le, 214, 662
  Thomas le, 189
Arnald, Peter, 108
Arnulf, monk of Bermondsey, 116, 613, 615
Aron, William, 704
Arras (Aras, Haraz)
  Eustace de, 667
  Giles de, 208, 294, 664; John & Robert his servants, 208
  Hubelin (Hubeletus) de, 292, 527
  Hubert de, 254, 570
  Ralph de, 257, 571
  Richard de, of Lincoln, 294, 663
  Robert de (I), 70; (II), sheriff, 294, 527, 532, 564, 663; (III), 475
  William de, 369, 739
Arrows, 61, 190, 315
Arson, 275, 280, 296
Arthur (Artur), Richard, 245, 564
Arundel, John de, 271
Ashbourne (Asseborne), Roger de, 264
Ashenden (Assendene, Assindon, etc.)
  Robert de, 272, 417, 579
  William de, 75, 445
Ashwell, Alexander de, 221
Aspele (Appeleye), Henry de, 273, 580
Assewy, *see* Eswy
Asshebof, William, 75
Assize: of cloth, 70, 294, 302, 469, 663–7; of wine, 292, 303, 527, 529; possessory, *see* Mort d'ancestor; Novel disseisin; Utrum
Aston
  John (de), 245, 564
  William, 564
Atenasse (Atteasse), John, 245, 564
Atepirie, *see* Attepyre
Attachment: article concerning, 321; contrary to custom, 87, 108; exceptions, 80, 190; not made, 24, 55, 70, 117, 119, 126, 133, 173, 177, 200, 203, 210, 215, 220, 230, 244; of appellees, 85, 222, 267, 273–4; of persons present at deaths, 15–260 *passim*; of returned fugitives, 230; practice concerning, 26, 29, 87, 108; prevented, 141
Attebrok, William, 245, 564
Atteclive, Solomon, 245, 564
Attecross (Ad crucem), John, 108, 610
Attediche, Nicholas son of Ralph, 233
Attegrove, William, 245, 564
Attehale (Atenhale)
  Richard, & Walter his brother, 280, 588
  William, 685
Attehegge (Atenhegge), John, 245, 564
Attehill (Atenhull, Attehull)
  Agnes daughter of Thomas, 275
  Richard, 245, 564
Attehoke (Atenhok, de Hoke)
  John, 245, 564
  Richard de, 245, 564
Atteknol, Agnes, 276
Attelane, Henry, 245, 564
Attelethe (Attelithe)
  Alice wife of Richard, 117
  Henry, 494
Attelowe, Maud, 470
Attemer(c)e, William, 245, 564

154

Index

Attemerk, Robert *alias* Walter, 245, 564
Atteponde, Robert, 245, 564
Attepyre (Atepirie), Richard, 245, 564
Attestile, Warin, 245, 564
Attestrande (Atestronde), John, 273, 580
Attewell (Etewell)
  Osbert, 245, 564
  Richard, 245, 564
  Robert, 245, 564
Attewode, Thomas son of Thomas, of Barton, 79, 597
Attewodecote, Robert, 264
Attorney, 472, 480, 484, 489, 493, 495, 514
Aubrey (Albredus), Adam & John, sons of, 7
Aubyn, *see* Albin
Audeley, Henry de, 340
Aunger (Aungier, etc.)
  John son of Roger de, 183, 642
  Peter, sheriff, 4, 105, 155–66, 243, 631–2; ward of, *see* Broad Street ward
Auvergne (Alverina, Alvernia), Anketin de, mercer, 31, 137, 194, 212, 215, 239, 252, 342, 500; ward of, *see* Farringdon ward
Avel, Richard, 521
Avelin, Richard son of, 61
Avener
  Ingebert le, 135
  Roger le, 288
Axes, 181, 200
Ayler, 83
Aylward, *see* Alward

Bacton (Boketon), John de, 216
Badencourt, *see* Batencourt
Bagard, Thomas, 105
Bagel, William, 227, 552
Bail (mainprise), 6, 16, 29, 37, 87, 116, 183, 200–1, 205, 208, 219, 227–8, 249, 284; article concerning, 324; by six pledges, 76, 266; custom concerning, 76, 324; in Middlesex, 279; sheriffs fail to answer for, 147
Baker (Pestour, Pistor), 48, 73, 108, 154, 240, 246, 287
  Adam, 103, 608
  Eve widow of Albin, 102
  Henry, 174, 637
  Ingolph le, 371
  Philip le, 75
  Simon, 366, 738
  Solomon, 193
  Terry, 665
  Walter le, 22
Bakynge, William de, 183
Baldersham, John son of Richard de, 112
Baldwin (son of Gerard or Jeremiah), Giles son of, 294, 664
Ballard

Austin, 27
  John, 167
Balsham (Balesham)
  Ralph de, 260, 272, 579
  Richard de, 272, 579
Balur, Stephen le, 700
Banbury, Robert de, 264
Barber (Barbator, Barbour, etc.)
  Adam le, 260, 573
  Alan le, 266, 576
  Andrew le, 252, 568
  Emma la, 292, 527
  Godfrey le, 264
  James le, 126
  John le (I), 165, 218, 544, 633; (II), by Newgate, 274, 581; (III), of St. Bartholomew's hospital, 685
  Laurence le, by the Temple, 244
  Reginald le (I), 86, 600; (II), 521
  Richard le, 252
  Roger le, 527
  Thomas le (I), 136, 292, 527, 621; (II), in Vintry, 237, 559
  William le, servant, 246, 565
Barber(i)e, Jakes de la, 294, 664
Barblegen, Henry de, 665
Bardolf, Michael son of John, 665
Baret, Peter, 199
Barking (Berkyngg)
  Agnes de, 21
  John de (I), 70; (II), currier, 468
  Nicholas de, 32
  Robert de, 102
  William de (I), 32; (II), 126
Barnet (Bernette, etc.), Middx., 20, 59, 285
  Richard de la, 292, 527
Baron, Thomas, *see* Carron, Thomas de
Barons: of London, 2, 18, 20–1; of the realm, 345
Barricades, 296
Bartholomew
  a boy named, 251
  parson of St. Michael Paternoster Royal, 503
Barton (Ba(r)thon), 79
  Robert de, precentor of St. Paul's, 344
  Thomas de (I), 37; (II), 316, 591
Bas, John le, 35
Basely, William, 173
Basing (Bassynges, etc.)
  Adam de, mayor, 3, 103, 237, 502, 517, 716
  Geoffrey de, 428
  Richard de, 13
  Thomas de (I), son of Adam de, 200, 502, 517, 716
  Thomas de (II), nephew of Adam de, sheriff, 4, 51, 70, 183, 205–19, 264, 296, 518, 522, 541, 542, 544, 654, 659, 661; ward of, *see* Candlewick ward

155

Index

Basingstoke, *see* White, Maud la
Basnet, 508
Basset
  Fulk, bishop of London, 55
  Ralph, & Walter his servant, 148, 623
Bassishaw ward, 178, 207
Bat (Bate), Nicholas, mayor & sheriff, 3, 4, 6–16, 499; ward of, *see* Bishopsgate ward; wharf of, 62
Batail, *see* Battle
Bateman, *see* Boatman
Batencourt (Badencourt), Luke de, sheriff, 4, 182–92, 254–69, 286, 316, 571, 572, 574–6, 591, 642, 644; Alice la Blund (or Maud), his widow, 182, 520
Batewell (Baterell)
  Richard de, 37
  William de, 37
Bath (Bathon)
  Henry de, 80; & John his son, 598
  Thomas, 294, 663
Batiler, William le, boatman of Greenwich, 220
Batour, John le, 209
Battery, 63, 89, 102, 117–18, 125, 127, 138, 141, 163, 180, 198, 208
Battle (Batail), Idonea sister of Richard de la, 120
Baud (Baude)
  Henry le, 99, 276
  Nicholas le, 111
Baudan, Terry, 294, 664
Baudri
  John, 665
  William, 48
Beams, 8, 35, 91, 101, 372, 376, 391, 455
Beaumund (Beaumount)
  Gunnilde, 422, 767
  Ralph de, 423
Beaupyne, Henry, 27
Bec (Beck, Bek)
  Anthony de, exchequer clerk, 588
  William de, 294, 663
Bed, death in, 47
Bedel, Faukes le, 159
Bedford
  Hugh de, 53
  Ralph de, 67, 593
  Richard de, 292, 527
  Roger de, 236
  William de, 53
Bedfordshire, 39, 290, 590, 650; sheriff of, 39
Beggars, 25, 27
Beille, *see* Beverley, William de
Bek, *see* Bec
Bekerannike, Ralph, 168
Bel (Bell)
  Andrew le, & Elena de Flete, his wife, 292, 527

Cristelot, 294, 664
Belfry, of St. Paul's, 162
Bell-tower, of St. Mary le Bow, 221
Bench, court of the, 447–8, 492, 510–11, 515
Benchesham, Denis de, 291
Bending, Walter, 448
Benekuk, *see* Bonebuk
Bengrant, William, 182
Bentley (Beney, Benleyhe, etc.)
  Adam de, 135, 619
  John de, & Isabel his wife, 261
Bentull, *see* Breteuil
Ber, John le, 134
Berand, William, 666
Berden, *see* Merdene
Bere
  John de, 75
  Robert de, 243
Bereman, 191, 246, 267, 270
  Geoffrey, 219
  Hugh, 197, 648
Berewe, William, 685
Berkeley, John de, 53
Berkhampstead
  John de, 198, 649
  Ralph de, 236
  Richard de, 109
Berkshire, 12
Berkweye, William de, 701, 706
Bermondsey, Surrey, prior & monks of, 116, 299, 613, 615
Bernard, Robert son of, kt., of Essex, 48
Berners, John de, 118
Bernette, *see* Barnet
Berwes, *see* Harrow
Bestenore, Alexander de, 262, 574
Betoyne (Bethoyne)
  Ingram de, 294, 663
  William de, 294, 663
Betteuil, *see* Breteuil
Beuvin (Beuwyn), Thomas, 294, 663
Beverley (de Beverlaco)
  Christine daughter of Simon de, 114
  Geoffrey de, 188, 644
  Reginald de, 28
  William de (*alias* William de Beille), 269, 292, 527
Bexley (Bix(e)le), William de, 174, 637
Beynin
  Gerard, 274, 581
  Roger, 294, 663
Bigod
  Hugh le (I), justice of gaol delivery, 152; (II), 521
  Roger, Earl Marshal, 456
  William, 481
Billing, Richard de, 36, 85
Billingsgate, 97, 299; ward, 26, 34, 48, 60, 63, 97, 220, 365–70

Index

Birkweye, *see* Berkweye
Birley, William de, 471
Bishop (Bissop, le Evesk)
  Andrew, 164
  Master Elias of the Jews, 296
  Roger, 163
  William, 245, 564
Bishopsgate: ditch outside, 45, 59; ward, 134, 343
  John de, 391, 751
  Nicholas de, 385
Bite: by a horse, 473; by a woman, 113
Bixle (Bixele), *see* Bexley
Black Friars, *see* Friars
Blakeney, Adam de, 292, 294, 527, 663
Blaket, Robert, 457
Blakethorn, John de, 25, 32, 109, 155; ward of, *see* Aldersgate ward
Blankmester, Robert de, 166
Blater, Thomas le, 132
Blauet, William, 243
Blaunker, John le, 665
Blereheye, Alice, 230
Bliburg, Roger de, 406
Blida, *see* Blythe
Blund (Blunde, Blunt)
  Alice la (I), widow of Luke de Batencourt, 14, 182, 520; (II), 119
  Edward le, sheriff, 4, 155–66, 178, 403, 631–2
  John son of Edward le, 155, 631–2
  Peter le, 41
  Ralph le, sheriff, 4, 258, 270–90, 481, 582, 585–6
  Solomon le, 296
  Walter le, 279
  William son of Edward le, 403
Blundel, William, 468
Blye, William de, 288
Blythe (Blida)
  Agnes de, 119
  William de, 272, 579
Board, 101
Boatman, 83, 139
Boats, 12, 46, 97, 122, 160, 184, 190, 220, 229, 251; *see also* Ships
Boby, Master Matthew, & Guyot his servant, 29
Boche, Ascelina de la, 437
Bocher, *see* Butcher
Bodele, *see* Budleigh
Bogays (Bogeys), Arnold, 411, 763
Bokeler
  Martin le, 288
  William le, 113
Bokerel, *see* Bukerel
Boketon, *see* Bacton
Bokez, Thomas, 119
Bolace, John, 235
Boldhed, William, 681

Bole
  Henry le, 279, 468
  James (*alias* Richard Pele), 292, 527
  Walter, 157, 630
Boleng', Richard son of Geoffrey, 9
Boles, Richard, 26
Bonacius, *see* Bonett
Bonac(o)urs, James, & Rembertin his son, 232, 556
Bonaventure, Richard, 260
Bonebroke, John, 294, 664
Bonebuk (*alias* Benekuk), Philip de, & John his brother, 294, 664
Bonenfaunt (Bonafaunt, Bonefaunt)
  Vincent, 15
  William (I), 222, 548; (II), 667
Bonett, *alias* Master Bonacius Lombardus, king's clerk, & William his servant, 226, 550
Bonfrani (Bonfreyn), Gerard, 294, 664
Bonin, Arnald, 665
Boniur (Bonior), Stephen, 183, 642
Bonnemi, Montere, 527
Bonvalet, John, 284
Books, ecclesiastical, 57, 521
Bord, Robert, 27
Bordeaux (Burdegal, Burdeus), Raymond de, 192, 260, 573; Peter his servant, 260, 573
Bordray, John de, canon of Holy Trinity, 55
Borham
  John de, 214, 655
  Richard de, 116, 615
Borser, *see* Burser
Bosco
  Peter son of Geoffrey de, 82
  William de, & John his son, 473, 481
Bosse
  John son of Geoffrey, 23
  Richard, 60
Botare (Boter), Adam le, 217, 543
Boteley, *see* Butley
Botiler, *see* Butler
Botoner
  Geoffrey le, 35, 192, 249
  Peter le, 35
Bow (de Arcubus)
  Geoffrey de, 181, 640
  John de, 280
Bowl, 69
Bows, *see* Arrows
Bowyer, 253
  Alexander le, 22
  William le, 289
Box
  Walter, 473
  William, king's purveyor, 474
Boxes, *see* Chests
Boxford, William de, 396, 754

Index

Boyland, Roger de, justice of gaol delivery, 41
Boys, William de (I), 252; (II), 294, 663
Braceresse, *see* Brewster
Brackley (Brakele, Brakeleye)
  Alice de, 182, 641
  Walter de, 165, 633
Bracour, *see* Brewer
Bradley (Bradele)
  Ralph de, 15
  Roger de, 441
Braeler, 228, 468
  Roger le, 209
Brakele (Brakeley), *see* Brackley
Bramleye, *see* Bromley
Brass, *see* Pot
Braunte, Nicholas, 133
Bray
  Peter le, 134
  Robert de, 30
Bread Street, 230; ward, 24, 53, 136, 212, 223, 230, 355–64
Brente, Nicholas de, 287
Bret
  Philip le, 288
  Robert, 114
  Roger le, 202
  William le, 256
Breteuil (Bentull, Brettevil, etc.), Anketin de, 221, 294, 481, 547, 663, 733
Breton, Thomas le, 190
Brevetour, John le, 381
Brewer (Bracour, Broiere)
  Hugh le, 244, 563
  John le, 201
  Walter le, 233
  William le, 244, 563
Brewster (Braceresse), 89
  Agaline the, 127
  Lucy, 89, 601
Breynford, John de, 195
Brian, Stephen, 239
Briancon (Brianzun, etc.), Bartholomew le, 340, 526; & John his servant, 190
Bribes, articles concerning, 302–3, 313; *see also Suet de prison*
Brichull, Edith de, 284
Brid
  Richard, 230
  Robert le, 109
  Thomas le, 109
  William, 245, 564
Bridge (de Ponte)
  Ailwyn de, 279, 583
  Daniel de, 279, 583
  John son of Robert de, 275
  Roger de, 279, 583
  Stephen de, & Geoffrey his servant, 279
  Thomas, goldsmith, 279
Bridge ward, 27, 73, 236

Bridges, broken, 334; *see also* London Bridge; Fleet bridge; Wharves
Brilond (Brylaunde), John de, 292, 294, 527, 663
Brinkley (Brinkele), Ranulf de, 26
Bristol (Brustowe)
  David de, 151
  Richard de, 273, 580
  William de, 98
Brittany, John de, 146
Broad Street, 125, 252; ward, 88, 105, 125, 143, 243
Brocher, *see* Broker
Broiere, *see* Brewer
Brok
  Adam de, canon of St. Paul's, 255
  Hugh son of Laurence de, 74
  Laurence de, justice of gaol delivery, 55, 74, 94, 128, 202, 203, 230, 235; his rolls, 94
Brokenford, John de, 174
Broker (Brocher, Brokour), 287
  Constantine le, 153, 625
  Laurence le, 37
Brokesburne, *see* Broxburne
Bromley (Bramleye, Bromle)
  Godfrey de, 119, 618
  Ralph de, 468
Brooches, 74, 261, 491; gold, 511
Broome (la Brome), Simon de, janitor of St. Bartholomew's priory, 201
Brothels, 119, 134, 137
Broxburne (Brokesburne), John de, 500
Bruning (Brouning, Brunyng, etc.)
  Adam de, sheriff, 4, 100–7, 152, 316; ward of, *see* Farringdon ward
  Henry de, & Avice his wife, 193
  John son of Adam, 4, 100
  Roger, 245, 564
  William, 245, 564
Brussels, Guy son of Walter de, 291
Brustowe, *see* Bristol
Bryton, Robert de, 493, 498
Bucher, *see* Butcher
Bucket, 191
Buckinghamshire, 262, 478, 493, 498
Buckle, 134
Budleigh (Bodele, Buddele), John de, sheriff, 4, 228–31, 554–5
Bukeler, 468
  Richard le, 249
Bukerel (Bokerel)
  Isabel, 118, 616
  Matthew, chamberlain and sheriff, 4, 63–85, 592, 594, 599
  Stephen, 108, 155, 296
  William son of Matthew, 4, 63, 88, 125, 143, 294, 663; ward of, *see* Broad Street ward
Bullok, Ralph, 35

Index

Bungay (Bungey), Bartholomew de, 109
Buntyng, William, 356
Burdegal (Burdeus), *see* Bordeaux
Burel, John, 46
Burel, surcoats of, 284
Bureller (Buryler, etc.), 209
   Henry le, 209
   Ralph le, 509
Burger, Henry le, 209, 657
Burgh, Austin de, 182
Burglary, 115, 262, 312
Burial, provision for, 505
Burinton, William de, 492, 497
Burne, John de la, 694
Burnell, Robert, chancellor, 240
Burser (Borser)
   Adam le, 269
   Richard, 279, 576
   Robert le, 266, 279, 374, 576
Burton, 174
   Stephen de, 277
Bury St. Edmunds, Suffolk, abbot of, 340
Buskele, John de, 665
But, Adam, 14
Butcher (Bocher, Bucher), 155, 228
   Hugh le, 78, 99
   Warin le, 16
Butler (Botiler, etc.)
   James le, 152
   John son of Reginald le, 163, 632
   Ralph le, 289
Butley (Boteley, Butteley), John de, kt., 51
Buttery, 501
Byflete (Biflete), Hugh de, 273, 580
Bynere, Alice de, 221

Caby, Alexander, 136
Cadaz, Walter, 264, 576
Cahors (Caword), 666
   Bernard de, servant of Sylvester of Anagni, 29
   Ponce son of Elias de, 666
Calabre, John de, 267, 577
Caldelond(e), Adam de, 245, 564
Caldwell (Caldelwell), Hugh, 234, 284, 557
Callere, William le, 183, 642
Camail(e), Robert de, 221, 294, 547, 663
Camberwell (Camerwell), Surrey, 115
Cambrai (Combray), France, 656
Cambray (Caumbrey), Peter de, 294, 664
Cambridge (Cantebrigia)
   Master Adam de, 415, 673
   Gilbert de, 31
   Richard de, 676
   Robert de (*alias* Robert le Petit), 312, 341
   Thomas de (I), 37; (II), 148
   William de, 169
Camelyn, William, 157
Cameys, John de, & Margery his wife, 495, 501

Campion, Oger le, 665
Cancellis, Master Philip de, Alice his sister, & Walter his squire, 39
Candle, 26
Candlewick Street, 51; ward, 51, 70, 183 264
Cane, Henry de, 122
Canner, Richard le, 156
Canon
   Gamelin, 284, 584
   Ralph, 32
   Ranulf, 32
   Reginald, 294, 663
   Richard le, 245, 564
Canterbury (Cantuaria), 312, 341
   archbishop of, *see* Kilwardby
   Henry de, 21
   John de, 176, 638
   Margery de, 498
   Reginald de, 176, 638
   see also Christchurch Canterbury
Canwode, William de, 236
Capeles, Walter de, chamberlain, 193–201
Capellarius, *see* Capper
Capeneshors, Thomas de, 209
Caperoun
   Reginald, 111
   Richard, 145
Capes, Adam, 27
Capons, 275
Capper (Capellarius, Chapeler), 96, 105, 137, 169, 174
   Adam le, 419, 766
   Hugh le, 239
   Lovekin le, 49
   Richard le, 174, 637
   Stephen le, 49, 468
   William le, 174, 637
Carbonel, Walter, 291
Cargoes: of hides, 493; of mill-stones, 130; of wine, 80, 246
Carlisle (Cardoil, Karl', etc.)
   Alan de (le), 159, 631
   John de, 159
   Margery, prostitute, 134
   Robert de, 67
Carpenter, 181, 195
   Bartholomew the, 195
   Gerard le, 294, 664
   John (I) son of Adam the, of Hythe, 57
   John (II) le, 114, 612
   Richard le, 232
   Robert le (I), & Christine his widow, 474; (II), son of Walter the, 172, 636
   Simon the, 64
   Thomas the, 222
   Master William le, 30, 422
Carpenton, Henry de, 426
Carron (Karon, Karroun)
   Matthew de, 237, 559

Index

Carron, *continued*
  Thomas de (*alias* Thomas Baron), 237, 292, 527, 559
Carter (Careter), 45, 227
  Hugh le, 109
  John le, 135
  Nicholas the, 45
  William le, 255
Carts, 45, 59, 227, 345; long, 521; *see also* Horses
Cassele, Michael de, 665
Castle (de Castello)
  Alan de, 78, 468
  Amaury de, 294, 664
  Bartholomew de, 212
  John de, potter, at the Tower, 258, 572
  Nicholas de, exchequer clerk, 526
  Robert de, ? exchequer clerk, 535
Castle Baynard, 78, 443; ward of, 91, 132, 165
  Richard de, 238
Catton, Ralph son of Robert de, 100
Caumpes, Geoffrey de, 51
Cauntyng (Cauntingg), Nicholas, 294, 664
Caword, *see* Cahors
Caxton, Thomas de, 215
Cecily, a woman named, & Juliana her maid, 13
Celebration, 60
Cellar (de Celario), Roger of the, 25
Cellars, 72, 356; windows of, 458
Cerne, Edward de, 468
Cesterhunte, *see* Cheshunt
Cestfeud, *see* Chesterfield
Cestr', *see* Chester
Chains, prisoner in, 55
Chairs, 216; steeple-jack's, 162
Chaloner
  Emma wife of Henry le, 117, 614
  Gilbert le, 210, 658
  Ranulf le, 210, 658
  Walter le, 365, 738
  William le, 210, 658
Chamberlain (Chaumberlain), Robert le, 272, 579
Chamberlain, king's: abjuration in his absence, 52; claims clergy, 18; defective list of, 5; distraint of heirs of, 18; during election of compurgators, 209; rolls of, 19, 24–6, 32, 37, 44, 87, 92, 115, 119, 133–7, 149, 159, 162, 177, 202, 215, 222, 246
Chambly (Chaumbliz), Oise, France, 508
Champvent, *see* Chauvent
Chancery: clerk, *see* Merston, Henry de; rolls, 208, 345
Chandler (Candeler, Chaundeler)
  Adam le, 222, 548
  Matthew le, 218, 544

Nicholas le (I), 284, 584; (II), of St. Bartholomew's hospital, 685
Reginald le, 292, 347, 527, 736
Richard le, 223
Roger le, 288
Simon le, 49
William le, 103, 404, 608, 759
Chaors, *see* Cahors
Chapel (de Capella), Bartholomew de, glover, 279, 292, 527, 583
Chapeler, *see* Capper
Chaplain (Capellanus, Chapeleyn)
  Ralph le, *see* Hackney
  Stephen le, 41
  Thomas the, 453
Chapman (Schapman)
  Bartholomew, 121
  Richard le, 245, 564
Charle, William, 245, 564
Charp, *see* Sharp
Charters, private, 291, 481, 502
Chasteloyne, Giles, clerk of Lorraine, & Nicholas & Theobald his servants, 231
Chattels: aliens', 310; detinue of, 496; Jews', 307, 336
Chattels of felons: concealed, 316; enquiry in eyre concerning, 72, 245; falsely valued by wards, 206, 223; of a suicide, 206; of abjurors, 9, 66, 79, 92, 112, 172, 186, 262; of outlaws, 37, 41, 50–1, 60, 75, 83, 89, 117, 125, 138, 148, 159, 163, 181, 183, 188, 194, 202, 215, 223, 228, 231, 234, 258, 264, 276, 284, 290, 316; released, 80; taken without warrant, 75; value of, App. C
Chaucer
  James le, 40
  John le (I), 180; (II) of St. Bartholomew's hospital, 685
Chaumbliz, *see* Chambly
Chauncy, Joseph de, treasurer of the exchequer, 786
Chauvent (Champvent)
  Peter de, keeper of the king's arms, 138
  William de, 465
Cheap ward, 65, 72, 101, 103, 128, 133, 147, 149, 171, 198, 241, 341, 468, 508; beadles of, 468
Cheapside (Forum, Westchep(e)), 24, 53, 104, 126, 128, 147, 179, 296
Chedworth (Cheddeworth), Alan de, 89
Chelmsford (Chelmereford), Amice daughter of Richard de, 523
Chendut(h), Agnes de, 174, 637
Chesewyke, *see* Chiswick
Cheshunt (Cesterhunte, Chestehunt), Herts., 197; prioress & nuns of, 349, 564
  John de (I), 75, 292, 503, 527; (II), 150
  Richard de, 109

160

Index

Chess, 48, 151
Chester (Cestr'): county, 116
   Maud, widow of Hemming de, 145
   Ralph de, 416, 765
Chesterfield (Cestfeud), Henry de, 37
Chests (boxes, coffers), 282, 498, 521
Chevendre, Roger de, 240
Chichester (Cycestre), bishop of, 18; dean & chapter of, 340
Child, Henry, 170
Chingford (Chingeforde), John de, 91
Chirographs, 134, 501, 521
Chiswick (Chesewyke), Roger de, 217, 543
Chrishall (Cristenhalle), Essex, 53
Christchurch, Jordan de, 50
Christchurch Canterbury, prior & convent, 221
Chubbe (Chobbe), Walter, 284, 584
Churches in the king's gift, 299
Churchyards, see St. Dunstan in the West; St. Paul's
Cippenham, Bucks., 478
Cirencester, Thomas de, 169
Cissor, see Tailor
Civil pleas, 470–523 passim
Civil War, crimes in time of, 170, 287
Clapham (Clopham), Hugh de, 399, 767
Clare
   Gilbert de, earl of Gloucester & Hertford, 17, 296, 357; household of, 189, 493
   Richard de, 78
   Thomas de, kt., 167, 230, 435, 481
Clere, Roger de, 316, 591
Clerk
   Athelard the, 452
   Christian the, 26
   Ellis the, 118
   German, without Aldgate, 527
   Gwiot (Wyotus), 272, 346, 579, 726
   Henry son of Stephen the, 187
   Hugh le, 195
   John le (the) (I), 54; (II), 499; (III), 196, 229, 647; (IV), 294, 664
   Leo the, 258, 572
   Michael the, 34
   Osbert the, 143
   Richard le (the) (I), 245, 564; (II), 263, 575
   Robert le, 409
   Roger the, 527
   Simon le (I), 236; (II), 246, 565
   William le, 252
   William son of Robert le, 9
Clerkenwell (Clerkewelle)
   priory and nuns of, 505
   Walter de, & Alice his wife, 87
Clerks: as witnesses, 488; not in frankpledge, 149, 192

Clerks, criminous: 18, 39, 55, 111, 116, 187, 256, 261, 264, 282; acquitted, 187, 256, 261, 282; convicted in secular court, 116, 264, 316; handed over to bishop, 39, 55, 116, 187, 264, ? 274, 282, 316, 479; outlawed, 149, 192
Cleve, Roger de, 209
Clifford, Roger de, the elder, 340
Clippers of coin, 11, 284, 309
Clive, Walter de, 227, 552
Clopham, see Clapham
Clopton
   Robert de, 527
   William de, 698
Cloth: 186; burel, 284; of gold & silk, 487; russet, 20; see also Assize of cloth
Clothing, 505; see also Brooches; Buckle; Dress; Girdle; Hood; Surcoats
Coal, 300
Cobbler, 141, 239
Cobham, John de, justice in eyre & justice of gaol delivery, 1, 146, 234, 243, 246, 249, 256, 265, 269, 583
Codeford (Godeford), Alexander (de), 267, 577
Cofferer, 214
   Godfrey le, 209, 690
   Henry le, 209
   John le, 341, 468, 521
   Richard le, 152
Coffers, see Chests
Coin, see Clippers of coin
Coiners, 309
Cokington, Henry de, kt., 481
Colchester (Colecestre)
   Adam son of William de, 177
   Gilbert de, tailor, 674; taverner, 279, 527
   John de, 201; king's almoner, 340, 526
Cole, John, 294, 663
Coleman
   Robert, 245, 564
   Walter, 130
Coleman Street ward, 83, 170
Coleworth, see Culeworth
Cologne (Colon'), 147
   Gocelin de, 11
   Lambert de, 39
Combe, see Coumbes
Combray, see Cambrai
Compurgators, election of, 209; see also Law
Conduit (de Conductu)
   Eleanor wife of Adam le Feroun, 292, 527
   Ellis de, 292, 527
   Thomas de, the elder, 292, 527
   Thomas de, the younger, 292, 527
Conduit, the great, 228, 464
Conin, John, 667

Index

Constable, *see* Dover castle; Tower of London
Contempt, 507
Convers, Nicholas le, 288, 306
Conyngham, *see* Coringham
Cook (Keu), 204, 214, 230, 250, 255
  Ailward le, 99
  Arnold the, 146
  Christine widow of Robert the, of Fleet, & Estrilda her maid, 231
  Master Geoffrey le, 214; & Thomas his servant, 541
  Godman, 49
  Henry le (the), 26, 48, 75
  Hugh the, 230
  James the, 252, 260, 573
  John the, 49, 257
  Lovekin the, 216
  Nicholas, 239
  Richard the, of Friday Street, 274, 581
  Robert the, 266, 576
  Roger the, 75
  Simon, cook of a canon of St. Paul's, 255
  Thomas le (I), 101; (II), 163
  William the, 170, 239, 243
Corder, 149, 284
  Roger le, 512, 714
Cordwainer (Corversarius), 114, 176, 222
  Geoffrey le, 154
  Gilbert le, 33
  Henry le, 108
  John le, 91, 102, 252, 602
  Richard le, 134; Juliana his wife, 151
  Robert le (I), 197; (II), 63, 266, 576
  Stephen le, 351, 728
  Thomas le, 142
Cordwainer ward, 35, 47, 56, 64, 131, 223, 238
Coringham (Conyngham), Robert de, 376, 743
Corn, 276, 313, 474
Corner (Cornere), 279
  William de la, 292, 527; Master, 340
  William le, 118, 616
Cornhill (Cornhull), 287–8; ward, 112, 185, 250, 495
  Robert de (I), sheriff, 4, 86–98, 205–19, 541, 542, 544, 601, 603, 661; (II), his son, 4, 205, 654
  Stephen de, draper, 221, 294, 458, 481, 547, 590, 663, 782
Cornmonger, Robert le, 36
Cornwall, Edmund (of Almain), earl of, 401, 481
Coroner's rolls, 37, 87, 222; *see also* Chamberlain, king's
Correour (Coureour), *see* Currier
Corteys (Cortois), *see* Curteys
Cosin (Cosyn), *see* Cusin
Cotiler, *see* Cutler

Coubely, John, 246
Coumbes (Co(u)mbe)
  Thomas de, 236, 292, 527
  Walter de, 48
Council, king's, 39, 484
County court, appeal in, 131
Coupere (Cuper), Richard le, 108, 228, 553, 610
Coureour, *see* Currier
Courts, *see* Bench; County; Curia Regis; Curia Romana; Husting
Courtyards, 91, 231, 256, 442
Covenants, 489, 492, 495, 501, 505
Coventry (Coventre), 23; prior of, 340, 526
  Henry de, sheriff, 4, 54, 100–8, 130, 192, 237, 246, 249, 258, 289, 292, 316, 468, 496, 506, 509, 519, 529, 565–6, 589, 591
  John de, 86, 287, 600
  Robert de, 95
  Roger de (I), 204, 652; (II), 292, 527
Coverer, *see* Cuver
Cows, 82, 276; *see also* Oxen
Crakehail (Crakehale), John de, treasurer of the exchequer, 104
Crammok, Maurice, 170
Crane, York, 665
Cranley (Cranlegh), John de, 237
Crapsy (Crapfy), Master Ralph (*alias* Adam), 432, 772
Cray, *see* Creye
Crek
  Geoffrey de, 152
  Master William de, 257
Crepiner, Henry le, 249
Crepyn
  Ralph, mayor's clerk, 523, 663 n. 12
  Roger, 43
Crespyn, *see* Crispin
Crete, William, 275
Creton, William de, 127
Creye (Cray)
  John de, 126
  Peter de, 70
Criour (Crior), Martin le, 267, 491
Cripplegate ward, 72, 120, 155, 211, 212, 234, 454, 504
Crispes (Crispus), Nicholas, 183
Crispin (Crespyn), Aaron, a Jew, 446, 777
Cristemes, John, 250, 567
Cristemeson, Robert, 276
Cristehalle, *see* Chrishall
Crok, Roger, 685
Croll (Cryol), William, 62, 540
Cross (Cruce)
  Hugh de, 227, 552
  John de, 392
  see also Attecross; Cruce Roes
Crosselin, Hugelot, 665
Crown & regalia, 300

Index

Crown pleas, 6–290 *passim*; held without warrant, 305
Cruce Roes, John de, 249
Crul, Simon, 48
Cryol, *see* Croll
Cufrere, Agnes la, 177
Culeworth (Coleworth, Culesworth), Richard de, justice of gaol delivery & constable of the Tower, 108, 112
Cullyng, Nicholas de, 200
Cuneyse, John le, 27
Cuper(e), *see* Coupere
Cups, gold & silver, 487; silver, 509
Curfew, 147, 500
Curia Regis, 152
Curia Romana, 498
Currier (Correour, Coureour), 214, 222, 468
  Gilbert le, 249
  Hugh le, 168, 635
  Miles le, 249, 496
  Nicholas le, 249
  Richard le, 239
  William le, 113
Curte, Nicholas, 294, 664
Curteney (Curtenay), Master Nicholas (de), 471, 488, 706, 708
Curteys (Corteys, Cortois)
  Richard, 99, 292, 527, 605
  Robert, 209, 294, 663
Cusin (Cosin)
  Gilbert, 228
  Peter, sheriff, 4, 243–5, 473, 481
Custody of prisoners: disputed, 98; pending pardon, 269; *see also* Imprisonment
Custom of the City, *see* Bail; First finder; Foreign warranty; Imprisonment; Inquests on corpses; Intrusion; Land; Neighbours; Sanctuary; Watch; Wills; Witnesses
Custom of the realm, 496
Customs, levied, 314
Customs & services, pleas of, 480, 483, 489, 495; claimed for husting, 483; covenant between parties, 489; parties agree, 480, 489
Cutler (Cotiler, etc.), 228
  Peter le, 192, 258, 572
  Ralph le, 209
  Solomon le, 214, 222, 548, 662
  William le, 742
Cut-purses, 20, 65
Cuver (Coverer, Cuverur)
  Alexander le, 129
  Hugh le, 168, 635
  John le, 185, 584 n. 3
  Richard le, 584
  Simon le, 33
  William le, 96

Cycestre, *see* Chichester
Cyphywast, Nicholas, kt., 481

Dagun, Robert, 34
Dakenes, Hubert de, 402
Damages: assessed, 471, 496, 519; claimed, 474, 483, 487–8, 491, 493, 495, 500, 505, 508–9, 511, 516
Damyas, *see* Amiens
Daniel
  Richard, 236
  Silvester, 16
  Walter, 392
Davy, Robert, 53
Daythef, Agnes, 38
De, Bertram de la, 108
Debt, plea of, 474; recognizances of, 475, 486, 490, 497–8
Decore, Richard le, 128
Default: articles concerning, 331–2; of common summons, 340, 526, 528
Defence of the realm, 491
Deneman, John, 183, 642
Deodands: grant of, 221; *loquendum* concerning, 130; not declared, 133, 253; not found, 122; taken without warrant, 162, 184, 240; value of, App. D; valued falsely, 32, 40, 43, 54, 67, 91, 129–30, 155, 178, 212, 220
Deodatus (Theodore), *see* Willame
Depe
  Arnold de, 292, 527
  John de, *alias* John de Dere, & John his servant, 236, 279, 292, 527, 583
  John de, mercer of Sopers Lane, 723
Deptford, Kent, 107
Derby (Derbi)
  earl of, *see* Ferrers, Robert de
  John de, 273
  Richard de, 368
  Robert de, *alias* Robert de Stroby, 159, 212, 656
  Roger de (I), 13; (II), 294, 663
  William de (I), 141; (II), 264
Dere, John de, *see* Depe, John de
Derkin, John, 116, 435
Despenser, Hugh le, justice of gaol delivery, 154, 163
Detinue: of charters, 510, 517; of chattels, 474
Deuben(e)y, Henry, 153, 625
Deusour, Richard, 292
Deveneys (Devenays), John de (le), 217, 543
Dibel (Dybel), William, 32, 37, 78
Dicer Lane (Dycereslane), 344
Dieulacres (Deulacres), Staffs., friar of, 521
Dikes, 392, 394
Dinton (Dynton), Gilbert de, 237

163

Index

Dishes, silver, 487
Distaflane, *see* Maiden Lane
Distraint, 9, 182, 258, 328–9, 510; death arising from, 70; in Essex, 6, 18, 520; in Yorks., 9; of prior of Bermondsey, 116
Ditches, 155, 157; *see also* Houndsditch
Docking, Osbert de, *alias* Osbert de Kent, 230
Doctor, *see* Physician
Doget (Doket)
 John, 292, 527
 William, 292, 527; & Isabel his wife, 516
Dogs, 345
Doneden, John, 666
Donewyz, *see* Dunwich
Dongon, Ralph, 340
Donstable, *see* Dunstable
Donstre, *see* Dunster
Donyngham, Simon de, 236
Door-keeper: in eyre, 2; of a priory, 201
Doors, 134; purpresture before, 392
Dormur, Walter le, 88
Dorset: county & sheriff of, 493
 Robert de, 292, 353, 527, 730
Douai (Douwai, Dowey)
 Lotimus de, 664
 Rykewin de, 294, 664
Dover, Kent, 115, 604; castle & constable, 203
 Robert de, 159, 631
Dower, pleas of, 477–8, 482, 484, 515; essoin allowed in, 513
Dowgate (Douegate) ward, 124, 253, 481
Dragon, Richard, 288
Draper, 287, 296, 481, 501
Drawer (Drauer)
 Fulk le, 99, 605
 Hamo (Hamond) le, 99, 605
 Henry le, 99, 605
Dress, woman's, 519
Drinkwater, Roger, 316, 591
Drowning, 19, 34, 211; in a ditch, 155, 157; in a pit, 18; in a well, 191; in the Fleet, 161; in the Thames, 10, ? 12, 36, 46, 62, 71, 93, 114, 122, 124, 132, 139, 144, 160, 184, 196, 217, 220, 240, 246, 248, 251, 259
Dubbur (Dubur)
 Henry le, 183, 642
 Wakelin le, 16
Duket, Laurence son of Humphrey, 207
Dumowe, *see* Dunmow
Dun, William, 170
Duncon, Nicholas de, 77
Dunelm, *see* Durham
Dung, obstructs a lane, 443
Dunhache, William de, 275
Dunkan, Peter, 32
Dunmow (Dumowe), Essex, 511

Edith de, 14
Dunolm, *see* Durham
Dunstable (Donstable)
 Hugh de, 175
 Thomas de, 91
Dunster (Donestre), Andrew de, 198, 649
Dunton(e)
 Alan de, 237
 Gilbert de, 292, 527
 Hugh de, 527, 693
 William de, 527
Dunwich (Donewyz), Roger de, 58
Durant (Duraunt)
 John, 209, 472, 485, 514, 669, 715
 Reyner, 219
Durham (Dunelm, Dunolm): London house of bishop of, 521
 Adam de, 238
 Bartholomew de, 209, 519
 Cicely widow of Jollan de, 209, 232, 511, 657
 Jollan de, 209, 232, 511, 657
 Peter de, 239
 William de, sheriff, 4, 14–16, 18–35, 53, 136, 193–204, 212, 223, 230, 355, 363, 481, 522, 531, 650; ward of, *see* Bread Street ward
Dusse, Alan, 245, 564
Dyer, 209
Dygon (Dykon), Richard, 408, 761
Dyting, Geoffrey, 236

Ear, loss of an, 473
Easements of hospitality, 501
Eastcheap (Estchep), 99, 218
 Thomas de (I), 288; (II), 682
Edelmeton, *see* Edmonton
Edelyre, John de, 665
Edeworth (Eddeworth, Edesworth), Stephen de, warden & chamberlain, 3, 202–3, 290, 519, 590, 728
Edith, a woman named, 124
Edmonton (Edelme(n)ton), Middx., 245, 279
 John son of Robert de, 245, 564
 Peter de, 91, 294, 663; ward of, *see* Castle Baynard ward
 Thomas de, 109
 William de, 208
Edmund, prince, son of Henry III, 208
Edrith, Roger & William, 36
Edward I (Lord Edward), 170, 208, 219, 293, 306, 309, 342, 470, 473, 476, 484, 521, 525, 567
Edwin (Edwyne), Reginald (*alias* Roger), 227, 552
Eggs, 275
Egrith, William, 34, 140, 288
Eleanor of Provence, queen of Henry III, 472, 485, 487, 495, 514

Eltham (Heltham), Thomas de, 96
Ely, William de, 135
Elylaund (Elilaund), John de, 288, 471, 488
Emeralds, 487
Emery, brother of Philip, parson of St. Mary Conyhop, 193
Enfield (Enefeld, Enefeud), Middx., 275, 279
  Alice de, 19
  Morkin de, 28
  William de, 232, 239, 257, 560, 571
English (Anglie, Engleis, Englys)
  Henry le, 36
  Walter le, 181, 292, 503, 527, 640
  William le, 250, 567
Erebourwe, Richer de, 16
Eriswell (Erwell), Geoffrey, son of Roger, 115
Escape from prison, 20, 37, 134, 257; allowed voluntarily, 289; article concerning, 316; confessions of, 204, 263, 316; from Aldgate, 153; from custody of sheriff of Middx., 280; from a house, 83, 204; from Newgate, 60, 62, 176, 208, 219, 257, 263, 316; sheriffs acquitted for, 316; *see also* Sanctuary, escapes from
Escheats, article concerning, 341; inquisition concerning, 75
Esert, Stephen le, 246
Eskirmeser, 260
Esperon (Esporon, Sporon), Thomas, chamberlain, 6–16, 18, 22, 73–6, 82–5
Espicer, Bartholomew le, 116, 360
Esprigonel (le Spigornel), Alexander, 213, 661
Essewell(e)
  Roger de, & John his servant, 122
  Walter de, 159
Essex: county, 42, 48, 92, 112, 493, 498, 511, 595, 657, 663, 702; sheriff of, 6, 18, 48, 520
  Robert de, 209, 657
  Walter de (? sheriff of Essex), 565, 747
  William de, 279, 583
  Wolmar de, 34, 63, 292, 527; ward of, *see* Billingsgate ward
Essoins, 513
Estbus, Gilbert de, 145
Estmor, Roger le, 292, 527
Eston, Hugh de, 428
Estrays (Estreis, Estreys)
  Herman le, 220, 279, 429, 583
  Maud le, 220
  Walter son of Gerard le, 220
Estreat, *see* Exchequer
Esture (Sture), Robert de, 147, 487, 622
Eswy (Essewy, Assewy, Hassewy)
  Joan, mother of Richard (II), 499
  Richard (I), broker, 287; (II), draper, 294, 499, 517, 663, 709, 716

William, mercer, sheriff, 4, 50–62, 73–6, 83, 203, 316, 537–8, 591; ward of, *see* Coleman Street ward
Etewell, Robert, 133; *see also* Attewell
Ethelburg, Juliana de, 200
Eure (Euere)
  Henry de, & Adam his servant, 279
  John son of Robert de, 186, 644
  Roger de, 209
Everard
  Henry son of Peter, 478
  Thomas, 33
  Walter, 294, 663
Evesham, William de, 37
Evesk, *see* Bishop
Ewell, Richard de, sheriff, 4, 73–6, 89, 94, 100, 102, 104, 132, 148, 167, 169, 206, 294, 595, 596, 663; ward of, *see* Farringdon ward
Ewer, Walter le, 174
Examination by the justices, 18, 54, 70, 146
Exchange, king's, 311
Exchequer: estreat of the eyre, 525–786; goods handed to, 234; order of, 182; Pipe Rolls, App. E; presentation of measures at, 468; record of, 468; treasurer & barons of, 182, 345
Excommunication, 333
Exemie, Alice de, 427, 770
Exeter (Exepote, Exeport): diocese of, 111
  Edmund de, 521
  Richard de, 271, 578
  Thomas de, 138
  Walter de, 37
Extortion, articles concerning, 326–9
Eye (Eya)
  Adam de, 208, 657
  Philip de, 442
Eyre of Middlesex, (of *1273–4*), 279–80
Eyres of London, 98
  of *1244*, 18, 52, App. A
  of *1251*, 2–3, 21, 295, 301, 321, 470, 503, 516
  of *1276*: articles of, 295–432, App. A; common summons & acquittance from 17, 340, 493; writ file, 74, 208
Eyt, Richard del, 700

Faggots, 220
Fairs, *see* Smithfield; Winchester
Falconel, Ingram, 294, 664
Falling sickness, 27, 30–1, 103, 215
Fanchirche, *see* St. Gabriel Fenchurch
Farnborough (Farenbergh), Roger de, 283
Farnham
  Henry de, 468
  Simon de, 292, 527
Farringdon ward, 31, 39, 41, 44, 67–8, 75, 89, 94, 100, 102, 104, 132, 137, 148,

165

Index

Farringdon ward, *continued*
  152, 167, 169, 194, 206, 212, 215, 239, 252, 342, 344, 346–54, 489, 500
Faukeham, William de, marshal of the king's household, 341
Faukes, Richard, 29; *see also* Fulk
Faversham, Kent, 20
  Henry de, 209
  William de, 26
Felice, a woman named, 89
Feltham, John de, 98
Ferar, *see* Ferrers
Ferebraz, Felice, 510
Ferol, Simon, 206, 634
Feroun (Ferun)
  Adam le, & Eleanor de Conductu his wife, 292, 527
  Henry le, 67
  Stephen le, 222, 548
  Walter le, 686
Ferrers (Ferar)
  Robert de, earl of Derby, 340
  William de, 296
Ferur
  Bartholomew le, 46
  Henry le, 75
  Walter le, 225
Fethermonger, John le, 209
Fever, 143; treatment of, 257
Fevere (Feverer)
  Alan le, 676
  Geoffrey le, 284
  Henry le, 236
  Ralph le, sheriff, 527, 548, 556, 564, 579, 583, 605, 663, 673, 677, 683–4, 717, 738, 744, 752, 770–1
  Richard le, 240, 562
  William le, 245, 564
  see also Smith
Fige, Henry (de), 227, 552
Fines, 287, 471, App. B
Finthard, *see* Fyntard
Fire in London, 296; prevention of, 344
First finder, custom concerning, 21
Fisherman, Peter the, 378
Fishing, unlawful, 339
Fishmonger (Pessoner), 159, 181, 209, 228, 273, 279
  Germain le, 383, 746
  William le, 48
Fishponds, 315
Fishtraps, 339
Fisicien, *see* Physician
fitz Mary, Joan, daughter of Simon, 84
fitz Otto, Hugh, warden, chamberlain & constable of the Tower, 3, 170, 204–19, 300, 309
fitz Richard, William, mayor & sheriff, 3, 4, 22, 40, 178–81; his heir, 640; Amis, widow of, 440, 776; ward of, *see* Tower ward
fitz Thedmar, Arnald, 60, 220; ward of, *see* Billingsgate ward
fitz Thomas
  Thomas, the elder, mayor & sheriff, 3, 4, 78–82, 102, 521, 597; ward of, *see* Queenhithe ward
  Thomas, the younger, 294, 663
Flagons, silver, 487
Flaoner
  Hugh le, 99
  Thomas le, 287, 587
  William le, 159, 287, 587
Fleet (Flete): stream, 231, 491, 533
  Ellen de, wife of Andrew le Bell, 292, 527, & Walter her son, 500
Fleet bridge, 500
Fleet prison & soke, 300
Fleg (Flegh), Peter de (le), 93, 604
Fleming (Flemyng, Flandrensis)
  Lambert le, 232
  Michael brother of Albod the, 60
Flemish merchants, *see* Merchants
Florence, Italy, 219
Flos, Gerard de, 294, 664
Fokkelape, *see* Fukelape
Folesham, *see* Fulham
Folkmoot at St. Paul's, 209
Food, 505
Forain, William, 37
Forbo(u)r, *see* Furber
Ford (de la Ford(e), de Lafford)
  Thomas, sheriff, 4, 142–54; Juliana his widow, 340, 526
  Walter de la, 253, 473, 569
Foreign pleas, 493, 511
Foreign warranty, 477–8, 482, 484–5, 494, 502, 513–15; custom concerning, 484; of a minor, 470; of a queen, 472, 485, 514
Forester, Henry le, 127
Forests, 315
Forgery of money, 11
Formager, *see* Fromager
Forner, John le, 667
Forshort, 489
Fos..., Henry, 257
Fot, William, 309, 341
Foucher (Fucher), William, 235, 558
Framlingham (Framelyngham, Fremingham), Suffolk, 263, 575
  Gilbert de, 118
  Ralph de, justice in eyre, 1
  William de, 262
Frank, Simon le, 30
Frankeleyn (Fraunkelein)
  Alexander le, 276, 582
  Henry, 284
  Jordan le, 15
  Richard, 80

166

Index

Frankpledge: felons in, 185, 250, 258; persons not in, because: clerks, 149, 192; itinerant, 51; living in church-precincts, 255; a minor, 158; strangers, 20–263 *passim*; vagrants, 61, 246; *see also* Mainpast
Frauncveys
  Andrew le, 29
  Isabel la, 258
  John le, 183
Frebodi, Walter, 45, 536
Freman, Thomas le, 245, 564
Fremingham, *see* Framlingham
Fremund, Master William le, 207
Frere
  John, 48, 91
  Richard, 45, 536
  Thomas, 243
  William, 105
Fresang, Jakes de, 294, 663
Fresharing (Fresheryng)
  Alexander, Margery his wife, & John their son, 95
  Reginald, 48, 95
Fressenede, William, 666
Friars
  Black Friars (Friars Preachers), 342
  Grey Friars (Friars Minor), church of, 106, 263, 316; friar of Dieulacres, 521
  Friars of the Sack (Friars of the Penitence of Jesus Christ), prior & brethren of, 472, 485, 514
Friday Street (Fridaistrate), 274
  Hugh de, 223
  Reginald de, 216, 358, 732
  Master Robert de, 166, 292, 527, 634
Fromager (Formager, Furmager)
  Ellis le, 392
  Godfrey le, 468
  Walter le, 185
  William le, 185
Frome (From), John de, 316, 591
Fros (Frosh)
  Geoffrey, 273, 580
  William, 34
Frowyk (Frouwyk)
  Henry de, sheriff, 4, 72, 120, 211, 234, 254–69, 286, 316, 434, 504, 520, 572, 574–6, 591; ward of, *see* Cripplegate ward
  John son of Laurence de, 4, 6
  Laurence de, sheriff, 4, 6–16, 39, 41, 44, 67–8; ward of, *see* Farringdon ward
  Peter de, 116
  Philip, 209
  Reginald de, 294, 663
  Walter de, 511
Fruter, 252
  Eustace le, 49
  Geoffrey le, 177, 639

Gregory le, 223
Jordan le, 668
Walter le, 152
Fuatard, John, 292, 527
Fucedame, Roger, 209
Fucher, *see* Foucher
Fugitives from justice: article concerning, 312
Fukelape (Fokkelape), Richard, 37, 533
Fulburn (Fuleburn), Stephen de, knight hospitaller, 306
Fulham (Fole(s)ham)
  Mahekin de, 209
  Walter de, 453
Fulk, Robert son of, 340, 528
Furber (Forbo(u)r, Furbur)
  Geoffrey le, 228, 553
  Gladwyn le, 222
  Osbert le, & Beatrice his wife, 281
  Peter le, 192, 214, 508, 655, 713
Furfeles, John de, 294, 664
Furmager, *see* Fromager
Fuster
  Adam le, 21
  Roger le, & Theobald his servant, 88
Fyntard (Finthard), Thomas, 260, 573

Gaddesden (Gatesden), John de (I), keeper of the queen's wardrobe, & Hawys de Nevill his wife, 495, 501; (II), 25
Galeys, *see* Waleys
Games, *see* Chess
Gandavo, Simon de, 473
Gandos, Adam de, 228
Ganter, *see* Gaunter
Gaol delivery, 55, 74–5, 230, 235–6; by jury, 152, 202–3, 243, 246, 256; by writ (or pardon), 6, 37, 108, 208, 219, 231; confirmed: by the justice, 243, 256, the mayor & aldermen, 55, 74, 152, the neighbourhood, 230; justices of, *see* Aguilon, William; Bigod, Hugh; Blund, Peter le; Boyland, Roger de; Broke, Laurence de; Cobham, John de; Culeworth, Richard de; Despenser, Hugh le; justices testify, 249, 269; pardon at instance of justice, 265; without warrant, 317
Gaol delivery rolls, 74, 94, 243, 256
Gardens, 18, 32, 232
Gardiner
  Peter le, 101
  Ralph le, 101
  Thomas le, 156, 627
  William le, 119, 618
Garsie, Arnato de, a Roman, 29, 531
Garskirke, *see* Gracechurch
Garst, John de, 37
Garzon, Adam le, 480

Index

Gascony, Bartholomew of, 67
Gask, Otto de (*alias* Odyn de Gare), & Geoffrey his servant, 257, 571
Gates: of a house, 225; of the City, 322; with locks, 344
Gatesden(e), *see* Gaddesden
Gatham, *see* Gotham
Gaugi, John, 130
Gaundone, Thomas de, 284
Gaunt, 665
   Abraham le, 665
   Baldwin de, 114, 612
   Bordin (Boydin) de, 294, 663
   John de, 260
   Simon de, 481
Gaunter (Ganter), 253, 279, 292
   Haukin le, 127
   John le, & Agnes his wife, 250, 567
   Walter, 153
Gavelet, 483
Gayste, Roger de, 123
Geddingg(es), Geoffrey de, & William de, his brother, 294, 663
Gedenare, Abraham, 665
Gent, Cresse son of, 672
Geoffrey, Philip son of, 149
Gerard, Robert son of, 59
Geraudun, Arnald de, chamberlain, 5–16, 18, 22
Giffard, William, 299
Gilbert, Richard, 245, 564
Gille, William, 37
Girdle, silk, 511
Girdler (Gerdeler)
   John le, 6
   Luke le, 113
   Robert le, 109
Gisburn (Giseburn), Adam de, 232
Gisors (Gysors, etc.)
   Bruyn de, 292, 527
   Hugh de, 306
   John de (I), chamberlain & mayor, 3, 19–54, 63–8, 72, 130, 159, 181, 628; wharf of, 130; (II), his son, 19, 24, 628
   Peter de, chamberlain, 78–81, 86–124, 292, 380, 527, 600
   Robert de, 527
Gloucester
   earl of, *see* Clare, Gilbert de
   Hugh de, 264, 500, 710
   Philip de, 72, 594
   Walter de, 216, 246, 565
   William de, 155, 626
Goblet, silver, 284
Godale, *see* Godhale
Godard, Alan, 212
Godeford, *see* Codeford
Godewe, Simon, 15
Godewin, Master, 352, 729
Godewyn, William, 227, 552

Godfrey, John son of, 159
Godgrom, Simon, 132
Godhale (Godale), John (I), 27; (II), 95
Goding (Godingg)
   Hugh & John, 245, 564
   William (de), 245, 564
Godington, John de, 159, 631
Godinou, Walter, 15
Gofeir, Gerard & John, 702
Gold, 487; *see also* Brooches; Cups; Rings
Goldrik, John, 249
Goldsmith (Aurifaber, Orfevre), 58, 85, 109, 158, 272, 279, 284, 309, 502
   Abel, 85
   Edmund the, 212, 660
   Hubert, 166
   Hugh le, 260
   Peter the, 95
   Reginald the, 375, 743
   Richard le, 171
   Robert the, 137
   Thomas the, of the Bridge, 279
   William the, 99
Goldsmiths, control of craft, 491
Goldston, John, 245, 564
Goldweys, John de, & Edith his wife, 197
Golet, Gilbert, 16
Good Neighbour, a Roman, 232
Gorel, Maurice, & Maud his wife, 275
Gorger
   Godfrey le, 219
   Peter le, 134
   Stephen le, 159, 631
Gorham (Goreham), Nicholas de, 252, 568
Gosewell, Albin & Robert de, 109
Gotele (Goteley)
   Robert de, 510
   Stephen de, 288
Gotham (Gatham)
   Henry de, 49
   Nicholas de, 260, 573
Gowiz (Gowys, Gouwyte)
   Brian de, 296
   Walter de, 294, 664
Goye, *see* Joie
Gracechurch (Garscherch, Garskirke etc.)
   Adam de, 15
   Austin de, 232
   Giles de, 527
   Philip de, 228
   Robert de, 279, 427
   Roger de, 292, 527
   see also All Hallows Gracechurch; St. James Garlickhithe
Gracechurch Street, 300, 305
Grapefig (Gratefige)
   Hugh le (I), 131, 438; (II), 686
   Robert, 241, 452, 561, 705
   William, sheriff, 4, 78–81, 597

Index

Gras
  Master John le, 104
  Robert le, & Isabel his wife, 261
Gravesend
  Dulcia de, 181
  William son of Robert of, 160
Gray, *see* Grey
Greenford (Greneford), Henry de, 279, 413, 505
Greenwich (Grenewyz), Kent, 220
  Alice de, 220
  John de, 135
Grene, Henry de, 685
Grescherche, *see* Gracechurch
Grey (Gray)
  John de (I), steward of the king's household, 146, 278, 287–8; (II), 249
  Reginald de, 340
  Roger de, 389
Grey Friars, *see* Friars
Greygrom
  Nicholas, 527
  William, 133
Greyhounds, *see* Dogs
Grimsby, Gilbert de, 204
Grosile (Grosyle), Warin, 245, 564
Gruyte, Baldewyn, 665
Guarinus, *see* Warin
Guilame (Gwilam), *see* Willame
Guildford (Guldeford), Surrey, 578
Guildhall (la Gildhall), 491
Gutters, 256, 357, 427–9, 463
Gylour, Geoffrey le, 94
Gynges
  Ellis de, 30
  John de, 221
Gypes, Geoffrey, 21
Gyrime, John, 665

Hache, John, 292
Hackney (Ageney, Haken(e)y), Middx., 245, 564
  Alan son of Philip de, 245, 564
  Benet de, 393, 752
  Peter de, 699
  Ralph de, chaplain (priest), 245
  Robert de (I), 222, 548; (II), cutler, 228
  William de, 103
Hadstock (Adestok, Hadestok)
  Joan, daughter of William de, 499, 502
  Robert de, 230, 555
  Simon de, 30, 33, 37, 49, 223, 459, 506, 519; erroneously listed as sheriff, 4; ward of, *see* Queenhithe ward
  William de, 220, 294, 499, 502, 517, 519, 622, 663; ward of, *see* Tower ward
Hak, Adam de, 99
Hakeborn, John de, 468
Hakeford (Aleford), Beatrice de, 292, 527
Haketon, Absolon de, 109

Hale, William del, 53
Hales, Thomas de, 48
Halistelle, Godfrey de, & John his son, 159
Haliwell, Middx., 245, 564; prioress of, 373, 378
  Godfrey de, 150
  Maud de, & Maud her niece, 221
  Walter de, 130
Halle, John, 665
Hallingbury (Hallynber')
  Geoffrey de, 24
  Nicholas de (I), 22; (II), 183
Halstead (Halstede, Hastede)
  James de, 183, 642
  Philip de, 521
  Thomas de, 50, 537
Halveclerk, Walter, 70
Hamelyn, William, sheriff of Warwickshire, 515
Hamiston, Peter de, 86
Hampshire (Sutht'), 51, 87
Hampton, Roger de, 486
Hanche, Thomas, 276
Hand, cutting off of a, 285
Hanging of felons, 188, 309; article concerning, 335; convicted at Canterbury, 312, 341; convicted at Newgate, 41, 49, 94, 128, 154, 163, 197, 202; convicted in eyre, 98, 146, 276–7, 284
Hannington (Hanningthon, Hanyngton)
  Alice de, 174
  Richard de, 174, 637
Harang, Isabel, 470
Haraz, *see* Arras
Harbouring of felons: alleged, 284, 286; arrest for, 279; articles concerning, 312, 315; by a master, 205; by a sheriff, 289; confession of, 28; in a priory, 116; in mainpast, 111; in the City, 109; in St. Clement's Lane, 312; in the Temple, 75; in wards, 29–258 *passim*; verdict of, 289
Harcourt (Harecourt), Saer de, 152
Hardel (Herdel)
  Avice, & Richard her servant, 292, 527
  John (I), 292, 527; (II), 702
  Laurence, wharf of, 246
  Nicholas, 108
  Ralph, mayor, 3
  Roger, 412
Haring, Roger, 43
Haringeye (Harenges), *see* Hornsey
Harpur, William le, 179
Harrow (Berwes, Herwes, etc.)
  Richard de (I), minor canon of St. Paul's, bishop's proctor, 39, 116, 187, 256, 261, 264, 282; (II), 274, 581
  Stephen de, 359, 732
  William de, 221

169

Index

Hartfield (Herefeud, Hertfeld), John de, & Thomas & William his servants, 202, 650
Haselbech, William de, chamberlain, 55–62, 69–71
Haslingfield (Haselyngfeud), Robert de, 36
Hassewy, *see* Eswy
Hastede, *see* Halstead
Hat, steel, 508
Hatche, John, 228
Hatfield (Hattefeld), Herts., 156
  Geoffrey de, 138
Hauberk, 508
Hautein (Hauteyn)
  Robert, 465, 468, 724, 774
  Stephen, 527
Hauvile (Huvil)
  Henry de, *alias* Henry de Lynnhull, 284, 585
  Simon de, 150
Haverhill (Haverhull)
  Isabel de, 35
  Margery de, 221
Havering (Haverynge)
  Richard de, 364
  William de, 13
Haversham (Haverham), William de, 174, 637
Hayes (la Haye), Middx., 58
Hayman, William, 183
Hayron, *see* Heyron
Hayward, *see* Heyward
Heaumer
  Robert le, 215
  Simon le, 215
Hede (Hese)
  John de, 227, 552
  Thomas, 685
Hegge, *see* Attehegge
Helmet, 306; *see also* Hat, steel
Heltham, *see* Eltham
Hendon, Middx., 127, 552
Hengham, Ralph de, chief justice, 484; his clerk, *see* St. Victor, James de
Henley (Henly), William de, exchequer clerk 182
Henry I, king, 345
Henry III, king, 6, 17–18, 72, 138, 170, 176, 207–8, 218–19, 221, 231, 279, 287, 299, ? 300, 341–5, 474, 484, 493, 508, 511, 514, 519, 521
Henry, Nicholas son of, attorney, 472
Hens, 275
Herdel, *see* Hardel
Herefeud, *see* Hartfield
Hereford
  Henry de, 292, 481, 527
  Thomas de, 209
  William de, 527
Herlauwe, *see* Hurly

Herlewyn, 588
Herlewyn, Nicholas, 696
Heron, *see* Heyron
Hert
  Adam le, 91
  William, 667
Hertfeld, *see* Hartfield
Hertford, 57, 88, 123, 565
  earl of, 493; *see also* Clare, Gilbert de
  Ellis de, 132, 350, 727
  Siward de, 37
  Walter de, 75
  William de, 284, 584
Hervey (Herevy, Hervi)
  Roger de, 362, 468, 735
  Thomas, 685
  Walter, mayor, sheriff & chamberlain, 3, 4, 133, 167–77, 193–204, 220, 221, 300, 468, 491, 508, 516, 636, 638, 646, 650; & Isabel his wife, 300
Herwes, *see* Harrow
Heryn, *see* Heyrin
Heryng
  Richard, 46
  Roger, 48
Hese, *see* Hede
Hewe
  Walter le, 285
  William, 292, 527
Hexham
  Master John de, 257
  Ranulph de, 257, 571
  Master Semann de, 257, 571
Heymonger, Edmund le, 364
Heyrin (Heryn), Gerard de, 294, 664
Heyron (Hayron, He(i)ron, Heyroun)
  Adam, 245, 564
  John (I), 272, 579; (II), 294, 663
  Paulin, 245, 564
  Ralph, 132
  Robert, 473, 527, 700
  Thomas, 209
  William, 60, 294, 490, 663
Heyward (Hayward), John (le), 212, 656
Hides, cargo of, 493
Hildersham (Hildringham), Isabel de, 149
Hocking (Ho(c)kyng)
  Gilbert de, 231
  Philip de, 231
  Walter de, 493, 498
Hodding, Ralph, 479
Hoder(e), 183
  Peter le, 183, 209, 642
Hodin, Robert, 271; *see also* Odyn
Hog (Hugge)
  John, 222
  William, 37, 533
Hoggelane (Hoggenelane), *see* Huggin Lane
Hoggenhore, Notekina, 119

Index

Hoke, *see* Atte hoke
Holborn (Holebo(u)rne, Holeburn), Middx., 67
  Salamon de, 665
  William de (I), & Beatrice his wife, 68; (II), 181, 640
Holebod, Ralph de, 12
Holy Trinity: Norman prior of, 345; prior & canons of, 55, 298–9, 345, 383, 477, 521; *see also* Bordray, John de; Portsoken
Holy Trinity the Less, parish, 61, 138
Home, Hamo, 97
Homicide, 7–281 *passim*; by Jews, 308; in Middlesex, 127, 279; in Surrey, 98, 116, 275
Honecote, Roger de, 697
Honey Lane (Honilane), 72
  Ellis of, 209
  Gilbert de, 688
  John de, 370
Hood, 74, 508
Hore, William le, 97
Hormade
  Adam de, 88
  Thomas de, 193
Horn
  Edmund, 279, 421
  John, sheriff, 4, 27, 73, 226, 232–48, 258, 270–90, 481, 522, 557, 582, 585–6; ward of, *see* Bridge ward
  Martin, 265, 516
  Nicholas, 279, 425, 769
Hornsey (Haringeye, etc.)
  Maud de, 87
  William de, 245, 564
Hors, Henry, & Cecily his wife, 163, 632
Horse-bite, 473
Horsemen, 24, 67, 345
Horsepol, John de, 256
Horses, 10, 67, 79, 144, 161, 178, 262, 276, 278, 284, 287–8, 471, 473; allegedly blind, 488; and carts, 45, 59, 227; king's, 146; unbroken, 227; valued, 511, App. D
Horse-trapper, 508
Horsham (Horsam), Robert de, 253, 569
Horton, John de, 75
Hosier, 214
Hospital, Gilbert of the, 14
Hospitality, 225, 495, 501
Hospitals in the king's gift, 298
Houndsditch (Hundesdiche, etc.), 45, 59
  Avice (Alice) de, 756; & Richard her husband, 400
  Geoffrey de, 629
  Stephen de, 156, 627
Household (*familia*), 104, 207–8, 214, 225, 235; *see also* Mainpast
Houses, 91, 138; built to the nuisance, 417, 434, 457; burnt or demolished, 275, 280, 296
Hoxton (Hoxston), Herion de, 245, 564
Hue and cry, 147; custom concerning, 24
Hugge, *see* Hog
Huggin Lane (Hoggelane, Hoggenelane), 90, 442
Hulder, Robert le, 197
Hull, Robert de (del), 245, 564
Hund(e), Nicholas, 37, 533
Hungrie
  Geoffrey son of John de, 189
  John de, 85
Huntingdon, Roger de, 153
Huntingfield (Huntyngfeud), Agnes de, 221
Huppehaldestere, *see* Upholder
Hurer (Huyrer)
  Alan le, 209
  Walter son of Adam le, & Robert his brother, 266, 576
  William le, 294, 663
Hurly (Herlauwe), Nicholas de, 25
Husting: annulment of wills in, 502, 517; appeals in, *see* Appeals; appeals remitted to, 120, 271; City's claim concerning civil pleas in, 483–4; justices in eyre hear plea in, 523; plaintiffs in eyre to sue in, 470, 484; plea quashed because not initiated in, 503; process concerning forshort in, 489; wife's renunciation in, 489
Hyde, Walter de la, 665
Hythe (Hithe, Huthe), 57
  William, 275

Imprisonment: articles concerning, 318, 326; custom concerning, 134; *hic cras*, 70; for wounding in self-defence, 147; in a priory, 55; in houses, 83, 204, 316, 509; of an appellor for withdrawal, 144; of clerks, 314, 316; of a defendant in a plea of trespass, 519; plea of wrongful, 496; satisfaction for wrongful, 522; *see also* Custody of prisoners; Gaol delivery; Prisons; *Suet de prison*
Incitement to felony, 39, 70, 140, ? 214, 219, 249
Indictments, 77, 98, 264, 275–6, 278, 281–2, 284–8; in the Middlesex eyre, 280; referred to, 289
Infalisation, 203
Inkel, Roger, 12
Inquests on corpses: adjudged inadequate, 70; custom concerning, 21–2; failure to hold, 124; irregularities in, 132, 177; record of, not found, 18
Inquests or inquisitions held: by a justice in Kent, 146; by the mayor & citizens, 37, 75, 473, 521, 523
Insanity, 253

Index

Intrusion, pleas of, 499, 504, 516; custom concerning, 516
Ipegrave, Thomas de, warden of the City, 3
Ireland, 580, 699
   Alan de, 90
   Miles de, 176, 638
   Nicholas de, 78
Iron, 508
Ironmonger (Ismonger, Ysemangere), John le (I), 263, 575; (II), 591 n.
Ironmonger Lane (Ismongerelane), 81, 84
   Adam de (I), 266, 527, 576; (II), 287
Islington (Iseldon), Middx., 245
Ispinelli, *see* Spinelli
Italian merchants, *see* Merchants
Ive, Hugh de, 396
Iverne, Frank, 665

Jakeford, Laurence de, 128
Jewels, 487, 491, 509
Jewry, 146, 287–8
Jews: agreements made without licence, 296; cruelty of, 308; fine of, 551; goods & chattels of, 307, 336; homicide by 308; houses of, 296; purprestures of, 775–6
Joce
   Richard, 272, 579
   Thomas son of, 694
John, a boy named, 16
Joie (Goye), Henry, 107
Jointe, *see* Junte
Jolinet, king's clerk, 193
Jordan, Thomas son of, 222
Joun, Edmund, 488
Jovene (Jouen, le Juvin, Jonior)
   John le (I), 51, 183; (II), 264; (III), 279
   Robert le, 183
   Roger le, 183
   Solomon le, 246, 565
   Thomas le, 70
Joynur, Ralph le, 37
Junte (Jointe), Donelin, 292, 527
Jur', Walter, 26
Jury & jurors: article concerning, 338; default of, 493; in inquests, 75, 473; licence to be tried by mayor & aldermen, 37, 70, 199, 222, 257; of twenty-four, 514, 523; of forty-two, 214, 233, 245, 249, 256, 261, 264; trial by, declined, 107; *see also* Trespass
Justices in eyre: in London, 1–2, 199, 222, 257, 470, 473, 484; party to a recognizance, 490; to visit Kent, 146; in Middx., 279
Justices of gaol delivery, *see* Gaol delivery

Karl', *see* Carlisle
Karon (Karroun), *see* Carron
Keddles, 339
Kedermenstre, *see* Kidderminster
Kelveden (Keleweden), William de, 209, 677
Kemefingg, Michael de, 384
Kemsing (Kemesyng), Stephen de, 198
Kendale, Hugh de, 471, 706
Kene, Lambert del, 667
Kenesherte, Alexander de, 118
Kensington (Kensingthon), Henry de, 181, 640
Kent: county, 694; sheriff of, 97, 107, 146, 510
   Alice de, 274, 581
   Henry de, 249
   John de, 156, 627
   Maud de, 268
   Osbert de, *alias* Osbert de Docking, 230, 555 n.
   William de, 116, 355, 468
Keu, *see* Cook
Keuter, William le, 174
Keylaston, Roger de, 235
Kidderminster (Kedermenstre), Robert de, 250, 294, 567, 663
Kilwardby, Robert, archbishop of Canterbury, 293, 476
King (Kyng)
   Alexander le, 275
   John le, 75, 291
King's chapel, yeomen of, 122
Kingsford (Kyngesfeld, Kynggeford), Richard, 15, 530
Kingston
   Richard de, 292, 527
   Robert de, 39
   William de, 165
Kirkstead, Lincs., abbot of, 340, 526
Kitchens, 141, 356, 501
Knight (Knith, Knyth), William, 102, 249, 607
Knives, 22, 26, 39, 48, 108, 133–4, 154, 156, 158, 189, 202, 230, 250, 260, 471
Kopherle, Robert de, 83
Kyse, Edmund, 245, 564
Kyvere, William le, 140

Ladder, 8, 64, 101
Lade, John de la, 159, 631
Lafford, *see* Ford
Lambourn (Lamburn), 22
   Adam de, 91
Lamenes (Laminess, Laymenes), Richard de, sheriff's bailiff, 256, 289, 589
Lance head, iron, 508
Land, pleas of, 470, 472, 485, 514, 523; by writ of right patent, 485, 514, 523; custom concerning, 514, 523
Landa (Lande), Jake(s) de, 294, 664
Lanes: grants to enclose, 342–4; obstructed, 409, 443; *see also* Paths

Index

Langbourn ward, 29, 117, 197, 256
Langford, William de, 66, 592
Langley
  Alexander de, 276
  Alice widow of Robert de, 72
  Richard de, 257
Lannes, Walter de, 725
Larceny, *see* Theft
Large, Ralph le, 83, 108, 610
Lastebyr', Robert de, 152
Laster, Thomas le, 21
Latimer, William le, 146, 278
Latten, rings of, 491
Laufare (Lauvare)
  Eustace de, 232
  Reginald de, 292, 527
  William de (I), 116; (II), 377, 744; (III), 684
Lavenham, Robert de, 218, 544
Law: great, 209; twelve-handed, 488
Laymenes, *see* Lamenes
Lead, 221; load of, 270; *see also* Vessels
Leather, 496; white, 508; *see also* Hides
Leden, Adam de, & Simon his servant, 142
Leges, Robert de, 506
Leicester, Agnes de, 38
Lemynstre, *see* Lyminster
Len, *see* Lynn
Leodegar, Master, 382
Lerenz, *see* Lorenz
Letherharde, Bette, 127
Letter, written in defendant's name, 278
Leuesham, *see* Lewisham
Leuis (Leuys), *see* Lewis
Leukenore
  Geoffrey de, justice in eyre, 1
  Roger de, 388, 750
Leuman, Simon, 15
Lewes, Sussex, battle of, 296
Lewis (Leuis, Leuys)
  Henry de, 145
  Richard, 245, 564
  William de, 294, 663
Lewisham (Leuesham, Louesham)
  Alexander de, 129
  William de, 32, 532
Liberty of the City, 279-80
Lichfield (Lichefeld), Alice de, 33
Lilystone (Lilleston), 127
Limeburner (Lymberne), Peter le, 392
Lincoln: bishop of, 18, 39, 316
  J. de, clerk, 671
  John de, & Christine his daughter, 85
  Matthew de, 274, 581
Lincolnshire, 52
Linde, *see* Lynde
Linton (Lynton)
  Master Adam de, Maud his wife, & Agnes her maid, 75, 596

Robert de, sheriff, 4, 50-62, 209, 294, 316, 370, 468, 481, 537-8, 591, 657, 663, 739
Lo, John de, & Peter his brother, 664-5
Loberg(e), Nicholas de, 294, 664
Lock, John, 236
Locks, on gate, 344
Loger (Logger), Hugh, 294, 664
Lokier (Lokyere), Maud, wife of Henry le, 163, 632
London: bishop of, 39, 55, 116, 187, 479, 527, 552, 564, 663; his proctor, *see* Harrow, Richard de (I)
London, Christine de, 247
London Bridge, 15, 45, 99, 107; Paul, warden of, 95
London Wall, 322, 345
Longe (Longman, Longus, le Lung)
  Geoffrey, 83
  Ives le, draper, 287
  John le, 159, 228
  Ralph le, 60, 539
  Robert le, 468
  William (I), 60, 539; (II), son of Ralph le, 245
Loquendum concerning: deodands, 130; enrolment of appeals, 137; escapes from churches, 20, 48; gaol delivery, 230; hue & cry, 24; inquests, 22; watch & ward, 20
Lorenz (Lerenz), John, 279, 300
Lorimer, 101, 272
  Nicholas le, 25
  Roger le, 209
  Terry le, 101
Lorraine (Lorianico), 231
Lou, Hugh le, 450, 780; *see also* Wolf
Louel, Emma, 256
Louesham, *see* Lewisham
Louman, Mabel, & Philippa her maid servant, 187
Louvain (Lovayne), Lyhussenere de, 665
Lovecote, Denise de, 234, 284, 584
Loveday, Roger, 340
Lucas, John, 249
Lucca, Italy
  Luke de, & his associates, 521, 666
  Theobald de, & his associates, 666
Ludgate, 137
  Simon de, 513
Lunatic, 253
Lung, le, *see* Longe
Lure, Ranulf, 288
Lyminster (Lemynstre), Simon de, 53
Lynde (Linde)
  Clarice, widow of John de, 484
  John de la, bailiff of the City & constable of the Tower, 3, 345, 508
Lyne, Ranulf, 99, 605

Index

Lynn (Len)
  Emma de, 212
  Nicholas de, 22
  see also Lyons
Lynnhull, *see* Hauvil, Henry de
Lyon, John de, 665
Lyons (Lynne), Bernard de, 294, 664
Lythfot, Roger, 316

Mace, Hugh, Florentine merchant, 219
Maiden Lane (Distaflane), 505
Mail, iron, 508
Mainpast, 7, 102, 131, 156, 190, 200–1, 208, 225–6, 244, 260; *see also* Household
Mainprise, *see* Bail
Makeheyte, Gilbert & Maud his widow, 181, 640
Makerel, John & Felice his wife, 21
Malefactors, unknown, 24, 26, 56, 86–7, 104, 126, 137–8, 146, 166–7, 177
Malemeyns, Thomas, 126
Malkse, Henry de, 665
Malling (Molling, etc.)
  Adam, 133, 410, 762
  Robert de, 237, 559
Malmesbury, John de, 236
Malon (Malur), Simon, & Geoffrey his servant, 257
Maneli, Laurence de, 387
Manhale (Mannahale), William de, 228, 288, 691
Mannec', William le, 93
Manors, *see* Southall; Thrafferton
Mansel (Maunsel), John, treasurer of York, 78, 521
Maplederfeld
  Henry de, 145
  William de, 145
Marbrer, John le, 222, 548
Marchaunt, Robert le (I), 31; (II), 245, 564
Marche, John de la, 249
Marcheys, Thomas le, 196
Mare (Mara)
  Matthew de (la), 80, 598
  William de, glover, 253, 569
Mareworth, Roger de, 183, 642
Margaret, queen of Scotland, 72
Mariner, 12, 80
  Ellis le, 420, 766
Markets & fairs, *see* Cheapside; Smithfield; Winchester
Marlborough (Marlebergh), Walter de, 102
Marmion, Philip, 340
Mars, Robert de, 473
Marshal (Marishall, etc.): 205; Earl, 456; king's, 501
  Alice, widow of Michael le, 245
  Geoffrey le (I), 180; (II), 231, 554; (III), 671
  Gilbert le, 105, 609
  Robert le (I), & Ismania his wife, 260, 573; (II) of St. Bartholomew's hospital, 685
  Roger le (I), 71, 181, 229, 503; (II), 228
  Thomas le (I), 228; (II), 464, 785
  Walter the (le), 51, 75
  William le (I), 455; (II), 704
Martilane, Henry de, 22
Martin's Lane (St. Martin Orgar Lane), 409
Mash, hot, 14, 95
Mason (Mazon), 91, 121
  Alan le, 268
  Master Andrew the, 91
  Emma widow of John le, 81, 84
  Ralph le, 406, 760
  Master Robert the, 121
Maunsel, *see* Mansel
Mauntel, Brouning, Laurence & Richard, 245, 564
May
  John, 214, 222, 662
  Nicholas, 222, 548
  Thomas, 121
Mayhem, 265
Mayor & aldermen (*or* barons *or* citizens), 18–517 *passim*
Mayors, list of, 3
Mayor's court, 491
Mazon, *see* Mason
Measurer, Nigel the, 69
Measures, 468
Megucer
  Humphrey le, 105, 609
  William le, 15, 105, 609
Melbourn (Meldeb(o)urne), Robert de, sheriff, 4, 170, 243–5, 722; ward of, *see* Coleman Street ward
Melker, Gilbert le, 99
Melkestrete, *see* Milk Street
Melton, Theobald de, 34
Mercer, 13, 50, 228, 272, 316, 468
  Anketin le, *see* Auvergne
  Edward, 222, 548
  Laurence le, 213
  Ralph le, & Alice his wife, 16
  Richard le, 153, 625
  William le, 89
Merchants, foreign, 119; Flemish, 663–5, 667; Italian, 74, 219, 521, 666
Merdene (Berden), Walter de, 449, 779
Merk(e), Adinett, 245, 564
Merston, Henry de, chancery clerk, & Robert de Kingston his servant, 39
Merton
  Roger de, & Beatrice his maid servant, 224
  Walter de, chancellor, 236
  William de, 195

Index

Mesendene, *see* Missenden
Mesme, John de, 665
Messager (Messeger)
  Robert le, 258
  Thomas le, 354, 730
  William le, 231
Messeday, Peter, 197
Messendene, *see* Missenden
Messer, John le, 200
Meystre, William le, 237
Micham (Michem), *see* Mitcham
Middlesex: county, 285, 527, 552, 559, 595; sheriff of, 28, 127, 180, 245, 280, 522; eyre in, 279–80, 564
Middleton (Middelton)
  John de, 91
  William de, 451
Midi, Baude de, 294, 664
Miles, Peter, 473
Milk Street (Melk(e)strete, etc.), 14, 72
  Christopher de, & Clement his brother, 120
  Henry de, 201
  Thomas de, 294, 663
Mill-stones, 130
Milnward (Milneward)
  Adam le, 169
  John (le), 37, 533
Mimms (Mimmis, Mymmes)
  John de, 222, 548
  Richard de, 468
  Thomas de, 468
Minors, 502, 511, 517, 519; not in frankpledge, 158
Mint, king's, 311; engraving die for, 300
Minur (Munur)
  Hankin le, 127
  John le, sheriff, 4, 18, 63–72, 592, 594; ward of, *see* Aldersgate ward
  William le, 22
  see also Moneyer
Missenden (Mes(s)endene), William de, 386
Mitcham (Micham, Micheham, Michem)
  Peter de, 70, 209, 673
  Thomas de, 8
Modingham, *see* Nottingham
Moler, Guillot le, 254, 570
Molling, *see* Malling
Molsham, Walter de, 668
Money, 509, 511; forgery of, 11; theft of, 289; *see also* Mint
Moneyer (Moneor), Hamo (Henry), 174, 637; *see also* Minur
Monpelers, *see* Montpellier
Monquey, Geoffrey, 159, 209
Monsorel son of Robert, 241
Montauban (de Montibus), James de, 511–12, 519, 714, 718
Montfort (de Monteforti)
  John de, 230
  Simon de, son of Simon de, earl of Leicester, 521
Montpellier (Monpelers, de Monte Pessulano, Mumpelers)
  Ralph de, 72
  Robert de (I), sheriff, 4, 116, 129–41, 147, 521; (II), 72
Mora, Ponce de, 258
More, Robert de la, 272, 579
Morket, Walter, & Alice his wife, 98
Mort d'ancestor, pleas of, 494, 502
Morton (Mutton), Thomas, 45, 536
Mote, Peter de la, 223, 549
Moyne
  Walter le, 183
  William le, 56
Mumpelers, *see* Montpellier
Munden(e)
  John de, 341
  Stephen de, 475
Muniments, royal, 521
Munur, *see* Minur
Murage, 322
Mus, Thomas son of William, 284
Musard, Walter, 294, 664
Mutton, *see* Morton

Nas, Henry le, 245, 564
Nasegor, William, 97
Nasinger, Roger de, 498
Nastok, John de, 226
Naun, Robert de, 106
Neighbours, attachment of: custom concerning, 87; irregular, 47, 53, 60, 80, 87–8, 101, 111, 134, 154, 159, 161–2, 165, 206; rule concerning, 26
Neuman (Norman)
  John, 294, 663
  Reginald le, 245, 564
Neverathom (Neverhethome)
  Adam, 292, 527
  Katherine de, 527
Nevil, Hawys (Helewys) de, wife of John de Gaddesden, 495, 501
New Hospital, *see* St. Mary Spital
New Temple, *see* Temple
Newark (Newerk, de Novo Loco)
  Alice daughter of Ralph de, 268
  Richard de, 292, 527
Newcastle, Robert de, 170
Newchurch (Neuchirch), Philip de, 96
Newenham, Devon, abbot of, 340, 526
Newgate prison, 6, 37, 41, 49, 55, 60, 62, 70, 74–5, 78, 94, 108, 113, 128, 152, 154, 163, 176, 183, 193, 197, 202–3, 208, 214, 219, 228, 234–6, 243, 246, 249, 256–7, 263, 269, 316, 496; keeper of, 219; William, keeper of, 491

Index

Newport (Neuport)
  John de, 161
  Nicholas de, 678
  Ralph de, 101
  William de, 35
Nichol (Nicol, etc.)
  John de, 294, 663
  Robert (I), 99, 606; (II), 245, 564
  Stephen son of, 109
  William, 12
Nogeriis, *see* Novarra
Noreis (Noreys), William le, 245
Norfolk, 100, 238
  Maud de, 119
  William de (I), 40; (II), 277
Norman
  John, mayor, 3, 56; ward of, *see* Cordwainer ward
  Roger, 209
  William, & Richard his son, 18
Normande, Alice le, 74
Normanton, Walter son of Henry de, 52
Northall (Northale), 276
Northampton (Northamton, etc.)
  Godfrey de, 459
  Hugh de, 185
  Isabel de, 284
  John de (I), sheriff, 4, 36–50, 108–18, 153, 219, 316, 460, 533–4, 591, 614, 783; (II), & Edith his wife, 197, 648
  Philip de, 405, 759
  Simon de, 37, 183, 642
  Thomas de, 101, 606
Northamptonshire, 238, 284, 477
Northawe, William de, 294, 663
Northbrook (Northbrok)
  Gilbert de, 213
  Richard de, 213
Northumberland, 263, 490, 492, 497, 575
Northwood (Northwode), John de, 292, 527
Norwich (Norwyco, etc.)
  Robert de, 287, 587
  Thomas de, 113, 249
Nothlethe, Philip de, 152
Nottingham (Notingham, Modingham, etc.)
  Gervase de, 109, 611
  Robert de, 7
  William de, 75
Nottinghamshire, 642
Novarra (Nogeriis), Reymund de, papal chaplain, 244
Novel disseisin, 321; *see also* Intrusion
Nuele, John de, a Fleming, 665

Oakley (Okele), William de, 12
Oath-swearing, 514
Oddington (Otington), Henry de, 341
Odekin (Odeken), Geoffrey son of, 294, 664
Odyn (Hodyn), Walter, 196, 647
Ogele, *see* Ugley
Okele, *see* Oakley
Old Fish Street, 443
Old Jewry, *see* Jewry
Opton, *see* Upton
Orbatour (Orlatour), 209
  Alexander le, 109
  Philip le, 230
Orfevre, *see* Goldsmith
Orwell (Orewell), William de, 60
Osbern, Richard, 245, 564
Oskin, Robert son of, 243
Ossulstone (Osolvestane), Middx., hundred, 245
Ostre, Robert del, & Rose his wife, 495
Otes, Robert, 145, 468, 473
Otington, *see* Oddington
Outlawry, 7–284 *passim*; articles concerning, 312, 316; in Essex, 48, 97; in Hampshire, 87; in Kent, 97; in Middlesex, 127, 245; in Staffordshire, 39; *see also* Waivery
Overseas, flight of felons, 75, 226
Oxen, 79, 92
Oxford (Oxonia), 38, 66
  Gilbert de, & Alice his wife, 478
  John de, 271, 578
  Nicholas de, 244, 563
  Roger de, 273, 580
  Walter de, 12, 21
Oynter, Michael le, 143, 288
Oysel, Audrey, 26
Oystergate (Oistergate)
  Stephen de, sheriff, 4, 56–62, 539–40
  Thomas de, 48
Oysterhull, Miles de, 279, 583
Oystermonger, 95

Pacbyndere, William le, 178
Packman, 231
Page
  Nicholas, 257
  Richard, 141
  William, 24, 174, 414, 754
Painasset, John, 566
Painmoyle, Sewall, 294, 664
Palfrayour, Alan & William le, of St. Bartholomew's priory, 141
Palisades, 353
Pantry, 501
Papal documents, 521
Papers, private, 521
Papworth (Pampesworth), Adam de, son of Roger de, 163, 632
Pardons: of homicide, 6, 72, 75, 78, 150, 170, 176, 189, 207–9, 218–19, 231; of trespasses, 265, 293, 476, 493; of usury, 306; offered, 521
Paris (Parys)
  Guylot de, 468

Index

John de, 272, 579
Peter de, 192
Richard de, sheriff, 4, 198, 228-31, 554-5
Robert de, 264, 444
William de, 468
Parker, Simon le, 152
Parks, 315
Parliament, 468
Parmenter (le Parchemener, Parchenarius, etc.), 67, 468
   Ambrose le, 67
   Godfrey le, 294, 664
   John le, 294, 664
   Kyng le, 67
   Luke le, 67
   Manasser le, 67
   Ralph le, 37, 533
   Richard le, 75
Parson (Person, Persone, etc.)
   John la, & Katherine (*alias* Katherine la Norreys) his sister, & Dulcia her maid, 87
   Richard la, 504
   Richard son of the, 15
   William la, 135
Party-wall, 121
Passelewe
   Robert, 273, 580
   Simon, 91
Paternoster (Paternostrer), 7
   Guilot le, & Lucy his wife, 215, 342
   John, 194, 646
   Nicholas, 194
   Ralph, 33
   Richard le, & Isabel his daughter, 212, 656
   Thomas le, 41, 468, 534, 724
   William le, 468, 724
Paths, obstructed, 345, 442, 459; *see also* Lanes
Patrik
   Richard, 245, 564
   Robert, 174
Pauchy, Gilbert, 71
Pauely, Andrew de, 237
Paumer
   Gerard le, 70
   John le, 165, 223, 236, 363, 633
   Ralph le, 222, 548
   Richard le, 232, 272, 468, 579
Pauncefot, Grimbald, 521
Pavement, 24
Payn, Thomas, 214, 655
Pears, 32; *see also* Trees
Pecche (Peche), Robert, 272, 579
Pecok, Edmund, 284, 584
Pe Dargent (Pe de Argent, Pedeargent)
   Belin, 294
   Walter, & Walter his son, 294, 664
Pede, *see* Pode

Peisorer, Fulk, 300
Peitel, Peter, 59
Pek, Richard de, 238
Pel (Pele), Richard (I), 228; (II), *alias* James Bole, 292, 527
Peleter, 209
   John le, 177, 639
   Robert le, 152
   Thomas le, 215
   see also Poleter
Pelham
   Alan de, 25
   Gervase de, 75
   Gilbert de, 273, 580
   John de, 75
   Ralph de, parson of St. Michael Bassishaw, 502
Pembroke, earl of, *see* Valence, William de
Pender(e), Walter le, 246, 565
Penkerk, Clementine wife of Robert de, 221
Penshurst (Pencestre), Stephen de (I), 145; (II), constable of Dover castle, 203
Pentecost, Edmund, 421
Pentecost Lane, 291
Pentices, 348-465 *passim*
Pepys (Pepes), William, 196, 647
Perdriz, Robert, 96
Perer, John del, 7
Perone, Peter de, 253
Perot
   Gerard, servant of James de Portu, 203
   Ralph, 521
Person(e), la Persone, *see* Parson
Pessoner, German le, 383, 746
Pestour, *see* Baker
Petche, Richard, 212
Peter
   Arnold son of, 316, 591
   Dunnyng, 223
Peterer [i.e. fisherman], 209
Peticors, Henry, 119
Petit (Petite)
   Henry le, & Margery his wife, 214
   Robert le, 312
   Roger le, sheriff's bailiff, 249, 566
Pevelesdon (Pevesdon), *see* Puleston
Peverer (Peuerer), 294
   Adam le, 131, 174
   James le, 116, 613
Phalizatus, 203
Physician (Fisicien, Fisicion), 257
   Robert le, le Petit, & Robert his son, 273, 580
Piacenza (Plesent'), Petrucche de, & his associates, 666
Picard (Pikard, Pykard)
   Adam, 132, 203, 657
   Ellis, 244, 563
   Hubert son of Richard, 108

177

Index

Picard, *continued*
   Richard, sheriff, 4, 36–49, 108–18, 316, 533–4, 614
   William, 46
Picot, Isabel widow of John, 271
Pictor, John, 192
Pig (Pighe, Pye, Pyg)
   Richard (I), 267; (II), 245, 564
   William, 245, 564
Piggesfles(h), Roger, 292, 294, 527, 663
Pigo (Pygon), Jordan, 418, 766
Pigs, 44, 155
Pikeman
   Ralph, & Robert his servant, 140
   Stephen, 279
   William, 48
Piket (Pikette)
   Thomas, 294, 664
   Wambert (Waubert), 294, 664
Pil (Pyl), John le, 245, 564
Pilate (Pylat), Bernard, 294, 664
Pills, as medication, 257
Pipe Rolls, App. E
Pistoia, 219, 545
Pistor, *see* Baker
Pit, 18
Plank of wood, 22
Plankes
   John de, 294, 664
   Wis (Wys) de, 294, 664
Plastrer
   Simon le, 217, 543
   William le, 217, 543
Plesent', *see* Piacenza
Plomer (Ploumer, Plumer)
   Hugh le, 212
   John le, *alias* Robert le, 273, 580
Plumstead (Plumstede)
   Henry de, 49
   Walter de, 91
Pode (Pede), John, 245, 564
Poel (Porcher), Hugh le, 227, 552
Pointel (Portel, Poyntel)
   Nicholas, 168, 635
   Reginald, 288
   Robert, 125, 290, 590
Poisoning, 209
Poleter (Poloter, Poluter, Puleter), 32, 67, 405
   Amisius le, 180
   Bartholomew le, 180
   John le, 221
   Osbert le, 185, 209, 288, 643
   Walter le, 284, 584
   see also Peleter
Poleyn, Baldwyn, & Jakem his son, 665
Ponte, de, *see* Bridge
Pontefract (de Pontefracto)
   Matthew de, 116, 613
   Robert de, 51, 538

Pope, Walter, 685
Porcher, *see* Poel
Porches, 352, 395
Porer, Thomas le, 494
Porteioye (Porteroye), John, 230, 555
Portel, *see* Pointel
Porteous (Purteus), Jo(ke)mes, 294, 664
Porter (Portur), 191
   John le, *see* Potter, John le
   Ralph le, 26
Porteroye, *see* Porteioye
Ports, assigned to abjurors, 115
Portsmouth (Portemuth), 115
   William de, 292, 527
Portsoken ward, 43, 111, 156, 163, 199, 300, 394
Portu, James de, & William de, 203
Portugal, 78
Portur, *see* Porter
Postel, John, 98
Pot, brass, 209, 496
Potente, Lambert de la, & Alexander his son, 294, 664
Poterel, Richard, 402, 758
Poteys, Geoffrey, 37
Potter (Poter), 222
   John le, *alias* Porter, 395, 754
   Laurence le, *alias* Gilbert le, 379, 745
   Michael, 419, 766
   Richard le, 209, 692
   Simon le, 135
   Walter le, sheriff, 4, 112, 185, 220, 232–42, 250, 495, 546; ward of, *see* Cornhill ward
Pourt (Purte, Purtre), Thomas le, 102, 232, 556, 607
Powerstock (Porstok, Purstok), William de, chamberlain, 132–48
Poygnant, Robert, 142, 149
Poytevin, John, 139
Prato, Robert de, 223
Premeditation, alleged, 147
Presbyter, Osbert, 447
Prest
   Thomas, 37
   William, 29
Preston
   Alice widow of Gilbert de, 477
   Laurence de, 477
Pretewse, Robert, *see* Prituse
Priories in the king's gift, 298
Prises, 319–20
Prisons: death in, 113, 193, 205; *see also* Aldgate; Custody; Fleet prison; Imprisonment; Newgate
Prituse (Pretewse), Robert, 245, 564
Privies, 428, 456
Privileges, *see* Custom of the City
Prostitutes, 119, 134, 137, 181
Proudman, William, 114

178

Index

Prudford, John, 550
Prus, William de, 665
Prute, Alan le, 154
Psalter, 521
Puleston (Pevelesdon, Pevesdon, Pyvelesdon), Thomas de, 129, 293, 296, 476; ward of, 129
Purgation, 187
Purprestures, in *1251*, 295; in *1276*, 342–467
Purstok, *see* Powerstock
Purte (Purtre), *see* Pourt
Purteus, *see* Porteous
Purveyor, king's, 239, 292, 474; *see also* Acatour, Joce le
Putney (Puttenheth), 98
Puys, Terry de, 665
Pye, *see* Pig
Pygon, *see* Pigo
Pyning, Nicholas, 16
Pynnot, Thomas, 43
Pyriton, Margery de, 119
Pystewell, Robert son of Hamo de, 214
Pysyng, John de, & Roger his servant, 177
Pyvelesdon, *see* Puleston

Quart measures, 468
Quays, *see* Wharfs
Queenhithe, 214; ward, 30, 33, 37, 49, 102, 223, 459, 506, 519
Queyfer, Lucy la, *see* Wysdarius
Quilter
  Walter le, 109
  William le, 126

Raban, Bartholomew de, 257
Racolf, John, 294, 663
Ramsey (Ramesey)
  Adam de, 255
  John de, 299
Randal, Thomas, 32
Randolf (Randulf)
  John, 32
  Robert, 245, 564
Rape, 74, 85, 519
Ravenescote, John de, 665
Reading (Reding(ges)), Robert de, 292, 527
Receiving stolen goods, 278
Recognizances of debt, 475, 486, 490, 497–8; justice in eyre party to, 490
Regalia, king's, 300
Reigate (Reygate), William de, 504, 711
Reliquary, 73
Rents, 483, 495, 499, 501–2, 517; arrears of, 489; clove-, 183, 291; held by serjeanty, 300; of assize, 138; quit-, 291; sold without warrant, 138
Respites: for default of jurors, 493; for foreign warranty, 477–8, 482, 484–5, 494, 502, 513–15

Retoundor, *see* Tundur
Retherhethe, *see* Rotherhithe
Return: permission to, 122, 139, 154, 181; without warrant, 312
Reus, *see* Rose
Reve (Rime), William, 183, 642
Reyley, John de, 273
Reyner, Christine, 292, 527
Reynham, Robert (*alias* Thomas) de, 294, 663
Richard
  John son of, 69
  William son of, 183
Richmond (Richemund)
  John, 468
  Peter de, 41
Richolda, prostitute, 230
Rime, *see* Reve
Ringerer, Robert le, 491
Rings: gold, 511; latten, 491
Robbery, 52, 145, 278, 287–8
Roberd, Richard, 197
Rochester (de Roff), Henry de, 260, 573
Rockingham (Rokyngham), Hugh de, 212
Rods, serjeants', 2
Roger, Robert, son of (I), 248; (II), of Hackney, 245, 564
Rokesle (Roqesley, Rotheley, etc.)
  Ellis de, 237, 559
  Gregory de, mayor, chamberlain & sheriff, 3, 4, 75, 142–54, 167, 221–7, 246, 270, 283, 291, 481, 522, 549, 623; ward of, *see* Dowgate ward
  Robert de, 473, 518, 717, 771
  William de, 481
Roman (Romayn, Romeyn)
  Besance, 104
  Frederico & Gentilio, Roman merchants, 74
  see also Garsie; Good Neighbour; Portu
Romney (Romoney), William de, 91
Rope, 130, 155, 162, 191, 206, 259
Roqesley, *see* Rokesle
Ros, Thomasina de, & Beatrice her servant, 182
Rose (Reus, Rous, Rus(s)e)
  Emma la, 454
  Gylot le, 222, 548
  Henry le, 288
  Hugh le, 108
  Isabel la, 119
  Maud la, 274
  Nicholas le, of Gaunt, 665
  Peter le, 108
  Richard le (I), 48; (II), 267, 577; (III), 111
  Robert le, 245, 564
  Roger le, 228
  Simon le, 26
  William le, 394, 695, 753

Index

Rotheley, *see* Rokesle
Rotherhill (Rotherhull), Robert de, 71
Rotherhithe (Retherhethe), 275
  Geoffrey de, 236, 487
  Robert de (I), 156, 627; (II), 246, 565
Rothing (Rothings, etc.)
  Geoffrey de, 209, 487, 657
  Henry de, 225
  Reginald de, 494
  Richard de, 243
Rous, *see* Rose
Roynges, Geoffrey de, 152
Rubies, 487
Rumford (Ryngefeld)
  Ralph de, 254, 570
  Richard de, 16
Rumpyng, Roger, 157
Rus (Russe), *see* Rose
Russel (Russell)
  Adam, 179
  Alexander, 239
  Henry, 159, 631
  John, 218, 544
  Nicholas, 99
  Richard, 219
  Robert (I), 12; (II), 292, 527; (III), 680
  William (I), 49; (II), 199; (III), 292, 527
Rye, Aaron de la, a Jew, 436, 775
Rylehale, *see* Wilehale
Ryngefeld, *see* Rumford

Sachier
  Geoffrey le, & Isabel his wife, 250
  Robert le, 34
Sadde, *see* Shadde
Saer (Saher, Seyre)
  John, 430, 473
  John son of John, 292, 527; Joan his widow, 482, 513, 515
Saffron Walden, Essex, abbey of, 225
Sage, Lambert le, 665
Saham, Richard de, 480
Saher, *see* Saer
St. Alban Wood Street, parish, 504
St. Albans, Herts.: abbot of, 431, 448, 504; Reginald, his *custos domorum*, 88
  John de, 266, 576
  Michael de, 499
  Thomas de, 96
St. Alphege London Wall, church, 299
St. Amand, William de, 294, 664
St. Andrew Holborn, parish, 502
St. Andrew Hubbard, church, 299
St. Audoen, church, 299
St. Augustine Papey (upon London Wall), church, 299
St. Augustine Watling Street, church, 299, 489
St. Bartholomew, Henry de, 685
St. Bartholomew the Less, church, 23, 52

St. Bartholomew's hospital, 363, 685, 737
St. Bartholomew's priory, 32, 141, 201, 298
St. Benet, parish, 121
St. Botolph, Richard de, 241, 292, 527, 561
St. Botolph Aldersgate, church, 42, 262; parish, 269
St. Brides, Robert de, 168, 635
St. Christopher le Stocks, church, William, rector of, 187
St. Clement's Lane, 312
St. Dionis Backchurch, William de, 508, 713
St. Dunstan in the West, churchyard, 39
St. Edmunds (de Sancto Edmundo)
  Fulk de, 183, 209, 657
  Michael de, 352
  Robert de, boatman, 139
  Robert de, cordwainer, 114
  Thomas de, 73, 88
St. Ermin, William de, 300
St. Gabriel (All Hallows) Fenchurch, church, 117, 299
St. Giles, Robert de, 155, 626
St. Giles without Cripplegate, church, 234, 262
St. Helen Bishopsgate, prioress & nuns of, 343, 390
St. Helens
  John de, agent of Gilbert de Clare, 493
  Robert de, 116
St. James Garlickhithe (Graschirche), church & Geoffrey, a clerk of, 264
St. Katherine by the Tower (without London): church, 28; hospital, 156, 627
St. Lawrence Jewry, church, 20, 65, 82
St. Lawrence Pountney, church, 79, 183
St. Magnus Martyr, church, 61, 299
St. Martin le Grand: dean & chapter of, 75, 295, 299, 340, 348, 526; special sessions at, 495, 520
St. Martin Orgar Lane, *see* Martin's Lane
St. Martin Pomeroy, church, 81, 84
St. Martin Vintry, church, 108
St. Mary Abchurch, church, 100; parish, 264
St. Mary Aldermary, church, 316
St. Mary at Hill, church, 48, 97
St. Mary Bothaw, parish, 481
St. Mary Colechurch, church & William, a clerk of, 192
St. Mary Conyhop, chapel & church, 57–8, 115, 193
St. Mary in Jewry, chapel, 299
St. Mary le Bow, church, 38, 221, 241
St. Mary Magdalen [? Old Fish Street], church, 194
St. Mary Spital, prior of the hospital, 386, 748

Index

St. Mary Woolchurch, church, 83, 92, 112, 123, 138, 149
St. Matthew Fridaystreet, church, 66
St. Michael Bassishaw, church, 262; parish, 265, 490; parson of, 502
St. Michael Cornhill, parish, 501
St. Michael Huggin Lane, church, 90
St. Michael le Querne, church, 41, 299
St. Michael Paternoster, church, 110; Bartholomew, parson of, 503; parish, 503
St. Michael Queenhithe, church, 457
St. Mildred (? Bread Street), church, 208
St. Nicholas Cole Abbey, parish, 505
St. Nicholas Lane, 291
St. Nicholas Shambles, church, 172; parish, 291
St. Osith, Henry de, 292, 527
St. Pancras Soper Lane, church, 508
St. Pauls
  Jordan de, 33
  Simon de, 56
St. Paul's cathedral: 11, 260, 282, 299; dean & chapter, 162; canons, 30, 255, 344; chaplain, 72; churchyard, 104, 146, 177, 209, 255; minor canon, *see* Harrow, Richard de; precentor, *see* Barton, Robert de
St. Peter (Sancto Petro), Peter de, 666
St. Peter in the Bailey, church, 299
St. Peter Paul's Wharf, church, 299
St. Peter Westcheap (of Woodstreet), church, 242
St. Saviour (de Sancto Salvatore)
  Geoffrey de, 236
  John de, 149
  Walter de, 75
St. Thomas Acon: church, 58; hospital, master & brethren of, 484, 720
St. Thomas London Bridge, chapel, 9, 73, 283
St. Victor, James de, clerk of Ralph de Hengham, 340, 526
Sakewell, *see* Shakewell
Sale, Thomas de la, 22
Salisbury (Sar'): bishop of, & his London house, 18, 161
  Philip de, 110
Salle, John de, 228
Salter (Saltere, Sautur)
  Geoffrey le, 136, 216, 621
  Stephen le, & Felice his wife, 216, 478
Samuel, William, 70, 365
Sanctuary: custom concerning, 20, 48; escapes from, 48, 61, 83, 108, 117, 149, 183, 194, 223, 234, 260, 316; taken by a clerk, 264; *see also* Abjuration
Sandwich (Sandwys, de Sandwyco)
  Henry de, 133
  Maurice de, 235, 558

Sanzdamage, Thomas de, 42
Sanztere, Walter, 61
Sapcote (Sapecote), Leics., 148
Sapphires, 491
Sarazin, Andrew le, 257
Saule, Walter, 267
Saumford, Nicholas de, 509
Sauncelina, a maid, 253, 569
Saunford, Walter de, sheriff of Middx., 280, 588
Sautur, *see* Salter
Sawyer, Henry le, & Amice his wife, 494
Say
  Adam de, 275
  William de, & Stacy his servant, 145
Scalding, death by, 13–14, 21, 43, 69, 95, 142, 174, 210, 212
Scarborough (Scardeborgh), Henry de, 229
Scaylon, Nicholas de, 294, 664
Schapman, *see* Chapman
Schoueler, *see* Scoueler
Scobir (Shobyr, Sobyre), Henry de, & Alice his wife, 480, 483, 489
Scot (le Escot, Skot, etc.)
  Adam, 37, 276, 284
  Alan le, 170
  David, 257, 571
  Henry, 185, 643
  Hugh, 158
  John, 134
  Richard, 263, 575
  Robert le (I), 228, 237, 559; (II), 270; (III), 292, 527; (IV), 703
Scotewy, *see* Sotewy
Scoueler (Schoueler), Henry le, 245, 564
Scrul, Isabel daughter of William, 217
Sealing: of a chirograph, 501; of measures, 468
Sealmaker (Factor sigillorum), Adam, 33
Seint Liz, *see* Senlis
Selds, 178, 241
Seler, 222, 272
  Richard le, 185, 643
  Roger le, 246, 565
Self-defence: slaying in, 269; wounding in, 147
Selketop, *see* Silketop
Sely, Nicholas, 16
Sempringham (Simplingham), Lincs., prior of, 340, 526
Sender, *see* Sondere
Senlis (Sancto Lycio, Seint Liz), Simon de, 292, 527
Serjeant (Seriaunt, Serviens)
  John le, 284, 584
  Ralph the, 488
Serjeanties, 300
Serjeants: in eyre, 2; sheriffs', 256, 289
Services, *see* Customs & services
Sevenhaunt, *see* Sovenaunt

181

Index

Sevenhode (Sevehod)
  Edward, 468
  Robert (I), 374, 742; (II), & Emma his wife, 468; (III) the younger, 468
  Walter, 468
Seyre, *see* Saer
Seyton, Master Roger de, justice in eyre, 1, 75, 108, 146, 470, 489, 490, 525
Shadde (Sadde), Ellis, 253, 569
Shakewell (Sakewell), Robert de, 245, 564
Shank, Walter, 236
Shankerton, Master Geoffrey de, clerk, 240
Shap, Thomas, 284
Sharp (Charp, Scharp), Richard, 76, 99, 423, 767
Shaylard, Roger, 236
Sheep, 9, 100, 123, 275
Shelfhanger (Shelfhangre), Walter, sheriff of Suffolk, 507, 712
Shepesheved, William, 256
Shepperton (Sheperton), Middx., 240
Sheriffs, *see* Bedfordshire; Dorset; Essex; Kent; Middlesex; Norfolk & Suffolk; Staffordshire; Surrey; Warwickshire; Worcestershire; Yorkshire
Sheriffs of London: account at exchequer, App. E, 525-786 *passim*; articles concerning, 324, 326; in crown pleas, 6-286 *passim*; list of, 4
Ships, 80, 130, 139, 240, 246, 248, 259, 493; *see also* Boats
Shobyr, *see* Scobir
Shops, 72, 241, 375, 464
Shoreditch, Middx., 45, 245, 564
  Alan de, keeper of Newgate, 316
  John de (I), 152; (II), 239; (III), 257
Showell, [a well near Shoe Lane], 342
Shrewsbury (Salopia), abbot of, 340, 387, 749
Silk, 75, 487, 511
Silketop (Selketop)
  John, 245, 564
  Warin, 245, 564
Silver, 509; *see also* Cups; Dishes; Flagons; Goblet; Spoons
Silves, Portugal, bishop of, 78
Simplingham, *see* Sempringham
Sipring, William, 259
Sire, Ralph, 16
Skanke, Henry, 667
Skete, Walter, 26
Skileman (Skyl(l)man)
  John (I), 102; (II), 154
  William, 412, 764
Skinner, 37, 209
  Richard le, 237
  William, 246
Skip (Skyp), John, 209, 292, 527
Slich (Slych), William (I), 284, 584; (II), 685

Slipertop, Lorekin, 16
Smalehunte, Ralph, 27
Smith (Faber, Feroun), 279
  Alexander le, 174
  Henry, 60, 539
  John, 114, 154
  Richard the, 174
  Thomas son of William, 20
  see also Fevere
Smithfield (West Smethefeld, etc.), 166, 206, 533; market & fair of, 471, 488
  John de, 584
  Stephen de, 91, 602
Snod, John, 235
Sobyre, *see* Sobir
Sodington, Master Thomas de, justice in eyre, 1
Sokes, 489; *see also* Fleet; Portsoken; Tovy, Roger de
Solars, 53, 72, 352-454 *passim*; above a gate, 116; fall of a, 54; overhanging, 349-50
Solio, Gailard de, & Gailard & John his servants, 108
Someter (Somoter)
  Alan le, 208
  John le, 179
Sondere (Sender), John le, 245, 564
Sone, Reginald, & Edith his wife, 504
Soper
  Thomas le, 91, 602
  Walter le, & Alditha his wife, & Amice their daughter, 44
Soper's Lane (Soperlane), 147
Sorel, William, & Alice his wife, 222
Sotewy (Scotewy), Richard, 244, 563
Soutere, Laurence, 99
Southall (Suthale, etc.): manor of, Essex, 511
  Hamo de, servant of Nicholas Bat, 10
Southampton (Sutht')
  John de, 159, 631
  Walter de, 159, 631
  see also Hampshire
Southwark (Suthwerk, Sutwerk), Surrey, 276, 527, 576
  Andrew de, 221
  John de (I), 77; (II), 162
  Thomas de, 153
Sovenaunt (Seven(h)aunt), Baude de, 294, 664
Sow, *see* Pigs
Spain, Michael de, 78
Sparling (Sperling, etc.)
  Gilbert, 417
  John (I), 34, 48; (II), 299; (III) & John his son, 367, 738
  Ralph, 26, 48, 97, 366; ward of, *see* Billingsgate ward
Spedel, Adam, 236

182

Index

Speleman (Spileman), William, 227, 552
Spendelove (Spendeluve, Spendellum)
   Adam, 246, 565
   John, 227, 552
Spereon, Andrew, 85
Spigornel, le, *see* Esprigonel
Spinelli (Ispinelli), Symonet (Simon), &
   Agnes his mistress, 219
Spirhard, Henry, 236
Spoons, silver, 511
Sporon, *see* Esperon
Sports & pastimes, *see* Archery; Chess;
   Wrestling
Springham, Robert de, 203, 651
Stables, 231, 473, 501
Stacey (Stacy), John, 157, 292, 527, 630
Staff, 24, 37, 53, 55, 80, 83, 140, 215
Staffordshire, & sheriff of, 39, 284
Staines (Stanes)
   Maud de, 265
   Muriel wife of William de, 196
   Peter de, 72
   Richard de, 502
Staleward, Gerard, & Thomas his brother,
   294, 664
Stanford (Staunford), 65
   Hugh de, 153, 625
   Isabel de, prostitute, 134
   John de, 292, 527
   Nicholas de, 289, 589
   Richard de, 289
   William de, the younger, 294, 663
Stanhard, Simon, 130
Stanstrate, John de, 665
Staples, 347
Starvation, death by, 25, 136, 165
Staumpeur, John le, 288
Staunford, *see* Stanford
Staunton (Staundon), Henry de, 67, 593
Stedeman, Roger le, 119
Steel, 508
Stench, 356
Stephen, William son of, 201
Stepney (Stebenhuth(e), Stypenhethe),
   Middx., 227, 245, 564
   John de, 43, 461, 535, 784
   Richard de (I), 144; (II), son of Peter de,
     245, 564
   Robert son of Peter de, 227, 552
Steps, 40, 68, 164, 175, 254, 347, 359, 393,
   430, 435–6, 462, 466; before a tavern,
   461; of a cellar, 356; on the king's
   highway, 446; to a solar, 358
Stilter, John le, 136
Stiwr, Roger le, 75
Stoil, William, 171
Stoke, James de, 282
Stonehall (Stonhale, Stonhall)
   John, Peter's brother, 239, 560
   Peter son of John de, 239

Stones, precious, 487, 491
Stoning, death by, 116
Stoppes, Roger de, 228
Stor
   John le (de), 245, 564
   Robert le, 287
Stortford (Storteford)
   Robert de, 368, 739
   William de, 279, 583
Strangers, extortion of, 301, 309
Strangulation, 231
Strata, Richard de, 272, 579
Stratford, abbot of, 340
   Ralph de, 159
   Thomas de, 159
Stratton (Stratone)
   Adam de, chamberlain of the exchequer,
     & John his clerk, 299, 468
   Ranulf de, 171
Strip, John, 227, 552
Stroby, Robert de, *see* Derby, Robert de
Strocton, Thomas de, 181, 640
Sture, *see* Esture
Sub muro, *see* Under Wall
Suche, *see* Zouche
Suer (Suur)
   John le, 155, 626
   Robert le, 165, 276
   Simon le, 128
Suet de prison, ? 257, 496
Suffocation, death by, 258
Suffolk, 115, 507, 712
   Alan de, 292, 527
   Edmund de, 246, 565
   Henry de (I), 223, 549; (II), 254
   Nicholas de, 169
   Osbert de, sheriff, 4, 129–41, 147, 292, 527
   Ralph de, 292, 527
   Reginald de, chamberlain, 149–92, 292,
     481, 527, 624, 757
   Robert de, 292, 527
   Roger de, 401
   Stephen de, 240, 562
   Thomas de, 209
   William de (I), 47; (II), 244, 563
Suicide, 206, 213
Suliz, John, 666
Summons, refusal to permit serving of, 337
Sunit, Richard, 191
Surcoats, 65, 486; of burel, 284; of russet, 20
Surgien (Surisien, etc.)
   Alfred le, 16
   Master Thomas le, 260, 573
Surrey, 485, 668, 698; sheriff of, 98, 489
Sussex, Notekin de, 255
Suthhale, *see* Southall
Sutht', *see* Southampton
Sutor
   Henry, 121
   William, 174

Index

Sutwerk, *see* Southwark
Suur, *see* Suer
Suzche, *see* Zouche
Swain (Swayn)
  Richard, 564
  Robert, 245, 564
Swath', Christine wife of William de, 113
Swetyng (Swthingg), Ralph, 227, 552
Swineford (Swyneford), John de, chamberlain, 125–31
Swomld, Geoffrey, 279
Swords, 41, 75, 151, 159, 214, 225; of Cologne, 147
Swynhog, William, 182
Syhen, John de, 665
Synod (Sinod, Synot)
  Nicholas, 30
  Ralph, & Maud his widow, 131
  William, 30
Syppond, Hugh, 159

Tadworth (Taddesworthe), Richard de, 224
Taillehaste, Richard, 261
Tailor (Cissor, Tayllur, etc.), 13–14, 21, 35, 154, 209, 228, 264
  Adinett, the king's tailor, 170
  Arnulf le, 184
  Austin le, 259, 574
  Bartholomew le, 53
  Ellis le, 493
  Geoffrey le, 294, 663
  Gilbert le, 53
  Godman the, 53
  Henry le (I), 53; (II), & Sarah his wife, 63
  Holdin le, 286, 586
  Hubert, 240, 244, 562
  Hugh le, of Lincoln, 294
  Humphrey le, 250, 567
  Jakett le, 189, 645
  John le, 244, 257, 292, 462, 527, 563, 571, 784
  Martin le, 83
  Maunsel the, 89
  Michael le, 252, 259–60, 568, 573–4
  Philip le (I), sheriff, 4, 116, 119–28, 134, 220, 291, 343, 481, 617; ward of, *see* Bishopsgate ward; (II), 278
  Ralph le, 53, 145
  Richard le, 24, 53, 445
  Robert le (I), 259, 574; (II), 380, 746
  Roger le, 379, 745
  Stephen le (I), 189, 645; (II), 679
  Thomas le, 177, 257, 639
  William le, 53, 101, 606
Takepeny, John, 95
Tallage, 323
Tallies, 474, 526–784 *passim*
Tame, Robert de, 243
Tanner (Tanur), 284
  Nicholas, 156

Stephen, 156
Tateregge (Taterig), John de, & Maud his wife, & Richard his brother, 6
Taverner (Tavernarius), 166, 228, 279, 292
  Edmund le, 237
  Eustace le, 292, 527
  Faukes le (Fulk), 209, 292, 527
  Geoffrey le, 256
  Henry le, 271
  Hugh le, 506
  James the, 292
  John le, 256, 500
  Nicholas le, 232, 556
  Ralph le, 236
  Walter le, 256
Taverns, 83, 192, 236, 258, 461
Tawyer, 120, 216, 273
  John le, 49
  Philip the, 266
  see also Megucer
Taxstede, *see* Thaxted
Teler (Tele)
  William son of Roger le, of Warwick, 65
  William le, brewer, 237, 559
Temple (Novum Templum), 39, 244; master of the, in England, 75, 184, 340, 526, 596
  Lambert de Templo, 665
Terring' (Therring'), Peter de, 273, 580
Ters, John, 36
Test, Nicholas, 666
Testard, Ralph, 284
Teyere, Richard le, 521
Teyford, Robert de, 238
Teynturer, Gilbert le, 113
Thames, 10–259 *passim*; bathing or washing in, 93, 124, 132; tides of, 86; water drawn from, 217; watering a horse in, 10, 144, 161; *see also* Drowning
Thames Street, 300
Thaxted (Taxstede), Ralph de, 125
Thedald (Thedap, etc.), Rusticald (Rustikell), 292, 294, 527, 663
Thefford, *see* Thetford
Theft, 74, 77, 87, 275–6, 282, 284, 287–9; confession of, 277; *see also* Abjuration
Thele, Roger de, canon of Holy Trinity, 55
Theoland, John, 29
Therring', *see* Terring'
Thetford (Thefford), Norfolk, prior of, 340, 526
Thirsk (Tresk), Yorks., 9
Tholosan, *see* Tolosan
Thorp, Paulin, 37
Thrafferton (Thrafferston), Northumberland, manor of, 492
Thurrok (Torrok, Turrok, etc.)
  Simon, 703
  Thomas de, 183

184

Index

Tiler (Tegulator, Tuler, etc.)
   Daniel le, 245, 564
   Godfrey le, 245, 564
   Hamund the, 392
   Henry le, 45, 536
   Richard le, 45, 536
   Roger le (I), 134, 620; (II), 156; (III), & Alice his wife, 176, 638
   Serle le, 67
   William le, 245, 564
Tilly, Philip, 221
Timber, 64, 221, 296, 522; yard, 195
Tirrel (Tyrel), Geoffrey, 159
Tolosan (Tholosan)
   Ellis, 486
   John de, mayor, 3
Tor, Gilbert le, 273, 580
Tornur, *see* Turner
Torp, Robert, 236
Torrington (Torington), William de, 98
Tottenham (Totenhale), Middx., 82, 280
   Robert de, 273, 580
Tottenham Court Road (Totenhalestrete), 127
Tour, de la, *see* Towers
Tovy (Thovy, Touvy, Tovi)
   Michael the elder, sheriff, 4, 16, 489
   Michael the younger, 146, 296
   Ralph de, 468
   Roger de, 480, 483, 489; soke of, 489
   Walter, 116
Tower of London, 1, 2, 190, 551, 672, 729, 775, 777; gate, 98, 112; barricades near, 296; constable of, 52, 98, 112, 508
Tower ward, 22, 40, 220, 459
Towers (de la Tour, de Turribus), John of the, 93, 604
Traiere (Traour), *see* Treyer
Travers, Thomas de, 96
Treasure-trove, 304
Trees, 394; pear, 32, 232
Trentemars, John, 85
Tresk, *see* Thirsk
Trespass, pleas of: for abduction, 511; asportation of chattels, 487, 491, 493, 508-9; battery & mayhem, 265; breaking & entering, 519; wounding, 471, 500, 508; wrongful imprisonment, 496
   adjournments in, 493, 511
   damages, *see* Damages
   dates alleged: after the summons of the eyre, 471, 500; before, 265, 487, 493, 508, 511, 519
   defendant: acquitted, 265, 487, 491, 500, 506, 508-9; defaults, 520; gaoled, 519; makes fine, 471
   juries: (mayor &) aldermen, 265, 487, 491, 509; foreign, 493, 511; of one ward, 500, 508; of two wards, 496, 506, 519; unspecified, 471
   licence to agree, 518
   plaintiffs fail to prosecute, 512
Tressere, Philip son of Richard le, 65
Treyer (Traiere, etc.)
   Abraham le, 249; & Brumania his wife, 265
   John le, 95
   Philip le, 292, 527
   Robert le, 292, 527
Treys, James de (le), 292, 527
Trille, Gilbert, 260
Tronour, Auncelin le, 209
Tropinel, Reginald, 228
Trossin (Trossyn, Troye), Copyn de, 294, 447, 663, 778
Trye
   Dulcia, 119
   Geoffrey de, 501
Tub, 224
Tuddehors (Tut dehors), William, 294, 664
Tuk, William le, & Constance his wife, 235, 558
Tuler, *see* Tiler
Tundur (Retoundor), William le, 294, 663
Turberville (Turbervile), Hugh de, 205, 653
Turgis, William, 245, 564
Turner (Tornur, Turnur)
   Albrhid (Aylbred) le, 397, 755
   Lovekyn le, 398, 755
Turribus, de, *see* Towers
Turrok, *see* Thurrok
Tut dehors, *see* Tuddehors
Twickenham (Tykenham), William de, 243
Tyeler (Tyveler, Tyweler), *see* Tiler
Tymbermonger, Baldwin le, 37

Ugley (Ogele, Uggle), William de, 183 (*bis*)
Under Wall (sub muro), Master Walter, 96
Upholder (Huppehaldestere), Margery la, 233
Upton (Opton), Wibert de, & William de, 91
Ushers in eyre, 2
Usurers, 306
Utrum, assize, 503

Vagabonds, 20, 23, 28, 38, 61, 83, 106, 245
Vair, *see* Veer
Valence
   John de, 207
   William de, earl of Pembroke, 340
Valet, Richard, 134
Vat, 247
Vaus (de Vallibus)
   John de, 75, 340
   Walter de, 53

Index

Veer (Vair, Ver, Veyre)
  John le, 245, 564
  Richard le (I), of Hackney, 245, 564; (II), 256
  William le, 245, 564
Vennair, Henry, 31
Versifier, Henry the, 39
Vessels, 142, 174; leaden, 13–14, 21, 43, 212
Veyre, *see* Veer
Viel (Vyel)
  Floria, widow of William, 361, 734
  John, 260
  Richard, 260
  Thomas, 147, 622
  William, 24; ward of, *see* Bread Street ward
Vile, Gerardin (Gerandin) de la, 294, 664
Vilein (Vileyn)
  Denise la, 505
  Gamelin le, 294, 664
  Richard le, 288
Vine, 437
Vinere, John le, 244
Vintner (Vineter), 228, 246, 464
  Peter le, 109, 611
  Richard le, 285
Vintry, 237; ward, 54, 108, 130, 159, 181, 237, 249, 258, 508, 519
Vivien, Robert, 15

Wade
  Master Geoffrey de la, 299
  John, 292, 468, 527
  William, 21
Waivery, 16, 84, 119, 134, 215, 250, 601; misdescribed, 117, 163
Wake, John, 209
Walbrook (Walebrok), stream, 521; as division of the City, 209; ward, 92
  Richard de, sheriff, 4, 119–28
Waldegrave
  Geoffrey de, 46
  John de, 45, 536
  Robert de, 288
Walden (Waldene)
  Martin de, 24
  Reginald de, 183
  Richard de, 228, 553
  see also Saffron Walden
Walebrok, *see* Walbrook
Walehop, William de, 102
Walemund, Henry de, sheriff, 4, 56–62, 204, 316, 539–40, 652
Walemyn (Wylemyn), John, 391, 751
Walerand (Walerant), *see* Walraund
Wales, 493
Waleton, *see* Walton
Waleys (Galeys)
  Henry le (I), mayor & sheriff, 3, 4, 35, 47, 64, 131, 164, 221–7, 238, 468, 481–2, 493, 499, 513, 515, 517, 522, 549; Geoffrey, his agent, 493
  Henry le (II), son of Henry le (I), 499, 502
  Lettice la, 30
  Robert le, 216
  Simon le, 244
  Thomas le, 67, 593
  Walter le, 731
  William le (I), 142, 216, 502; (II), 75
Walls, 195, 346, 366–7; party-, 121; stone, 89; *see also* London Wall
Walraund (Walerand, Wal(e)rant)
  John, warden of the City, 3, 345
  Robert, 214, 541; Maud his widow, 340, 526, 541
  William de, 564
Walsingham (Walsyngham), Adam de (I), 116; (II), 253, 569
Waltham (Wautham)
  Geoffrey de, 69
  John de (I), 153; (II), 294, 663; (III), master of St. Bartholomew's hospital, 685
  Miles de, 685
  Morris de, 141, 209
  Ranulf de, & Roger his servant, 235
  Reginald de, 46, 235
  Richard de, 243
  Robert de, 424, 768
  William de (I), 118, 616; (II), 217; (III), 284, 584; (IV), 543
Walton (Waleton), Henry de, 48
Wan, Walter, 184
Wandsworth (Wendlesworth), Surrey, 184
Wapping (Warpenbur'), Thomas de, 482, 513, 515
Warage (Warrache), William, 292, 527
Warden of the City, 3, 345
Wardrobe, king's: muniments of, 521; rolls of, 474; value of chattels to be paid into, 309; wheat rendered to, 474
Wards, unidentified, 16, 129
Wardship, 297, 511, 519
Ware, Herts.: prior of, 340, 526
  Adam de, 228
  Henry de, 246, 565
  Ralph de, 190
  Richard de, (I), 228, 246, 565; (II), 296
  Robert de, 246, 565
  William de, 53, 239
Warenne, John de, earl of Surrey, 225
Warin (Guarinus)
  a man named, 93
  Michael son of, 210
  William, 245, 564
Warpenbur', *see* Wapping
Warrache, *see* Warage
Warranty: foreign, *see* Foreign warranty; in a plea of dower, 515

Index

Warwick, 65
  Robert de, 91
Warwickshire, 23, 482; sheriff of, 515
Wasem, William, 236
Wastmel, John de, 227
Watch (& ward), 146; according to custom, 20, 138, 159
Watelyn, Jakes, 667
Waterbolkere, John, 665
Watford (Wateford)
  Richard de, 372, 741
  Rose, widow of William de, 495, 501, 719
Wautham, *see* Waltham
Waylaund, John, 705
Waymue, *see* Weymouth
Weapons, *see* Anlace; Axes; Arrows; Knives; Staff; Swords
Weder, 264
  Robert le, 264
Weights & measures, 468
Welles, Walter de, 250, 567
Wells, 191, 438; *see also* Showell
Welnouth, Godfrey de, & Gerard, 665
Wenden (Wendene), William de, 48
Wendlesworth, *see* Wandsworth
Weng, 96
Wengham, *see* Wingham
Wenham, Nicholas de, 239
Wenlock (Wenlocke), Salop, prior of, 454, 781
Werblynton, Master William de, & Margery his wife, 498
Weringe, Geoffrey le, 246
Werkeman, William le, 94
Werry (Werte), Richard, 245, 564
West Ham (Westhamme), Henry de, 24
West Smethefeld, *see* Smithfield
Westchepe, *see* Cheapside
Westden, William de, 501
Westle, John de, 272, 579
Westminster, 139, 184; abbot of, 299, 340
  Katherine de, 213
  Ralph de, & Cecily his sister, 137
Weston (Westone), Nicholas de, 292, 527
Weymouth (Waymue), Dorset, 493
Wharves, *pons*, 196; *see* Bat, Nicholas; Gisors, John de (I); Hardel, Laurence
Wheat, 276, 474
Whitby (Witeby, Wyteby)
  Adam de, 7
  Alecot de, 41, 534
  Ralph de, 31
White (Whyte, Wyt(e))
  Maud la, of Basingstoke, 230, 555
  Robert le, 468
  William le (I), 292, 527; (II), 236
Whiting, Geoffrey, & Alice his wife, 256, 267, 572, 577
Whitsone (Wytsone), John, 227, 552

Wife, renunciation by, 489
Wilde, John, 15
Wildelyf, Richard, 15
Wilehale (Rylehale, Wylehale)
  Agnes de, 292, 527
  John de, 294, 663
  Richard de, 294, 481, 663
Wilekin, Roger, 413
Wilinghale, *see* Willingale
Willame (Guilame, Gwilam)
  Peter, 267, 577
  Theodore (Deodatus, etc.), Florentine merchant, 292, 294–5, 487, 527, 663, 707
Willesden (Wyllesende), John de la, 473
William, Thomas son of, & Agnes daughter of Thomas son of, 492, 497
Willingale (Wilinghale), Richard de, 67
Wills: annulled, 502, 517; custom concerning, 517; inspected in court, 499; production of, by clerks, 488
Wimbledon (Wilmbeldon, etc.)
  Gilbert de, 32
  Henry de, 32, 532
Wimborne (Wymbourn, etc.)
  Michael son of Thomas, 14
  Thomas de, sheriff, 4, 14–6, 18–35, 116, 145, 531
Wimpler (Wympler), Henry le, 241, 468, 561, 721
Wimpole (Wynepol), Adam de, 154
Winchelsea (Wynchelesee)
  Oliver de, 80, 598
  Theywyn de, 468
Winchester (Winton', Wynton'), 263, 575; fair of, 180
  Adam de, 243
  Beatrice de, prostitute, 134
  Hubert de, 145
  John de, 191
  Juliana de, 230, 555
  Nicholas de, sheriff, 4, 29, 117, 234, 246–53, 256, 481, 512, 565; ward of, *see* Langbourn ward
  Peter de, 468
  Philip de, 25, 70
  Robert de, 166
  William de, 294, 663
Windows, 253, 398–9; of a cellar, 458
Windsor (Wyndeso(u)res)
  Geoffrey de, 12
  Hugh de, 209, 433, 773
  John de, 359
Wine: cargo of, 80; loading of, 246; putrid, 303; *see also* Assize of wine
Wingham (Wengham)
  Henry de, dean of St. Martin le Grand & king's chancellor, 75
  Margaret de, 262
Winter, Walter, 268

Index

Winton', *see* Winchester
Witham (Wytham), John de, 145
Witnesses, custom concerning, 488
Woburn (Wouborn, Wouburne), William de, 294, 663
Wodecote, *see* Attewodecote
Wodeford, *see* Woodford
Wodeham
  John de, 292, 527
  Walter de, 243
Wodeman, John, 83, 599
Wodemanger (Wodemongere), Robert le, 439, 776
Wodere
  Richard le (I), 245, 564; (II), 512, 714
  Walter le, 683
Wodestrate, *see* Wood Street
Wodeward, Walter le, 245, 564
Wokenden (Wokyndon), Henry de, 92, 603
Woking, Robert de, 689
Wolf (Lou)
  Hugh le, 209
  Roger le, 32
Wollemanger, Richard le, 16
Wolmarchirch, *see* St. Mary Woolchurch
Women, quarrelsome, 39, 119, 138, 230; *see also* Abjuration; Appeals; Prostitutes; Waivery; Wife
Wood, load of, 12; *see also* Faggots; Plank; Timber
Wood Street (Wodestrate), 72, 89, 261
Woodford (Wodeford)
  Isabel de, 385
  John de, 243
Wool Lane [in Billingsgate ward], 26
Wool-merchant, 76
Worcester, Nicholas de, 119, 618
Worcestershire, 172
Worsted (Worstede, Worthstede), Ralph de, 41, 534
Wouborn (Wouburne), *see* Woburn
Wounding, 166, 473; self-inflicted, 22, 133; *see also* Appeals; Trespass
Wovere (Wowere), Henry le, bereman, 246, 565

Wranghorn, William, 245, 564
Wrestling, 116
Writs, 80, 108, 221, 309, 345, 470, 483–4; exchequer summons, 525, 786; of mainprise, 37, 219, 246; of right patent, 37, 219, 246
Wrotham, Austin de, 26
Wybert (Wyberd), Robert, 203, 651
Wycombe (Wicombe, Wycumbe)
  Aubrey de, 173
  Richard de (I), 69; (II), 241
  William de, 274, 581
Wylemyn, *see* Walemyn
Wylton, Nicholas de, 687
Wymondham (Wymundeham), Norfolk, 90
Wynepol, *see* Wimpole
Wynteringt(h)on, William de, 209, 657
Wyrenale (Wylernale), Nicholas de, 294, 664
Wysdarius [woadmonger], Lucy widow of Adam de, *alias* Lucy la Queyfer, 218
Wysman, Walter, 272, 579
Wyt (Wyte), *see* White
Wyteby, *see* Whitby
Wyther
  Colin, 149
  John, 271, 578
Wytside, Reginald, 26
Wytsone, *see* Whitsone
Wyttefiz, John, 384

Yeregasse, William, 444
York (Ebor'), William of (I), justice in eyre, *1244*, 18, 52; (II), 699
Yorkshire: 42; sheriff of, 9, 490
Ypre, Lambert de, 663
Ysemangere, *see* Ironmonger

Zouche (Suche, Suzche, Zuche)
  Alan la, warden of the City, 3, & his household, 235
  Eudo la, 340
  Ivor la, 15
  William la, 15

LONDON RECORD SOCIETY

The London Record Society was founded in December 1964 to publish transcripts, abstracts and lists of the primary sources for the history of London, and generally to stimulate interest in archives relating to London. Membership is open to any individual or institution; the annual subscription is £3·15, which entitles a member to receive one copy of each volume published during the year and to attend and vote at meetings of the Society. Prospective members should apply to the Hon. Secretary, Mr Brian Burch, c/o Leicester University Library, University Road, Leicester.

The following volumes have already been published:
1. *London Possessory Assizes: a calendar*, edited by Helena M. Chew (1965)
2. *London Inhabitants within the Walls, 1695*, with an introduction by D. V. Glass (1966)
3. *London Consistory Court Wills, 1492–1547*, edited by Ida Darlington (1967)
4. *Scriveners' Company Common Paper, 1357–1628, with a continuation to 1678*, edited by Francis W. Steer (1968)
5. *London Radicalism, 1830–1843: a selection from the papers of Francis Place*, edited by D. J. Rowe (1970)
6. *The London Eyre of 1244*, edited by Helena M. Chew and Martin Weinbaum (1970)
7. *The Cartulary of Holy Trinity Aldgate*, edited by Gerald A. J. Hodgett (1971)
8. *The Port and Trade of Early Elizabethan London: documents*, edited by Brian Dietz (1972)
9. *The Spanish Company*, by Pauline Croft (1973)
10. *London Assize of Nuisance, 1301–1431: a calendar*, edited by Helena M. Chew and William Kellaway (1973)
11. *Two Calvinistic Methodist Chapels, 1743–1811: the London Tabernacle and Spa Fields Chapel*, edited by Edwin Welch (1975)
12. *The London Eyre of 1276*, edited by Martin Weinbaum (1976)

Price to members £3·15 each, and to non-members £4·50 each (vols. 1–11) and £8·00 (vol. 12).

The following Occasional Publication is also available:
London and Middlesex Published Records, compiled by J. M. Sims (1970)
Price: free to members, and to non-members £1.

A leaflet describing some of the volumes in preparation may be obtained from the Hon. Secretary.